D1286847

HULK
PLANET SKAAR

HULK: PLANET SKAAR. Contains material originally published in magazine form as SKAAR: SON OF HULK #7-12 and PLANET SKAAR PROLOGUE. First printing 2009. ISBN# 978-0-7851-3986-7. Published by MARVEL PUBLISHING. INC., a subsidiary of MARVEL ENTERTAINMENT, INC. OFFICE OF PUBLICATION: 417 5th Avenue, New York, NY 10016. Copyright © 2009 Marvel Characters, Inc. All rights reserved. $29.99 per copy in the U.S. (GST #R127032852); Canadian Agreement #40668537. All characters featured in this issue and the distinctive names and likenesses thereof, and all related indicia are trademarks of Marvel Characters, Inc. No similarity between any of the names, characters, persons, and/or institutions in this magazine with those of any living or dead person or institution is intended, and any such similarity which may exist is purely coincidental. **Printed in the U.S.A.** ALAN FINE, EVP - Office Of The Chief Executive Marvel Entertainment, Inc. & CMO Marvel Characters B.V.; DAN BUCKLEY, Chief Executive Officer and Publisher - Print, Animation & Digital Media; JIM SOKOLOWSKI, Chief Operating Officer; DAVID GABRIEL, SVP of Publishing Sales & Circulation; DAVID BOGART, SVP of Business Affairs & Talent Management; MICHAEL PASCIULLO, VP Merchandising & Communications; JIM O'KEEFE, VP of Operations & Logistics; DAN CARR, Executive Director of Publishing Technology; JUSTIN F. GABRIE, Director of Publishing & Editorial Operations; SUSAN CRESPI, Editorial Operations Manager; ALEX MORALES, Publishing Operations Manager; STAN LEE, Chairman Emeritus. For information regarding advertising in Marvel Comics or on Marvel.com, please contact Mitch Dane, Advertising Director, at mdane@marvel.com. For Marvel subscription inquiries, please call 800-217-9158.

10 9 6 7 6 5 4 3 2 1

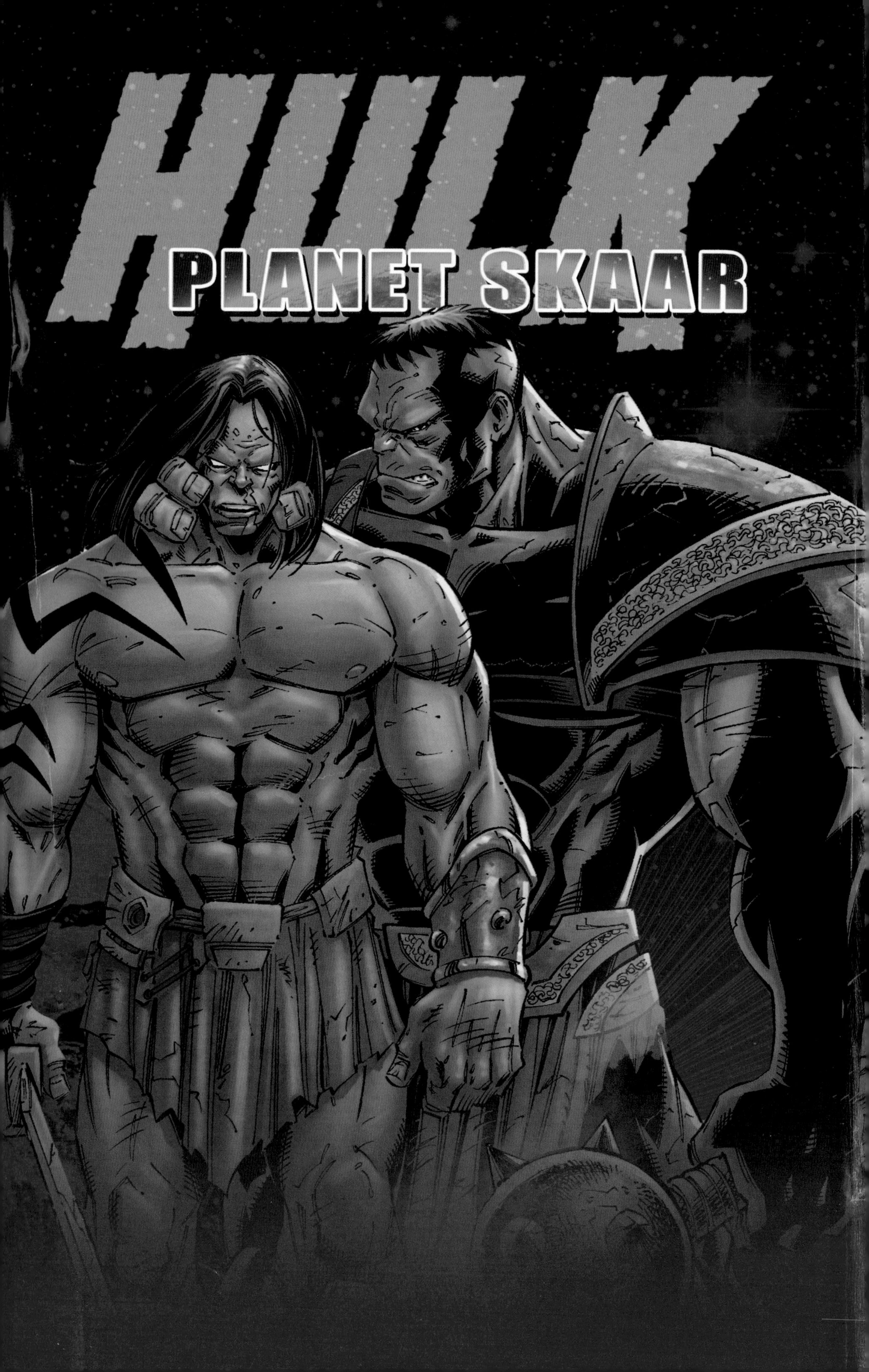
HULK
PLANET SKAAR

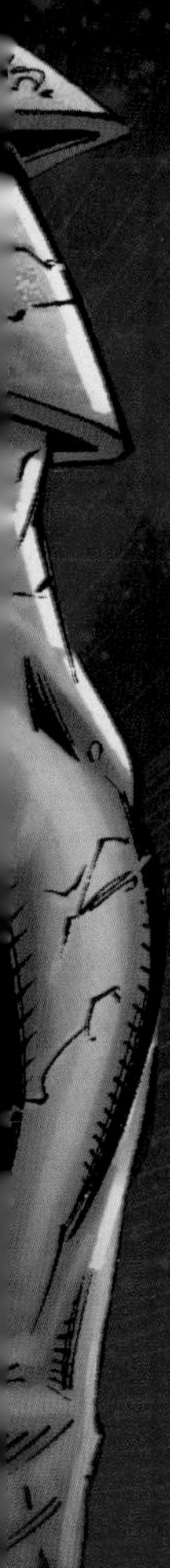

Writer
GREG PAK

Pencils
BUTCH GUICE, RON LIM & DAN PANOSIAN

Inks
BUTCH GUICE, CORY HAMSCHER, TERRY PALLOT, GREG ADAMS & DAN PANOSIAN

Colors
ELIZABETH BREITWEISER, WES DZIOBA, JUNE CHUNG, SOTOCOLOR'S A. STREET & KELSEY SHANNON

Letters
VIRTUAL CALLIGRAPHY'S JOE CARAMAGNA WITH JEREMY ELIOPOULOS

Cover Art
ED MCGUINNESS, DEXTER VINES & GURU eFX; DAVID YARDIN & MOOSE BAUMANN; ALEX GARNER; AND TRAVIS CHAREST

Assistant Editor
JORDAN D. WHITE

Editor
MARK PANICCIA

Collection Editor
ALEX STARBUCK

Assistant Editor
JOHN DENNING

Editors, Special Projects
JENNIFER GRÜNWALD & MARK D. BEAZLEY

Senior Editor, Special Projects
JEFF YOUNGQUIST

Senior Vice President of Sales
DAVID GABRIEL

Book Design
SPRING HOTELING

Production
JERRY KALINOWSKI

Editor in Chief
JOE QUESADA

Publisher
DAN BUCKLEY

Executive Producer
ALAN FINE

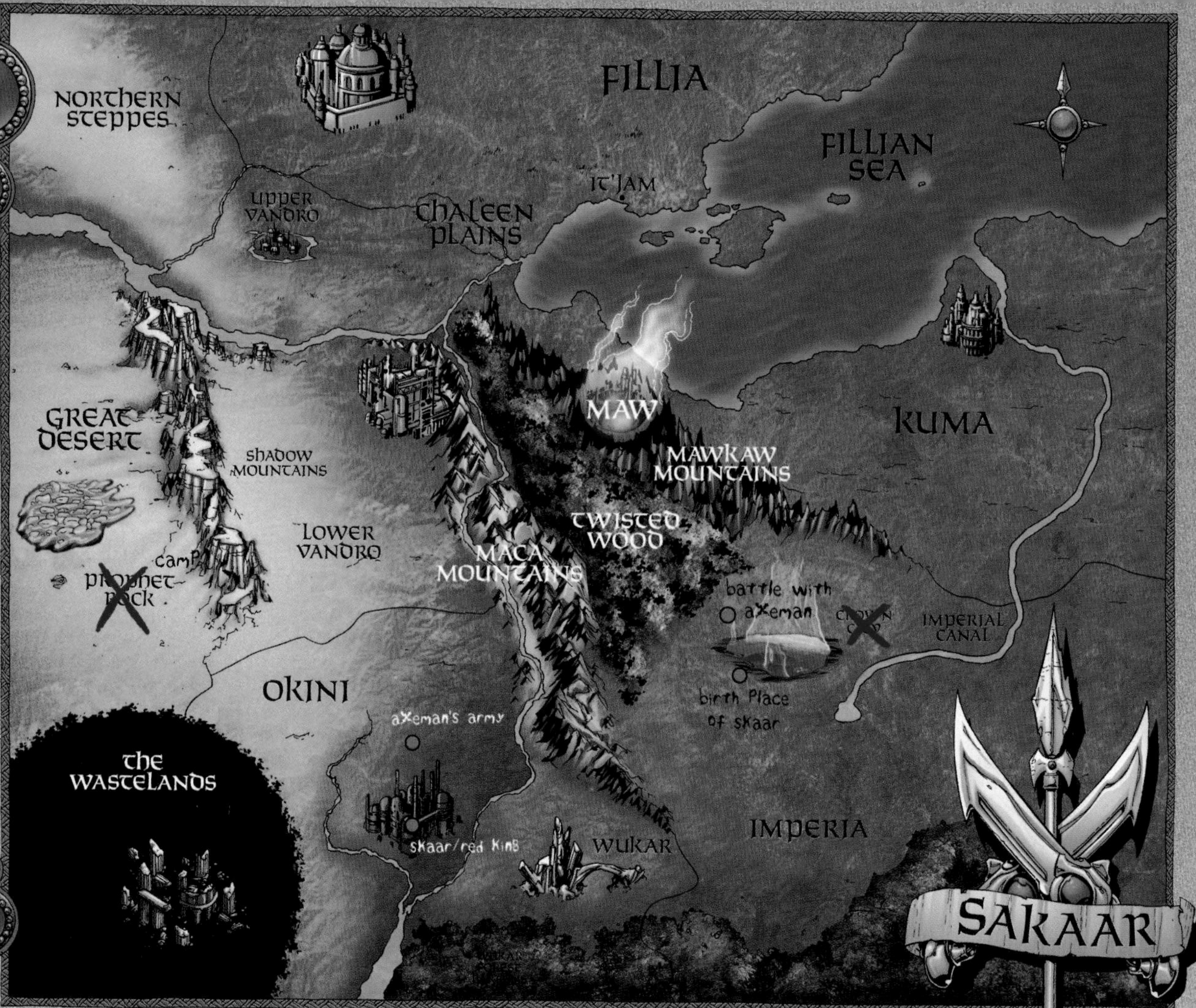
FILLIA
NORTHERN STEPPES
FILLIAN SEA
IT'JAM
UPPER VANDRO
CHALEEN PLAINS
MAW
KUMA
GREAT DESERT
SHADOW MOUNTAINS
MAWKAW MOUNTAINS
TWISTED WOOD
LOWER VANDRO
MACA MOUNTAINS
camp
battle with aXeman
IMPERIAL CANAL
OKINI
birth Place of skaar
aXeman's army
THE WASTELANDS
IMPERIA
WUKAR
skaar/red kinB
SAKAAR

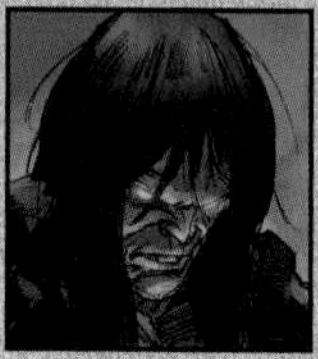
SKAAR,
Son of Hulk

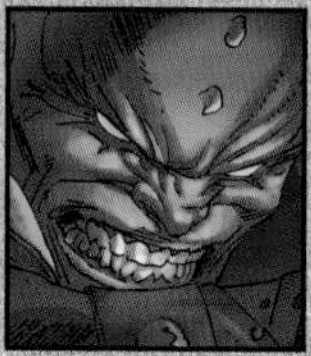
AXEMAN BONE,
barbarian invader

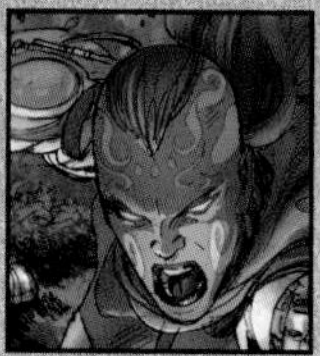
PRINCESS OMAKA,
Hero Protector of the people of Sakaar

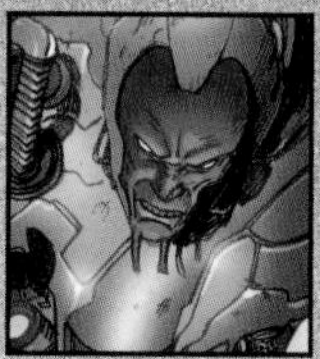
RED KING,
former ruler of Imperia

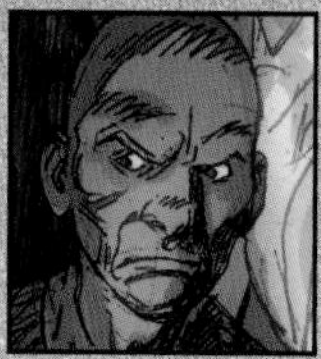
OLD SAM,
the clear-eyed Shadow who knows the secrets of the Old Power

The refugees and believers of planet Sakaar dream of the coming of the Sakaarson, who will save them from the horrors of their war-torn world. And all their prophecies point to Skaar, Son of Hulk, the savage born in the explosion that destroyed Crown City.

But from the day of his fiery birth, Skaar has known nothing but blood and pain and craves only the strength to defeat his enemies -- led by the barbarian invader Axeman Bone, who has slaughtered thousands in his campaign to destroy Skaar and conquer the continent.

Now, with the help of the Red King, his father's greatest enemy, Skaar has finally seized the ancient Old Power of his mother's people. And his former allies, Princess Omaka and the wise sage Old Sam, tremble with fear. For Skaar's terrible wrath promises nothing but more destruction.

And the silver savior who appears on the horizon may only make things worse...

Skaar: Son of Hulk
#7

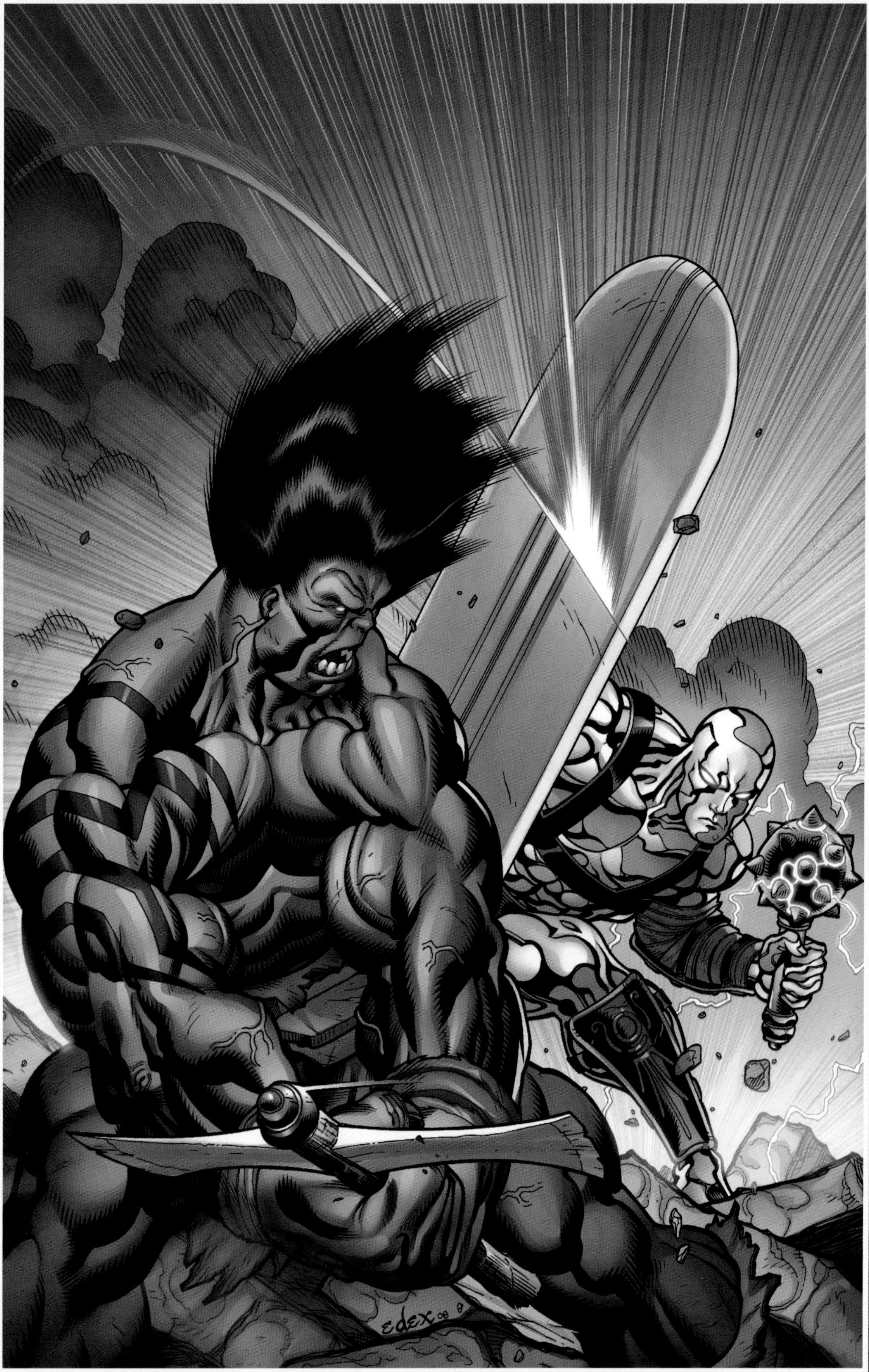
EDEX 08

Skaar: Son of Hulk #7 Variant Cover

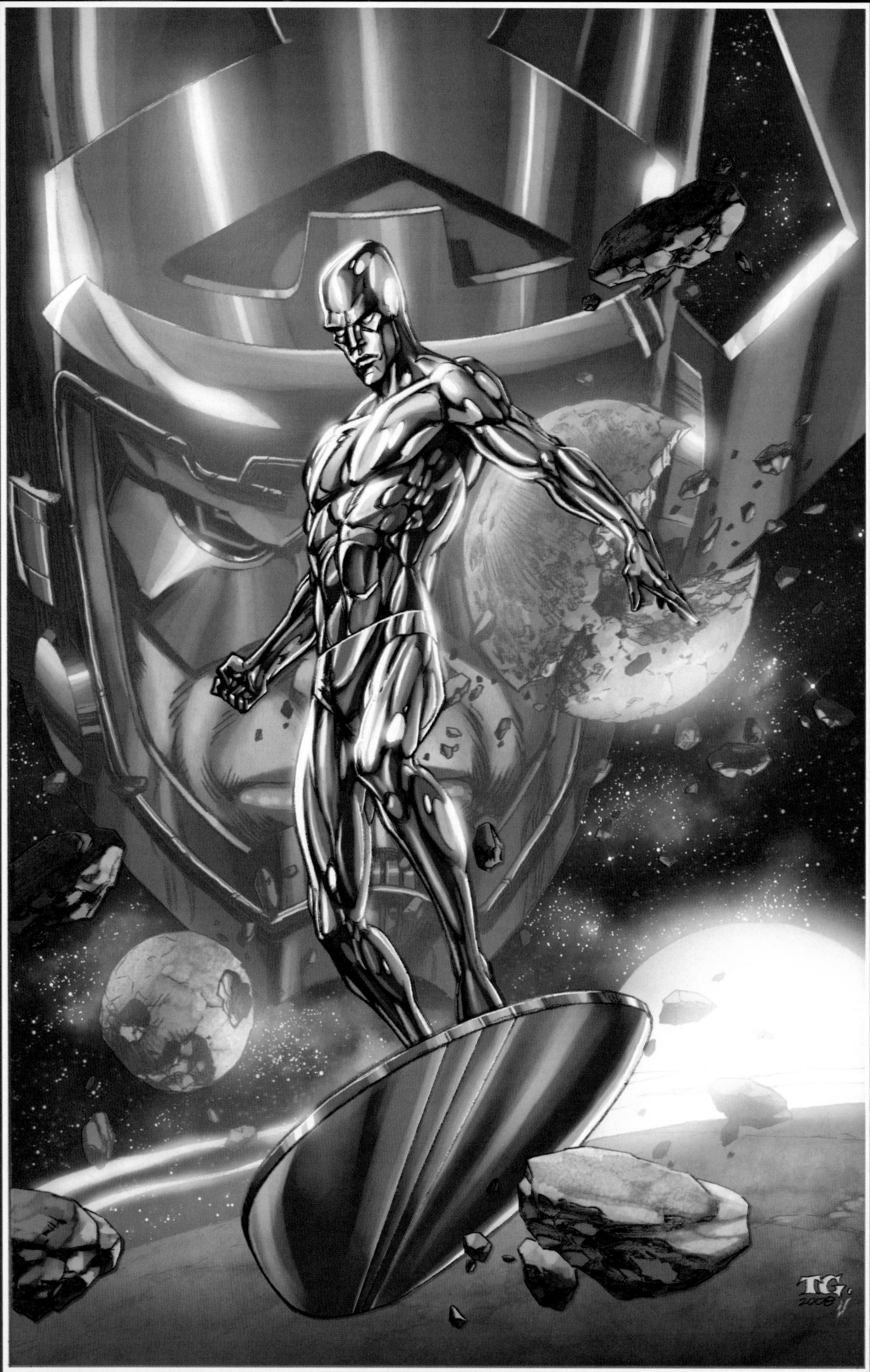
TG. 2008

by Tom Grummett & Ulises Arreola

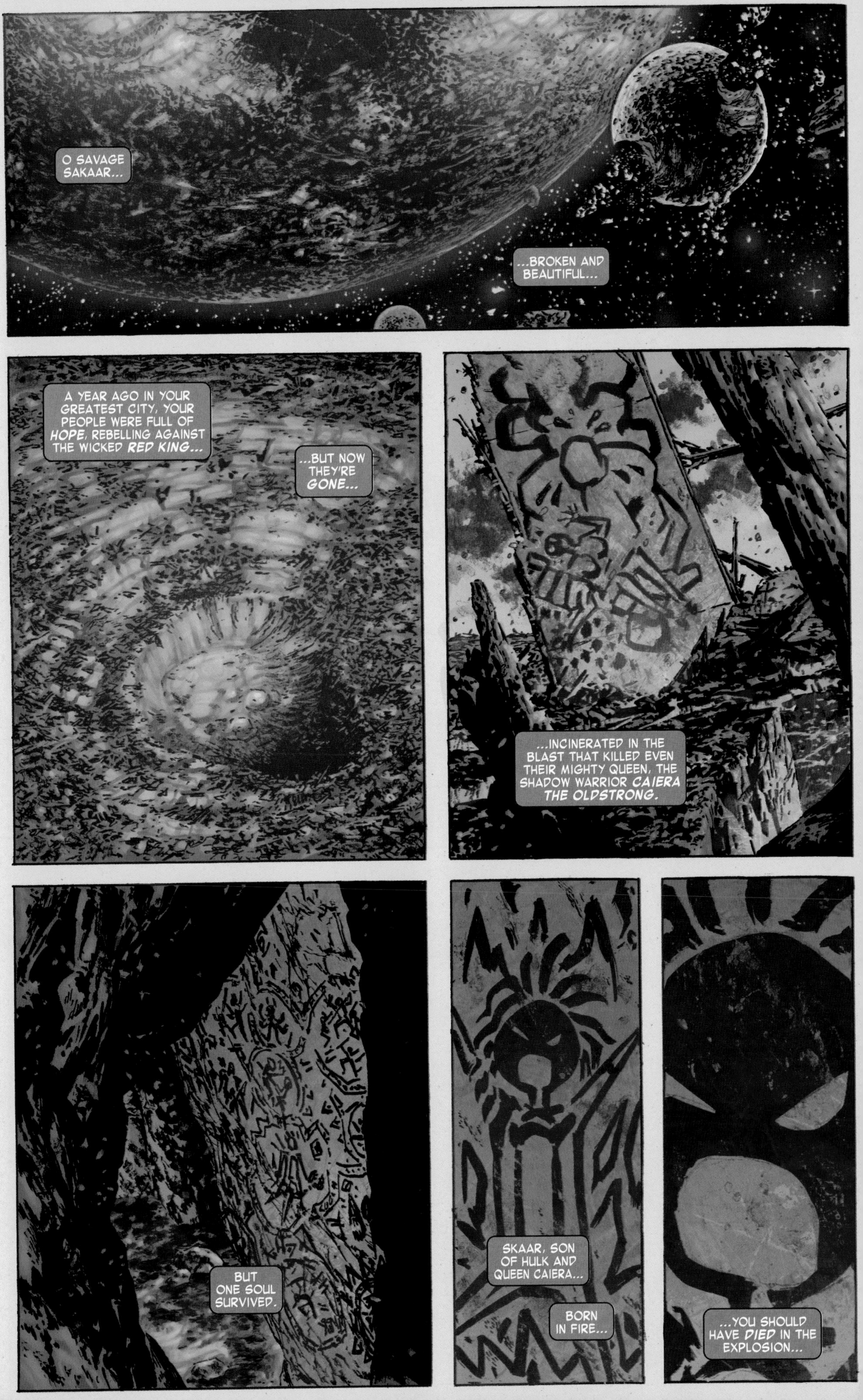
O SAVAGE SAKAAR...
...BROKEN AND BEAUTIFUL...
A YEAR AGO IN YOUR GREATEST CITY, YOUR PEOPLE WERE FULL OF HOPE, REBELLING AGAINST THE WICKED RED KING...
...BUT NOW THEY'RE GONE...
...INCINERATED IN THE BLAST THAT KILLED EVEN THEIR MIGHTY QUEEN, THE SHADOW WARRIOR CAIERA THE OLDSTRONG.
BUT ONE SOUL SURVIVED.
SKAAR, SON OF HULK AND QUEEN CAIERA...
BORN IN FIRE...
...YOU SHOULD HAVE DIED IN THE EXPLOSION...

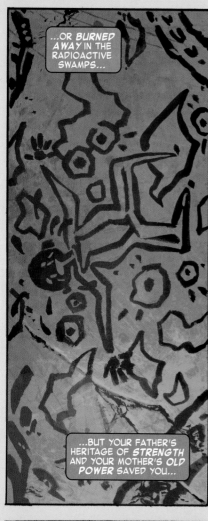

...OR BURNED AWAY IN THE RADIOACTIVE SWAMPS...

...BUT YOUR FATHER'S HERITAGE OF *STRENGTH* AND YOUR MOTHER'S *OLD POWER* SAVED YOU...

...LONG ENOUGH FOR YOU TO BE ATTACKED BY STARVING *MONSTERS*...

...HUNTED BY INVADING *BARBARIANS*...

...AND SCARRED BY FANATICAL *PRIESTS* WHO SAW IN YOUR *POTENTIAL* THE HARBINGER OF THEIR *DESTRUCTION*.

AND PERHAPS THEY WERE *RIGHT*.

FOR ALL YOU HAVE EVER KNOWN IS *PAIN* AND *BLOOD*...

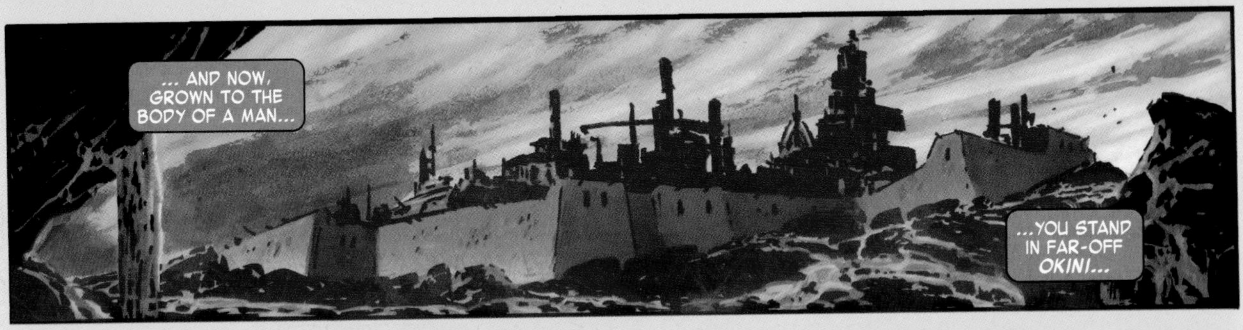
... AND NOW, GROWN TO THE BODY OF A MAN...
...YOU STAND IN FAR-OFF OKINI...

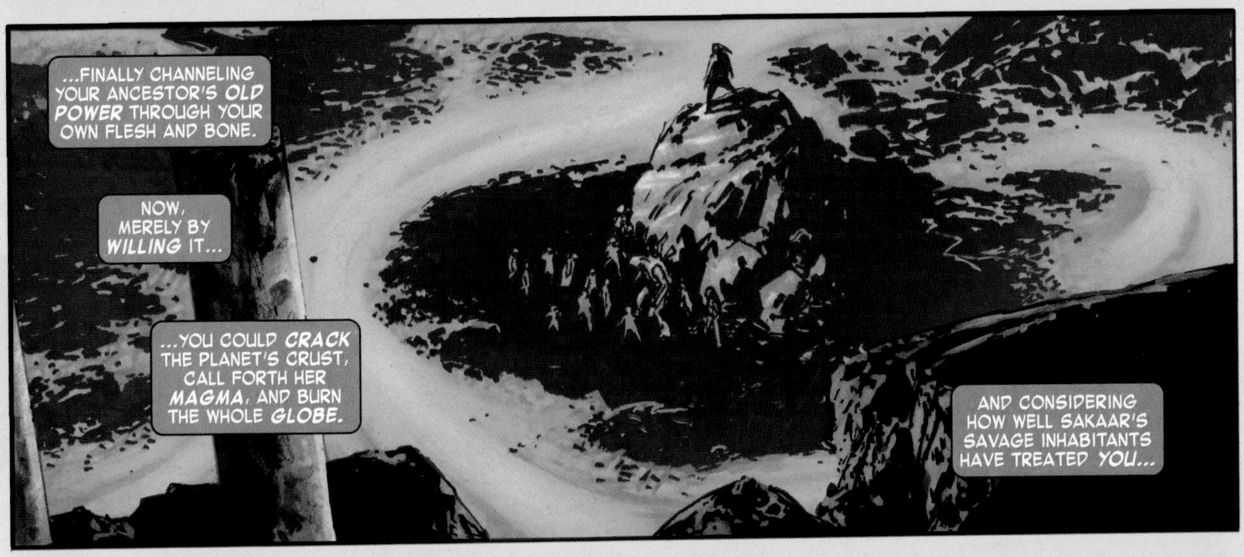
...FINALLY CHANNELING YOUR ANCESTOR'S OLD POWER THROUGH YOUR OWN FLESH AND BONE.
NOW, MERELY BY WILLING IT...
...YOU COULD CRACK THE PLANET'S CRUST, CALL FORTH HER MAGMA, AND BURN THE WHOLE GLOBE.
AND CONSIDERING HOW WELL SAKAAR'S SAVAGE INHABITANTS HAVE TREATED YOU...

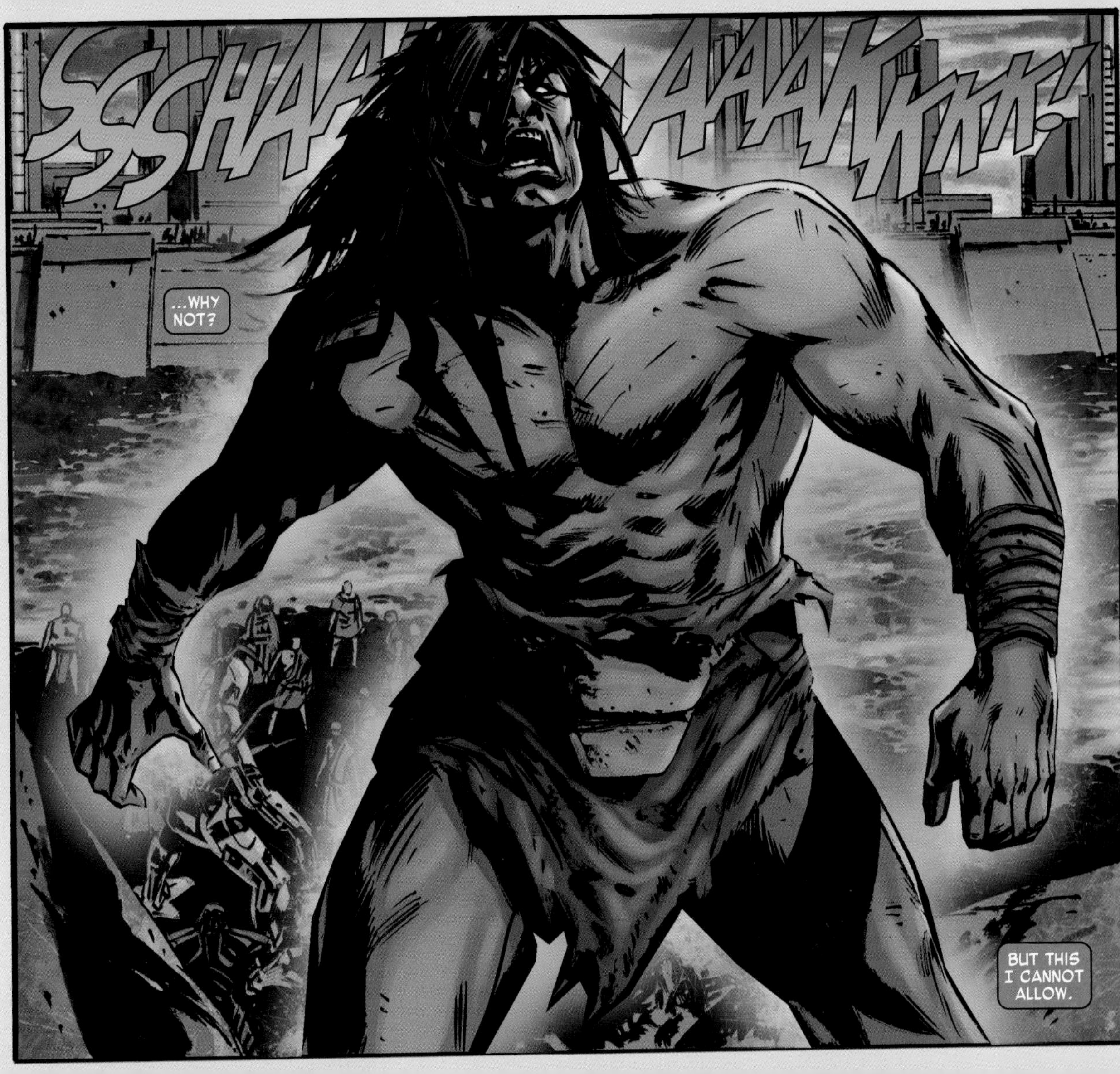
...WHY NOT?
BUT THIS I CANNOT ALLOW.

FOR I AM THE SILVER SURFER, THE HERALD OF GALACTUS...
...AND TO MY MASTER ALONE BELONGS THE RIGHT...
...TO DESTROY YOU AND YOUR WHOLE WORLD.
SON OF HULK
RETURN OF THE SILVER SAVAGE

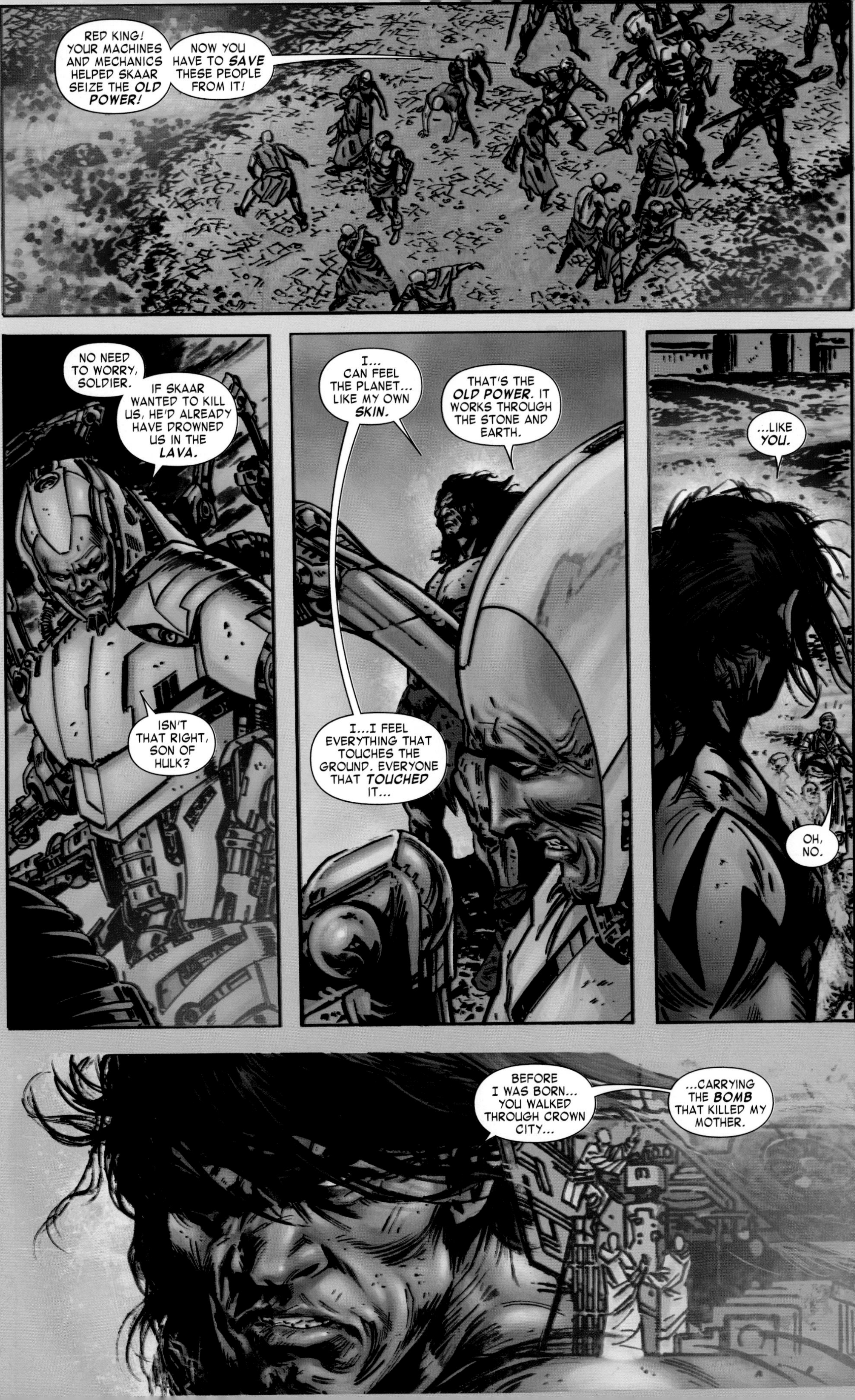
RED KING! YOUR MACHINES AND MECHANICS HELPED SKAAR SEIZE THE OLD POWER!
NOW YOU HAVE TO SAVE THESE PEOPLE FROM IT!
NO NEED TO WORRY, SOLDIER.
IF SKAAR WANTED TO KILL US, HE'D ALREADY HAVE DROWNED US IN THE LAVA.
ISN'T THAT RIGHT, SON OF HULK?
I... CAN FEEL THE PLANET... LIKE MY OWN SKIN.
THAT'S THE OLD POWER. IT WORKS THROUGH THE STONE AND EARTH.
I...I FEEL EVERYTHING THAT TOUCHES THE GROUND. EVERYONE THAT TOUCHED IT...
...LIKE YOU.
OH, NO.
BEFORE I WAS BORN... YOU WALKED THROUGH CROWN CITY...
...CARRYING THE BOMB THAT KILLED MY MOTHER.

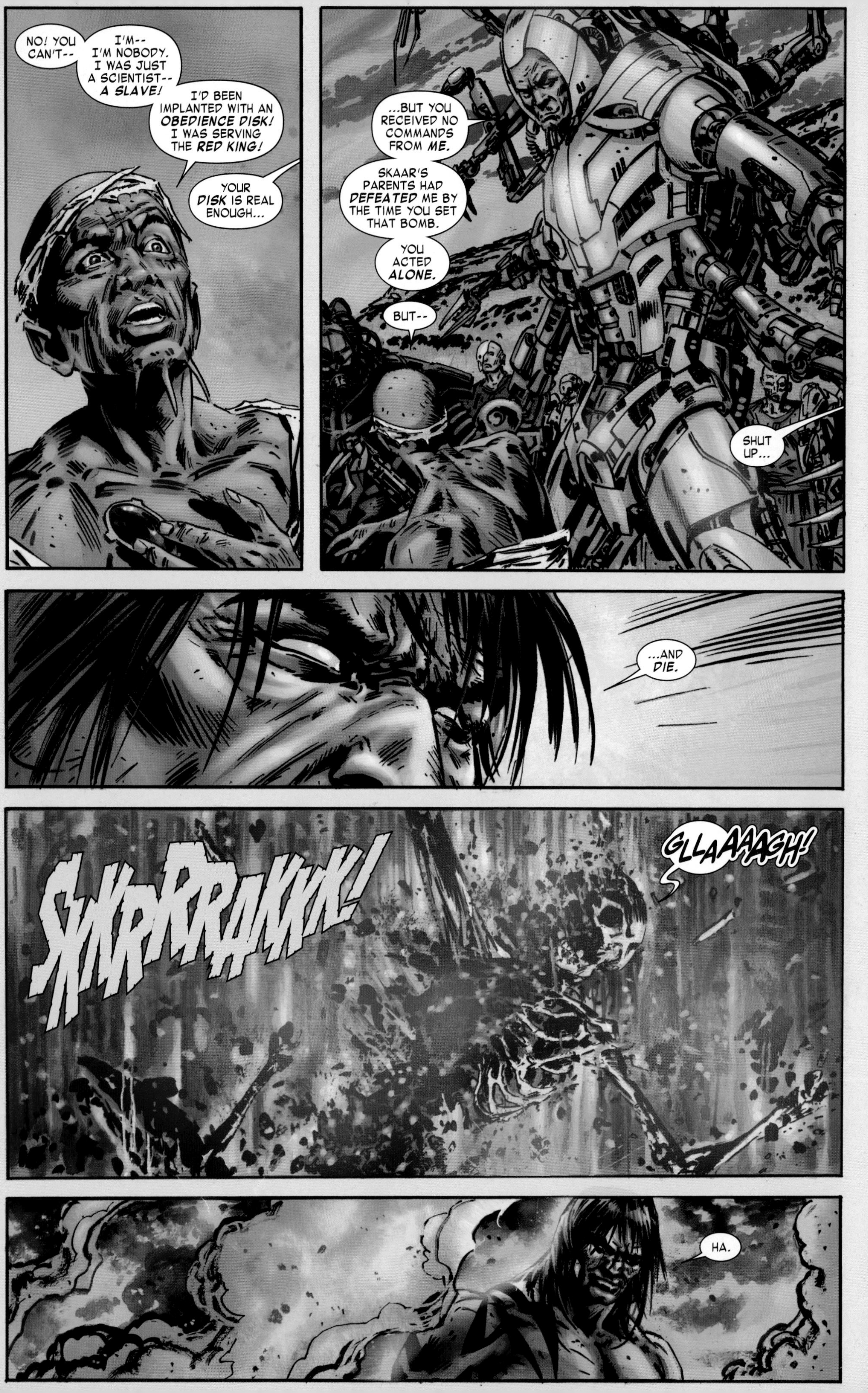
NO! YOU CAN'T--
I'M-- I'M NOBODY. I WAS JUST A SCIENTIST-- A SLAVE!
I'D BEEN IMPLANTED WITH AN OBEDIENCE DISK! I WAS SERVING THE RED KING!
YOUR DISK IS REAL ENOUGH...
...BUT YOU RECEIVED NO COMMANDS FROM ME.
SKAAR'S PARENTS HAD DEFEATED ME BY THE TIME YOU SET THAT BOMB.
YOU ACTED ALONE.
BUT--
SHUT UP...
...AND DIE.
SKKRRRAKKK!
GLLAAAAGH!
HA.

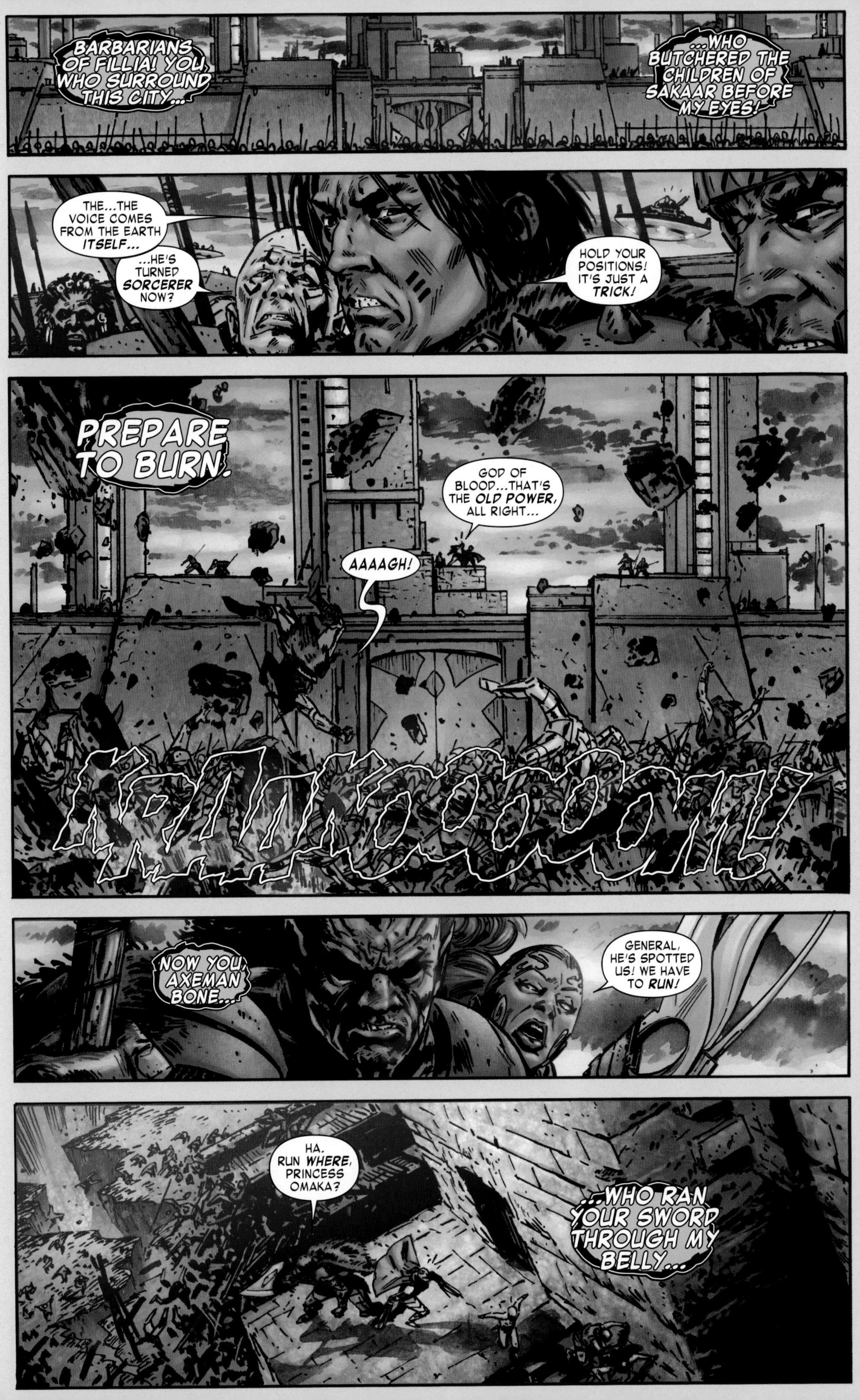
BARBARIANS OF FILLIA! YOU, WHO SURROUND THIS CITY...
...WHO BUTCHERED THE CHILDREN OF SAKAAR BEFORE MY EYES!
THE...THE VOICE COMES FROM THE EARTH ITSELF...
...HE'S TURNED SORCERER NOW?
HOLD YOUR POSITIONS! IT'S JUST A TRICK!
PREPARE TO BURN.
GOD OF BLOOD...THAT'S THE OLD POWER, ALL RIGHT...
AAAAGH!
KRAKOOOOM!
NOW YOU, AXEMAN BONE...
GENERAL, HE'S SPOTTED US! WE HAVE TO RUN!
HA. RUN WHERE, PRINCESS OMAKA?
...WHO RAN YOUR SWORD THROUGH MY BELLY...

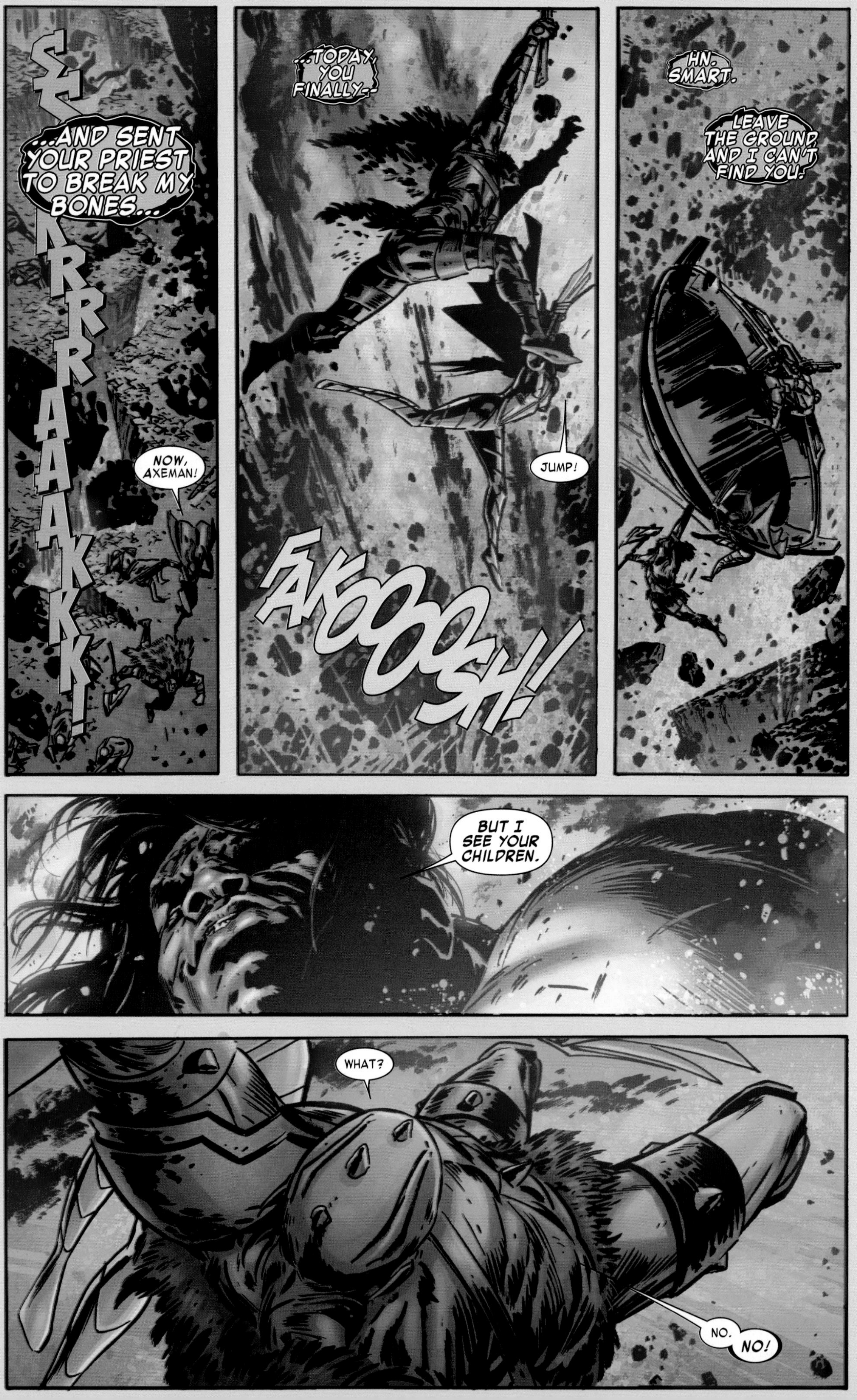
...AND SENT YOUR PRIEST TO BREAK MY BONES...
SKRRRAAAAKKK!
NOW, AXEMAN!
...TODAY, YOU FINALLY--
JUMP!
FAKOOOOSH!!
HN. SMART.
LEAVE THE GROUND AND I CAN'T FIND YOU.
BUT I SEE YOUR CHILDREN.
WHAT?
NO.
NO!

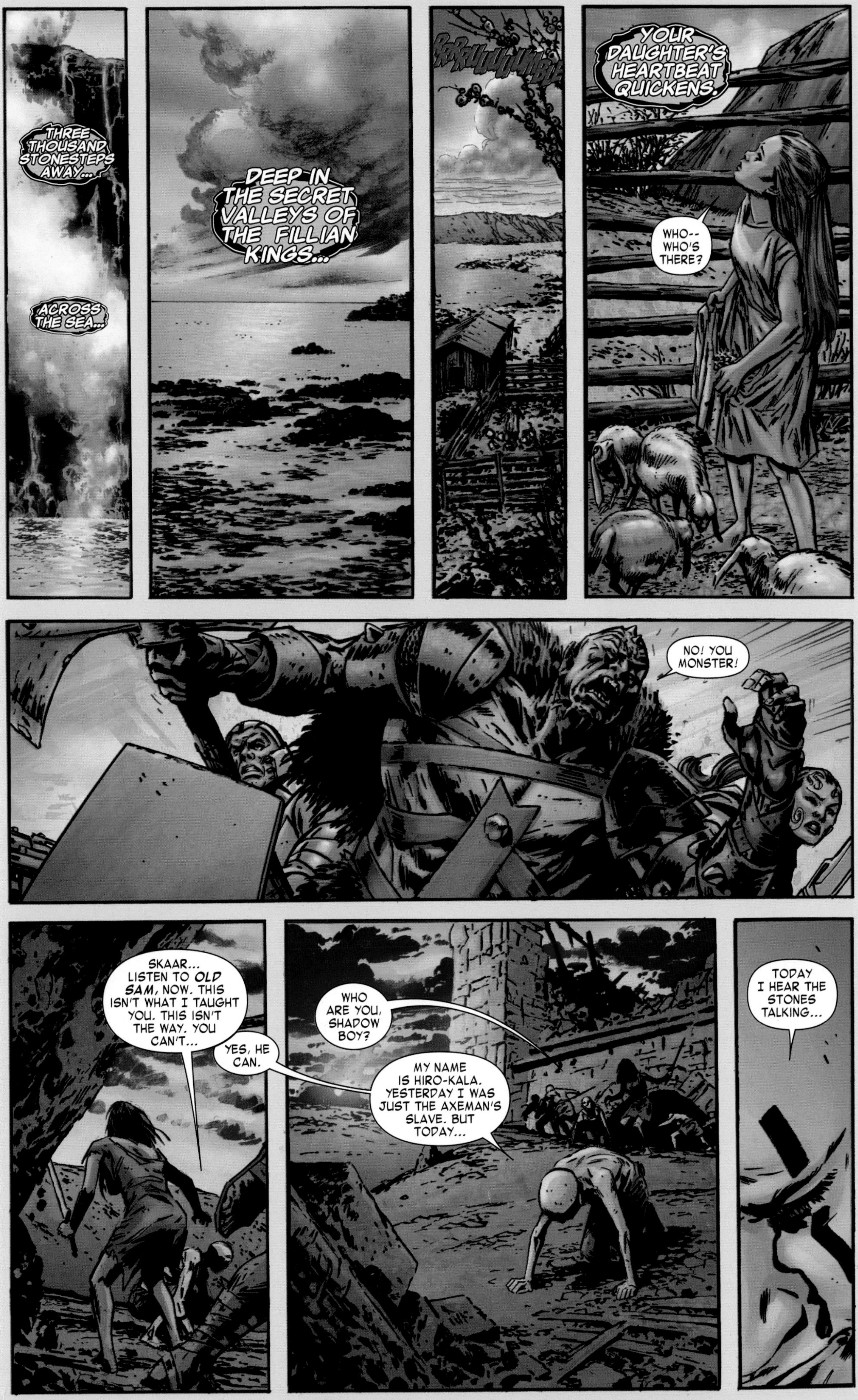
THREE THOUSAND STONESTEPS AWAY...
ACROSS THE SEA...
DEEP IN THE SECRET VALLEYS OF THE FILLIAN KINGS...
RRRRUUUUUMBLE
YOUR DAUGHTER'S HEARTBEAT QUICKENS.
WHO-- WHO'S THERE?
NO! YOU MONSTER!
SKAAR... LISTEN TO OLD SAM, NOW. THIS ISN'T WHAT I TAUGHT YOU. THIS ISN'T THE WAY. YOU CAN'T...
YES, HE CAN.
WHO ARE YOU, SHADOW BOY?
MY NAME IS HIRO-KALA. YESTERDAY I WAS JUST THE AXEMAN'S SLAVE. BUT TODAY...
TODAY I HEAR THE STONES TALKING...

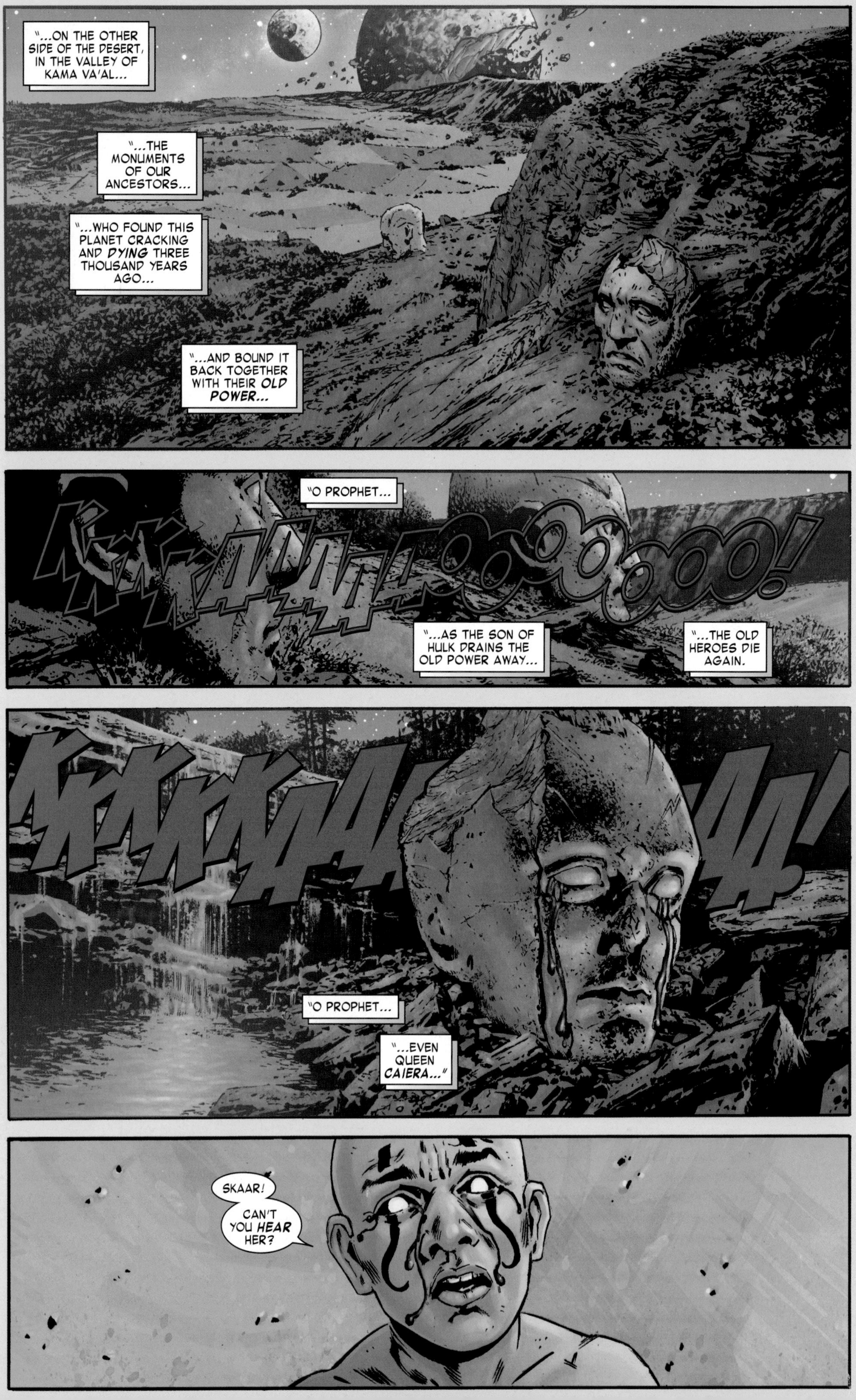
"...ON THE OTHER SIDE OF THE DESERT, IN THE VALLEY OF KAMA VA'AL...
"...THE MONUMENTS OF OUR ANCESTORS...
"...WHO FOUND THIS PLANET CRACKING AND DYING THREE THOUSAND YEARS AGO...
"...AND BOUND IT BACK TOGETHER WITH THEIR OLD POWER...
"O PROPHET...
KRKRAKAKOOOOOOOOO!
"...AS THE SON OF HULK DRAINS THE OLD POWER AWAY...
"...THE OLD HEROES DIE AGAIN.
KRKRKRAAAAA!
"O PROPHET...
"...EVEN QUEEN CAIERA..."
SKAAR!
CAN'T YOU HEAR HER?

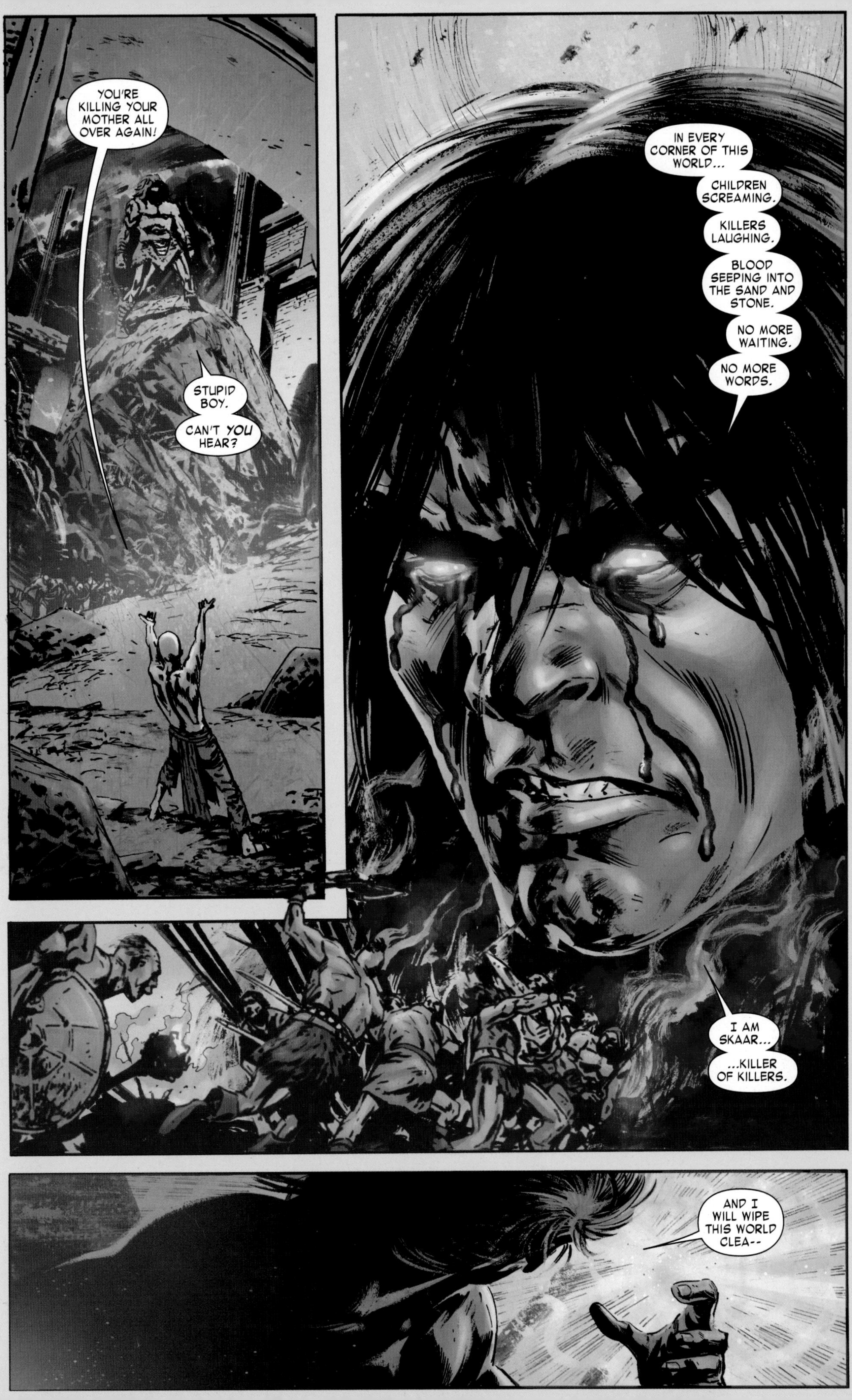
YOU'RE KILLING YOUR MOTHER ALL OVER AGAIN!
STUPID BOY.
CAN'T YOU HEAR?
IN EVERY CORNER OF THIS WORLD...
CHILDREN SCREAMING.
KILLERS LAUGHING.
BLOOD SEEPING INTO THE SAND AND STONE.
NO MORE WAITING.
NO MORE WORDS.
I AM SKAAR...
...KILLER OF KILLERS.
AND I WILL WIPE THIS WORLD CLEA--

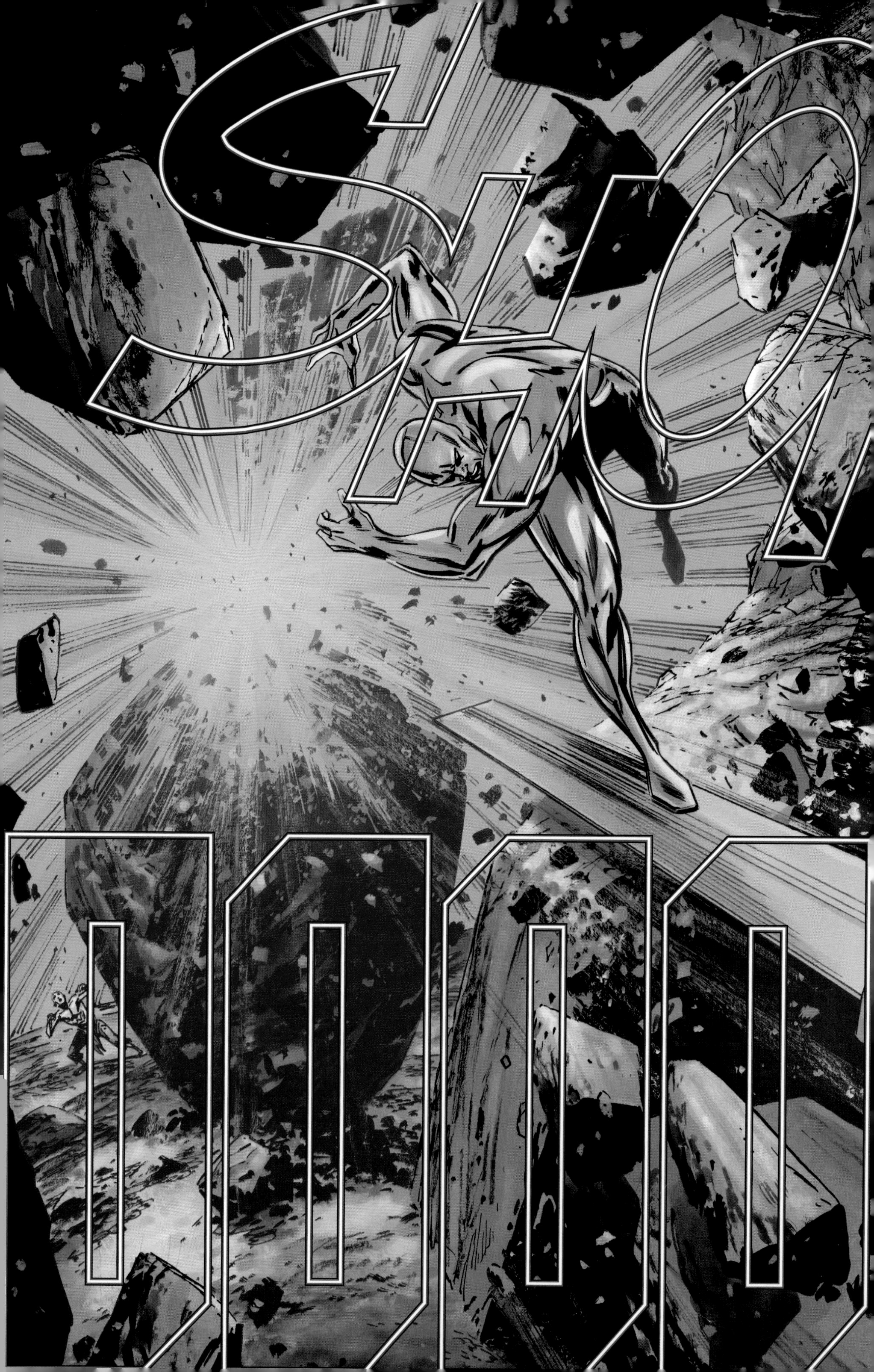

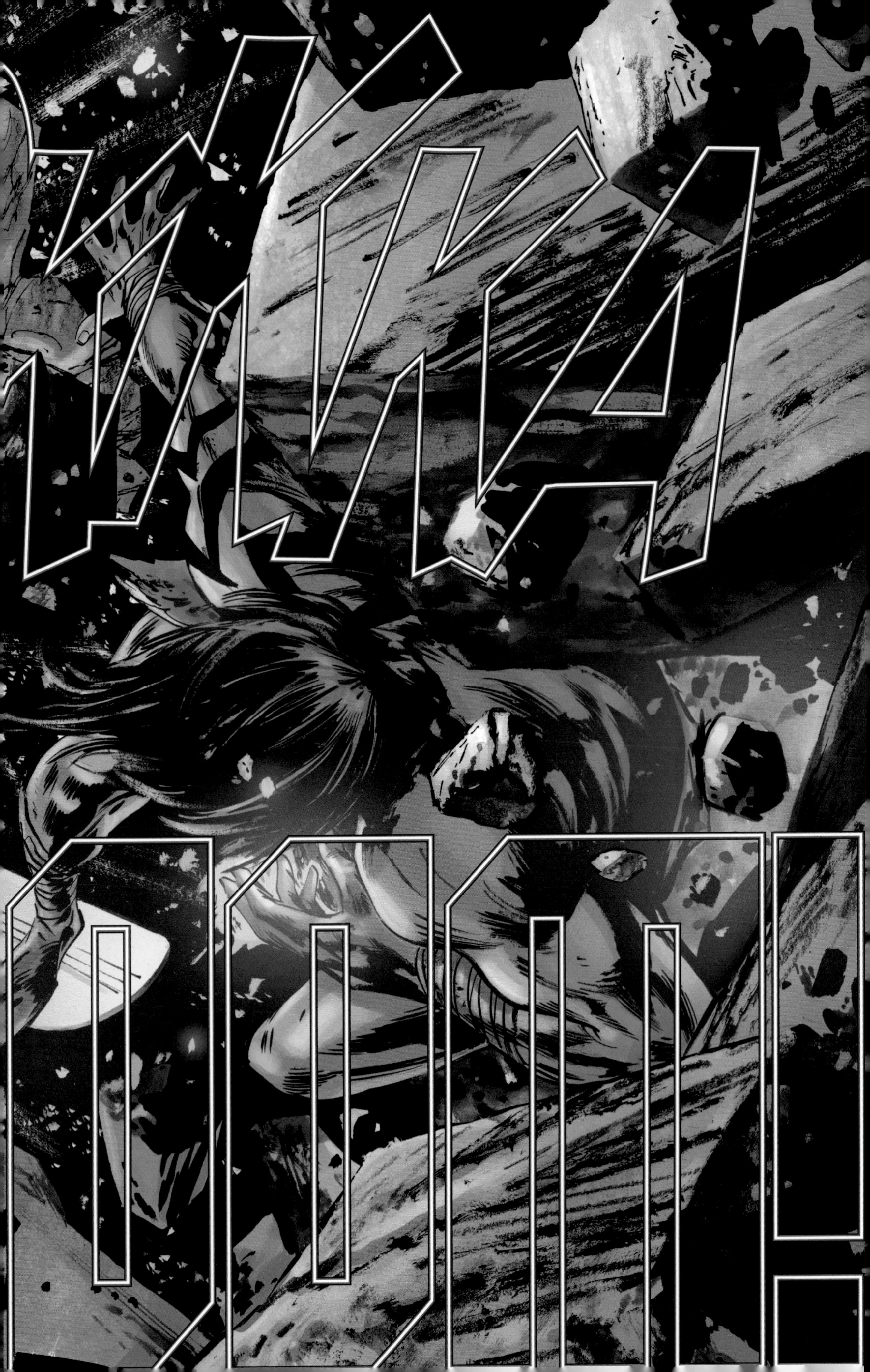
OOM!

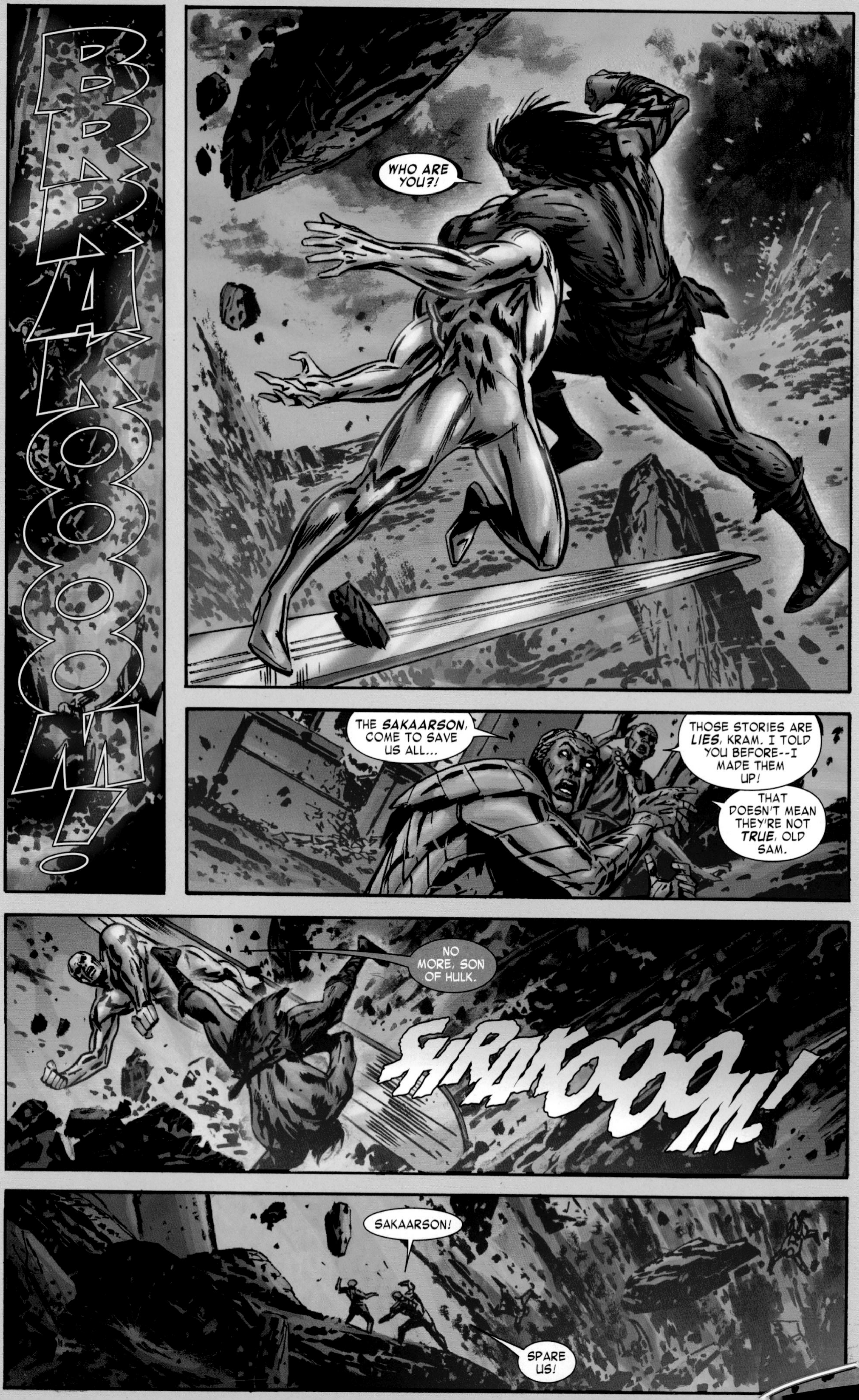
BRRAKOOOOOM!
WHO ARE YOU?!
THE SAKAARSON, COME TO SAVE US ALL...
THOSE STORIES ARE LIES, KRAM. I TOLD YOU BEFORE--I MADE THEM UP!
THAT DOESN'T MEAN THEY'RE NOT TRUE, OLD SAM.
NO MORE, SON OF HULK.
SHRAKOOOOM!
SAKAARSON!
SPARE US!

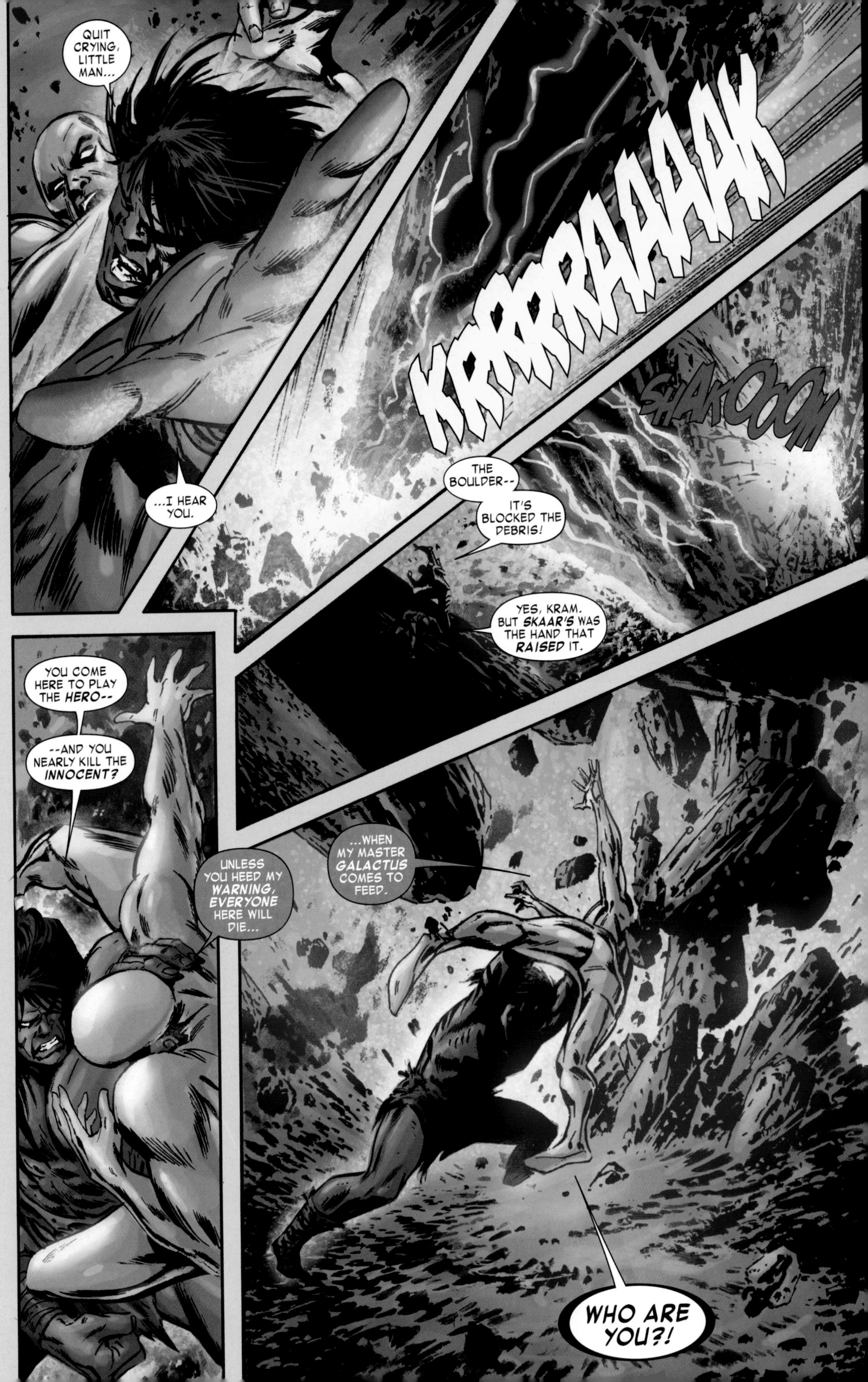
QUIT CRYING, LITTLE MAN...
...I HEAR YOU.
KRRRRRAAAAK
SHAKOOOM
THE BOULDER--
IT'S BLOCKED THE DEBRIS!
YES, KRAM. BUT SKAAR'S WAS THE HAND THAT RAISED IT.
YOU COME HERE TO PLAY THE HERO--
--AND YOU NEARLY KILL THE INNOCENT?
UNLESS YOU HEED MY WARNING, EVERYONE HERE WILL DIE...
...WHEN MY MASTER GALACTUS COMES TO FEED.
WHO ARE YOU?!

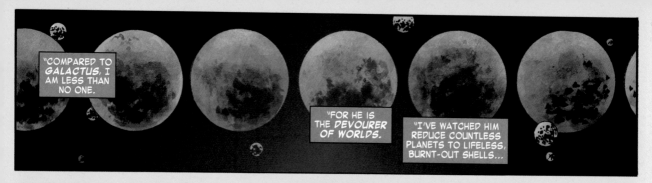

"COMPARED TO *GALACTUS*, I AM LESS THAN NO ONE.

"FOR HE IS THE *DEVOURER OF WORLDS*.

"I'VE WATCHED HIM REDUCE COUNTLESS PLANETS TO LIFELESS, BURNT-OUT SHELLS...

"...BUT NEVER HAS HE CONSUMED A WORLD SO FULL OF ANCIENT POWER AS *SAKAAR*.

"SO IF YOU TRULY CARE ABOUT THE INNOCENT, SON OF HULK...

"... LET YOUR MOTHER'S SHADOW PEOPLE READY THEIR STONE SHIPS AND EVACUATE THE SURVIVORS TO THE STARS.

"THEN I WILL HAIL MY *MASTER*...

"... AND THE *OLD POWER* WILL SATE HIM FOR A *HUNDRED THOUSAND YEARS*...

"... AND *BILLIONS* ACROSS THE *UNIVERSE* WILL HAIL YOU AS THEIR *SAVIOR.*"

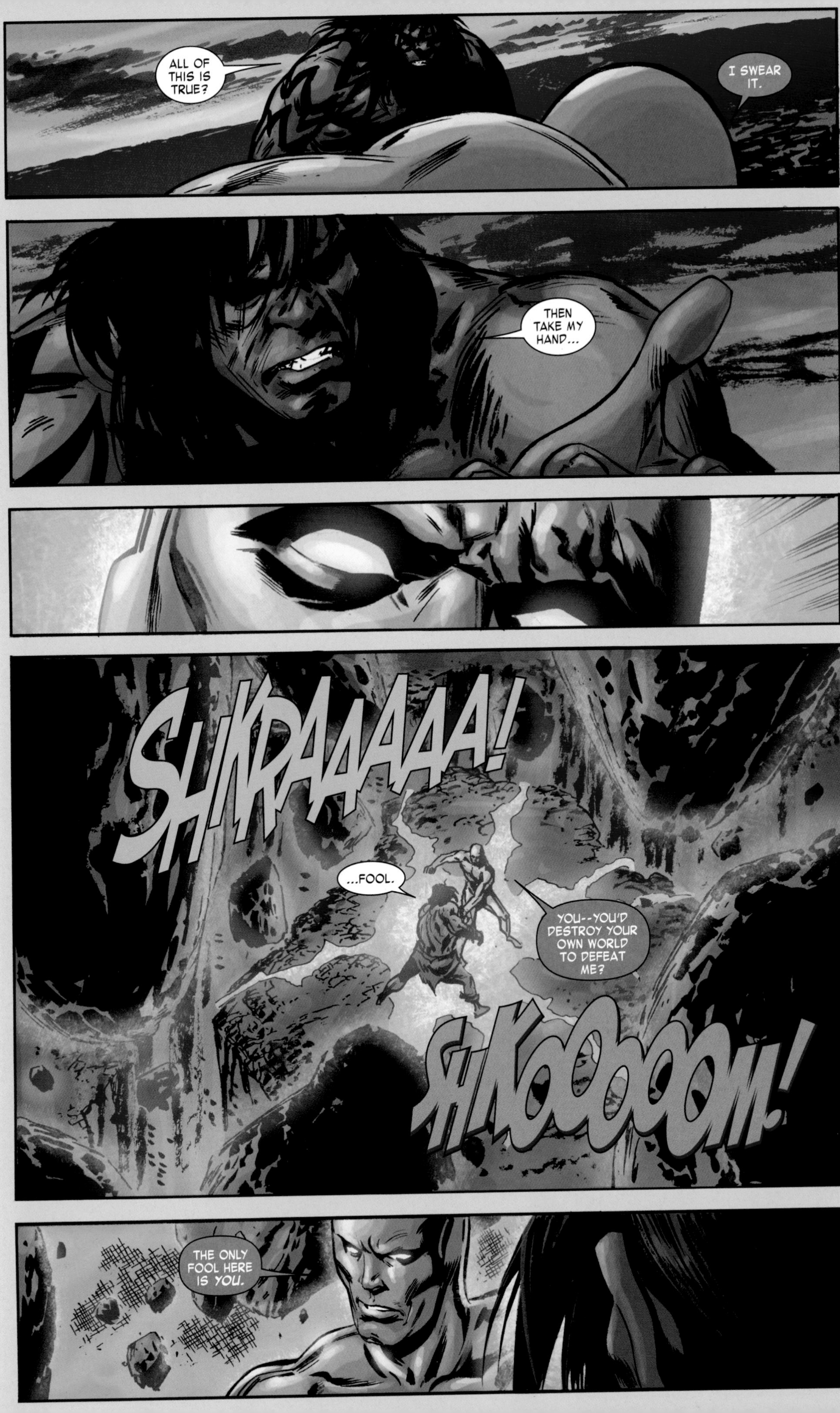
ALL OF THIS IS TRUE?
I SWEAR IT.
THEN TAKE MY HAND...
SHKRAAAAAA!
...FOOL.
YOU--YOU'D DESTROY YOUR OWN WORLD TO DEFEAT ME?
SHKOOOOOM!
THE ONLY FOOL HERE IS YOU.

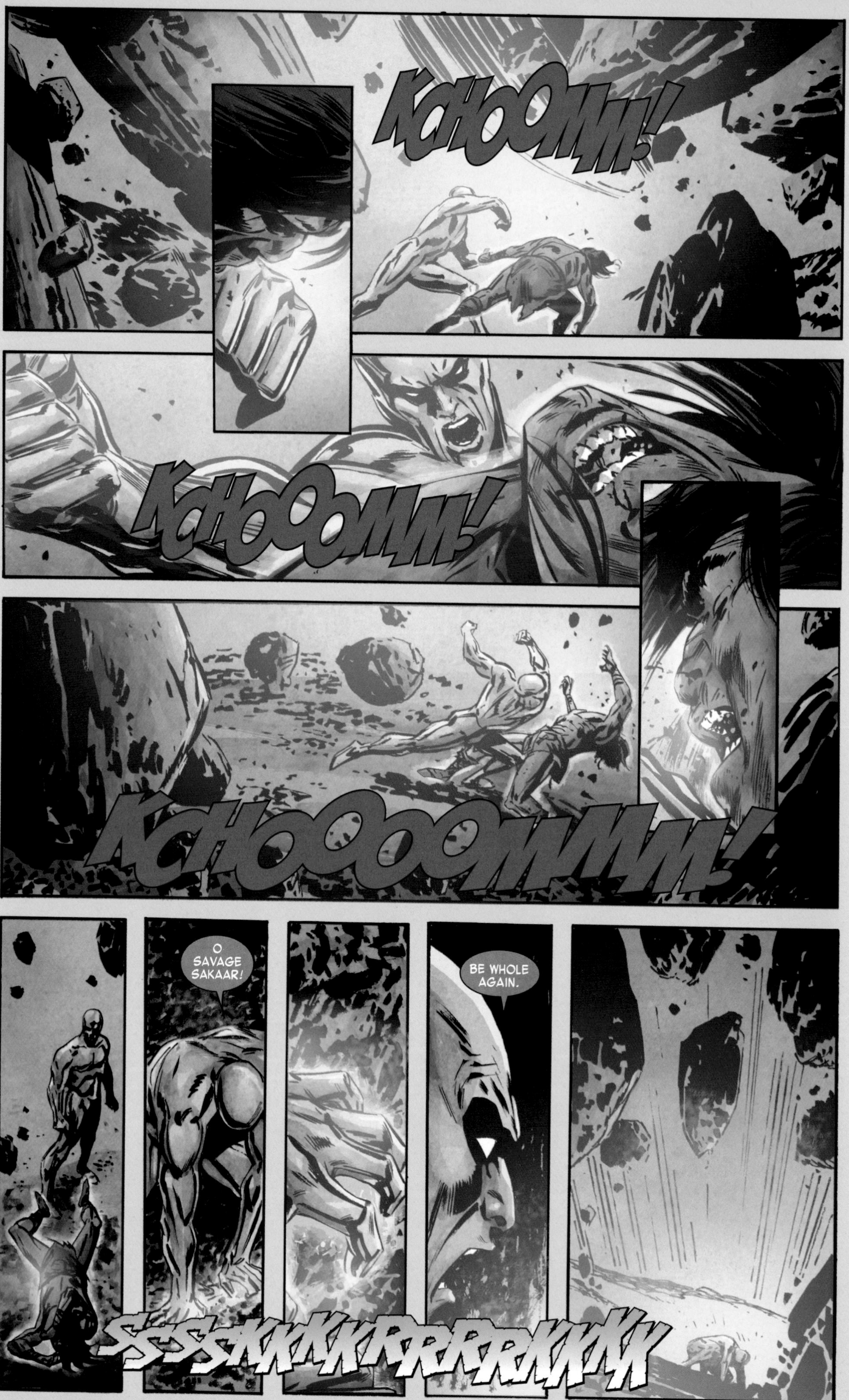
KCHOOMM!
KCHOOOMM!
KCHOOOOMMM!
O SAVAGE SAKAAR!
BE WHOLE AGAIN.
SSSSKKKKRRRRRKKKK

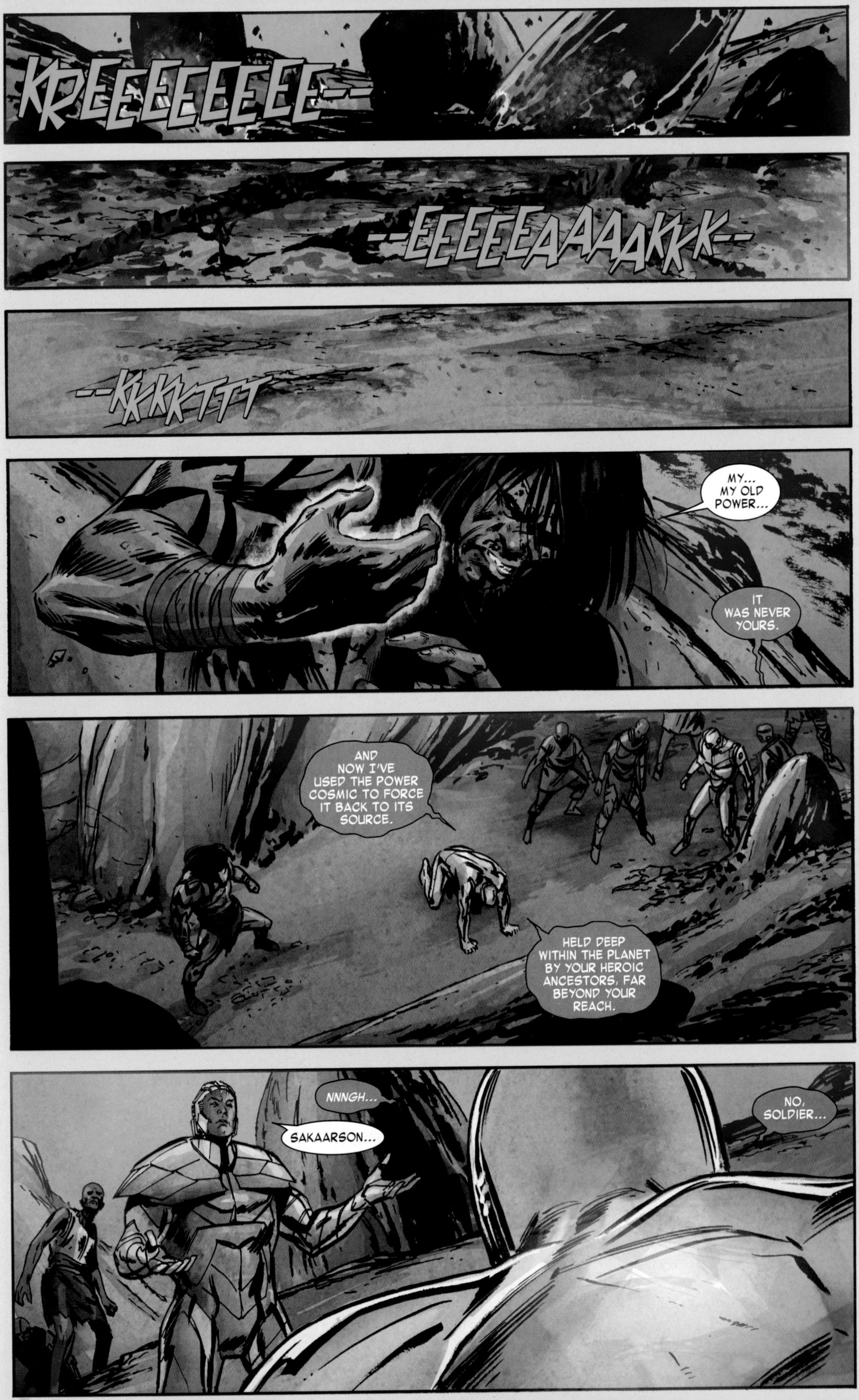
KREEEEEEEE--
--EEEEEAAAAKKK--
--KKKKTTT
MY... MY OLD POWER...
IT WAS NEVER YOURS.
AND NOW I'VE USED THE POWER COSMIC TO FORCE IT BACK TO ITS SOURCE.
HELD DEEP WITHIN THE PLANET BY YOUR HEROIC ANCESTORS, FAR BEYOND YOUR REACH.
NNNGH...
SAKAARSON...
NO, SOLDIER...

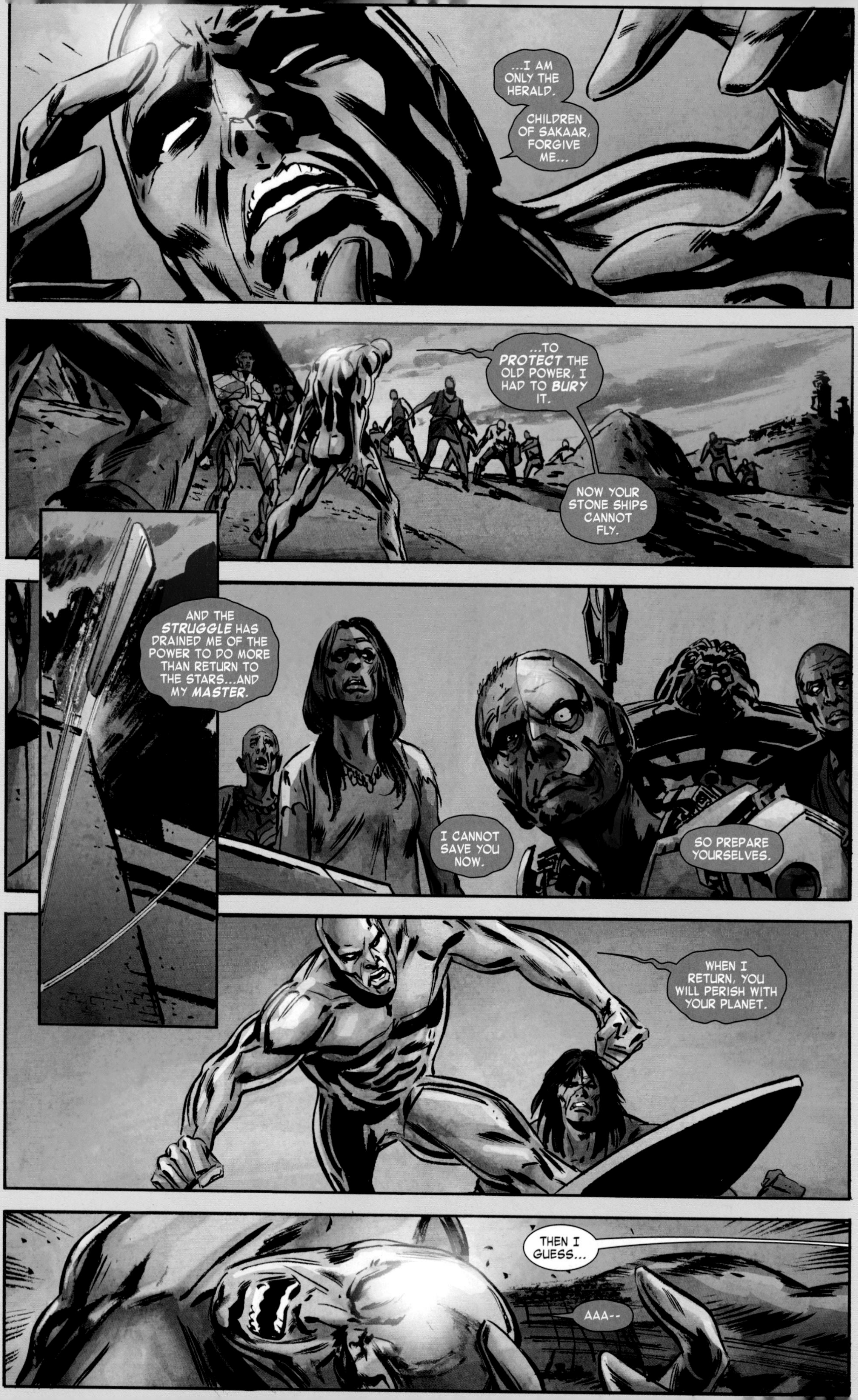
...I AM ONLY THE HERALD.
CHILDREN OF SAKAAR, FORGIVE ME...
...TO PROTECT THE OLD POWER, I HAD TO BURY IT.
NOW YOUR STONE SHIPS CANNOT FLY.
AND THE STRUGGLE HAS DRAINED ME OF THE POWER TO DO MORE THAN RETURN TO THE STARS...AND MY MASTER.
I CANNOT SAVE YOU NOW.
SO PREPARE YOURSELVES.
WHEN I RETURN, YOU WILL PERISH WITH YOUR PLANET.
THEN I GUESS...
AAA--

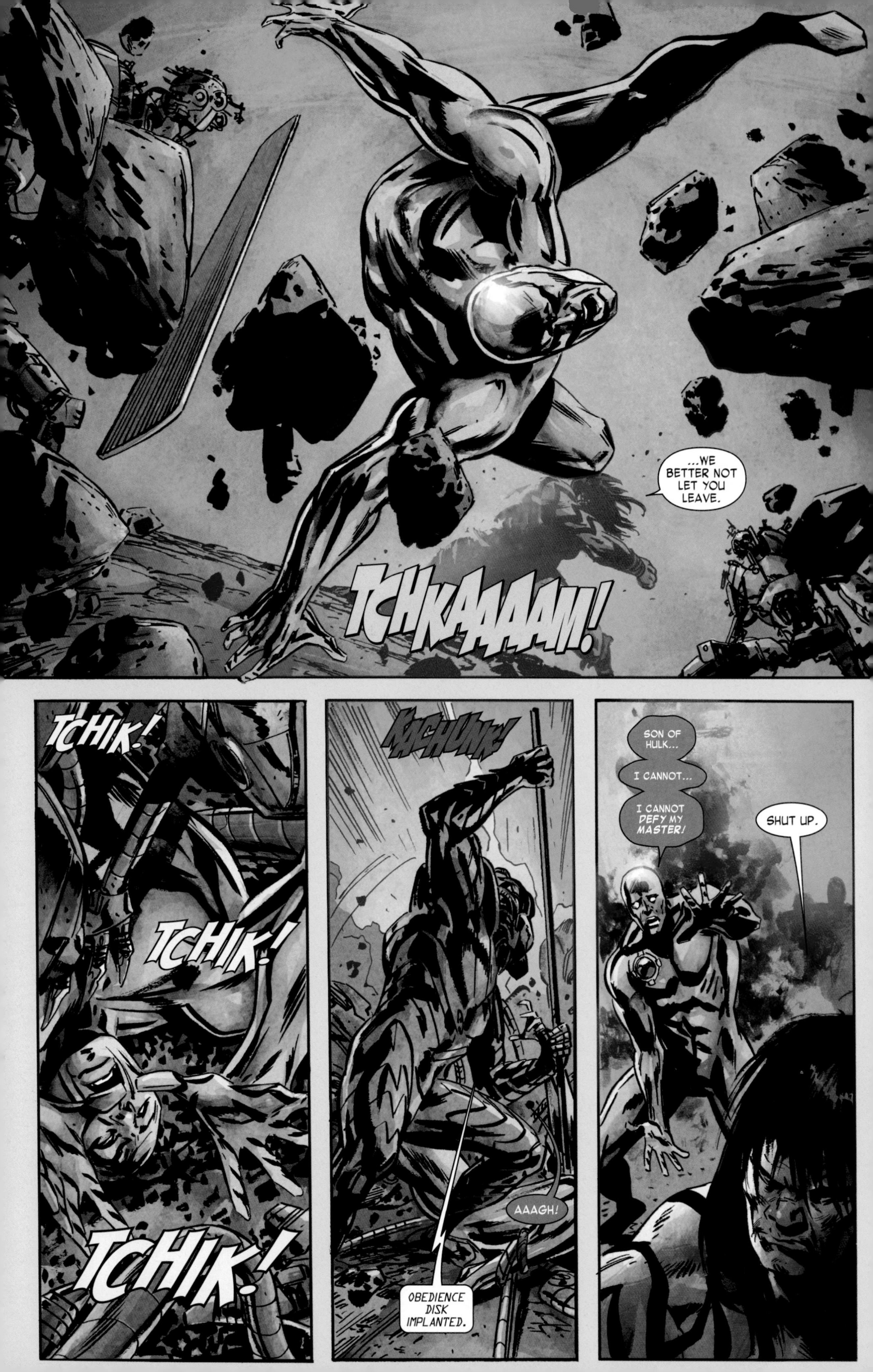
...WE BETTER NOT LET YOU LEAVE.
TCHKAAAAM!
TCHIK!
TCHIK!
TCHIK!
KACHUNK!
AAAGH!
OBEDIENCE DISK IMPLANTED.
SON OF HULK...
I CANNOT...
I CANNOT DEFY MY MASTER!
SHUT UP.

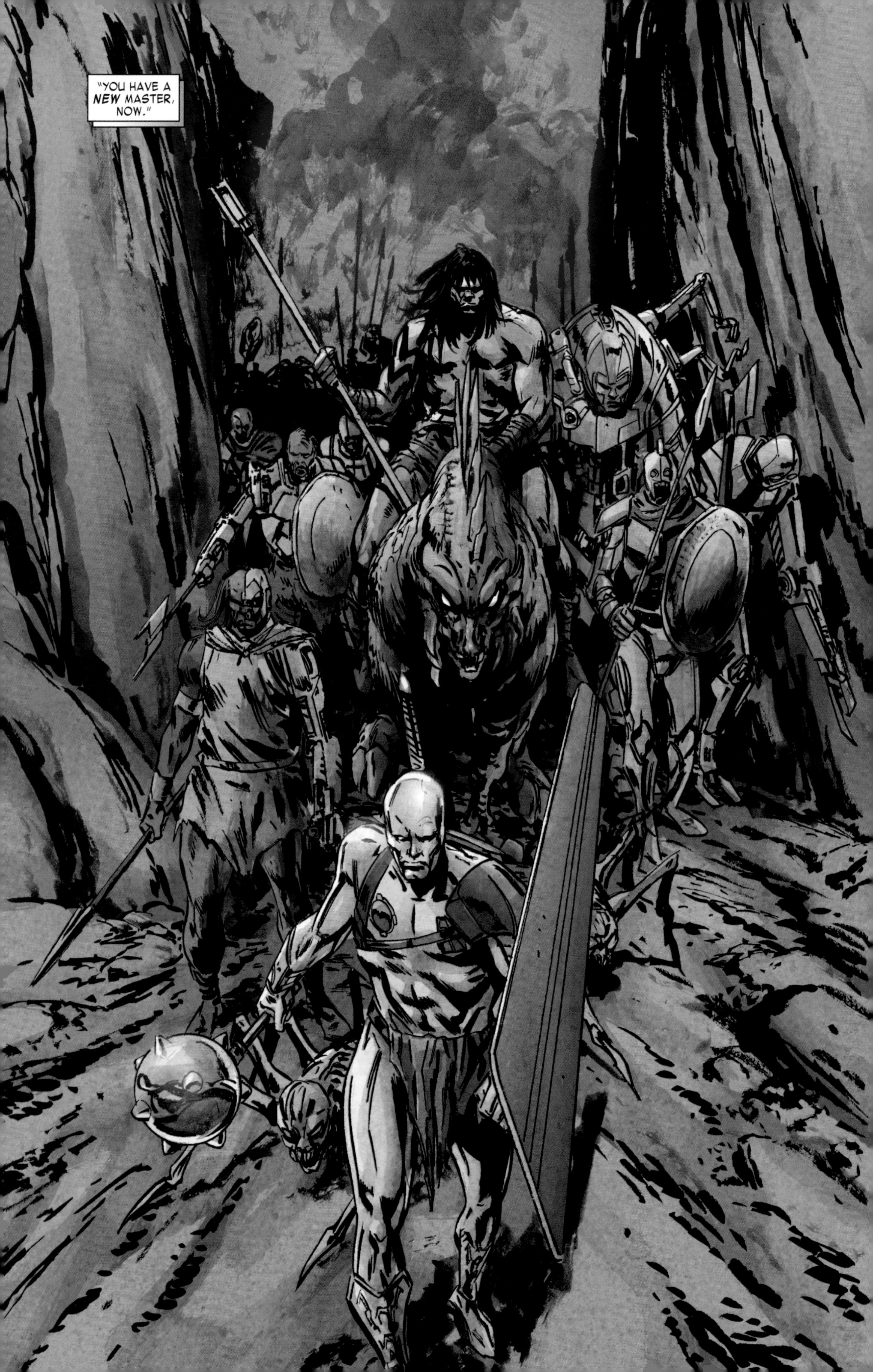
"YOU HAVE A NEW MASTER, NOW."

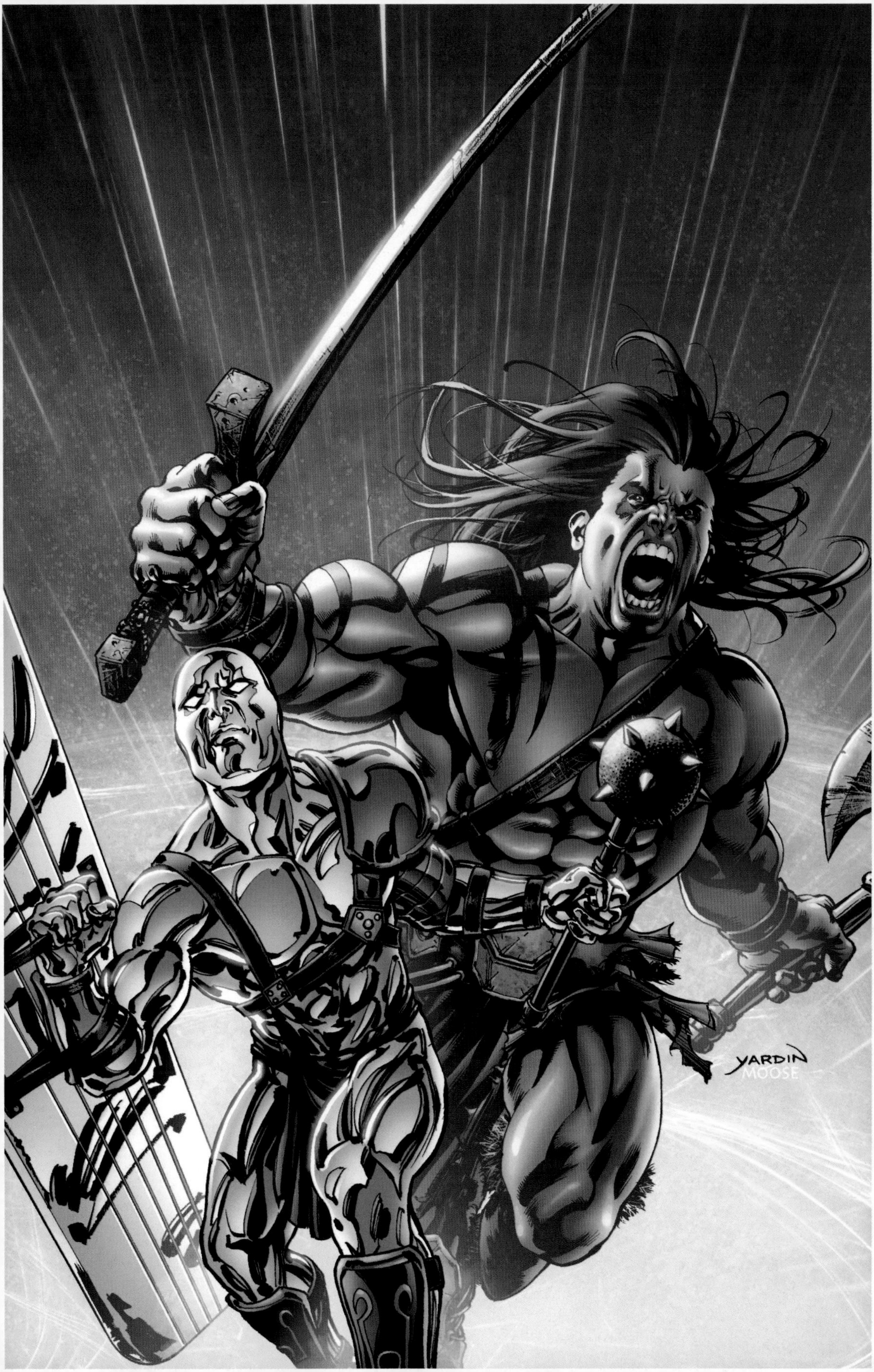
YARDIN
MOOSE

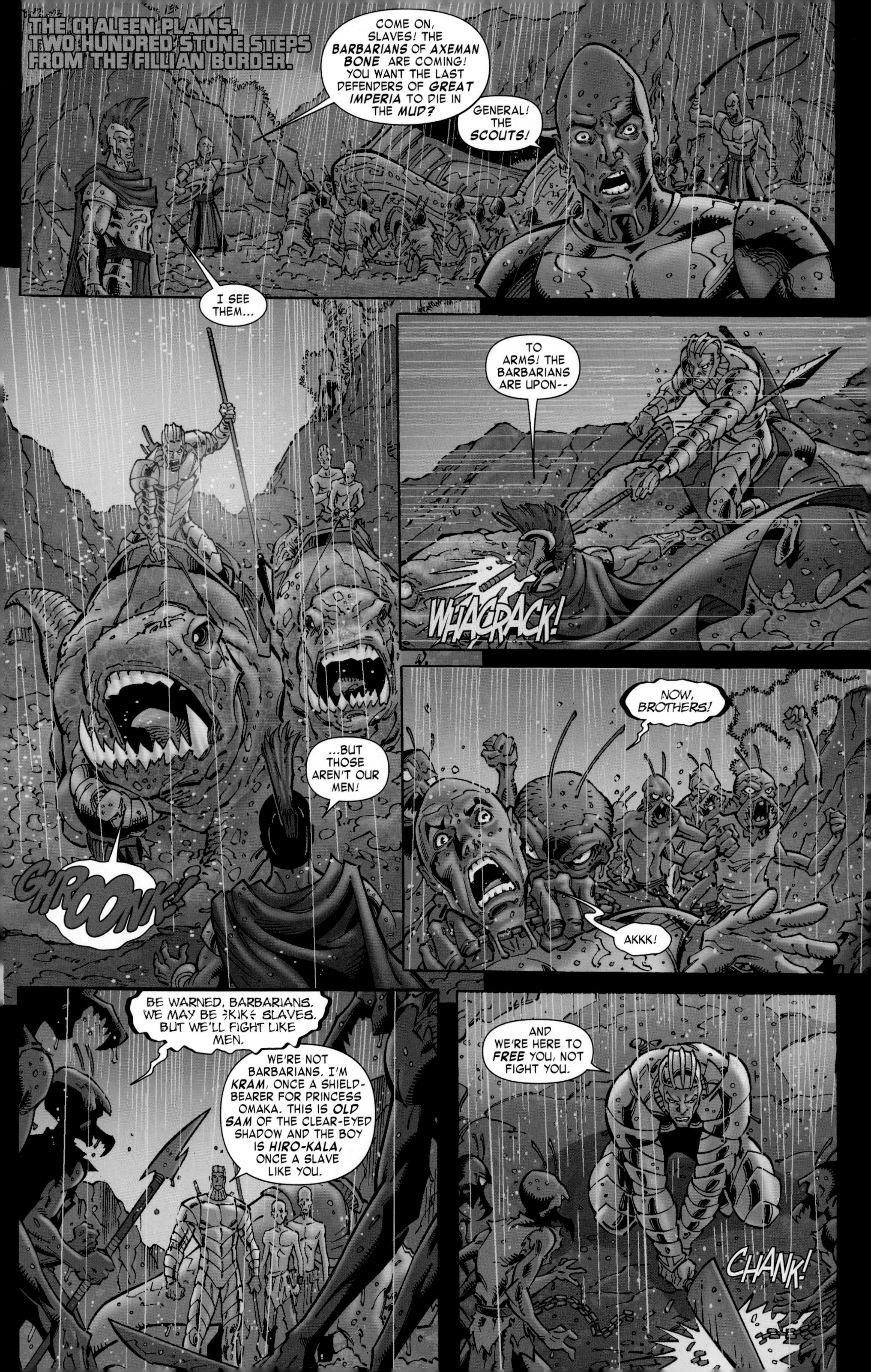
THE CHALEEN PLAINS. TWO HUNDRED STONE STEPS FROM THE FILLIAN BORDER.
COME ON, SLAVES! THE BARBARIANS OF AXEMAN BONE ARE COMING! YOU WANT THE LAST DEFENDERS OF GREAT IMPERIA TO DIE IN THE MUD?
GENERAL! THE SCOUTS!
I SEE THEM...
TO ARMS! THE BARBARIANS ARE UPON--
WHACRACK!
...BUT THOSE AREN'T OUR MEN!
GHROONK!
NOW, BROTHERS!
AKKK!
BE WARNED, BARBARIANS. WE MAY BE KIK SLAVES. BUT WE'LL FIGHT LIKE MEN.
WE'RE NOT BARBARIANS. I'M KRAM, ONCE A SHIELD-BEARER FOR PRINCESS OMAKA. THIS IS OLD SAM OF THE CLEAR-EYED SHADOW AND THE BOY IS HIRO-KALA, ONCE A SLAVE LIKE YOU.
AND WE'RE HERE TO FREE YOU, NOT FIGHT YOU.
CHANK!

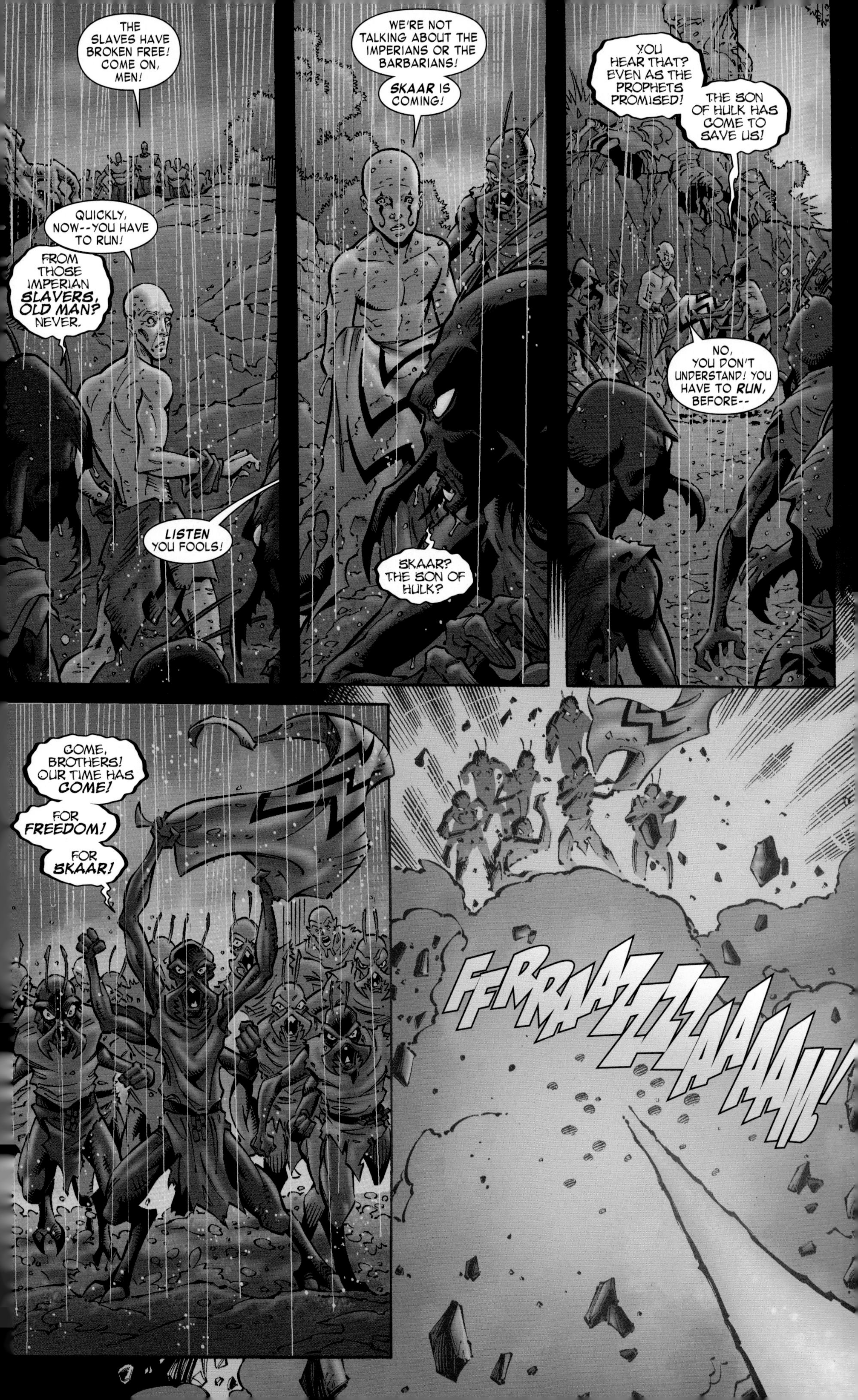
THE SLAVES HAVE BROKEN FREE! COME ON, MEN!
QUICKLY, NOW--YOU HAVE TO RUN!
FROM THOSE IMPERIAN SLAVERS, OLD MAN? NEVER.
LISTEN YOU FOOLS!
WE'RE NOT TALKING ABOUT THE IMPERIANS OR THE BARBARIANS!
SKAAR IS COMING!
SKAAR? THE SON OF HULK?
YOU HEAR THAT? EVEN AS THE PROPHETS PROMISED!
THE SON OF HULK HAS COME TO SAVE US!
NO, YOU DON'T UNDERSTAND! YOU HAVE TO RUN, BEFORE--
COME, BROTHERS! OUR TIME HAS COME!
FOR FREEDOM!
FOR SKAAR!
FFRRAAZZZAAAM!

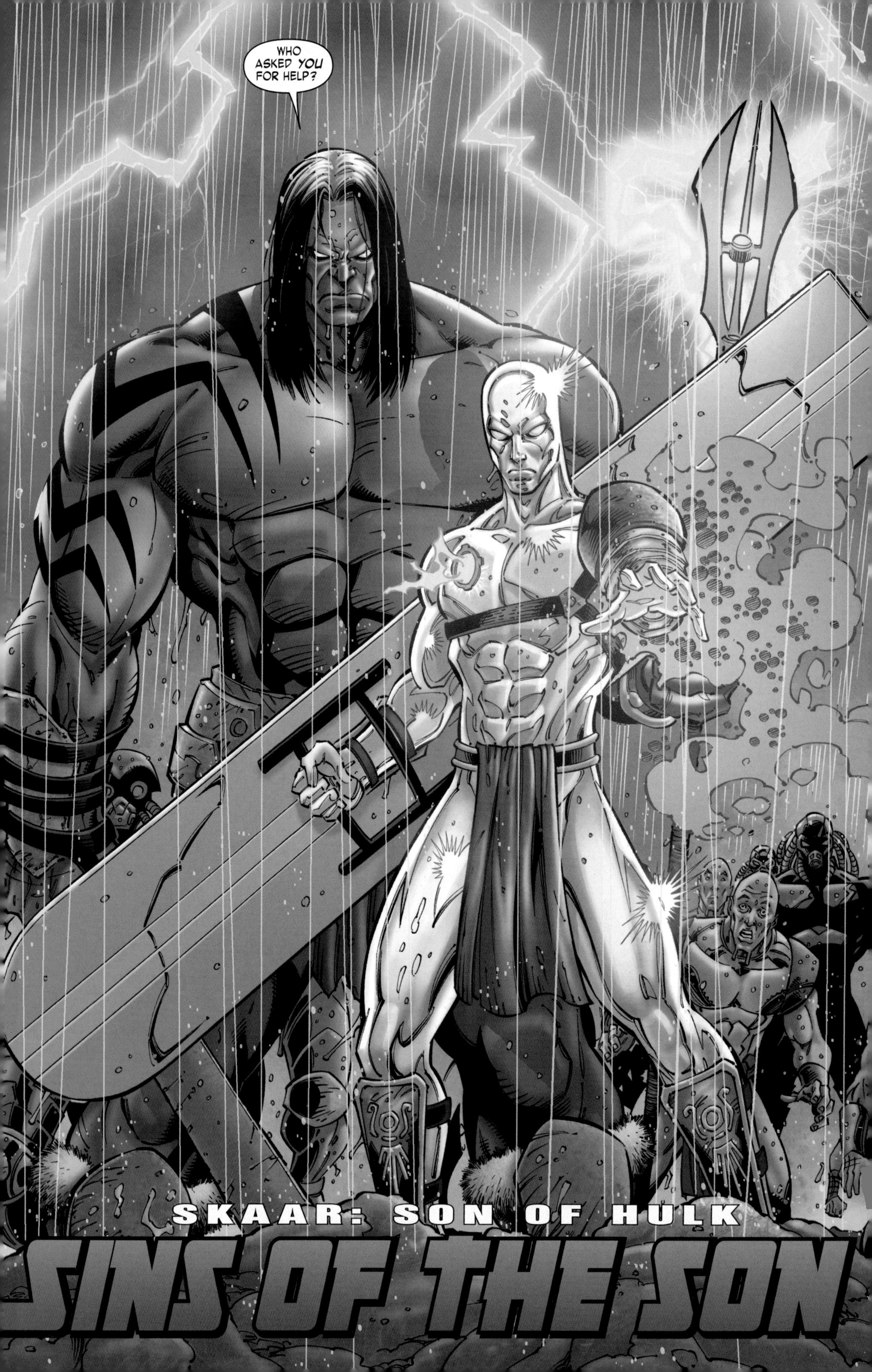
WHO ASKED YOU FOR HELP?
SKAAR: SON OF HULK
SINS OF THE SON

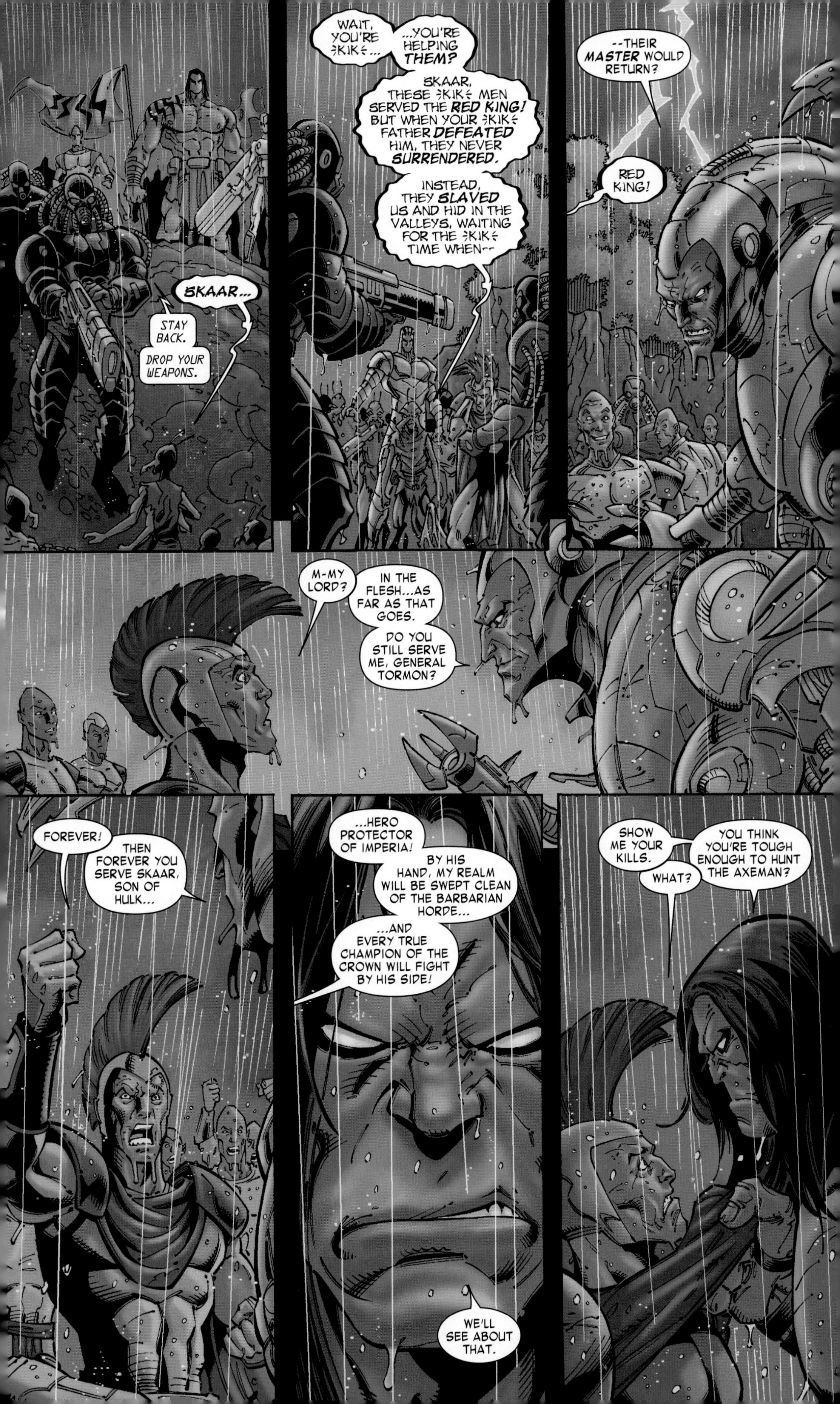

STAY BACK.
DROP YOUR WEAPONS.
SKAAR...
WAIT, YOU'RE ⸗KIK⸗...
...YOU'RE HELPING THEM?
SKAAR, THESE ⸗KIK⸗ MEN SERVED THE RED KING! BUT WHEN YOUR ⸗KIK⸗ FATHER DEFEATED HIM, THEY NEVER SURRENDERED.
INSTEAD, THEY SLAVED US AND HID IN THE VALLEYS, WAITING FOR THE ⸗KIK⸗ TIME WHEN--
--THEIR MASTER WOULD RETURN?
RED KING!
M-MY LORD?
IN THE FLESH...AS FAR AS THAT GOES.
DO YOU STILL SERVE ME, GENERAL TORMON?
FOREVER!
THEN FOREVER YOU SERVE SKAAR, SON OF HULK...
...HERO PROTECTOR OF IMPERIA!
BY HIS HAND, MY REALM WILL BE SWEPT CLEAN OF THE BARBARIAN HORDE...
...AND EVERY TRUE CHAMPION OF THE CROWN WILL FIGHT BY HIS SIDE!
WE'LL SEE ABOUT THAT.
SHOW ME YOUR KILLS.
WHAT?
YOU THINK YOU'RE TOUGH ENOUGH TO HUNT THE AXEMAN?

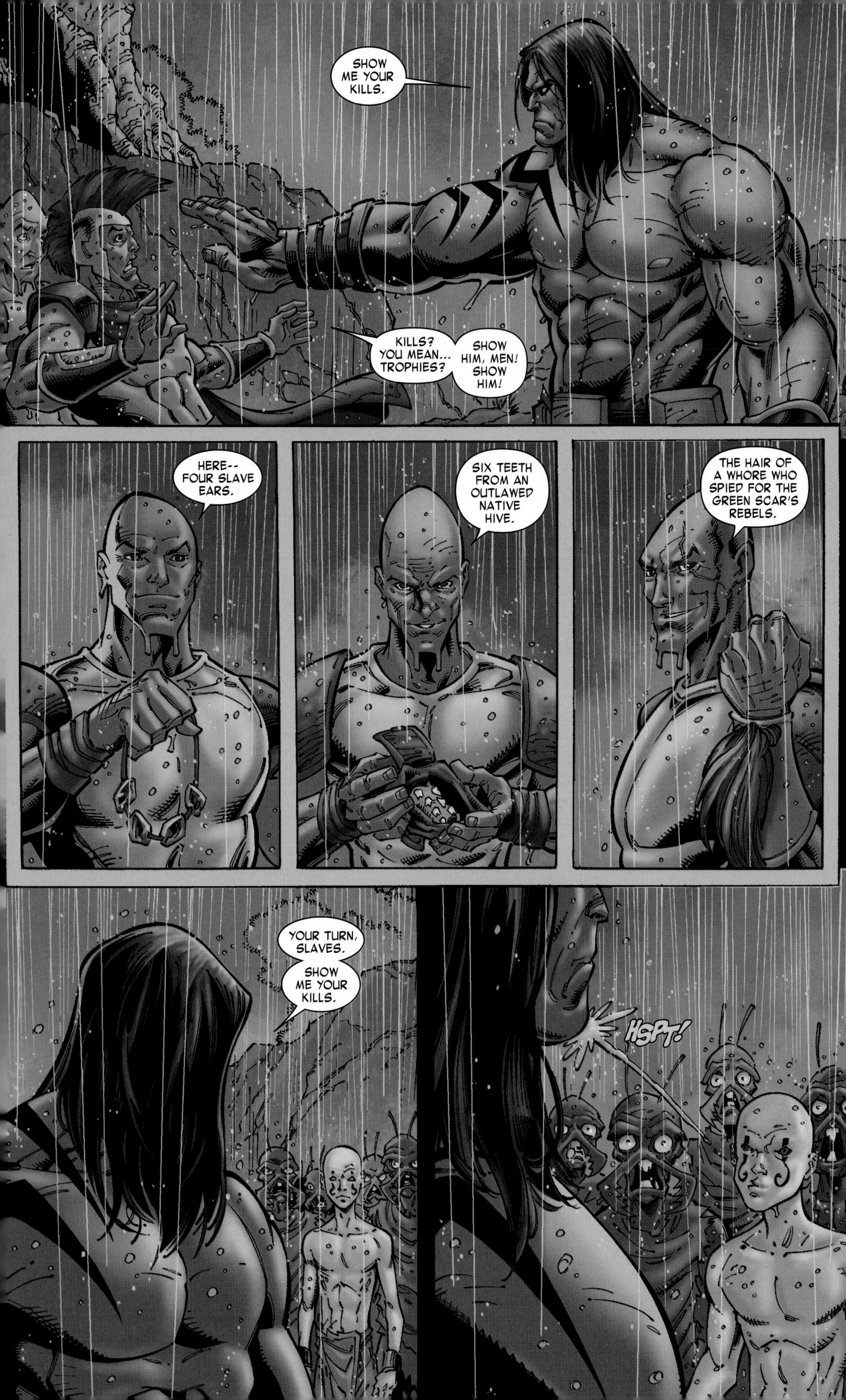
SHOW ME YOUR KILLS.
KILLS? YOU MEAN... TROPHIES?
SHOW HIM, MEN! SHOW HIM!
HERE-- FOUR SLAVE EARS.
SIX TEETH FROM AN OUTLAWED NATIVE HIVE.
THE HAIR OF A WHORE WHO SPIED FOR THE GREEN SCAR'S REBELS.
YOUR TURN, SLAVES.
SHOW ME YOUR KILLS.
HSPT!

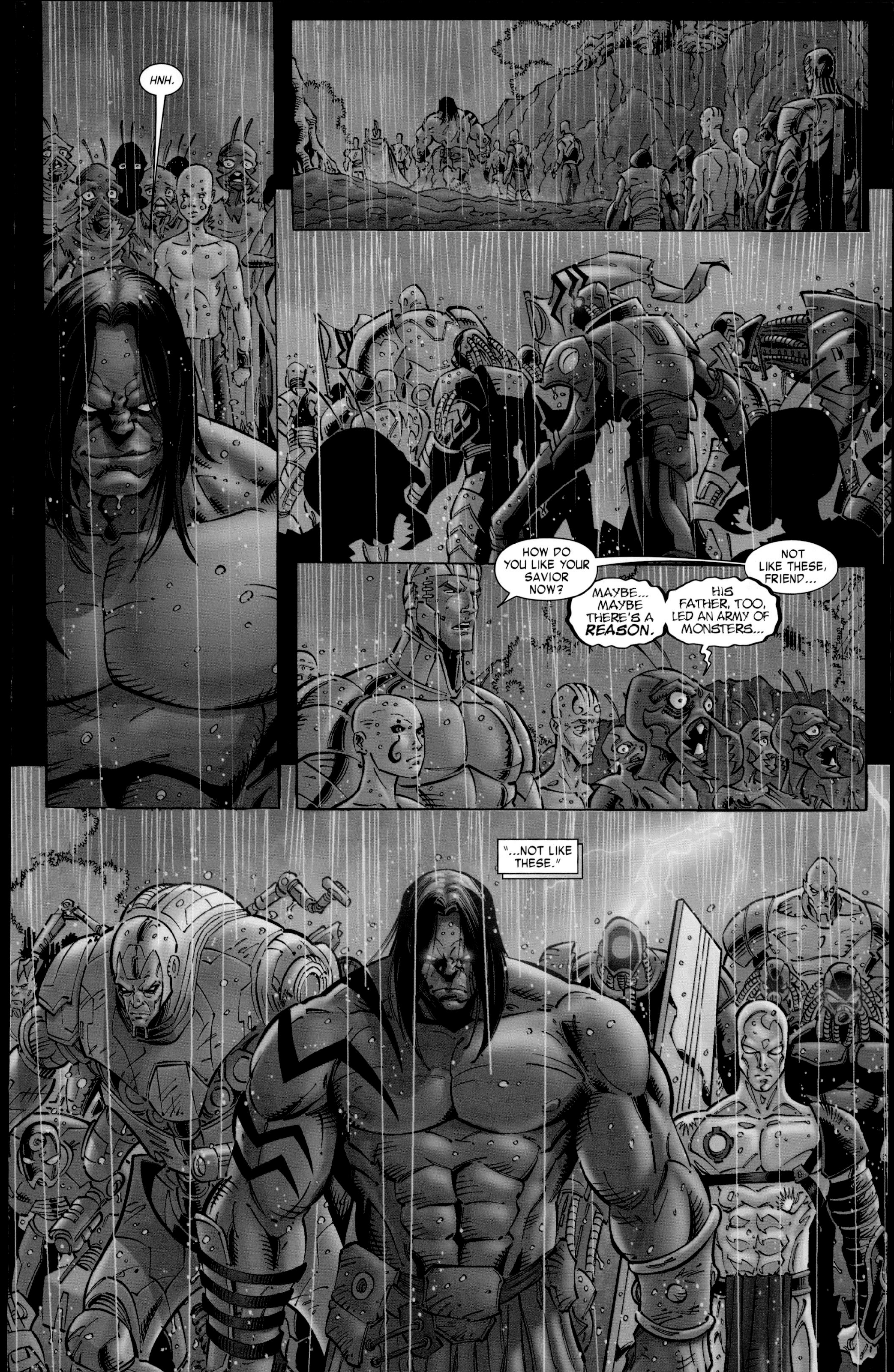

HNH.
HOW DO YOU LIKE YOUR SAVIOR NOW?
NOT LIKE THESE, FRIEND...
MAYBE... MAYBE THERE'S A **REASON.**
HIS FATHER, TOO, LED AN ARMY OF MONSTERS...
"...NOT LIKE THESE."

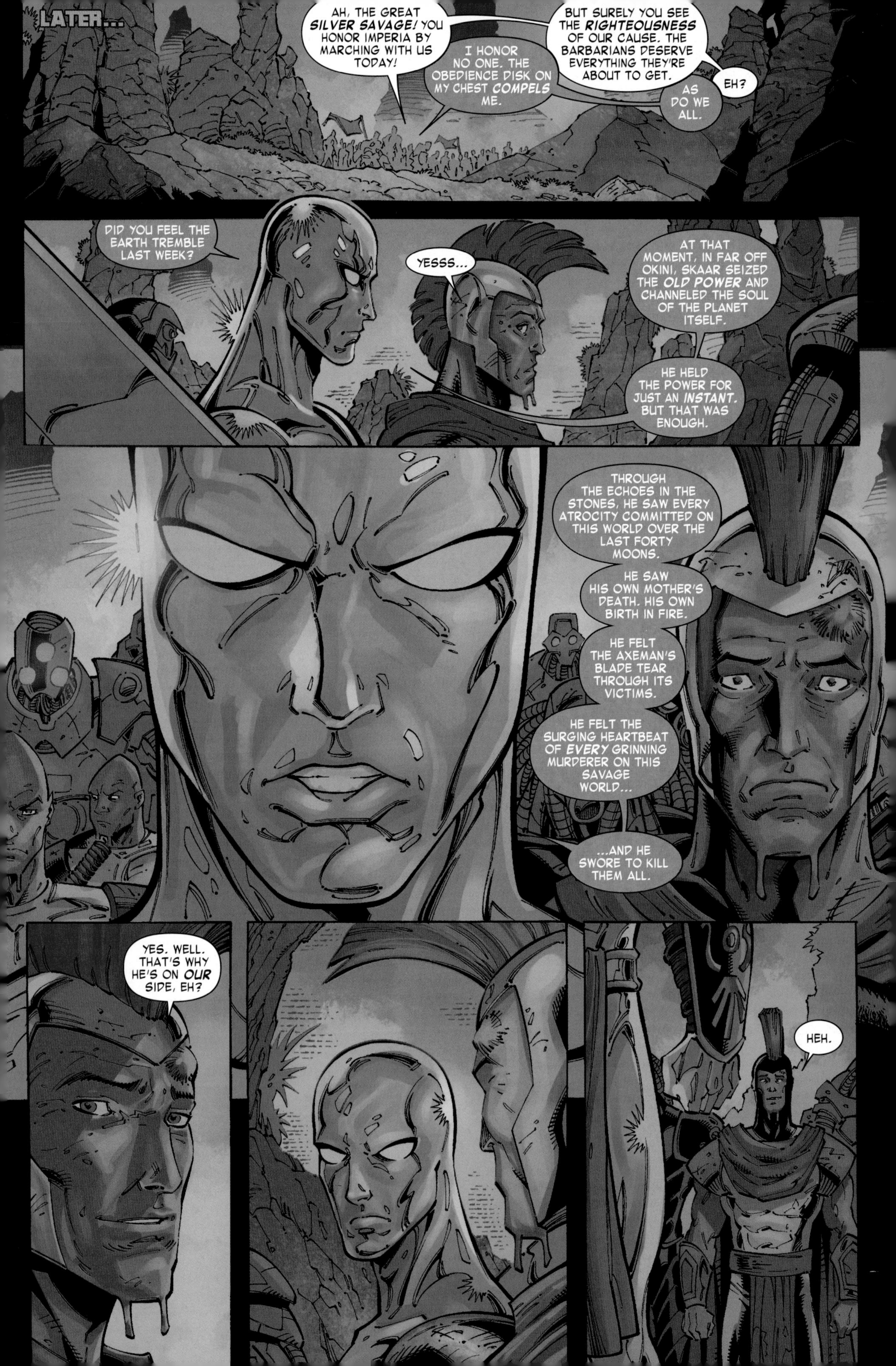
LATER...
AH, THE GREAT SILVER SAVAGE! YOU HONOR IMPERIA BY MARCHING WITH US TODAY!
I HONOR NO ONE. THE OBEDIENCE DISK ON MY CHEST COMPELS ME.
BUT SURELY YOU SEE THE RIGHTEOUSNESS OF OUR CAUSE. THE BARBARIANS DESERVE EVERYTHING THEY'RE ABOUT TO GET.
AS DO WE ALL.
EH?
DID YOU FEEL THE EARTH TREMBLE LAST WEEK?
YESSS...
AT THAT MOMENT, IN FAR OFF OKINI, SKAAR SEIZED THE OLD POWER AND CHANNELED THE SOUL OF THE PLANET ITSELF.
HE HELD THE POWER FOR JUST AN INSTANT. BUT THAT WAS ENOUGH.
THROUGH THE ECHOES IN THE STONES, HE SAW EVERY ATROCITY COMMITTED ON THIS WORLD OVER THE LAST FORTY MOONS.
HE SAW HIS OWN MOTHER'S DEATH. HIS OWN BIRTH IN FIRE.
HE FELT THE AXEMAN'S BLADE TEAR THROUGH ITS VICTIMS.
HE FELT THE SURGING HEARTBEAT OF EVERY GRINNING MURDERER ON THIS SAVAGE WORLD...
...AND HE SWORE TO KILL THEM ALL.
YES. WELL. THAT'S WHY HE'S ON OUR SIDE, EH?
HEH.

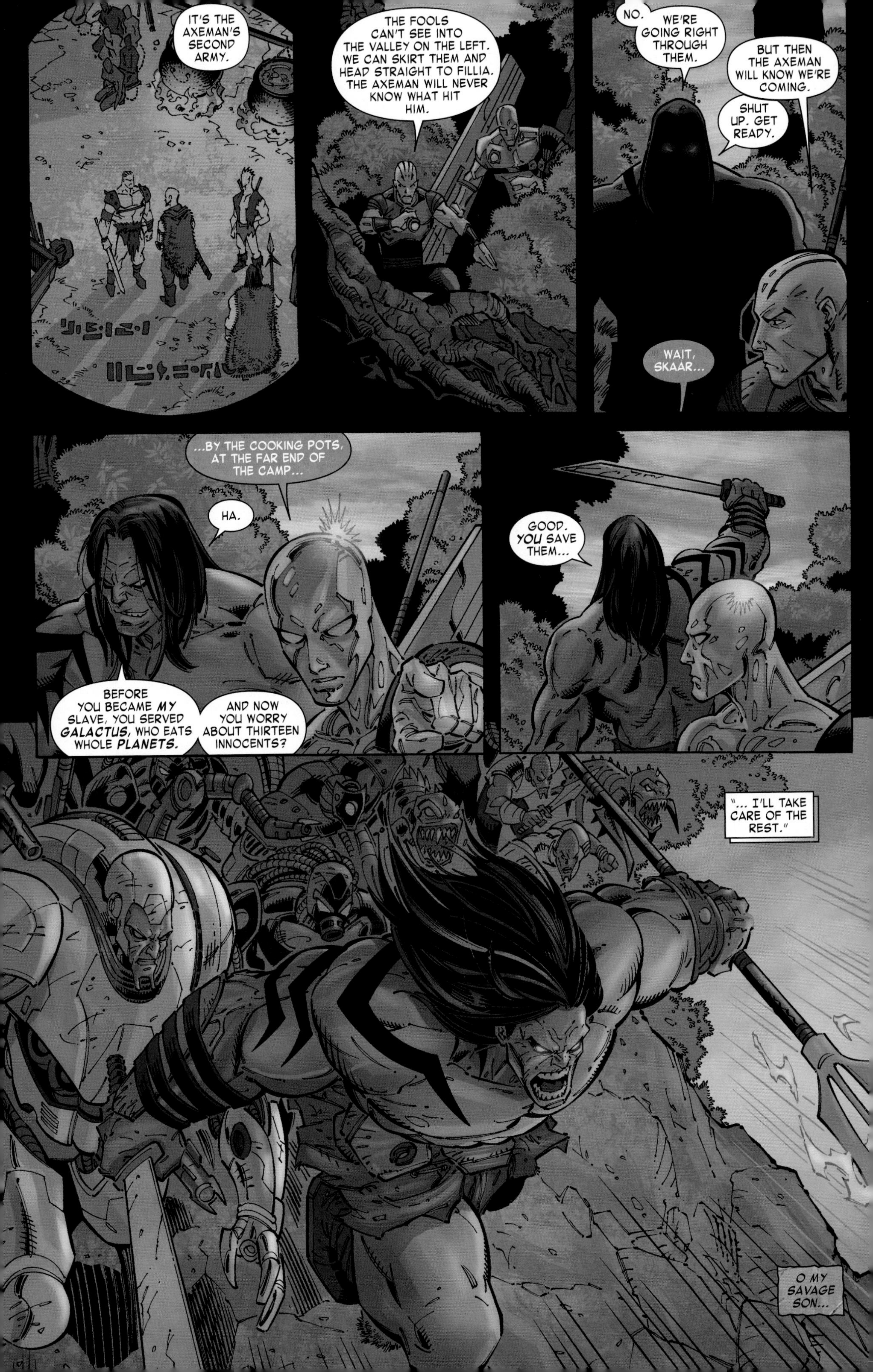
IT'S THE AXEMAN'S SECOND ARMY.
THE FOOLS CAN'T SEE INTO THE VALLEY ON THE LEFT. WE CAN SKIRT THEM AND HEAD STRAIGHT TO FILLIA. THE AXEMAN WILL NEVER KNOW WHAT HIT HIM.
NO.
WE'RE GOING RIGHT THROUGH THEM.
BUT THEN THE AXEMAN WILL KNOW WE'RE COMING.
SHUT UP. GET READY.
WAIT, SKAAR...
...BY THE COOKING POTS, AT THE FAR END OF THE CAMP...
HA.
BEFORE YOU BECAME MY SLAVE, YOU SERVED GALACTUS, WHO EATS WHOLE PLANETS.
AND NOW YOU WORRY ABOUT THIRTEEN INNOCENTS?
GOOD. YOU SAVE THEM...
"... I'LL TAKE CARE OF THE REST."
O MY SAVAGE SON...

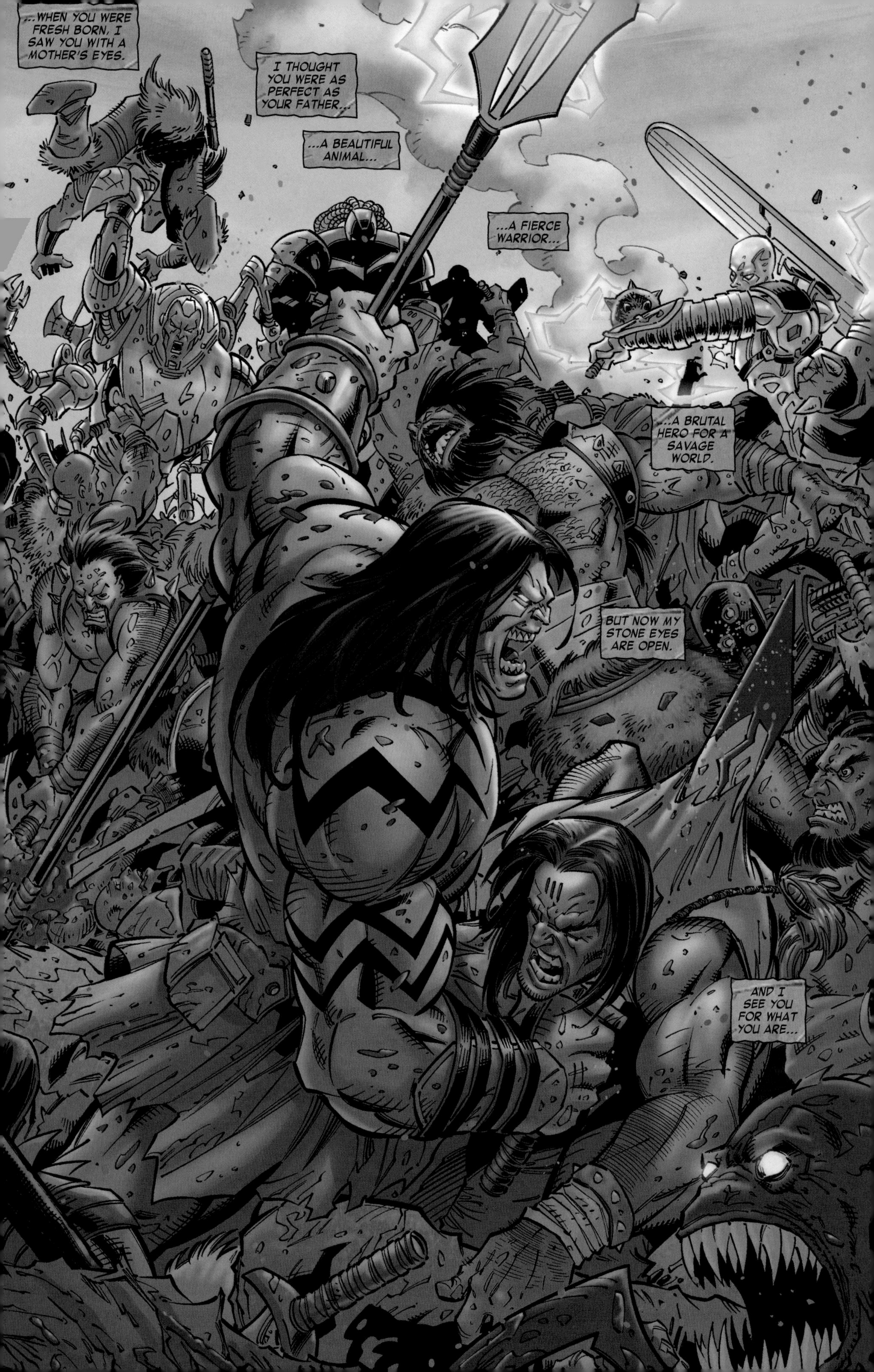
...WHEN YOU WERE FRESH BORN, I SAW YOU WITH A MOTHER'S EYES.
I THOUGHT YOU WERE AS PERFECT AS YOUR FATHER...
...A BEAUTIFUL ANIMAL...
...A FIERCE WARRIOR...
...A BRUTAL HERO FOR A SAVAGE WORLD.
BUT NOW MY STONE EYES ARE OPEN.
AND I SEE YOU FOR WHAT YOU ARE...

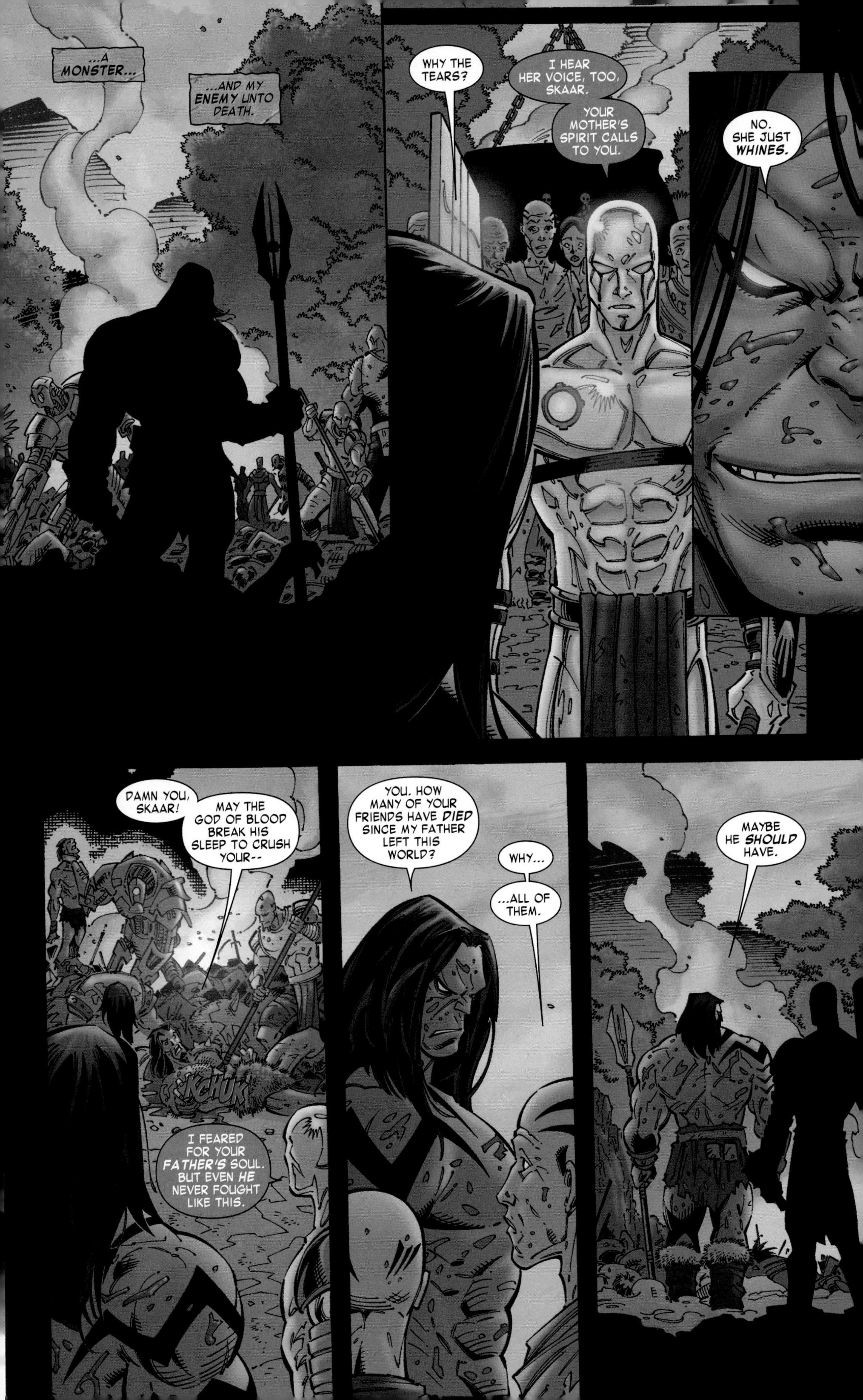
...A MONSTER...
...AND MY ENEMY UNTO DEATH.
WHY THE TEARS?
I HEAR HER VOICE, TOO, SKAAR.
YOUR MOTHER'S SPIRIT CALLS TO YOU.
NO. SHE JUST WHINES.
DAMN YOU, SKAAR!
MAY THE GOD OF BLOOD BREAK HIS SLEEP TO CRUSH YOUR--
SKCHUK
I FEARED FOR YOUR FATHER'S SOUL. BUT EVEN HE NEVER FOUGHT LIKE THIS.
YOU. HOW MANY OF YOUR FRIENDS HAVE DIED SINCE MY FATHER LEFT THIS WORLD?
WHY...
...ALL OF THEM.
MAYBE HE SHOULD HAVE.

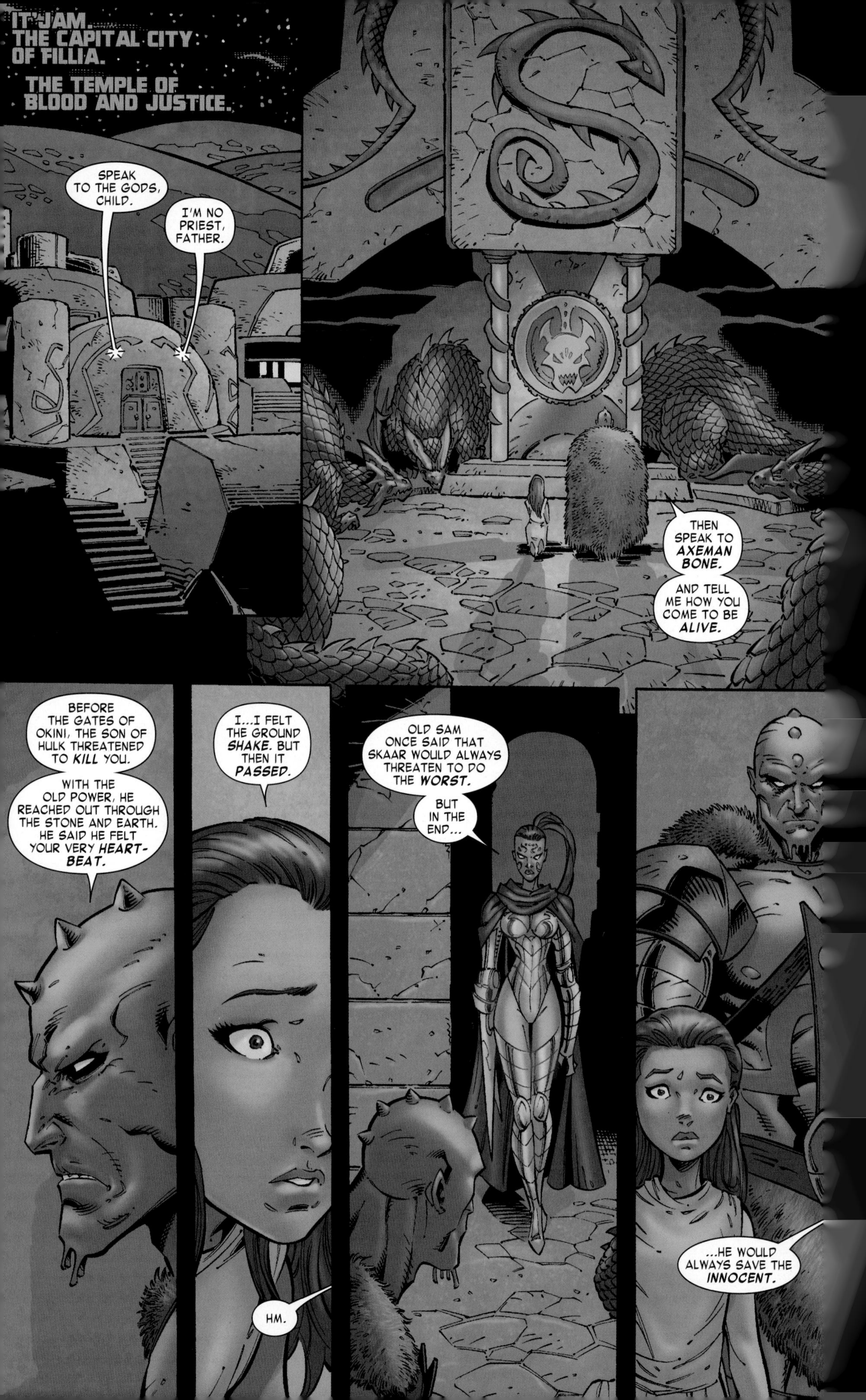
IT'JAM. THE CAPITAL CITY OF FILLIA.
THE TEMPLE OF BLOOD AND JUSTICE.
SPEAK TO THE GODS, CHILD.
I'M NO PRIEST, FATHER.
THEN SPEAK TO AXEMAN BONE.
AND TELL ME HOW YOU COME TO BE ALIVE.
BEFORE THE GATES OF OKINI, THE SON OF HULK THREATENED TO KILL YOU.
WITH THE OLD POWER, HE REACHED OUT THROUGH THE STONE AND EARTH. HE SAID HE FELT YOUR VERY HEART-BEAT.
HM.
I...I FELT THE GROUND SHAKE. BUT THEN IT PASSED.
OLD SAM ONCE SAID THAT SKAAR WOULD ALWAYS THREATEN TO DO THE WORST.
BUT IN THE END...
...HE WOULD ALWAYS SAVE THE INNOCENT.

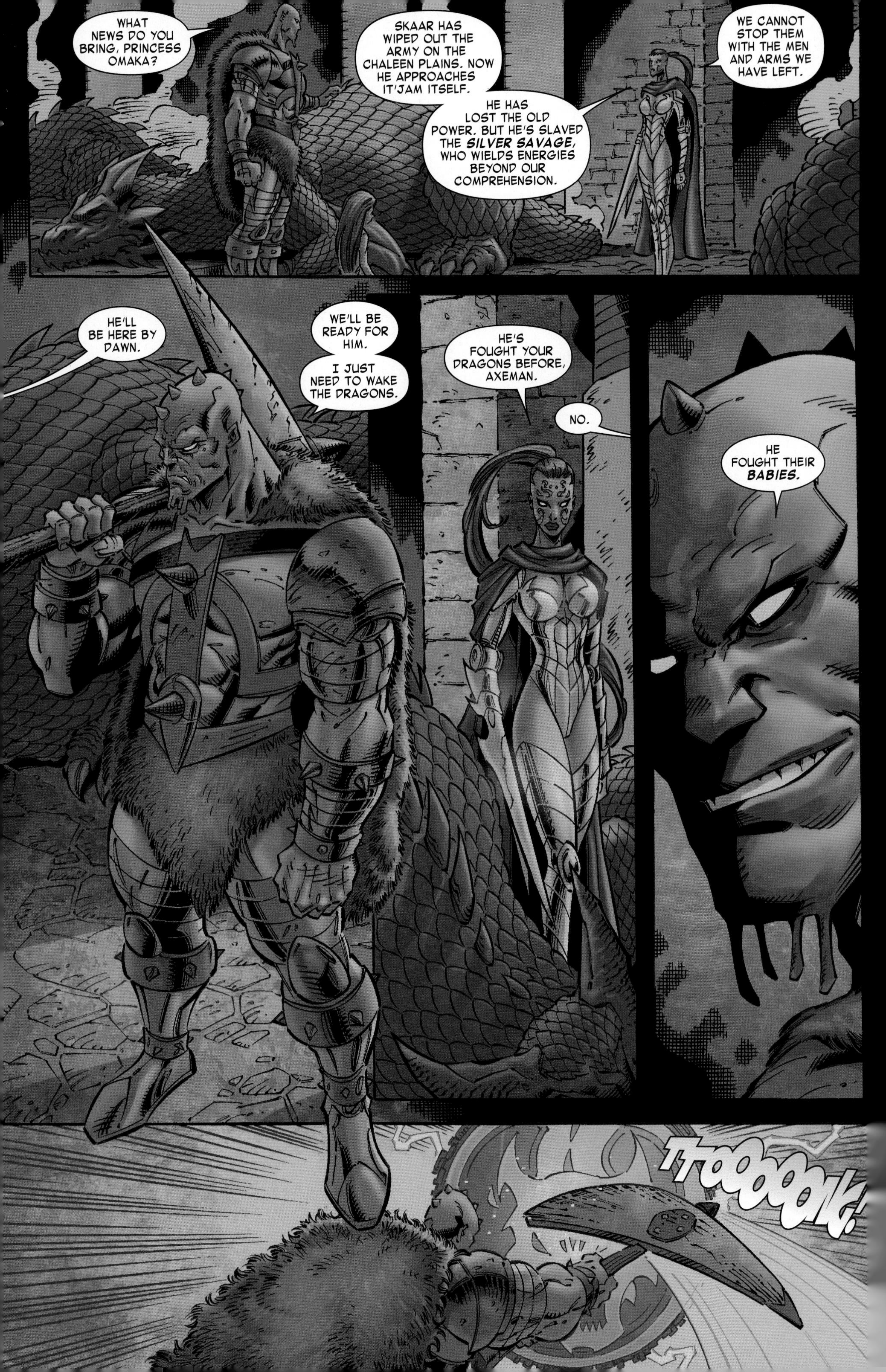
WHAT NEWS DO YOU BRING, PRINCESS OMAKA?
SKAAR HAS WIPED OUT THE ARMY ON THE CHALEEN PLAINS. NOW HE APPROACHES IT'JAM ITSELF.
HE HAS LOST THE OLD POWER. BUT HE'S SLAVED THE SILVER SAVAGE, WHO WIELDS ENERGIES BEYOND OUR COMPREHENSION.
WE CANNOT STOP THEM WITH THE MEN AND ARMS WE HAVE LEFT.
HE'LL BE HERE BY DAWN.
WE'LL BE READY FOR HIM.
I JUST NEED TO WAKE THE DRAGONS.
HE'S FOUGHT YOUR DRAGONS BEFORE, AXEMAN.
NO.
HE FOUGHT THEIR BABIES.
TTOOOOOM!

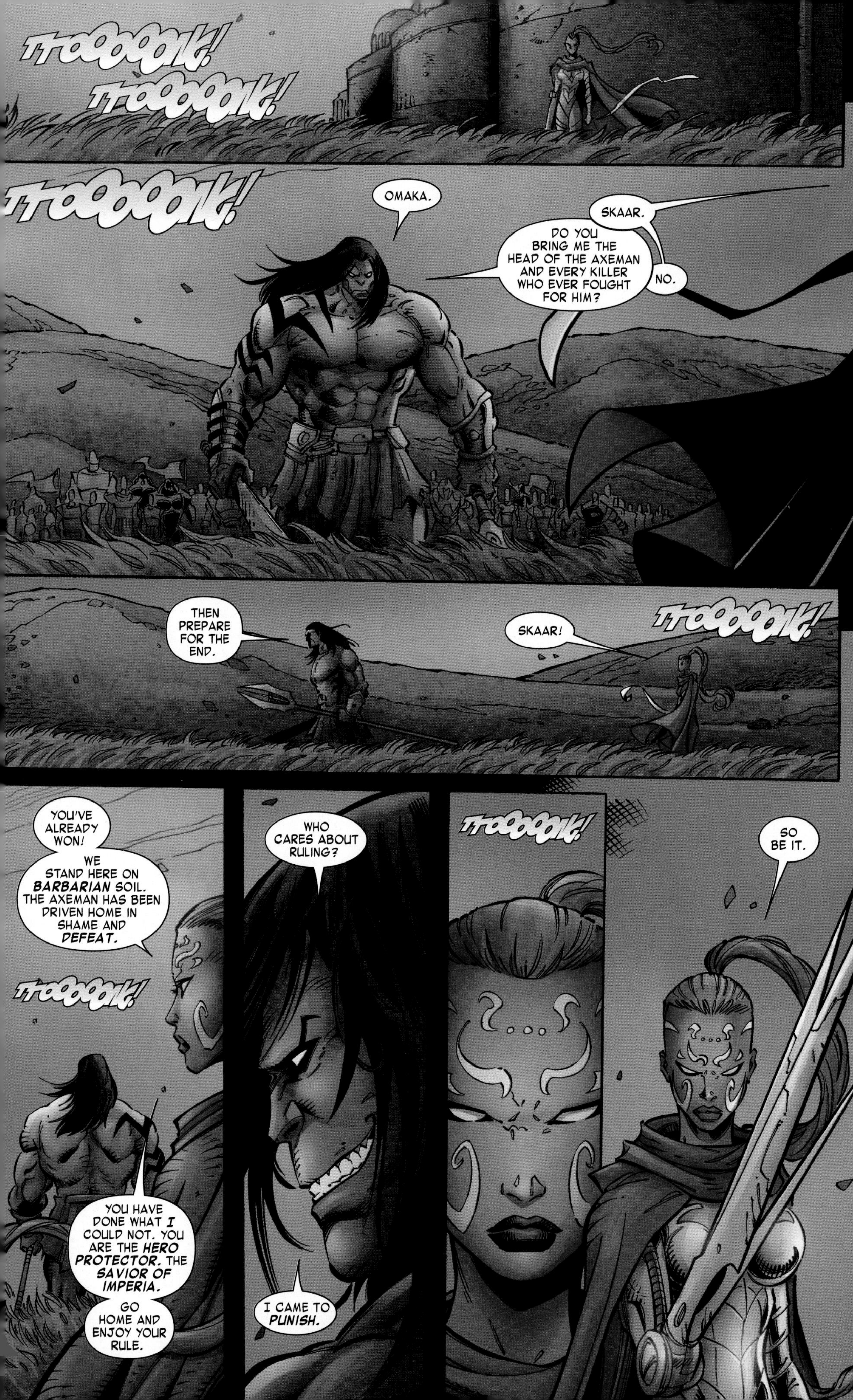
TTOOOOONK!
TTOOOOONK!
TTOOOOONK!
OMAKA.
SKAAR.
DO YOU BRING ME THE HEAD OF THE AXEMAN AND EVERY KILLER WHO EVER FOUGHT FOR HIM?
NO.
THEN PREPARE FOR THE END.
SKAAR!
TTOOOOONK!
YOU'VE ALREADY WON!
WE STAND HERE ON BARBARIAN SOIL. THE AXEMAN HAS BEEN DRIVEN HOME IN SHAME AND DEFEAT.
TTOOOOONK!
YOU HAVE DONE WHAT I COULD NOT. YOU ARE THE HERO PROTECTOR. THE SAVIOR OF IMPERIA.
GO HOME AND ENJOY YOUR RULE.
WHO CARES ABOUT RULING?
I CAME TO PUNISH.
TTOOOOONK!
SO BE IT.

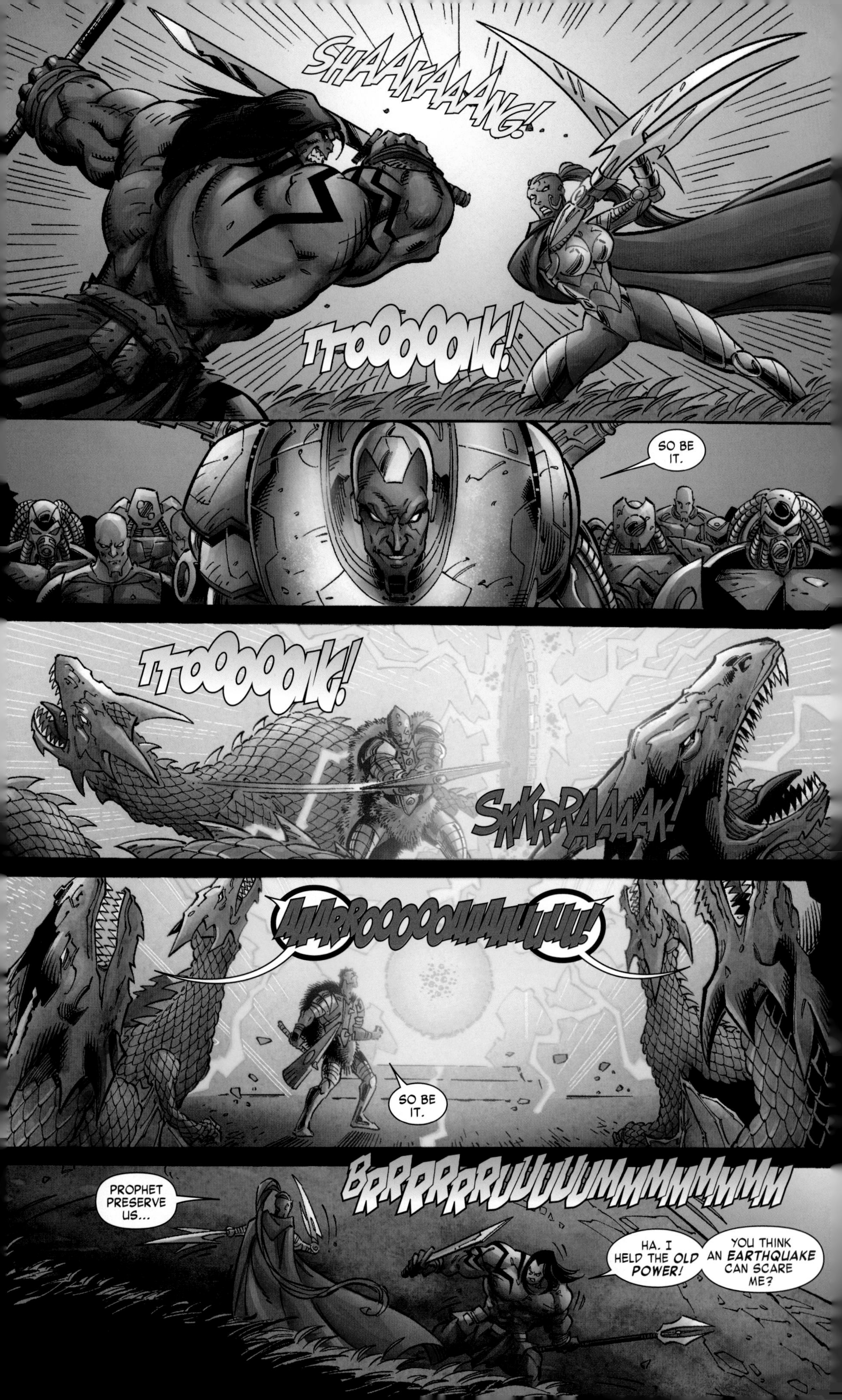
SHAAKAAANG!
TTOOOOOOM!
SO BE IT.
TTOOOOOOM!
SKKRRAAAAK!
AAARROOOOOOAAAUUUU!
SO BE IT.
BRRRRRRUUUUUMMMMMMMMM
PROPHET PRESERVE US...
HA. I HELD THE OLD POWER!
YOU THINK AN EARTHQUAKE CAN SCARE ME?

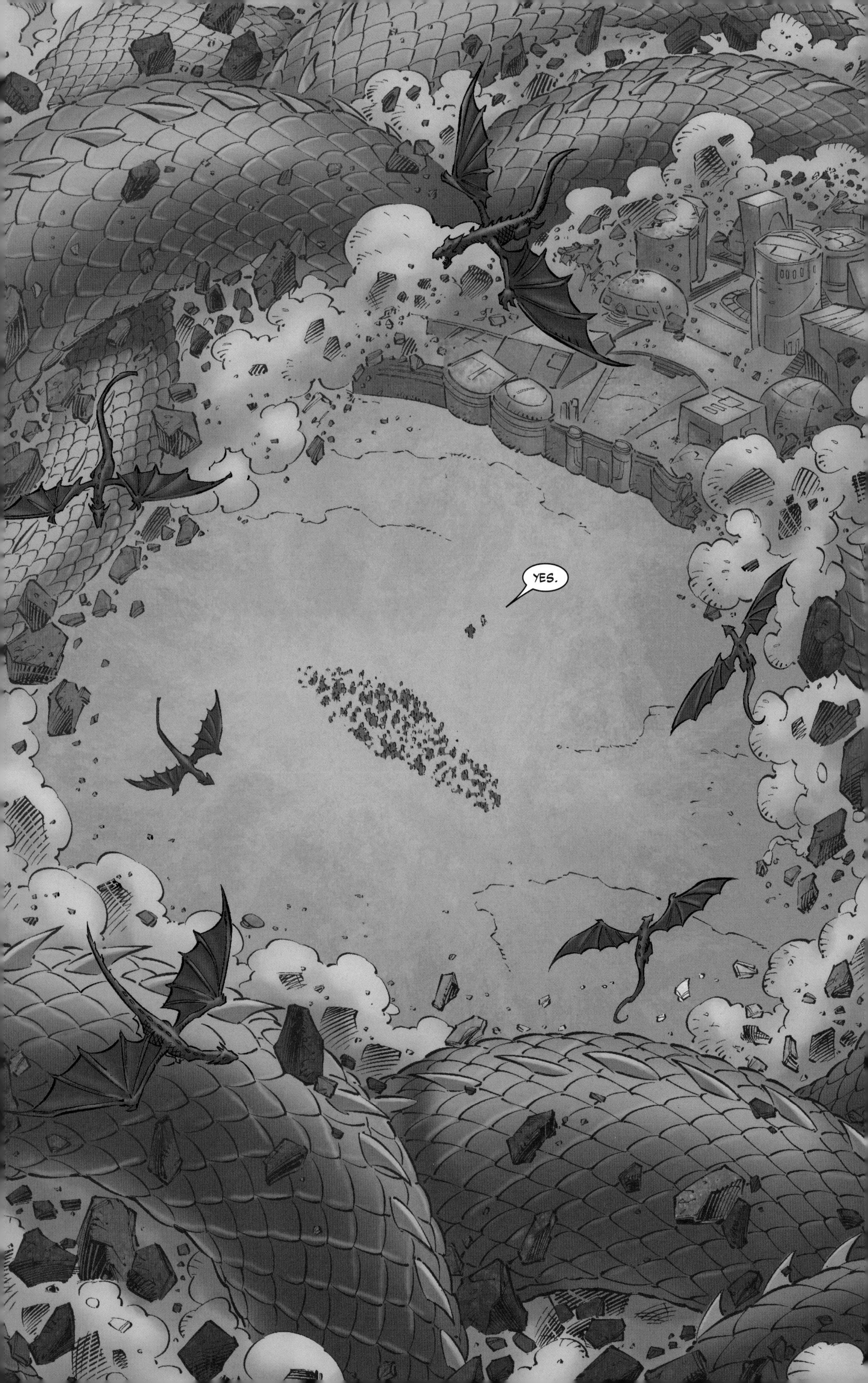
YES.

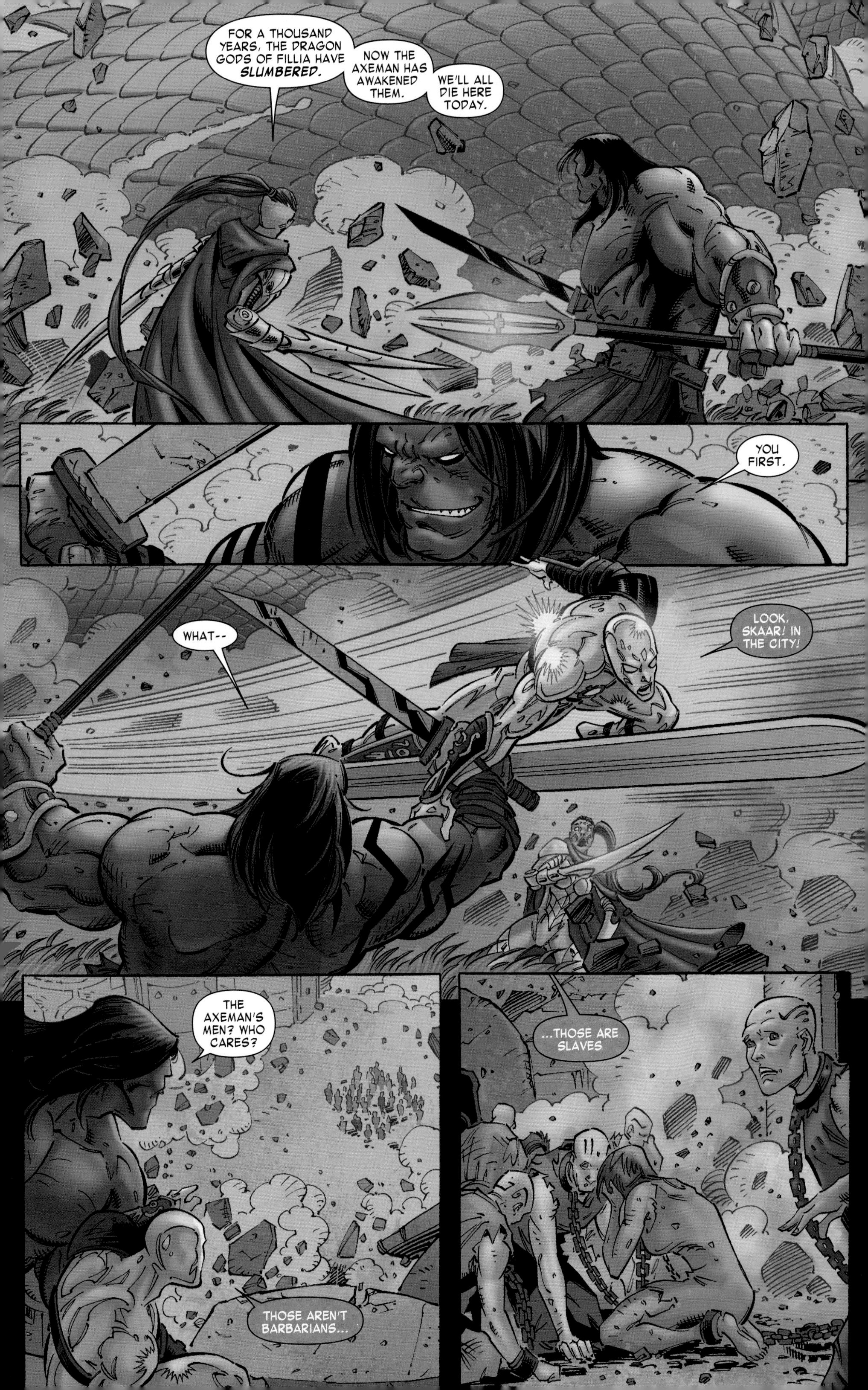
FOR A THOUSAND YEARS, THE DRAGON GODS OF FILLIA HAVE SLUMBERED.
NOW THE AXEMAN HAS AWAKENED THEM.
WE'LL ALL DIE HERE TODAY.
YOU FIRST.
WHAT--
LOOK, SKAAR! IN THE CITY!
THE AXEMAN'S MEN? WHO CARES?
THOSE AREN'T BARBARIANS...
...THOSE ARE SLAVES

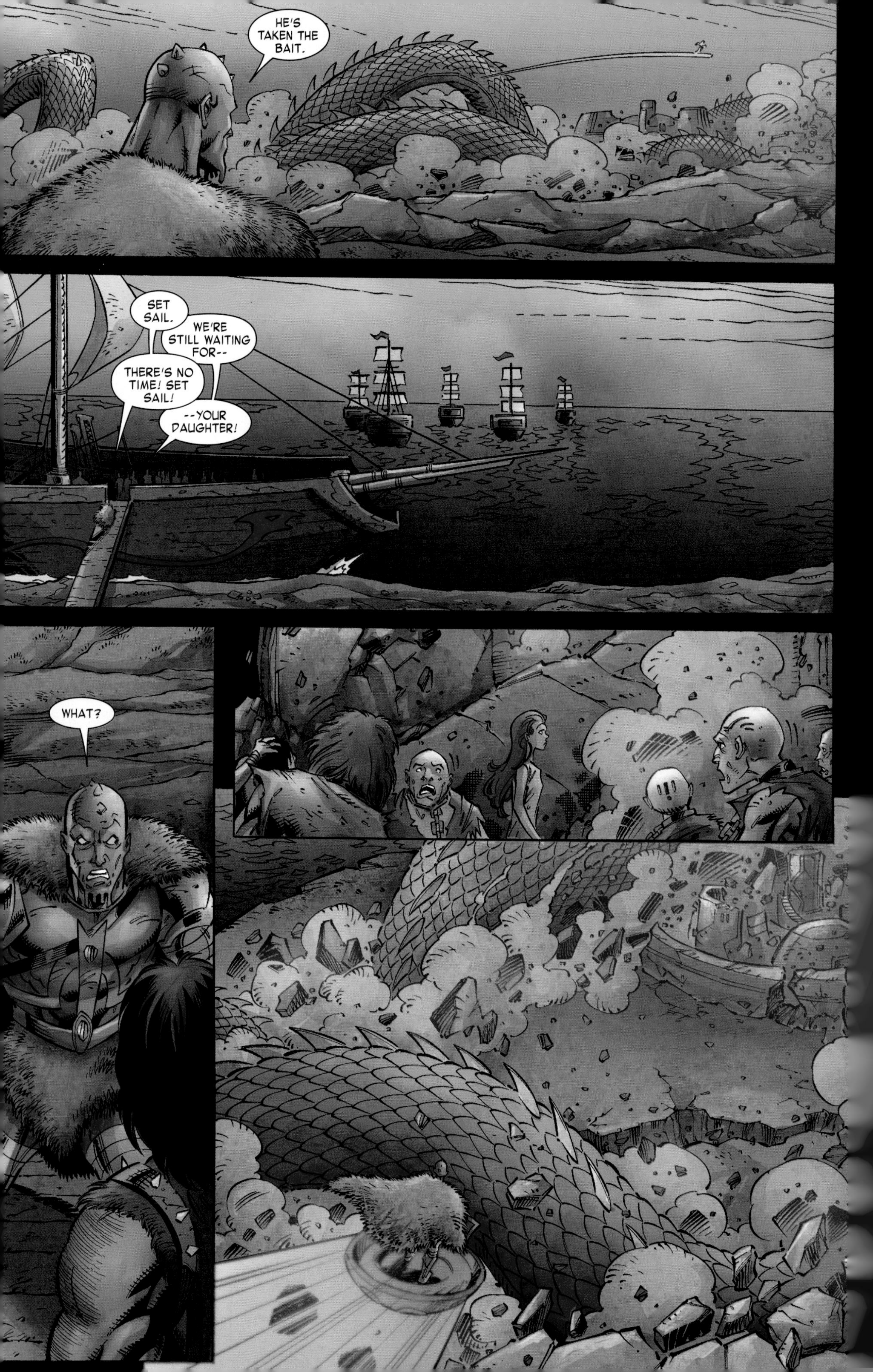

HE'S TAKEN THE BAIT.
SET SAIL.
WE'RE STILL WAITING FOR--
THERE'S NO TIME! SET SAIL!
--YOUR DAUGHTER!
WHAT?

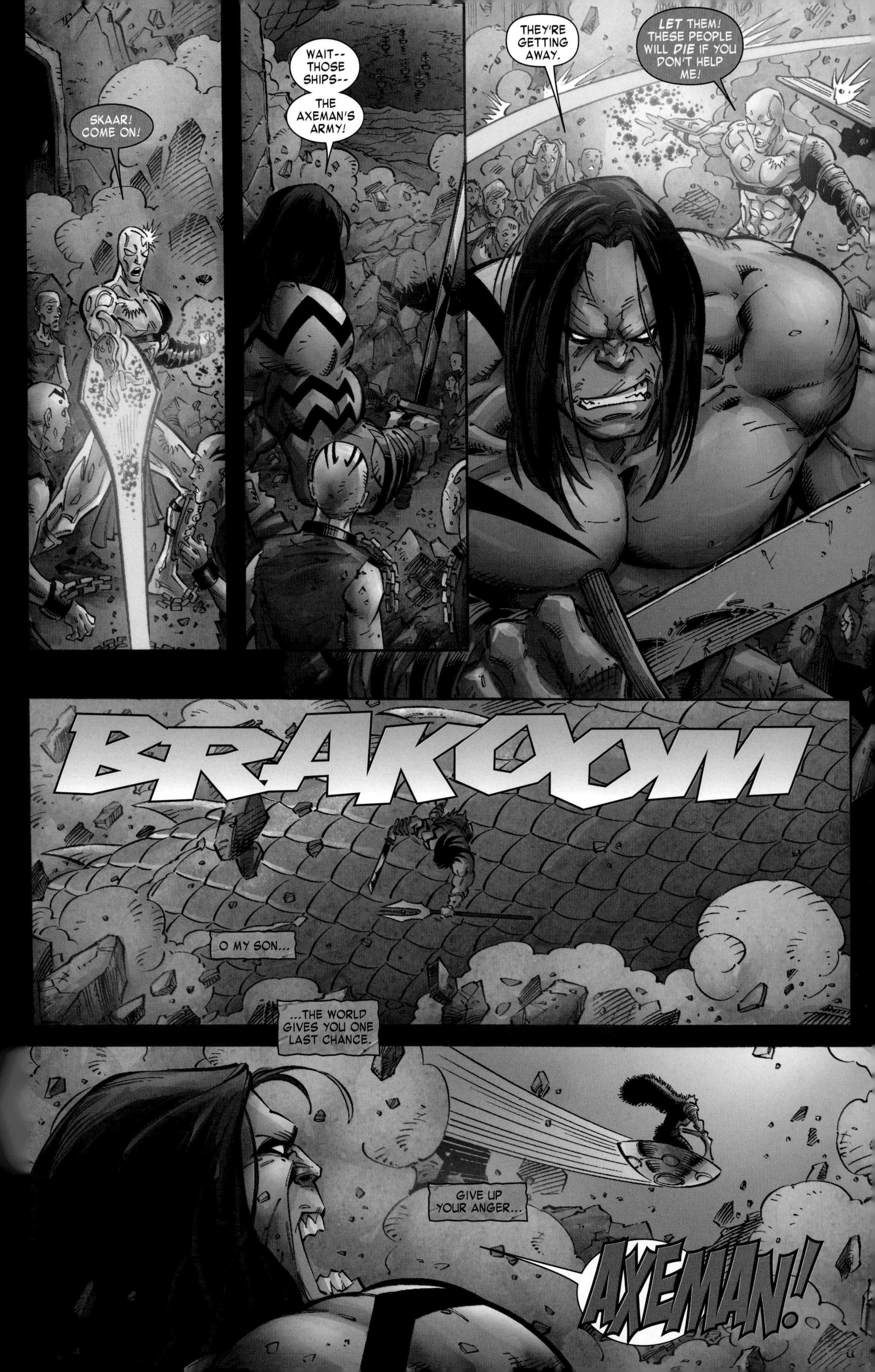
SKAAR! COME ON!
WAIT-- THOSE SHIPS--
THE AXEMAN'S ARMY!
THEY'RE GETTING AWAY.
LET THEM! THESE PEOPLE WILL DIE IF YOU DON'T HELP ME!
BRAKOOM
O MY SON...
...THE WORLD GIVES YOU ONE LAST CHANCE.
GIVE UP YOUR ANGER...
AXEMAN!!

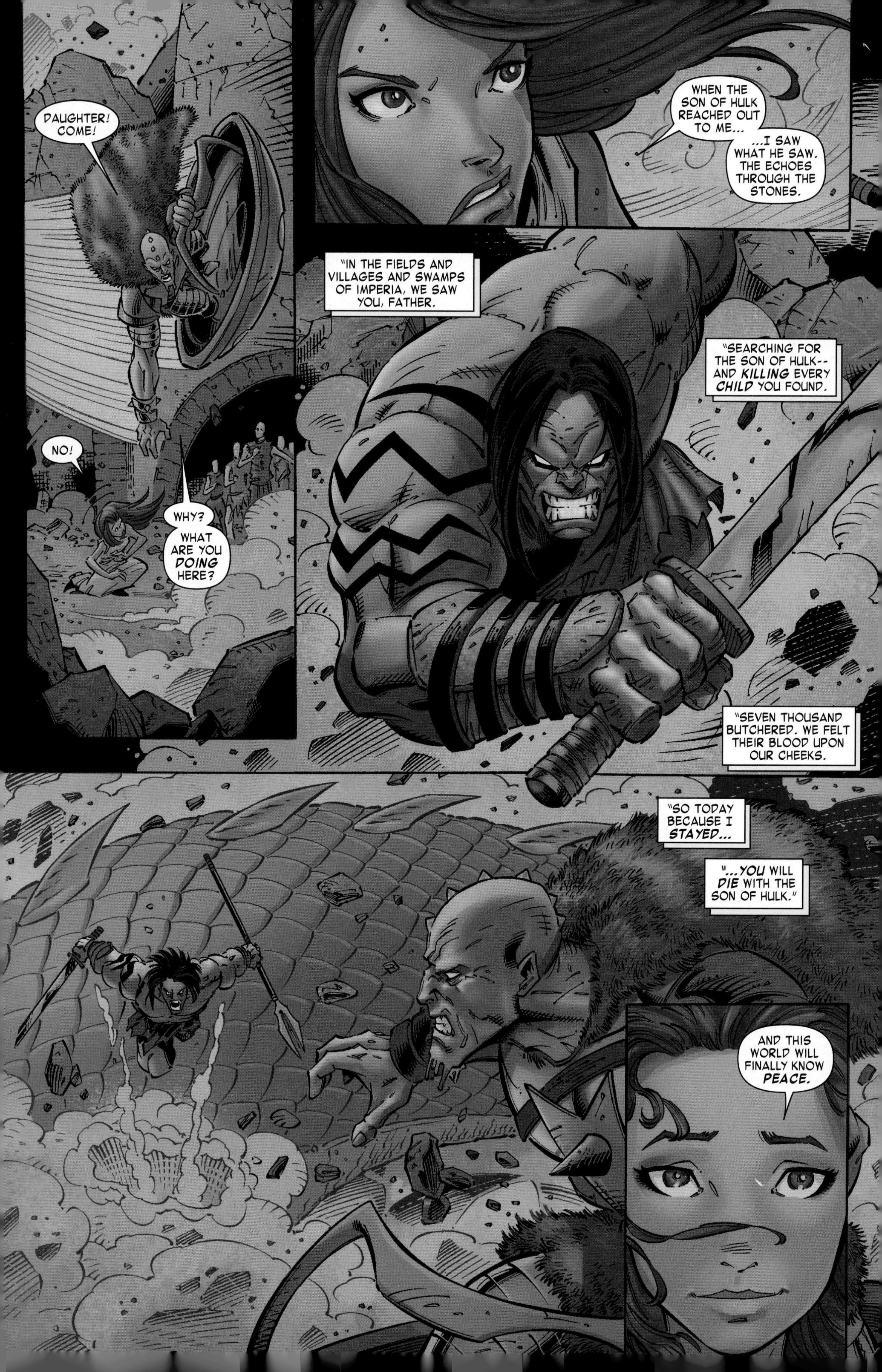
DAUGHTER! COME!
NO!
WHY? WHAT ARE YOU *DOING* HERE?
WHEN THE SON OF HULK REACHED OUT TO ME...
...I SAW WHAT HE SAW. THE ECHOES THROUGH THE STONES.
"IN THE FIELDS AND VILLAGES AND SWAMPS OF IMPERIA, WE SAW YOU, FATHER.
"SEARCHING FOR THE SON OF HULK-- AND *KILLING* EVERY *CHILD* YOU FOUND.
"SEVEN THOUSAND BUTCHERED. WE FELT THEIR BLOOD UPON OUR CHEEKS.
"SO TODAY BECAUSE I *STAYED*...
"...*YOU* WILL *DIE* WITH THE SON OF HULK."
AND THIS WORLD WILL FINALLY KNOW *PEACE.*

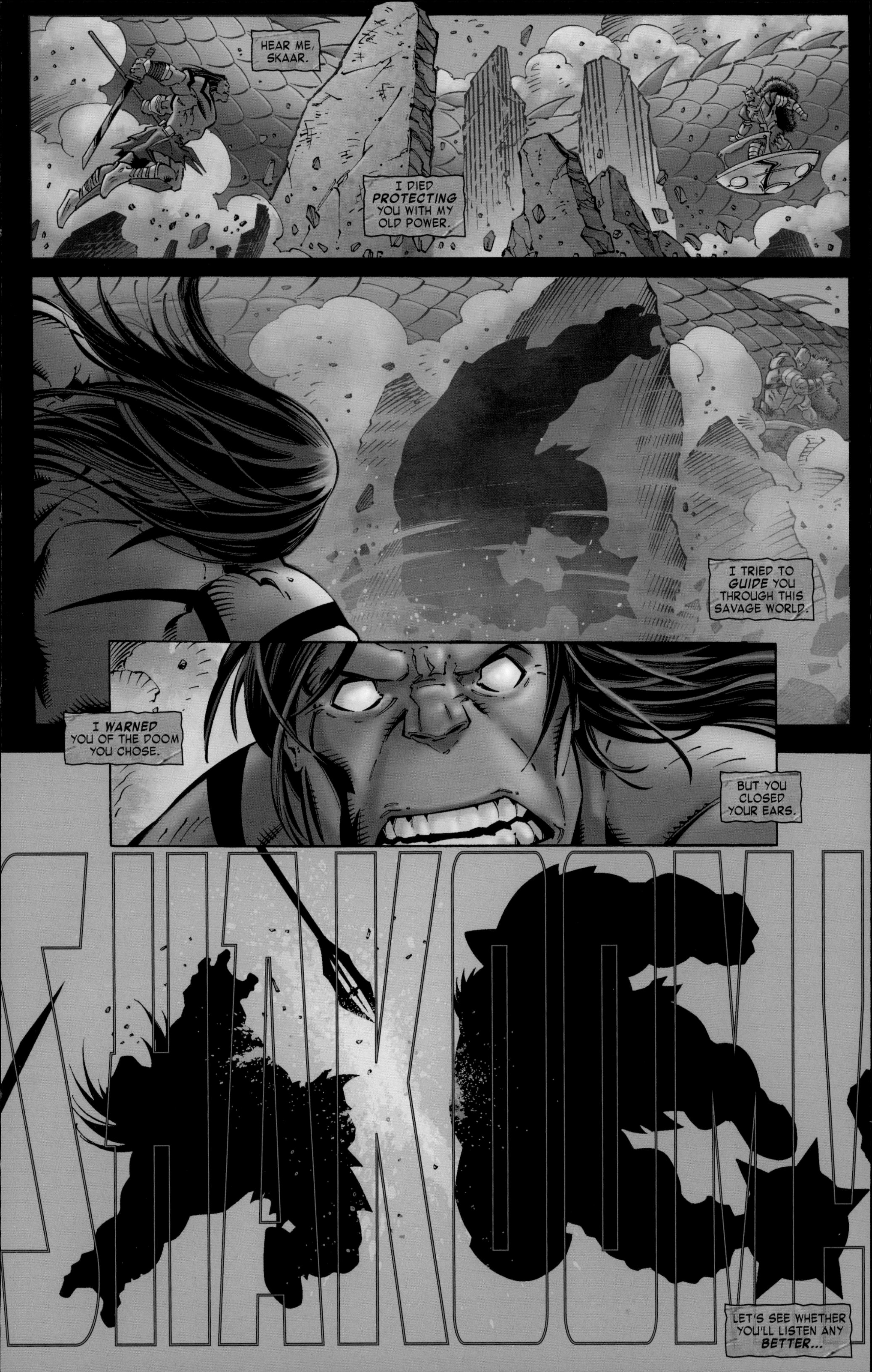
HEAR ME, SKAAR.
I DIED PROTECTING YOU WITH MY OLD POWER.
I TRIED TO GUIDE YOU THROUGH THIS SAVAGE WORLD.
I WARNED YOU OF THE DOOM YOU CHOSE.
BUT YOU CLOSED YOUR EARS.
SHAKOOM!
LET'S SEE WHETHER YOU'LL LISTEN ANY BETTER...

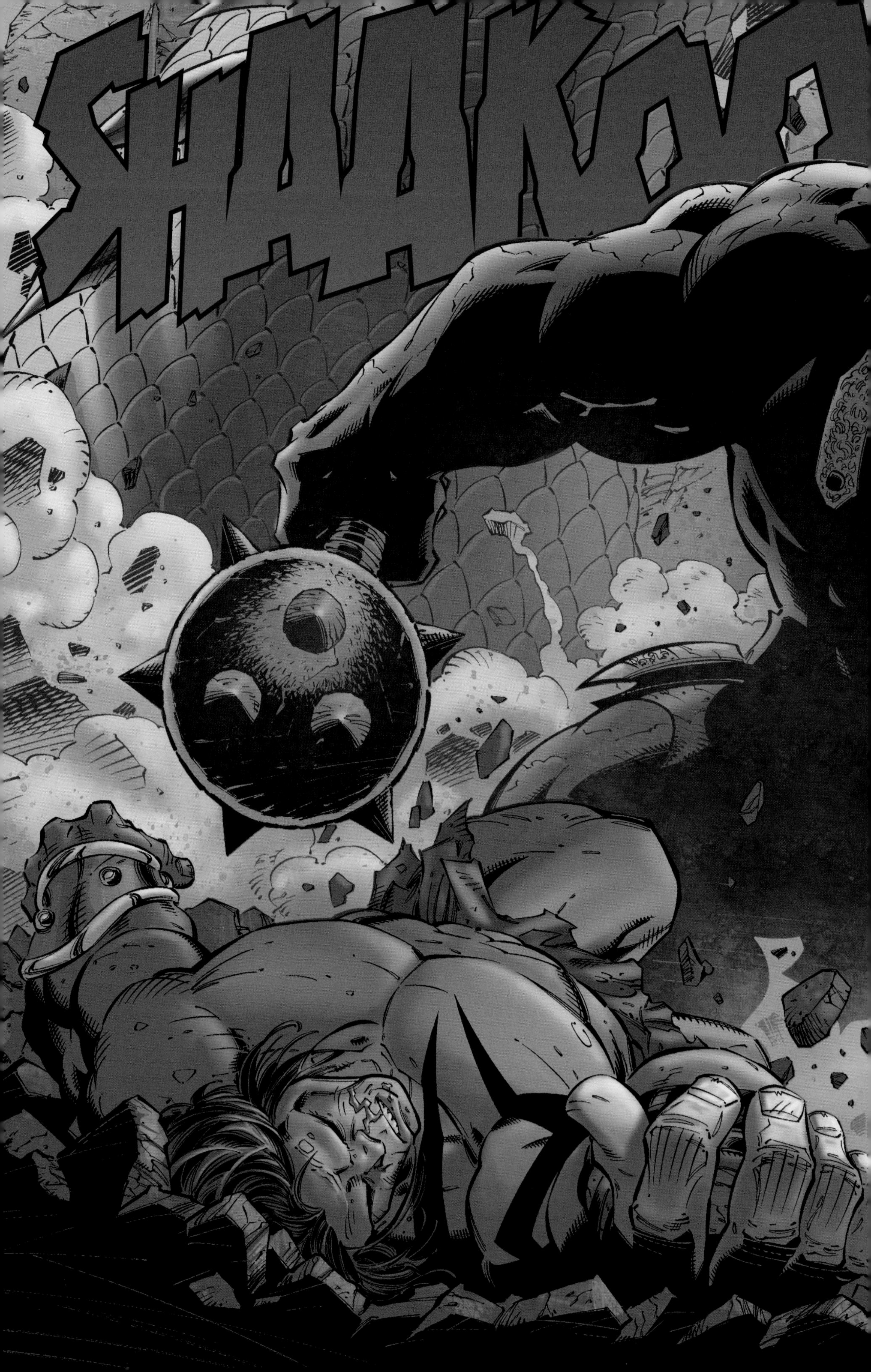
SHAAKO

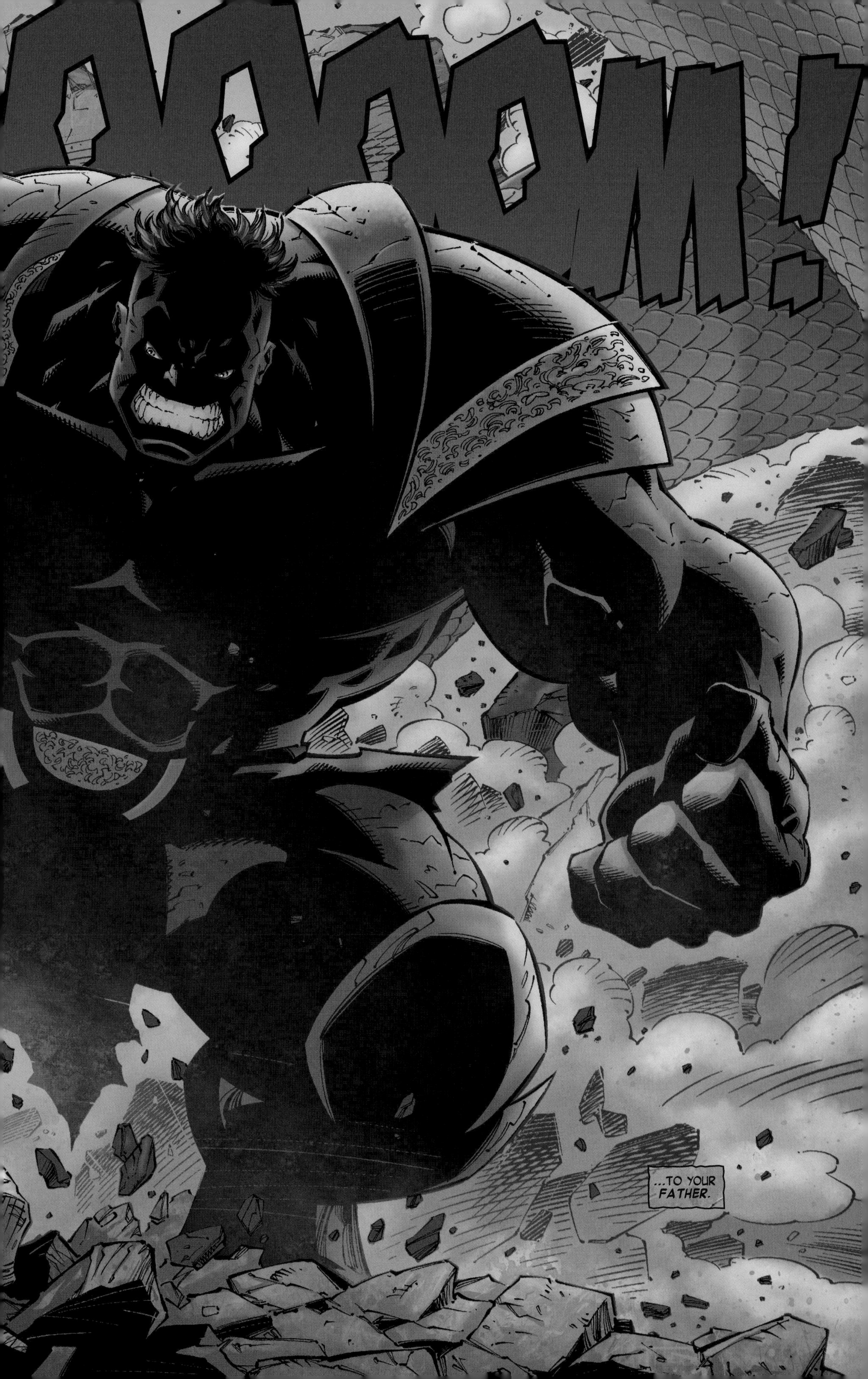
...TO YOUR *FATHER.*

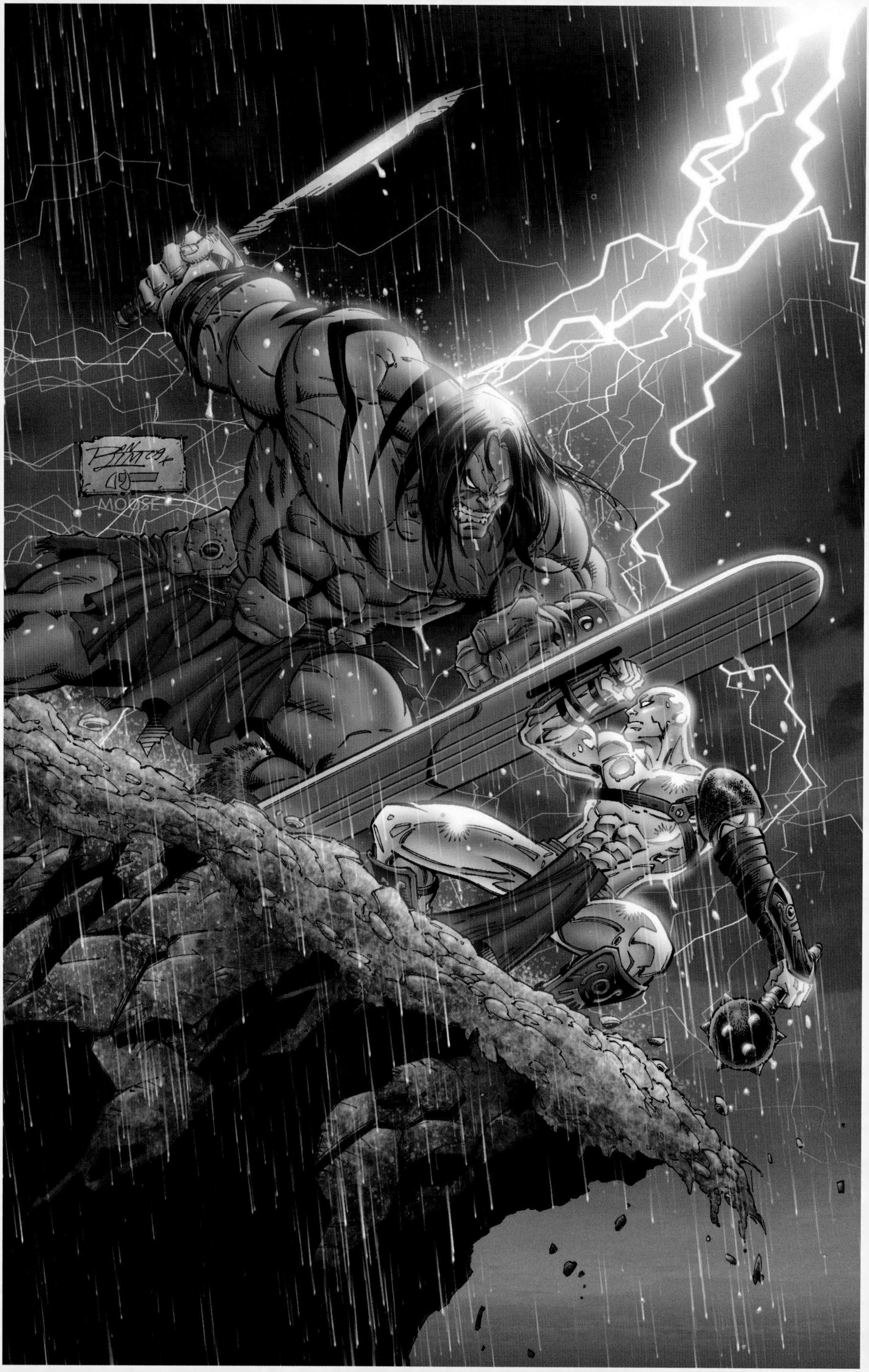
MOOSE

Skaar: Son of Hulk
#9

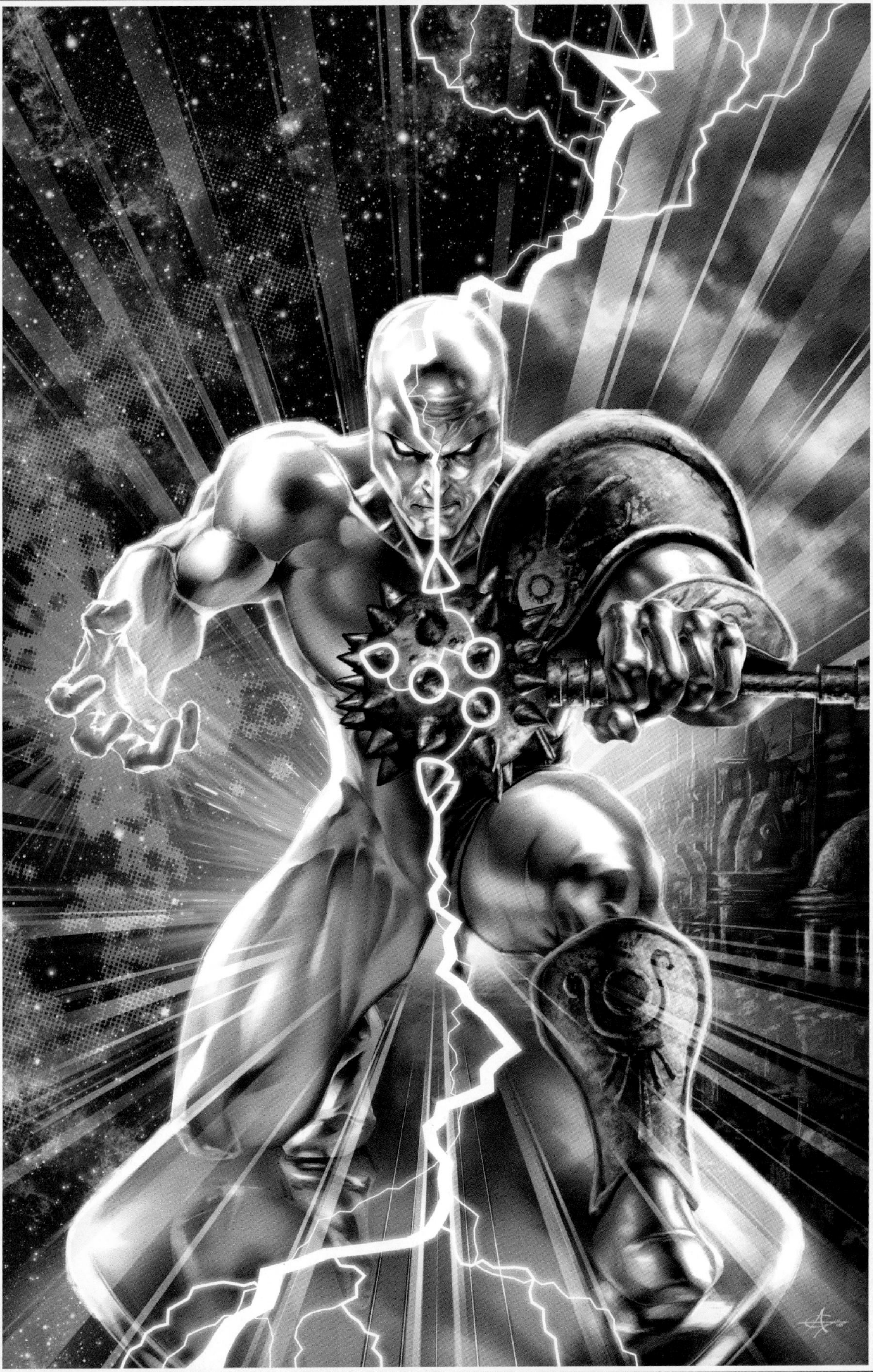

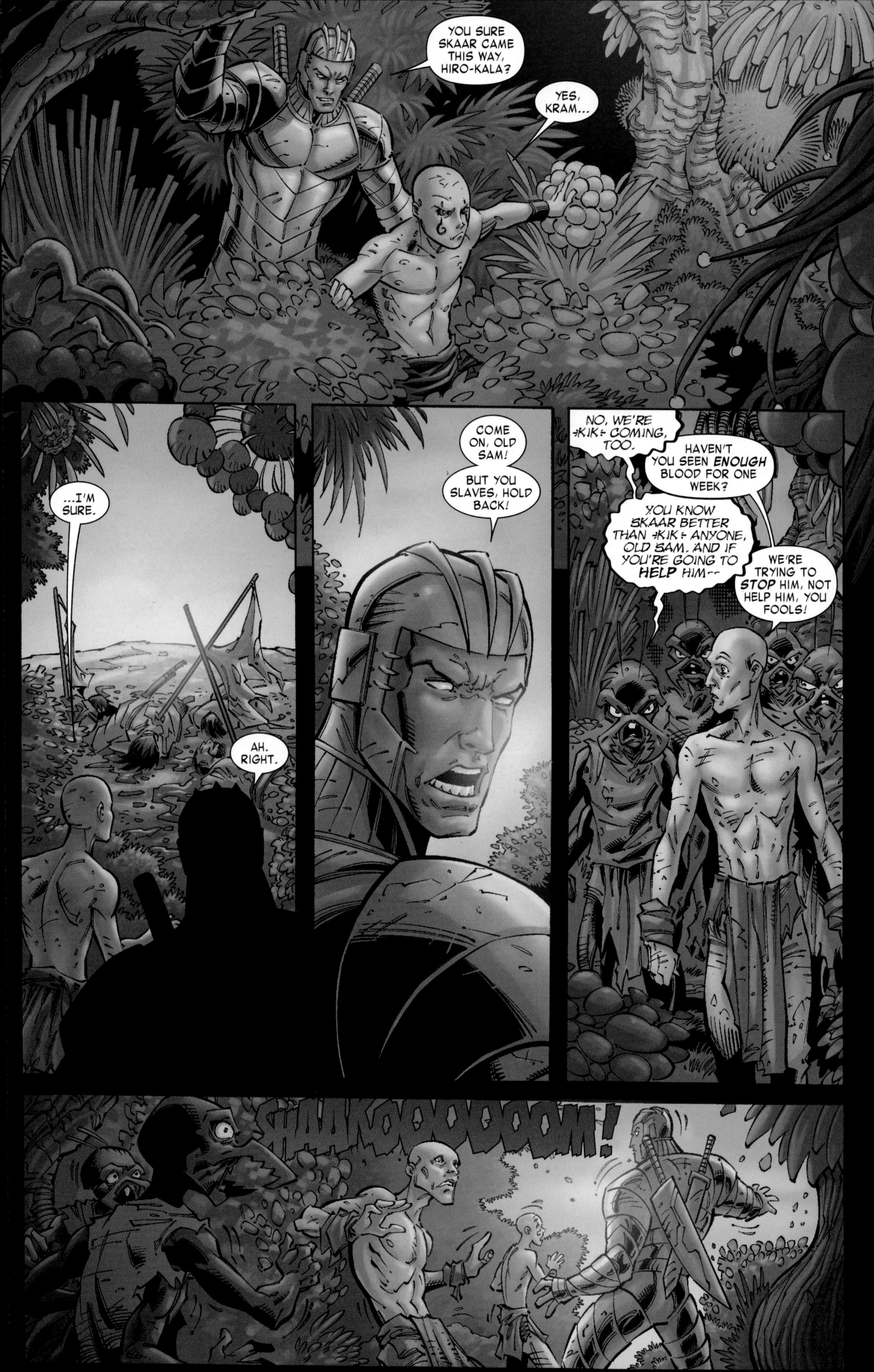
YOU SURE SKAAR CAME THIS WAY, HIRO-KALA?
YES, KRAM...
...I'M SURE.
AH. RIGHT.
COME ON, OLD SAM!
BUT YOU SLAVES, HOLD BACK!
NO, WE'RE ≠KIK≠ COMING, TOO.
YOU KNOW SKAAR BETTER THAN ≠KIK≠ ANYONE, OLD SAM. AND IF YOU'RE GOING TO HELP HIM--
HAVEN'T YOU SEEN ENOUGH BLOOD FOR ONE WEEK?
WE'RE TRYING TO STOP HIM, NOT HELP HIM, YOU FOOLS!
SHAKOOOOOOOM!

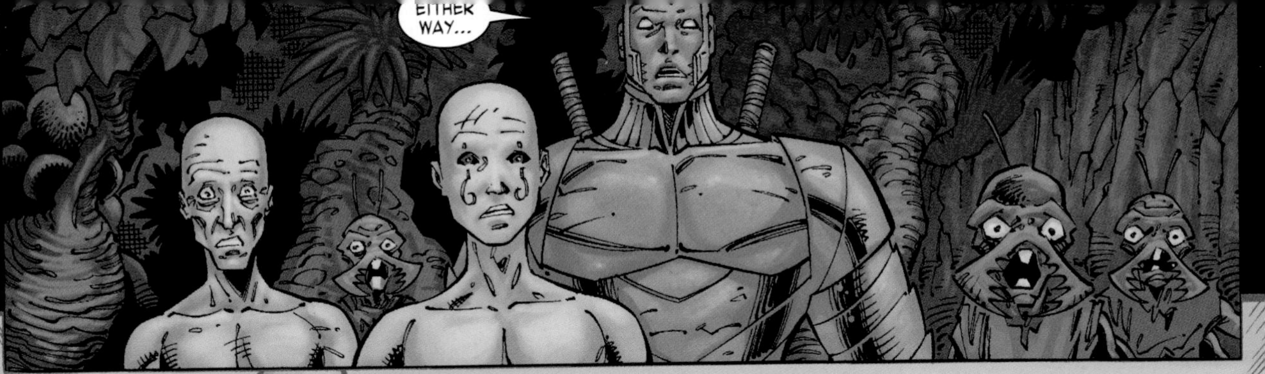
EITHER WAY...

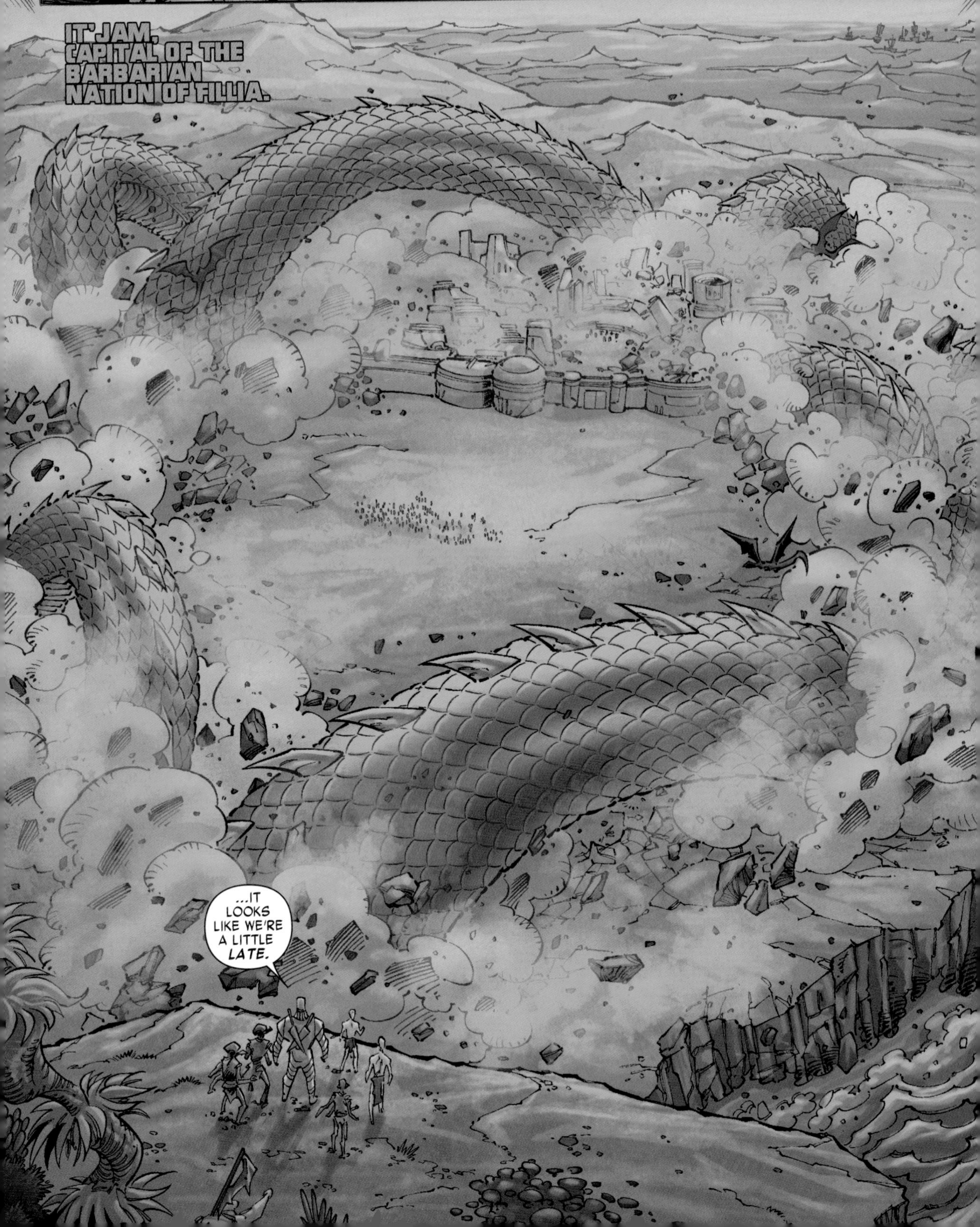
IT'JAM, CAPITAL OF THE BARBARIAN NATION OF FILLIA.
...IT LOOKS LIKE WE'RE A LITTLE LATE.

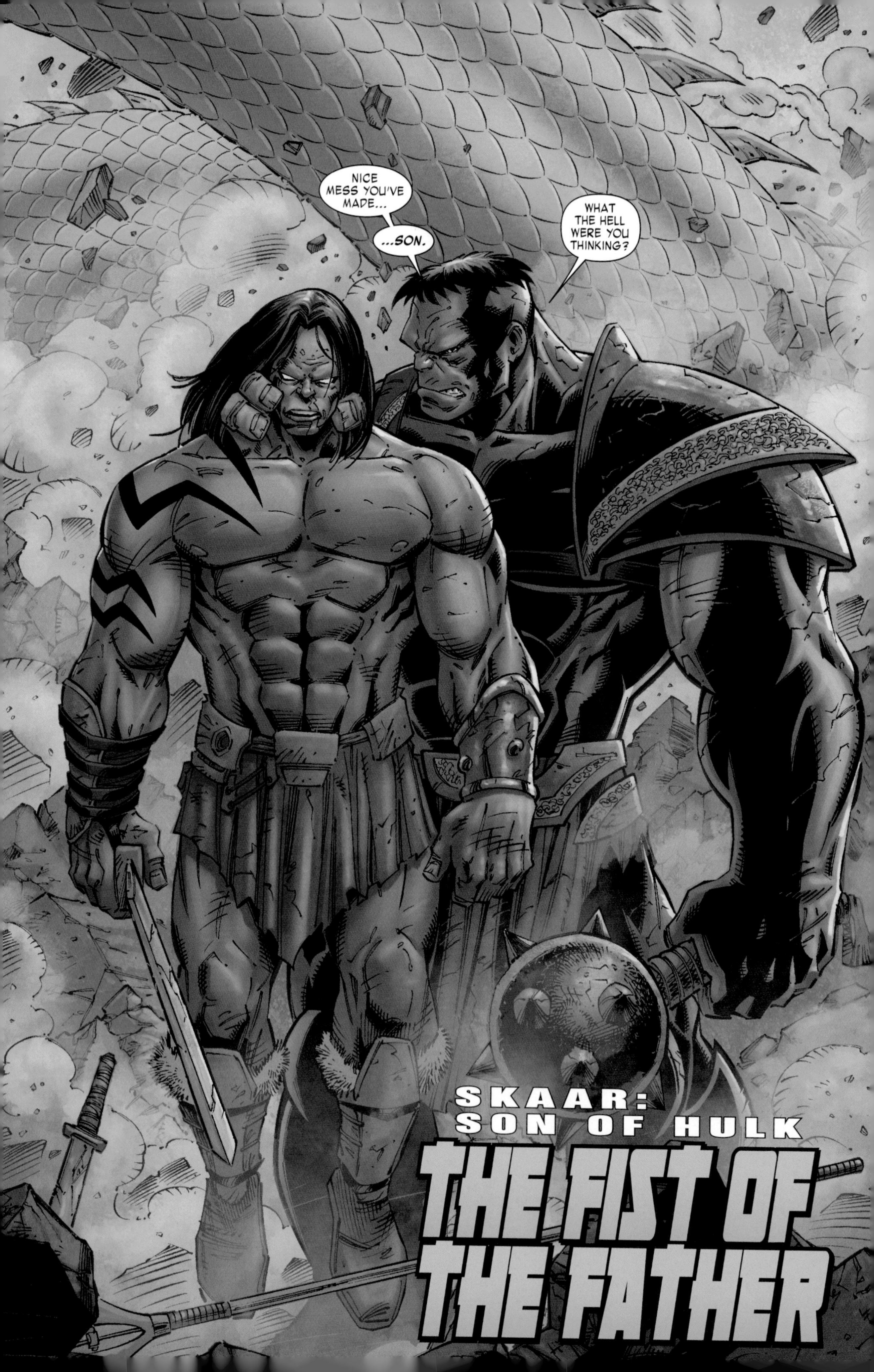
NICE MESS YOU'VE MADE...
...SON.
WHAT THE HELL WERE YOU THINKING?
SKAAR: SON OF HULK
THE FIST OF THE FATHER

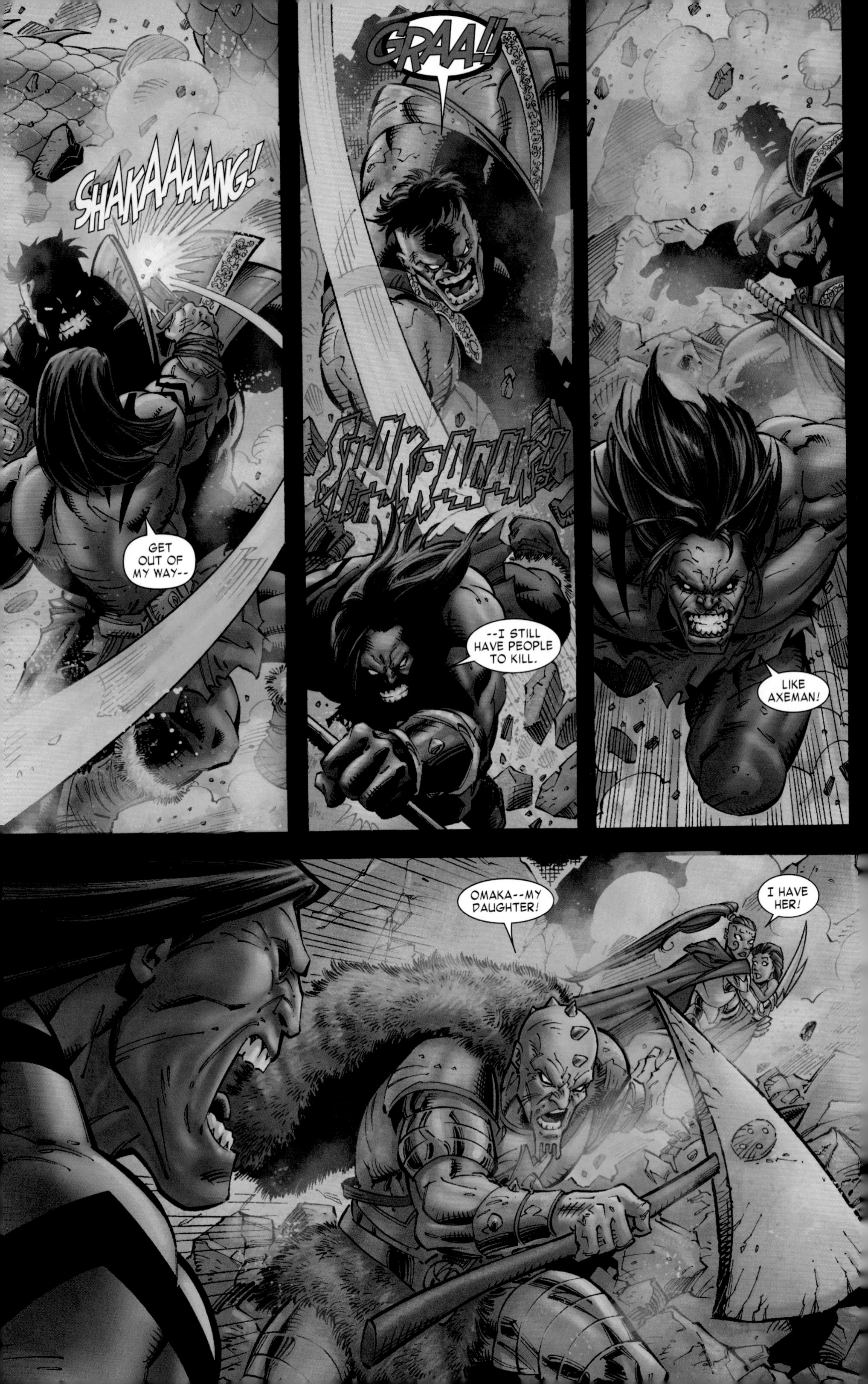
SHAKAAAANG!
GET OUT OF MY WAY--
GRAA!!
--I STILL HAVE PEOPLE TO KILL.
LIKE AXEMAN!
OMAKA--MY DAUGHTER!
I HAVE HER!

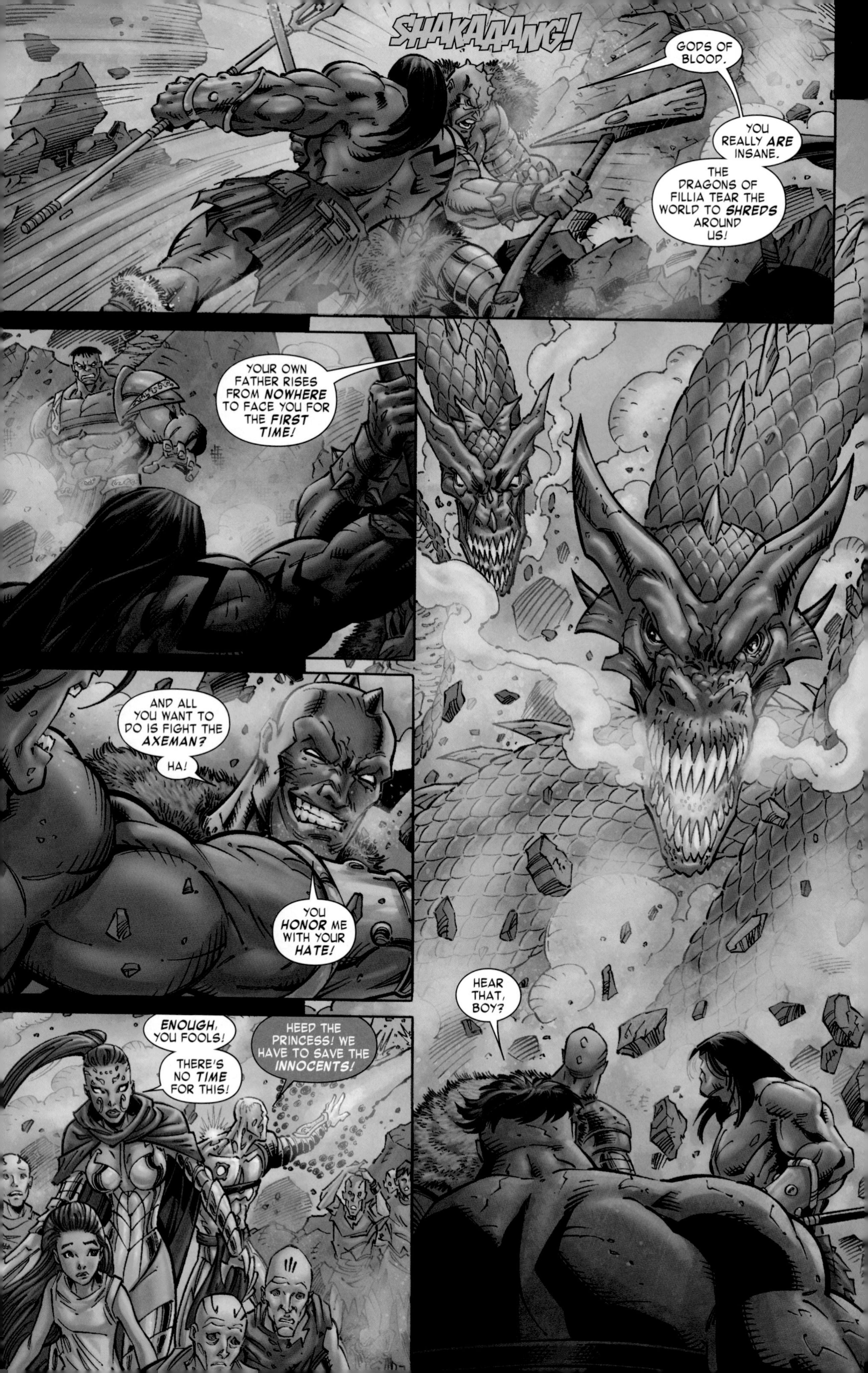
SHAKAAANG!
GODS OF BLOOD.
YOU REALLY ARE INSANE.
THE DRAGONS OF FILLIA TEAR THE WORLD TO SHREDS AROUND US!
YOUR OWN FATHER RISES FROM NOWHERE TO FACE YOU FOR THE FIRST TIME!
AND ALL YOU WANT TO DO IS FIGHT THE AXEMAN?
HA!
YOU HONOR ME WITH YOUR HATE!
ENOUGH, YOU FOOLS!
THERE'S NO TIME FOR THIS!
HEED THE PRINCESS! WE HAVE TO SAVE THE INNOCENTS!
HEAR THAT, BOY?

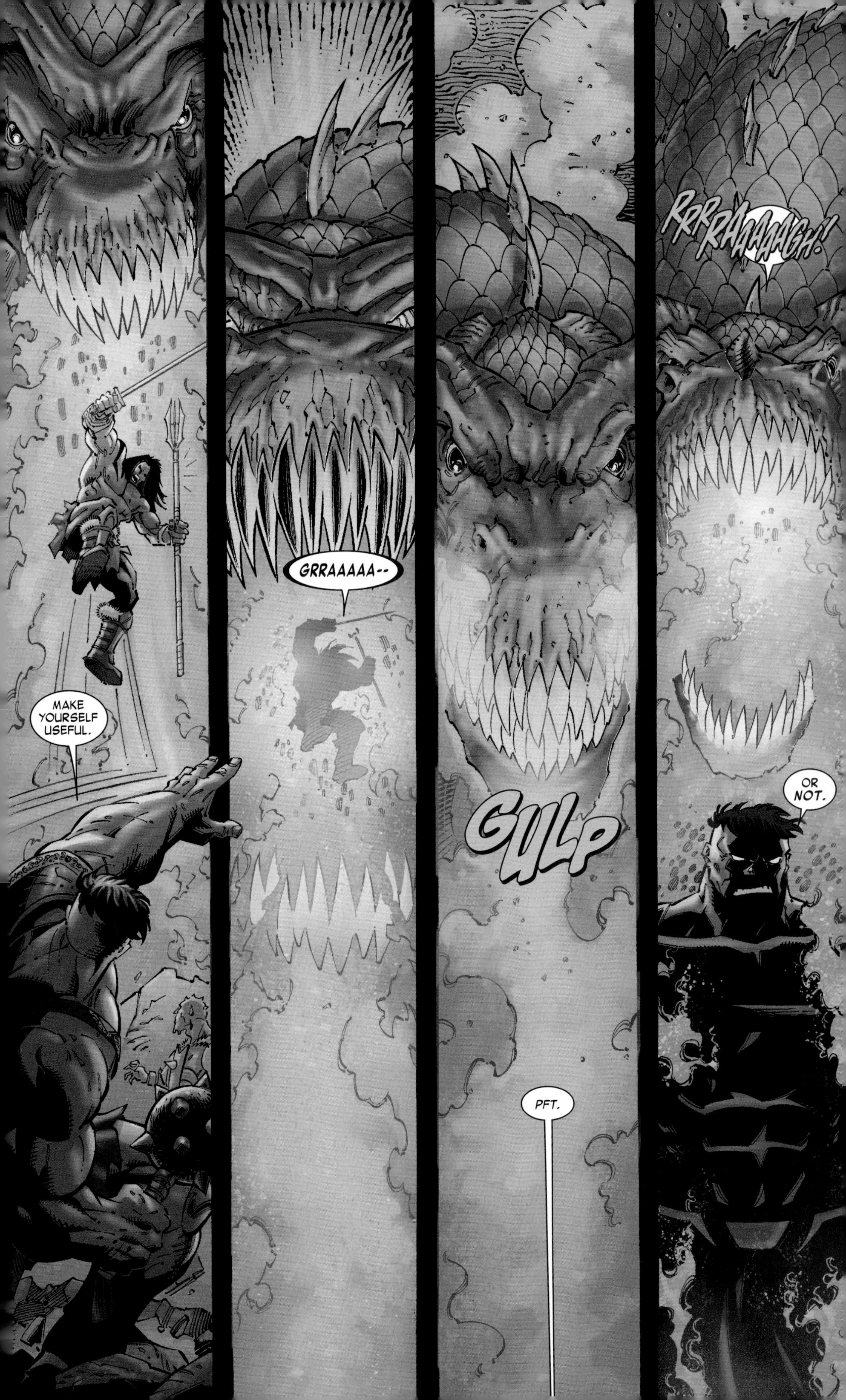
MAKE YOURSELF USEFUL.
GRRAAAAA--
GULP
PFT.
RRRRAAAAAAGH!
OR NOT.

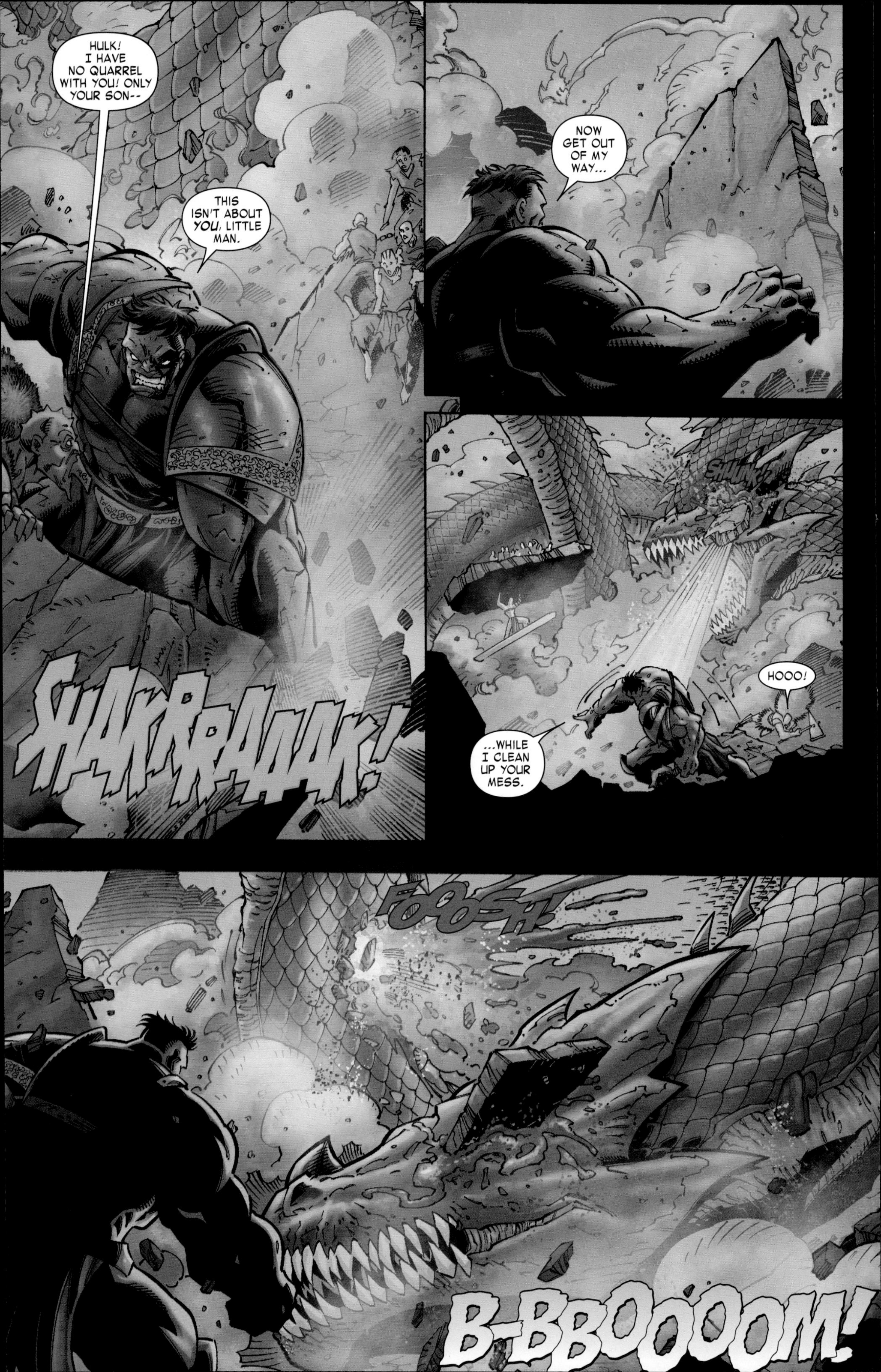

HULK! I HAVE NO QUARREL WITH YOU! ONLY YOUR SON--
THIS ISN'T ABOUT YOU, LITTLE MAN.
SHAKRRAAAAK!
NOW GET OUT OF MY WAY...
...WHILE I CLEAN UP YOUR MESS.
HOOO!
FOOOSH!
B-BBOOOOOM!

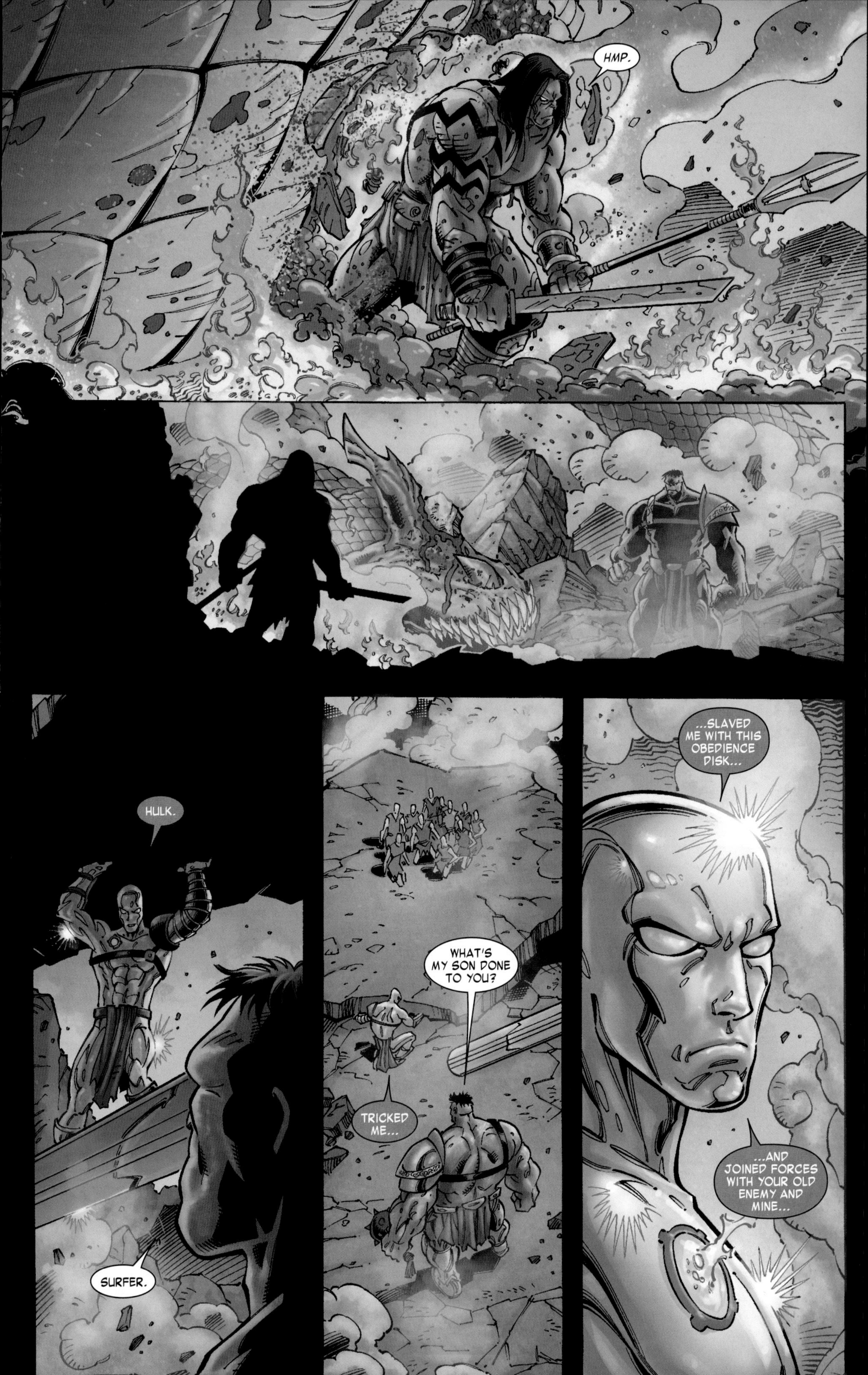
HMP.
HULK.
SURFER.
WHAT'S MY SON DONE TO YOU?
TRICKED ME...
...SLAVED ME WITH THIS OBEDIENCE DISK...
...AND JOINED FORCES WITH YOUR OLD ENEMY AND MINE...

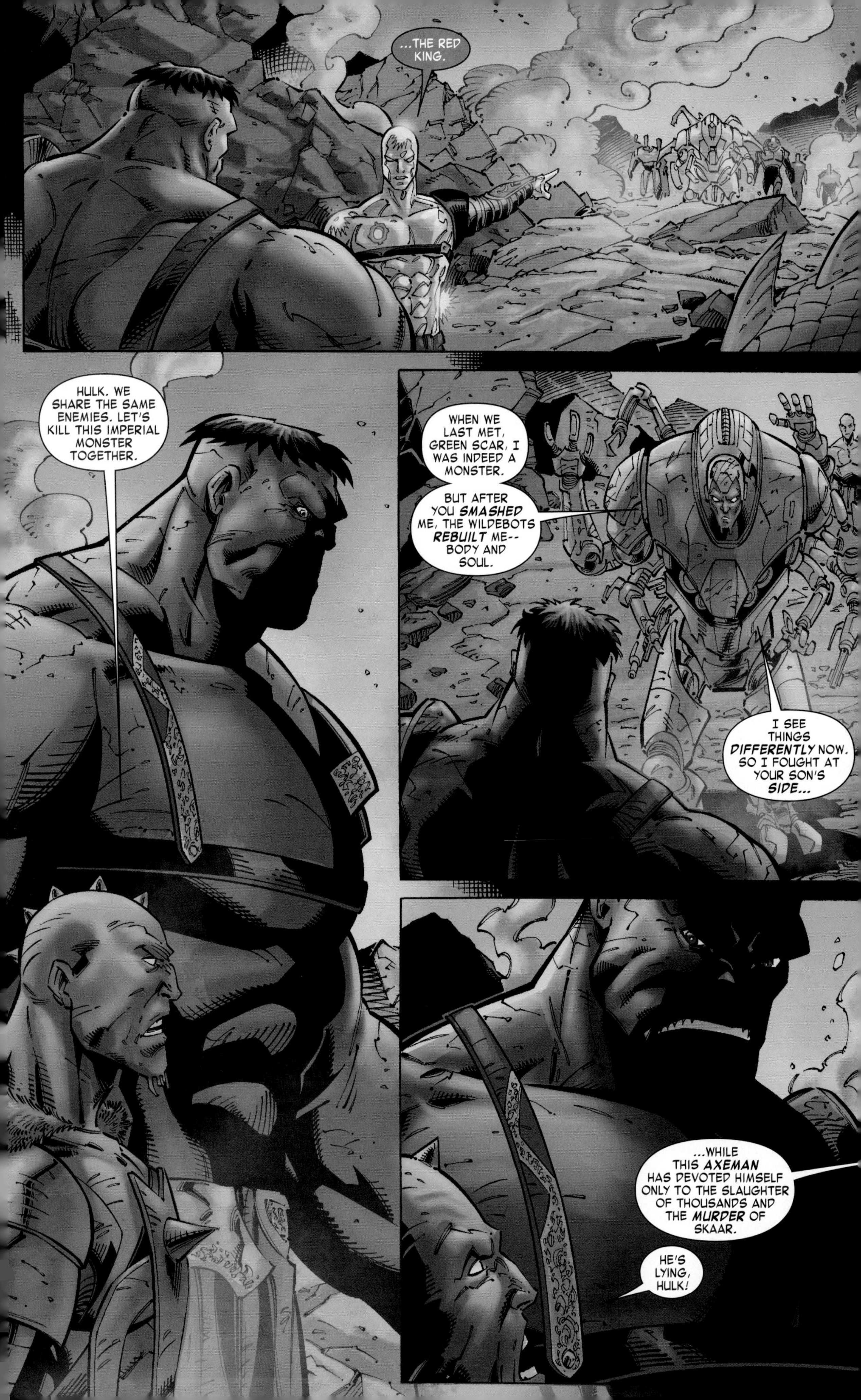
...THE RED KING.
HULK. WE SHARE THE SAME ENEMIES. LET'S KILL THIS IMPERIAL MONSTER TOGETHER.
WHEN WE LAST MET, GREEN SCAR, I WAS INDEED A MONSTER.
BUT AFTER YOU SMASHED ME, THE WILDEBOTS REBUILT ME-- BODY AND SOUL.
I SEE THINGS DIFFERENTLY NOW. SO I FOUGHT AT YOUR SON'S SIDE...
...WHILE THIS AXEMAN HAS DEVOTED HIMSELF ONLY TO THE SLAUGHTER OF THOUSANDS AND THE MURDER OF SKAAR.
HE'S LYING, HULK!

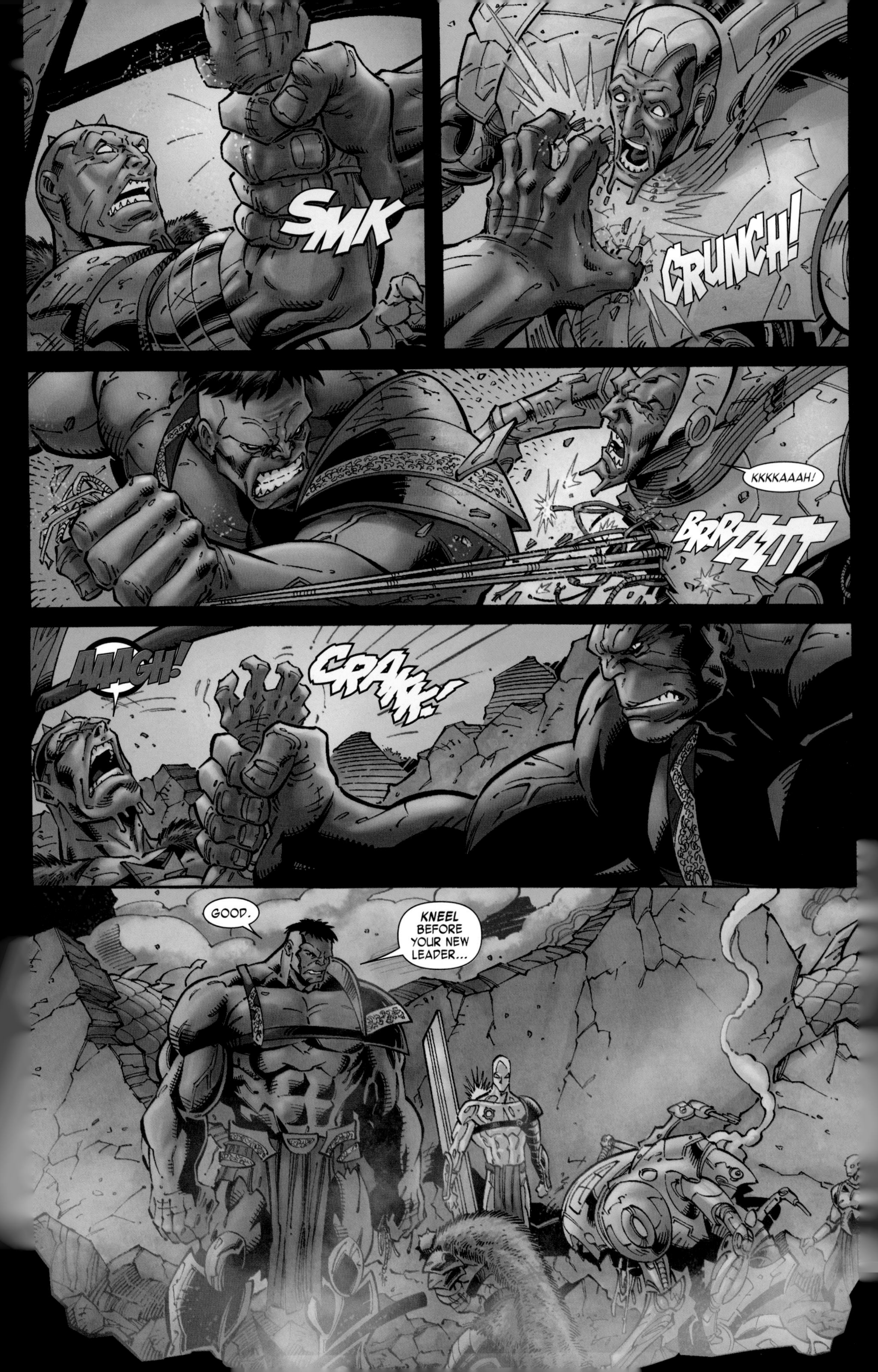
SMK
CRUNCH!
KKKKAAAH!
BRRZZZTT
AAAGH!
CRAKK!
GOOD.
KNEEL BEFORE YOUR NEW LEADER...

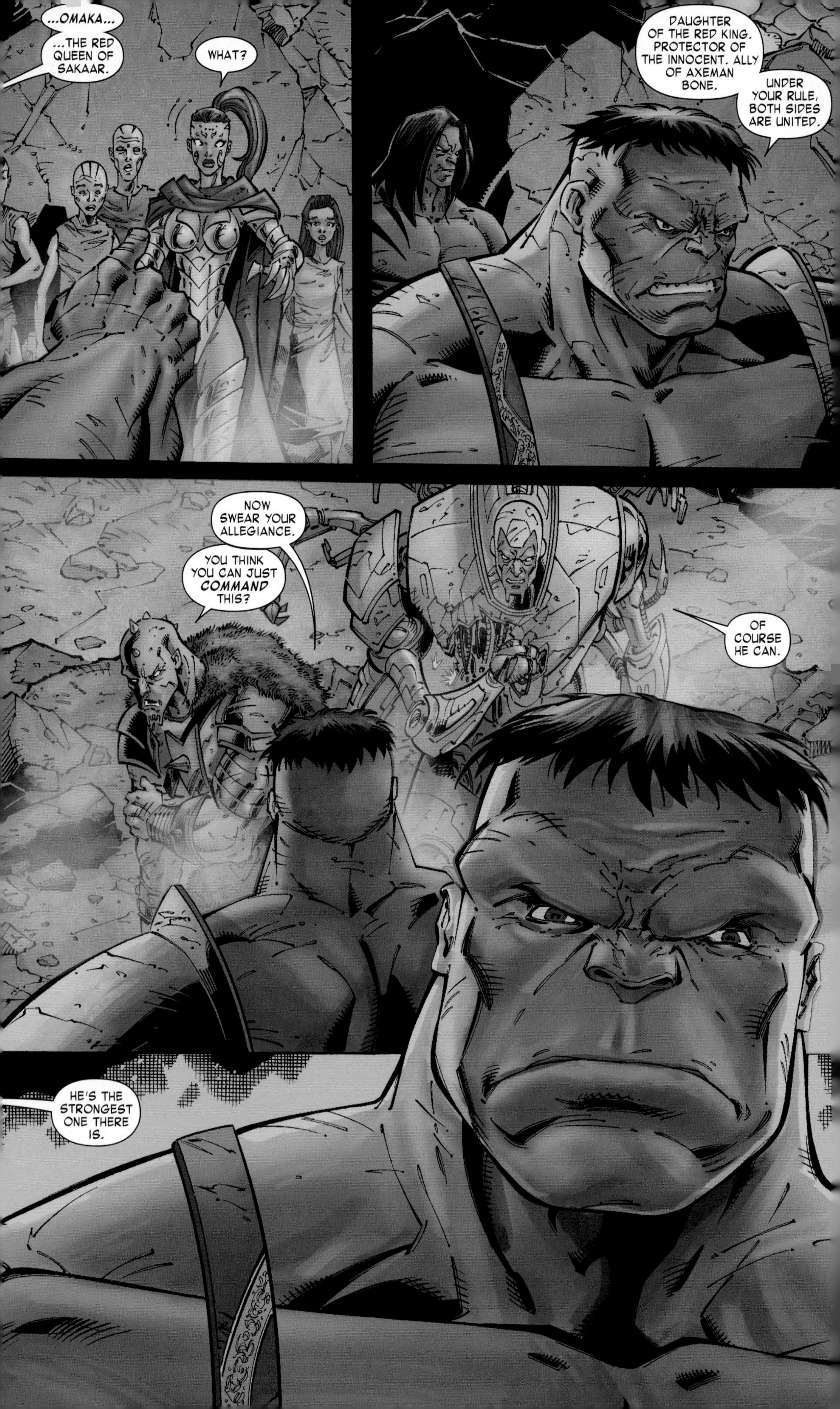
...OMAKA...
...THE RED QUEEN OF SAKAAR.
WHAT?
DAUGHTER OF THE RED KING. PROTECTOR OF THE INNOCENT. ALLY OF AXEMAN BONE.
UNDER YOUR RULE, BOTH SIDES ARE UNITED.
NOW SWEAR YOUR ALLEGIANCE.
YOU THINK YOU CAN JUST COMMAND THIS?
OF COURSE HE CAN.
HE'S THE STRONGEST ONE THERE IS.

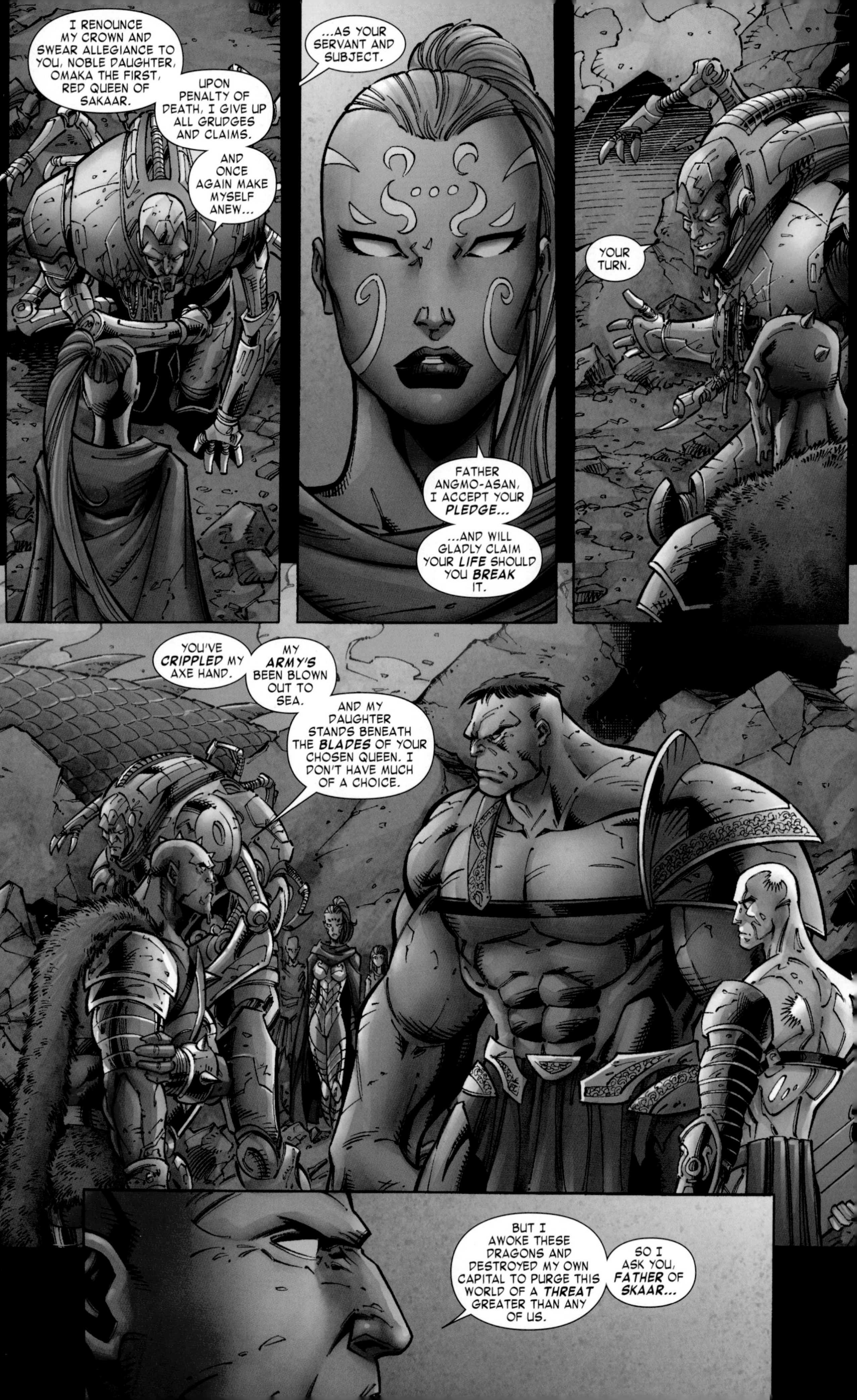
I RENOUNCE MY CROWN AND SWEAR ALLEGIANCE TO YOU, NOBLE DAUGHTER, OMAKA THE FIRST, RED QUEEN OF SAKAAR.
UPON PENALTY OF DEATH, I GIVE UP ALL GRUDGES AND CLAIMS.
AND ONCE AGAIN MAKE MYSELF ANEW...
...AS YOUR SERVANT AND SUBJECT.
FATHER ANGMO-ASAN, I ACCEPT YOUR PLEDGE...
...AND WILL GLADLY CLAIM YOUR LIFE SHOULD YOU BREAK IT.
YOUR TURN.
YOU'VE CRIPPLED MY AXE HAND.
MY ARMY'S BEEN BLOWN OUT TO SEA.
AND MY DAUGHTER STANDS BENEATH THE BLADES OF YOUR CHOSEN QUEEN. I DON'T HAVE MUCH OF A CHOICE.
BUT I AWOKE THESE DRAGONS AND DESTROYED MY OWN CAPITAL TO PURGE THIS WORLD OF A THREAT GREATER THAN ANY OF US.
SO I ASK YOU, FATHER OF SKAAR...

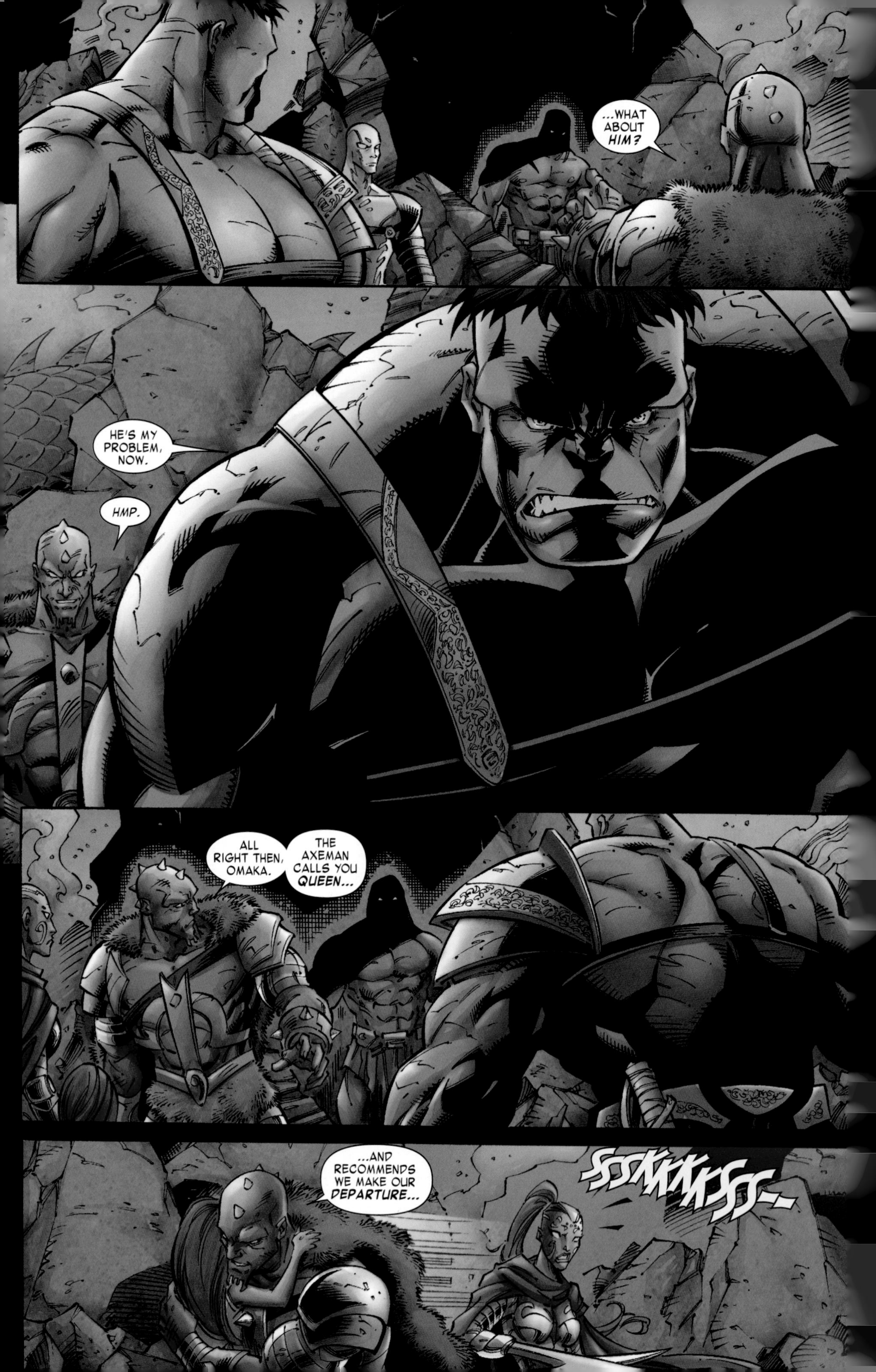
...WHAT ABOUT *HIM*?
HE'S MY PROBLEM, NOW.
HMP.
ALL RIGHT THEN, OMAKA.
THE AXEMAN CALLS YOU *QUEEN*...
...AND RECOMMENDS WE MAKE OUR *DEPARTURE*...
SSSKKKKSSS--

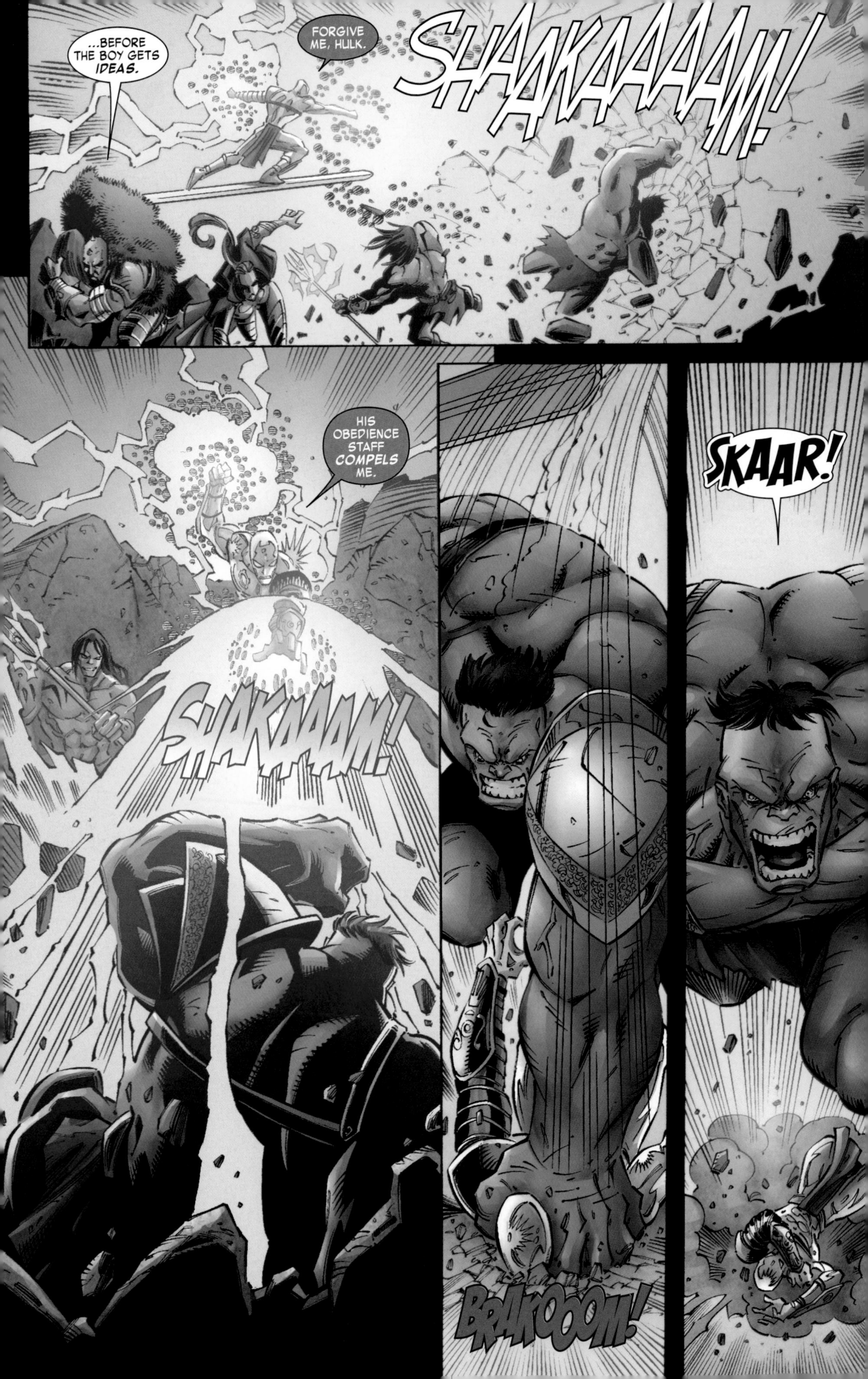
...BEFORE THE BOY GETS IDEAS.
FORGIVE ME, HULK.
SHAKAAAAAM!
HIS OBEDIENCE STAFF COMPELS ME.
SHAKAAAM!
SKAAR!
BRAKOOOM!

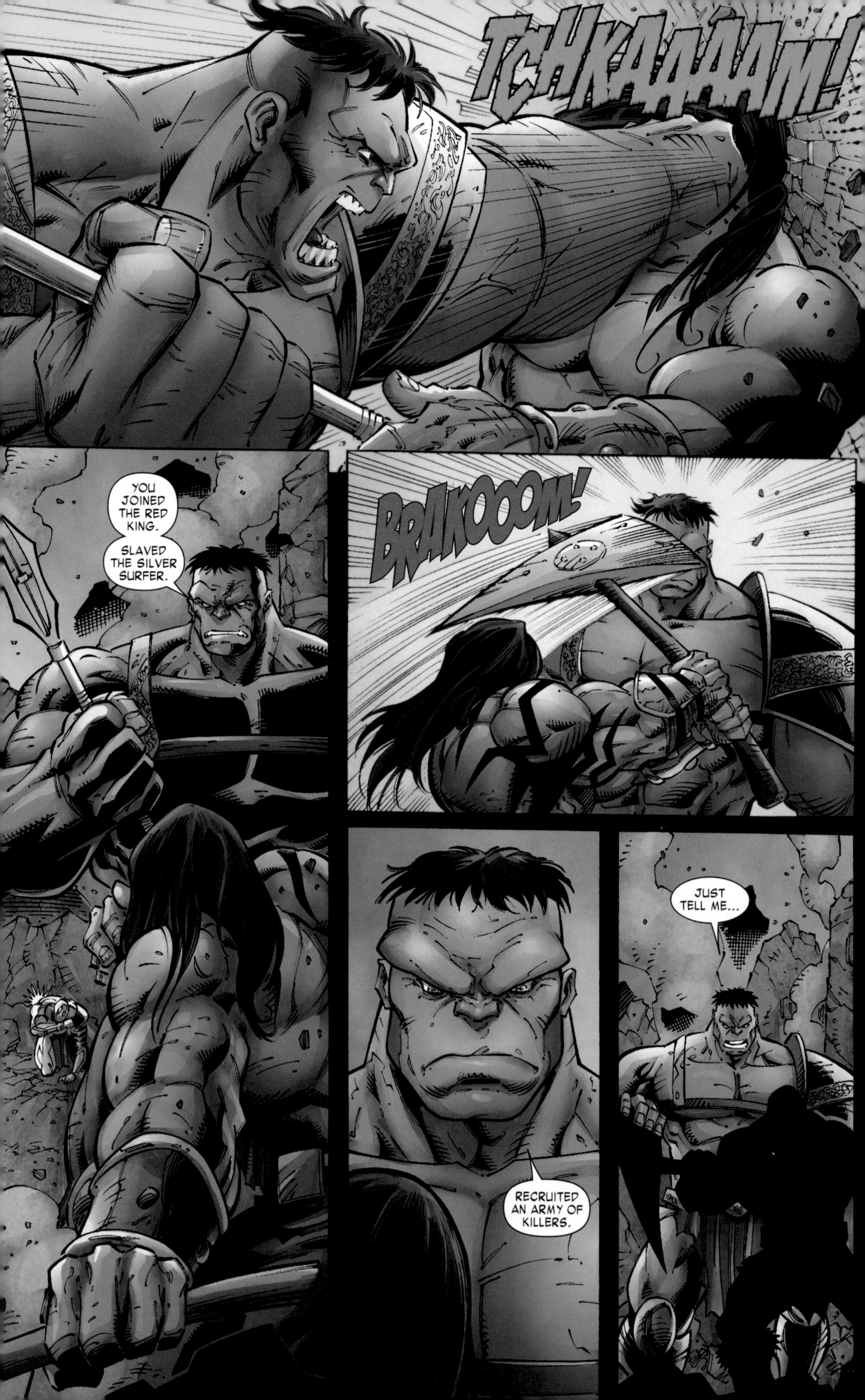
TCHKAAAAAM!
YOU JOINED THE RED KING.
SLAVED THE SILVER SURFER.
BRAKOOOM!
RECRUITED AN ARMY OF KILLERS.
JUST TELL ME...

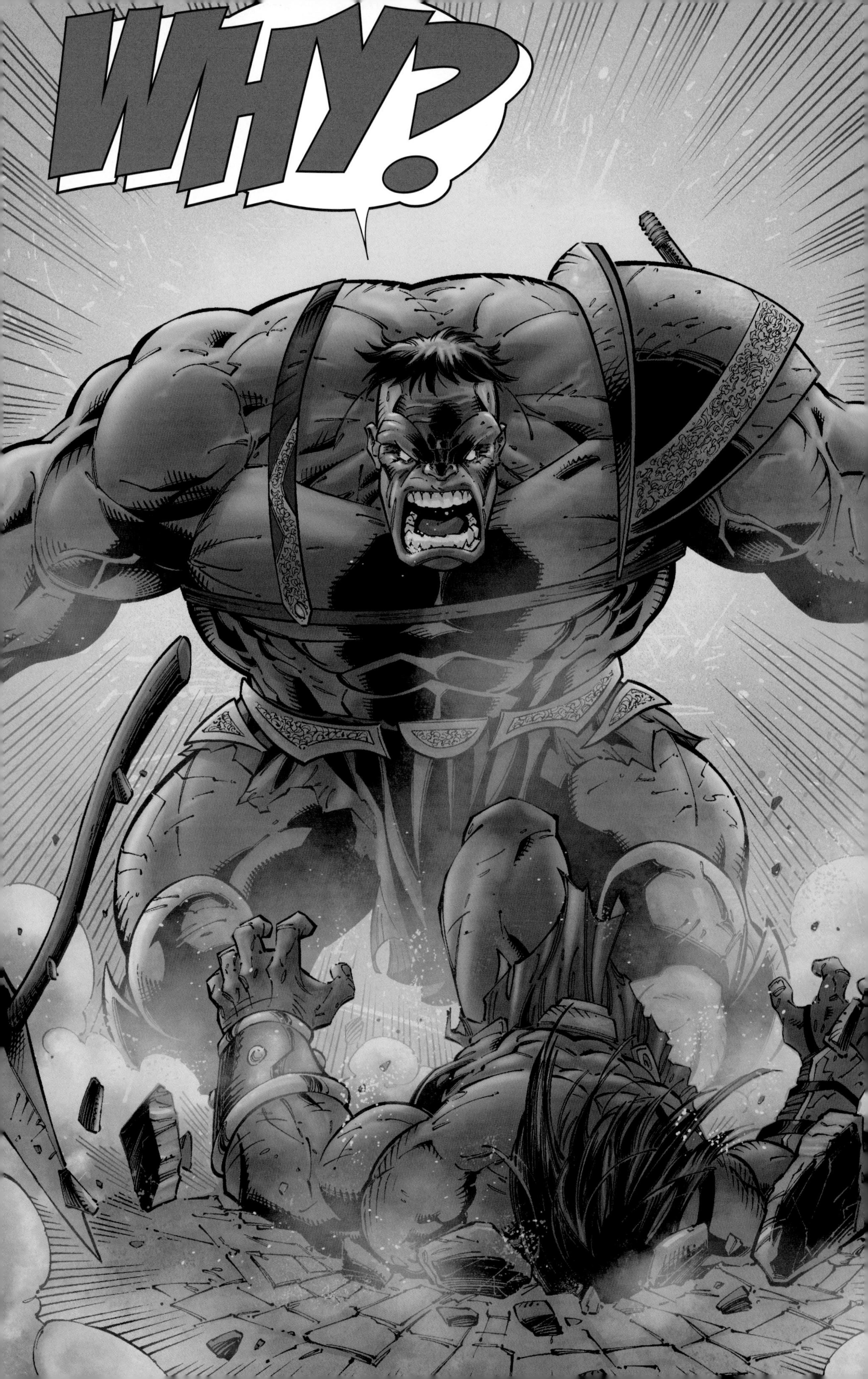
WHY?

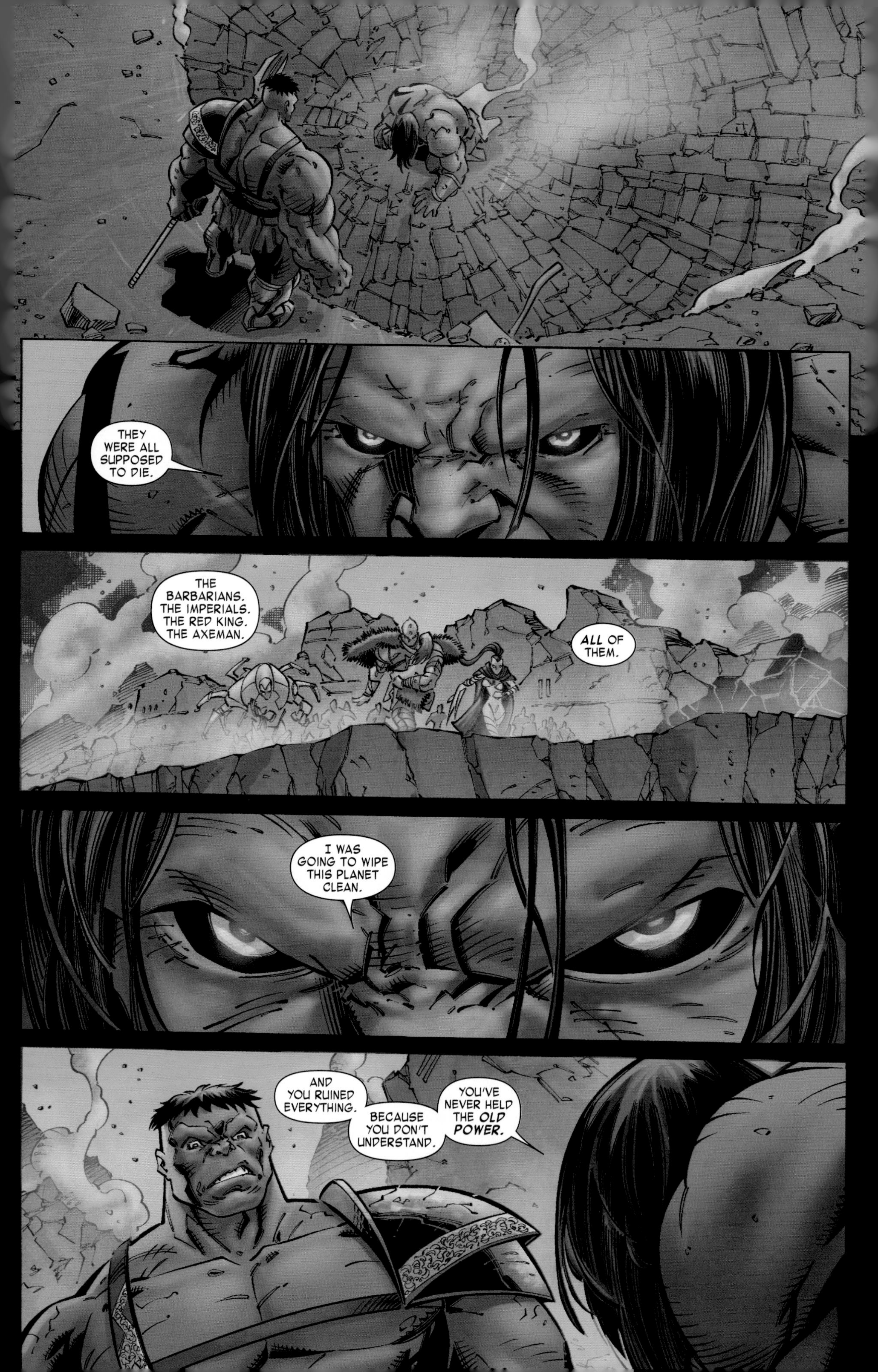
THEY WERE ALL SUPPOSED TO DIE.
THE BARBARIANS. THE IMPERIALS. THE RED KING. THE AXEMAN.
ALL OF THEM.
I WAS GOING TO WIPE THIS PLANET CLEAN.
AND YOU RUINED EVERYTHING.
BECAUSE YOU DON'T UNDERSTAND.
YOU'VE NEVER HELD THE OLD POWER.

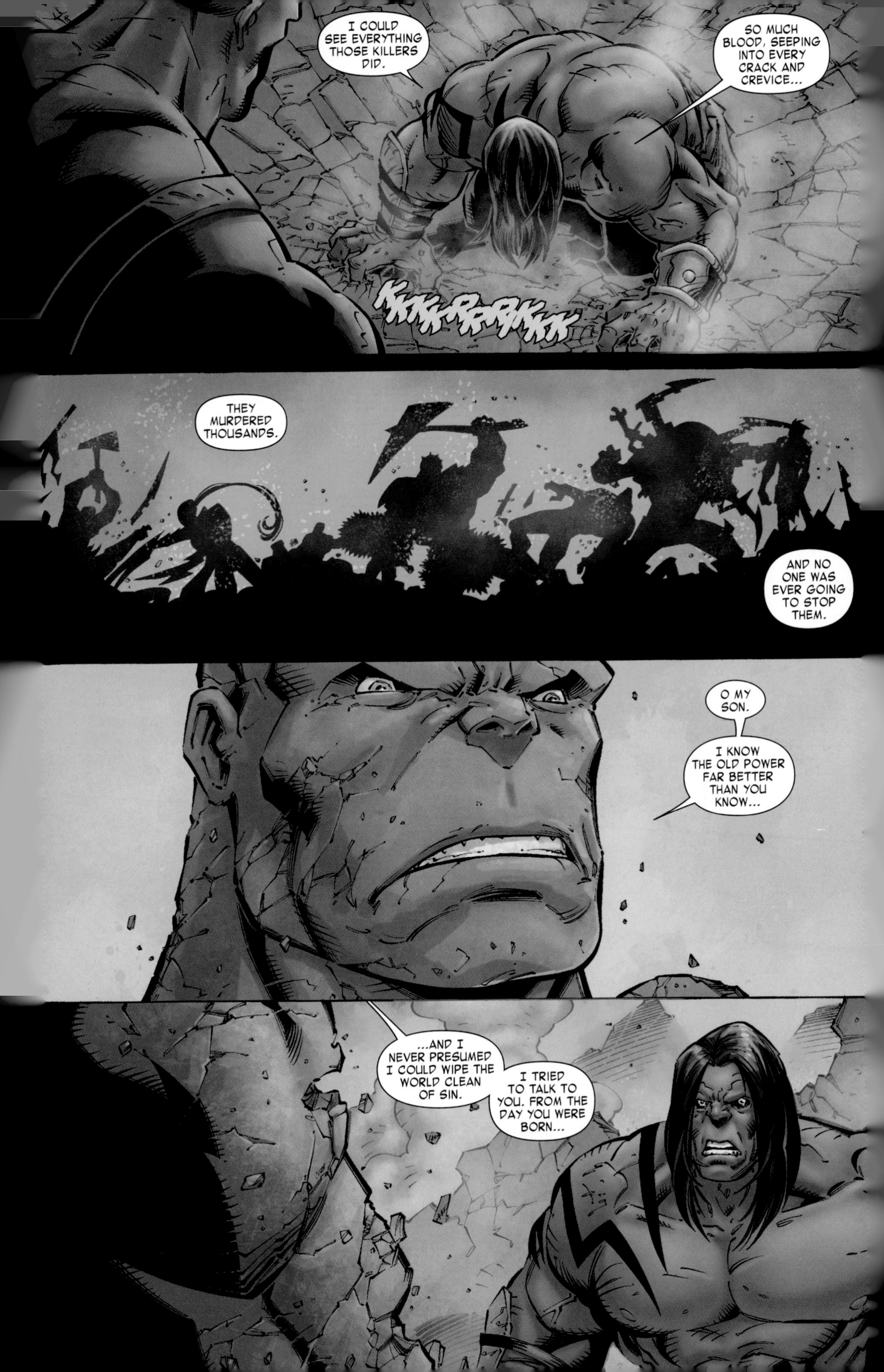
I COULD SEE EVERYTHING THOSE KILLERS DID.
SO MUCH BLOOD, SEEPING INTO EVERY CRACK AND CREVICE...
KKKKRRRKKKK
THEY MURDERED THOUSANDS.
AND NO ONE WAS EVER GOING TO STOP THEM.
O MY SON.
I KNOW THE OLD POWER FAR BETTER THAN YOU KNOW...
...AND I NEVER PRESUMED I COULD WIPE THE WORLD CLEAN OF SIN.
I TRIED TO TALK TO YOU. FROM THE DAY YOU WERE BORN...

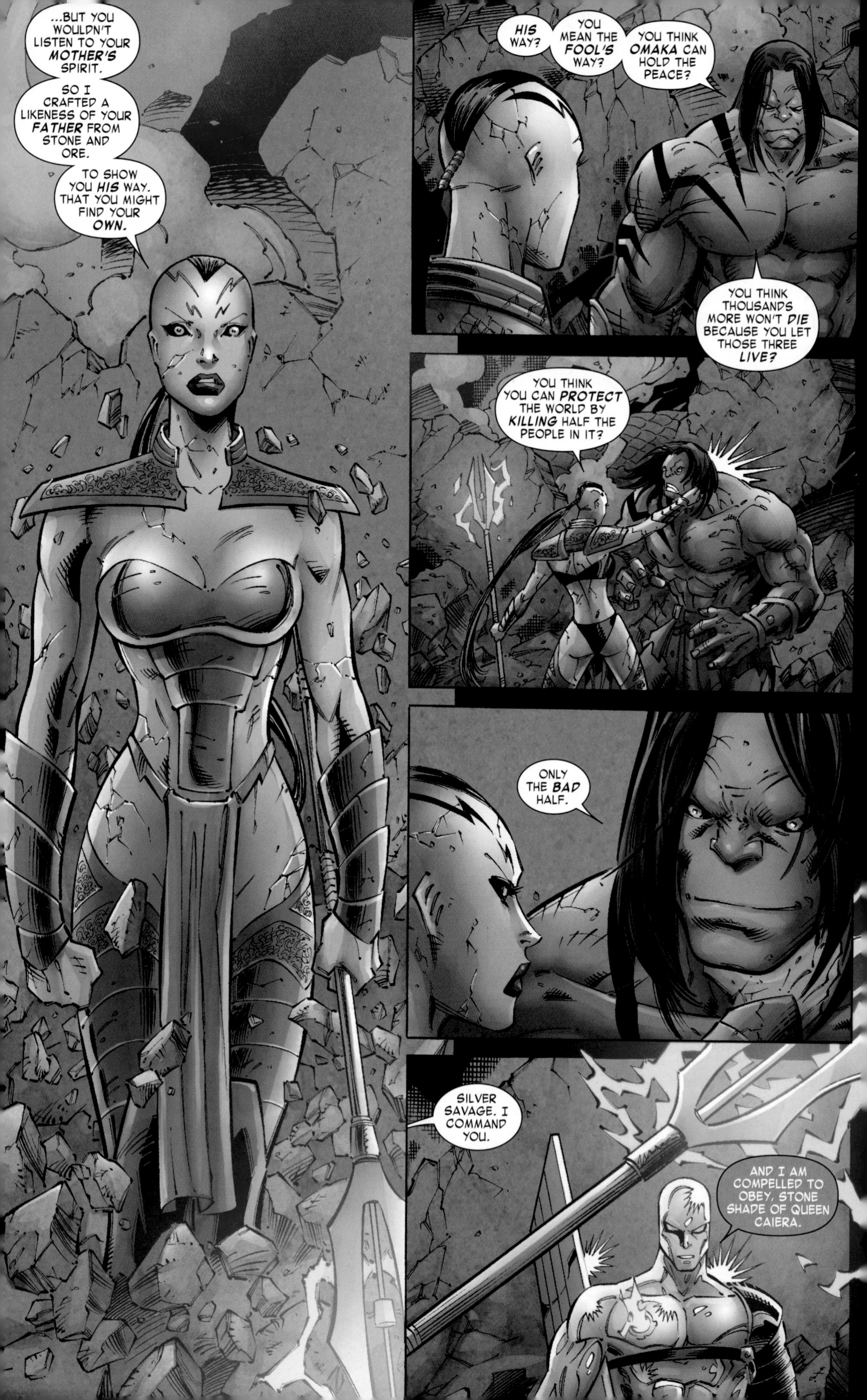
...BUT YOU WOULDN'T LISTEN TO YOUR MOTHER'S SPIRIT.
SO I CRAFTED A LIKENESS OF YOUR FATHER FROM STONE AND ORE.
TO SHOW YOU HIS WAY. THAT YOU MIGHT FIND YOUR OWN.
HIS WAY?
YOU MEAN THE FOOL'S WAY?
YOU THINK OMAKA CAN HOLD THE PEACE?
YOU THINK THOUSANDS MORE WON'T DIE BECAUSE YOU LET THOSE THREE LIVE?
YOU THINK YOU CAN PROTECT THE WORLD BY KILLING HALF THE PEOPLE IN IT?
ONLY THE BAD HALF.
SILVER SAVAGE. I COMMAND YOU.
AND I AM COMPELLED TO OBEY, STONE SHADE OF QUEEN CAIERA.

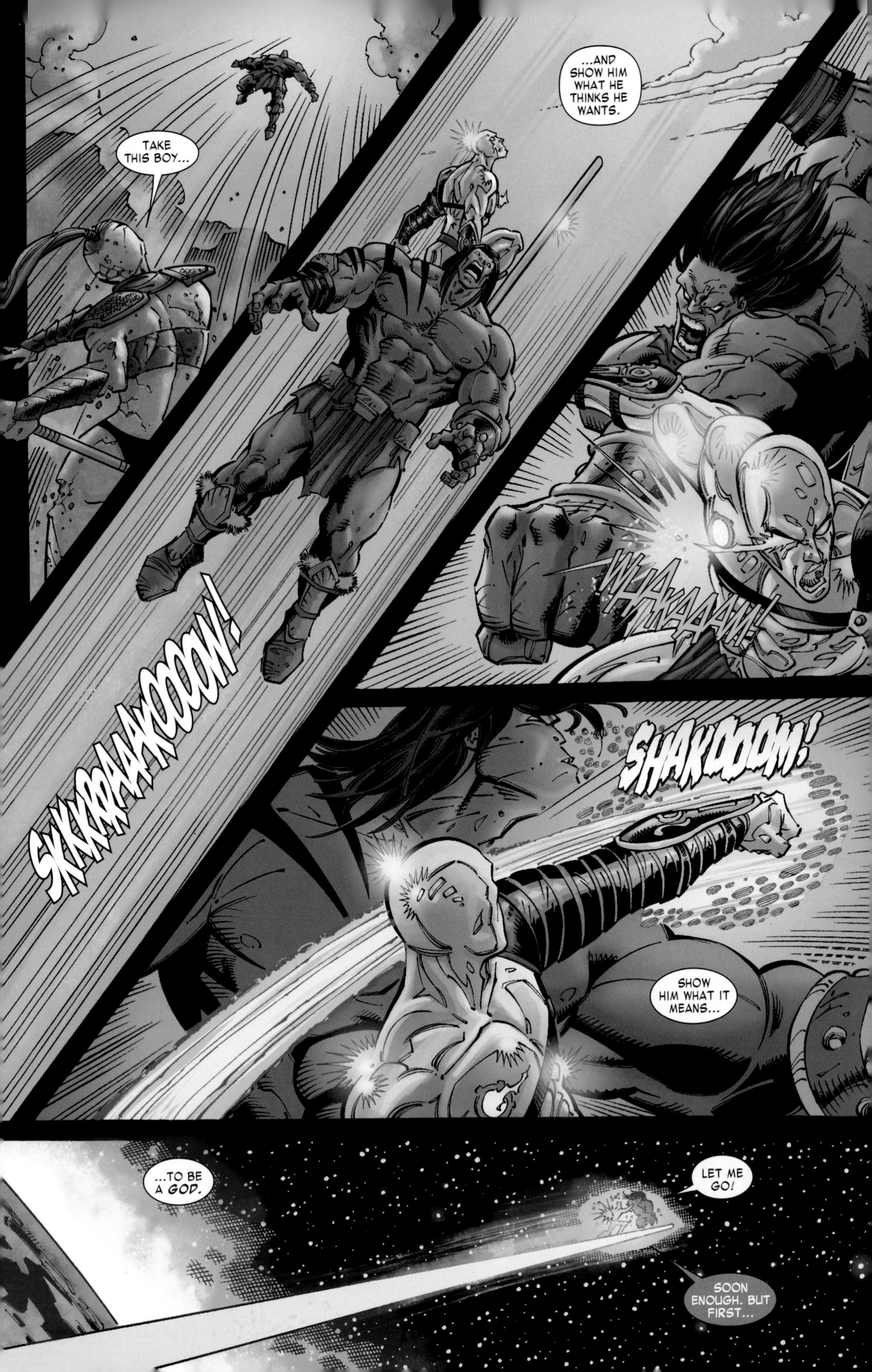
TAKE THIS BOY...
...AND SHOW HIM WHAT HE THINKS HE WANTS.
SKKRRAAKOOOOM!
WHAKAAAM!
SHAKOOOM!
SHOW HIM WHAT IT MEANS...
...TO BE A *GOD*.
LET ME GO!
SOON ENOUGH. BUT FIRST...

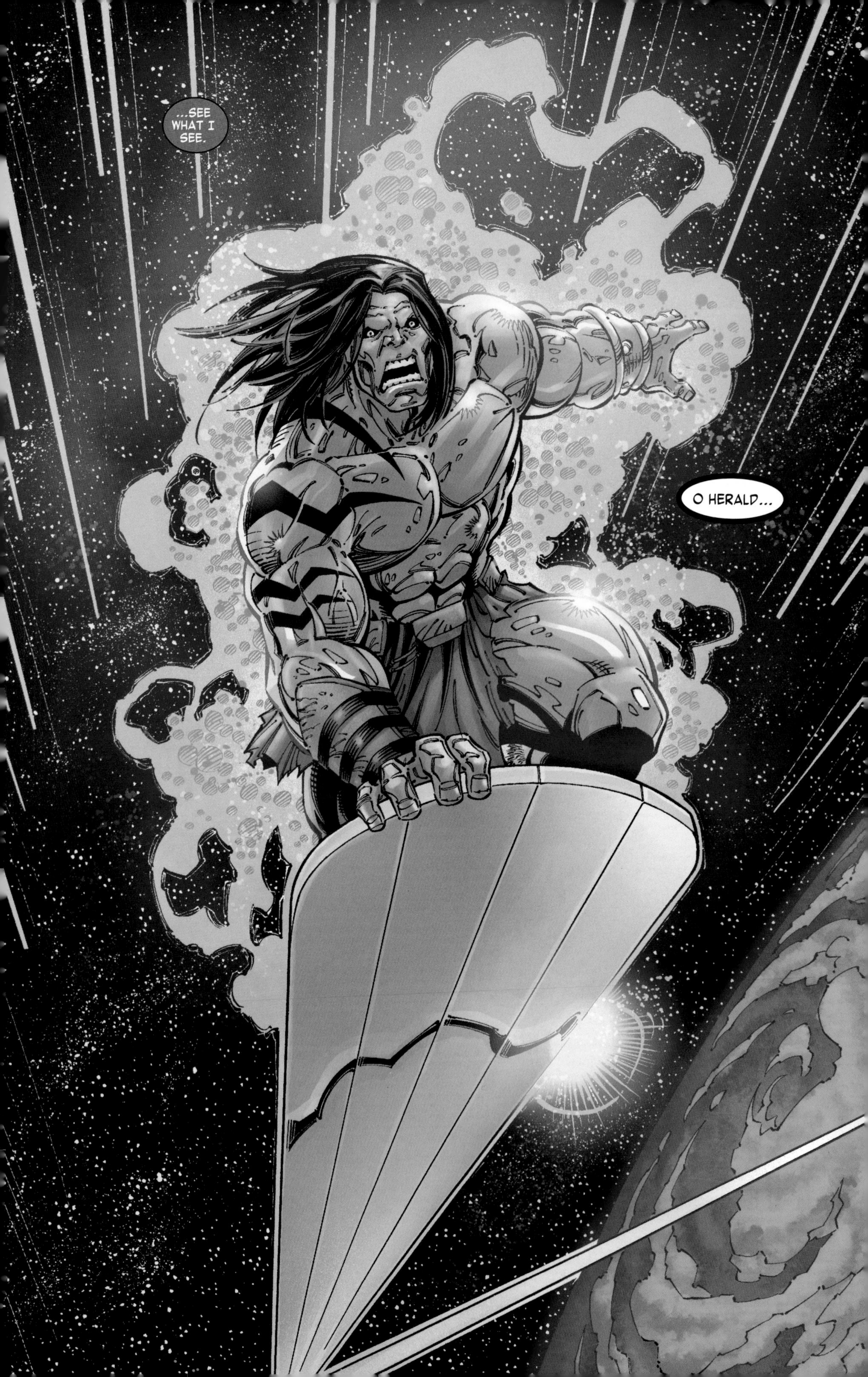
...SEE WHAT I SEE.
O HERALD...

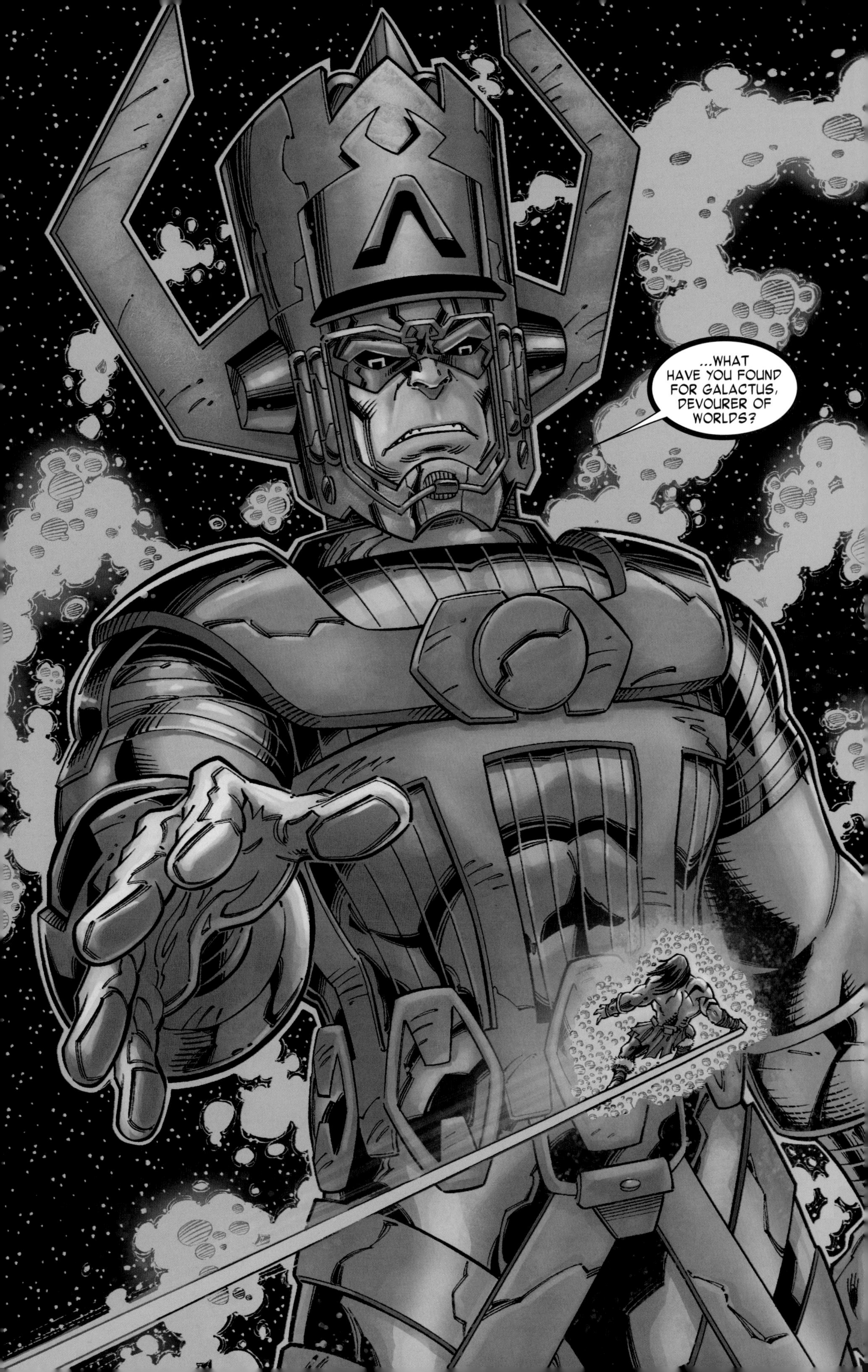
...WHAT HAVE YOU FOUND FOR GALACTUS, DEVOURER OF WORLDS?

Skaar: Son of Hulk #10

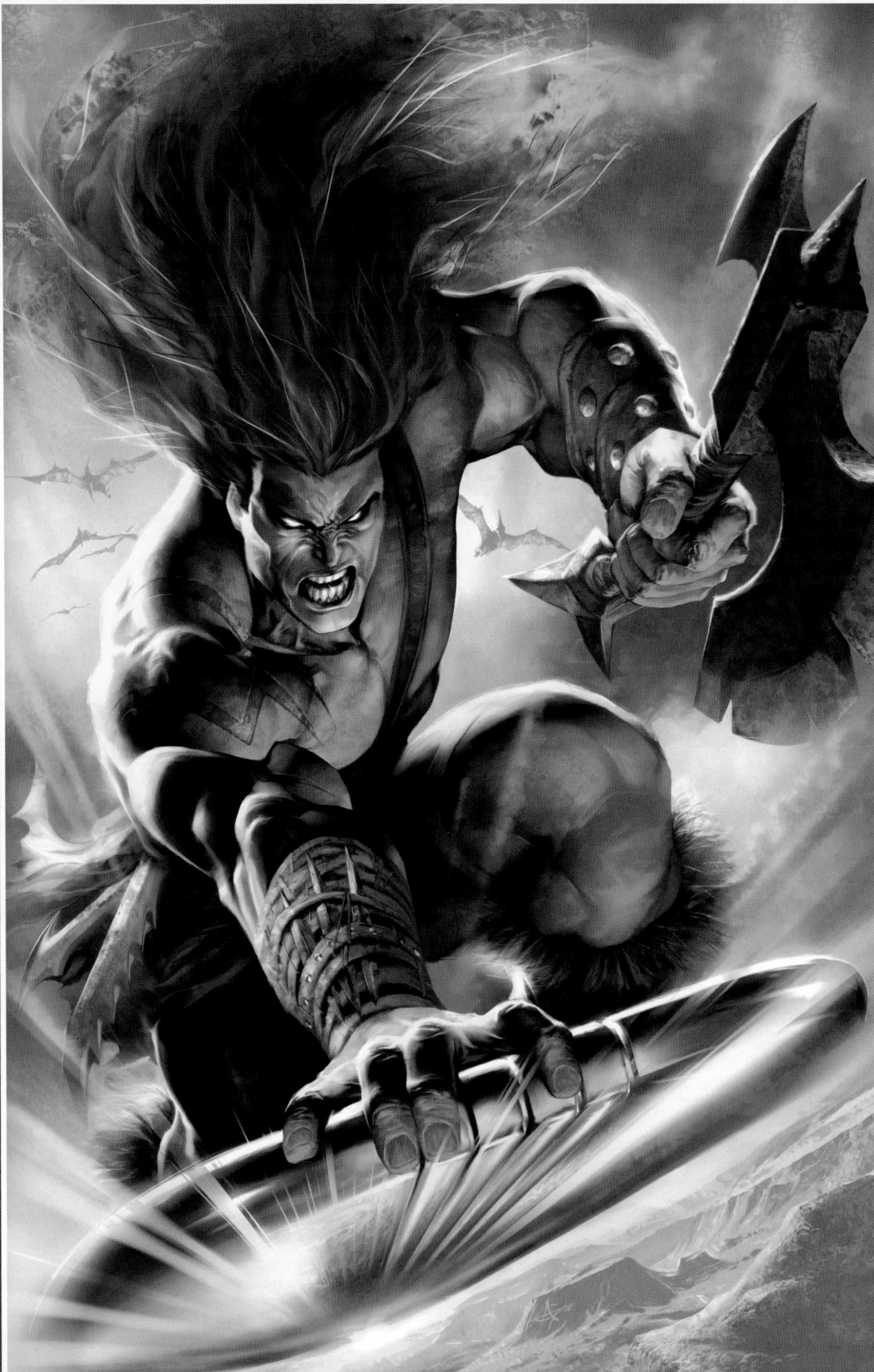

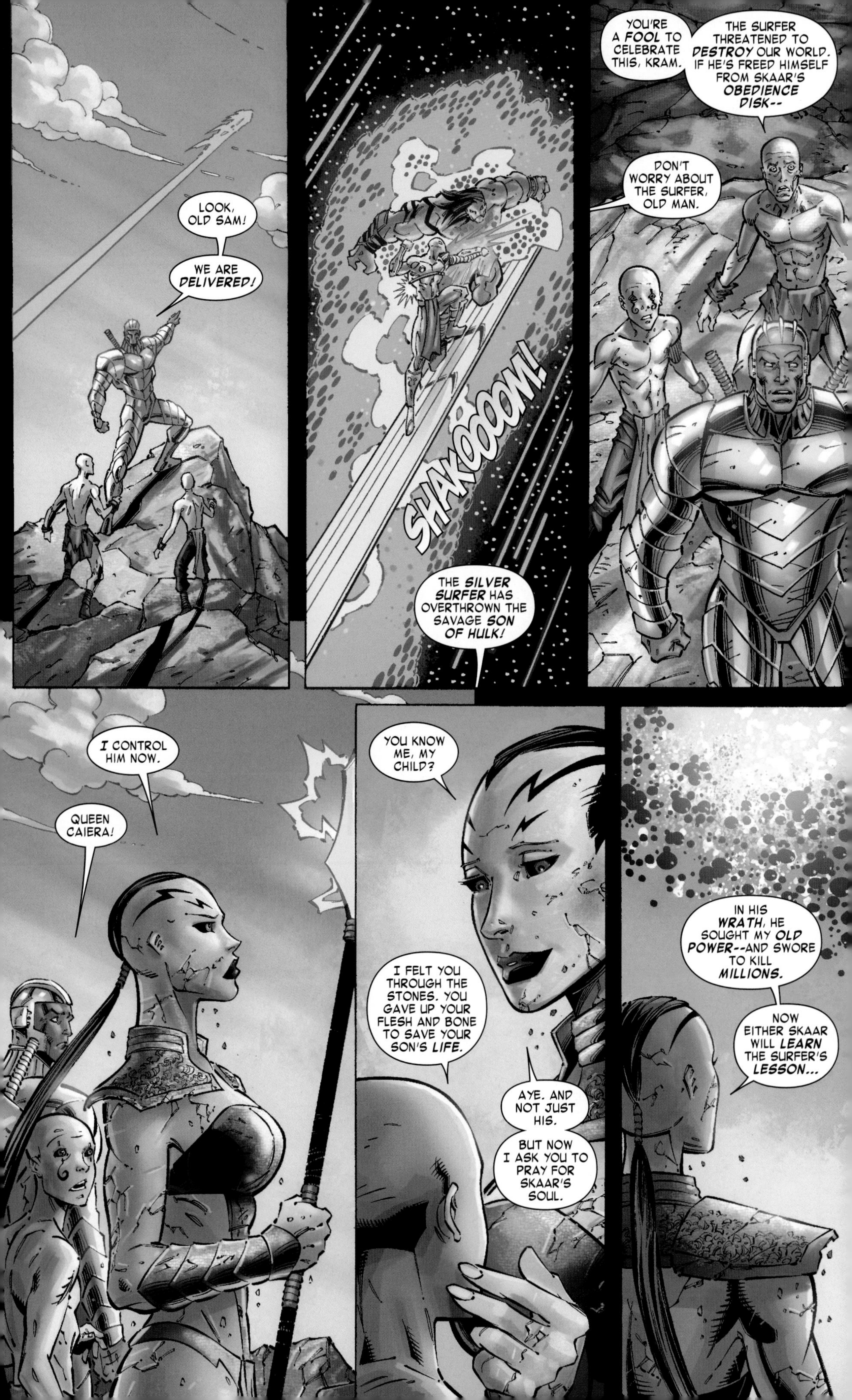
LOOK, OLD SAM!
WE ARE DELIVERED!
SHAKOOOOM!
THE SILVER SURFER HAS OVERTHROWN THE SAVAGE SON OF HULK!
YOU'RE A FOOL TO CELEBRATE THIS, KRAM.
THE SURFER THREATENED TO DESTROY OUR WORLD. IF HE'S FREED HIMSELF FROM SKAAR'S OBEDIENCE DISK--
DON'T WORRY ABOUT THE SURFER, OLD MAN.
I CONTROL HIM NOW.
QUEEN CAIERA!
YOU KNOW ME, MY CHILD?
I FELT YOU THROUGH THE STONES. YOU GAVE UP YOUR FLESH AND BONE TO SAVE YOUR SON'S LIFE.
AYE. AND NOT JUST HIS.
BUT NOW I ASK YOU TO PRAY FOR SKAAR'S SOUL.
IN HIS WRATH, HE SOUGHT MY OLD POWER--AND SWORE TO KILL MILLIONS.
NOW EITHER SKAAR WILL LEARN THE SURFER'S LESSON...

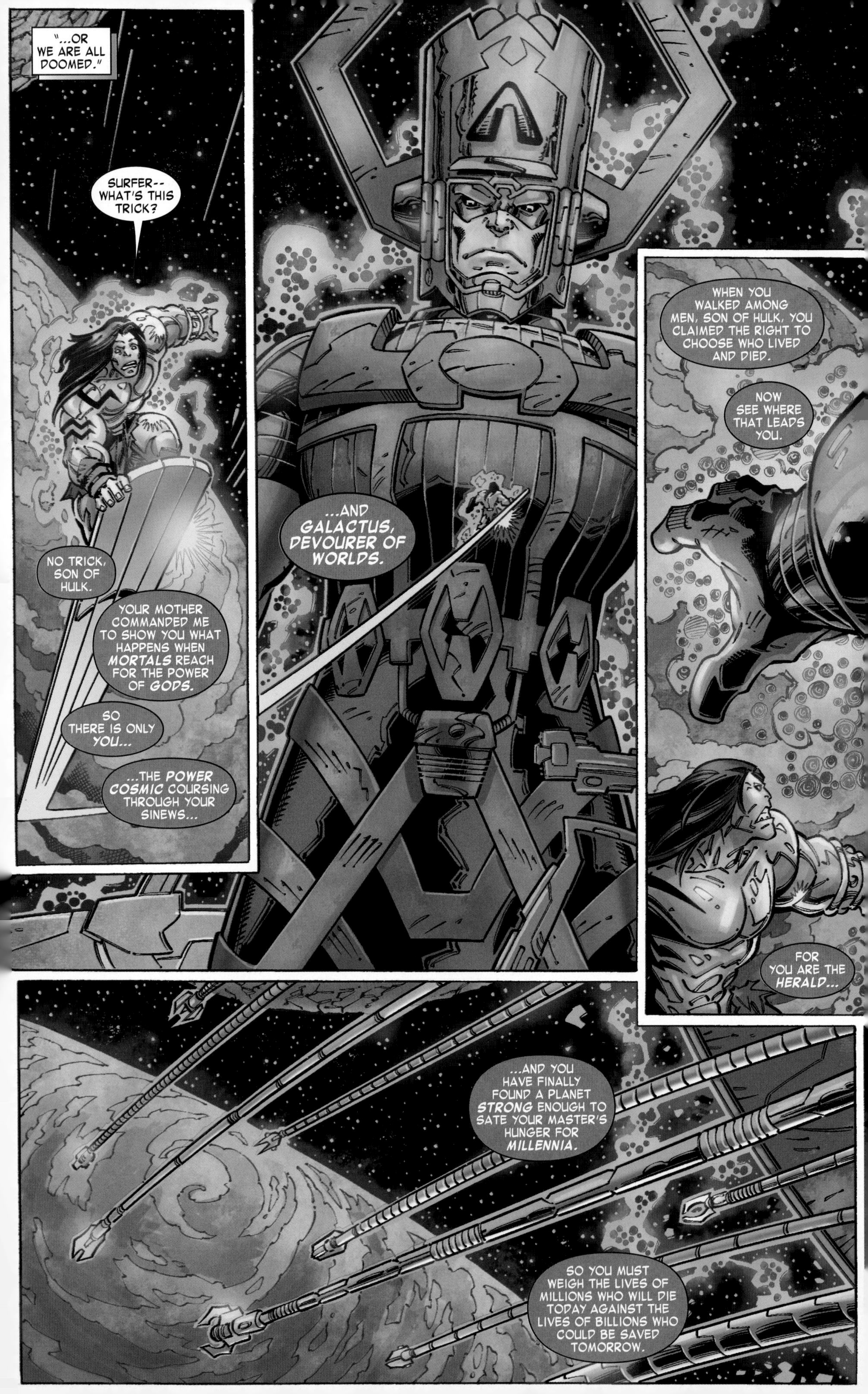

"...OR WE ARE ALL DOOMED."
SURFER-- WHAT'S THIS TRICK?
NO TRICK, SON OF HULK.
YOUR MOTHER COMMANDED ME TO SHOW YOU WHAT HAPPENS WHEN MORTALS REACH FOR THE POWER OF GODS.
SO THERE IS ONLY YOU...
...THE POWER COSMIC COURSING THROUGH YOUR SINEWS...
...AND GALACTUS, DEVOURER OF WORLDS.
WHEN YOU WALKED AMONG MEN, SON OF HULK, YOU CLAIMED THE RIGHT TO CHOOSE WHO LIVED AND DIED.
NOW SEE WHERE THAT LEADS YOU.
FOR YOU ARE THE HERALD...
...AND YOU HAVE FINALLY FOUND A PLANET STRONG ENOUGH TO SATE YOUR MASTER'S HUNGER FOR MILLENNIA.
SO YOU MUST WEIGH THE LIVES OF MILLIONS WHO WILL DIE TODAY AGAINST THE LIVES OF BILLIONS WHO COULD BE SAVED TOMORROW.

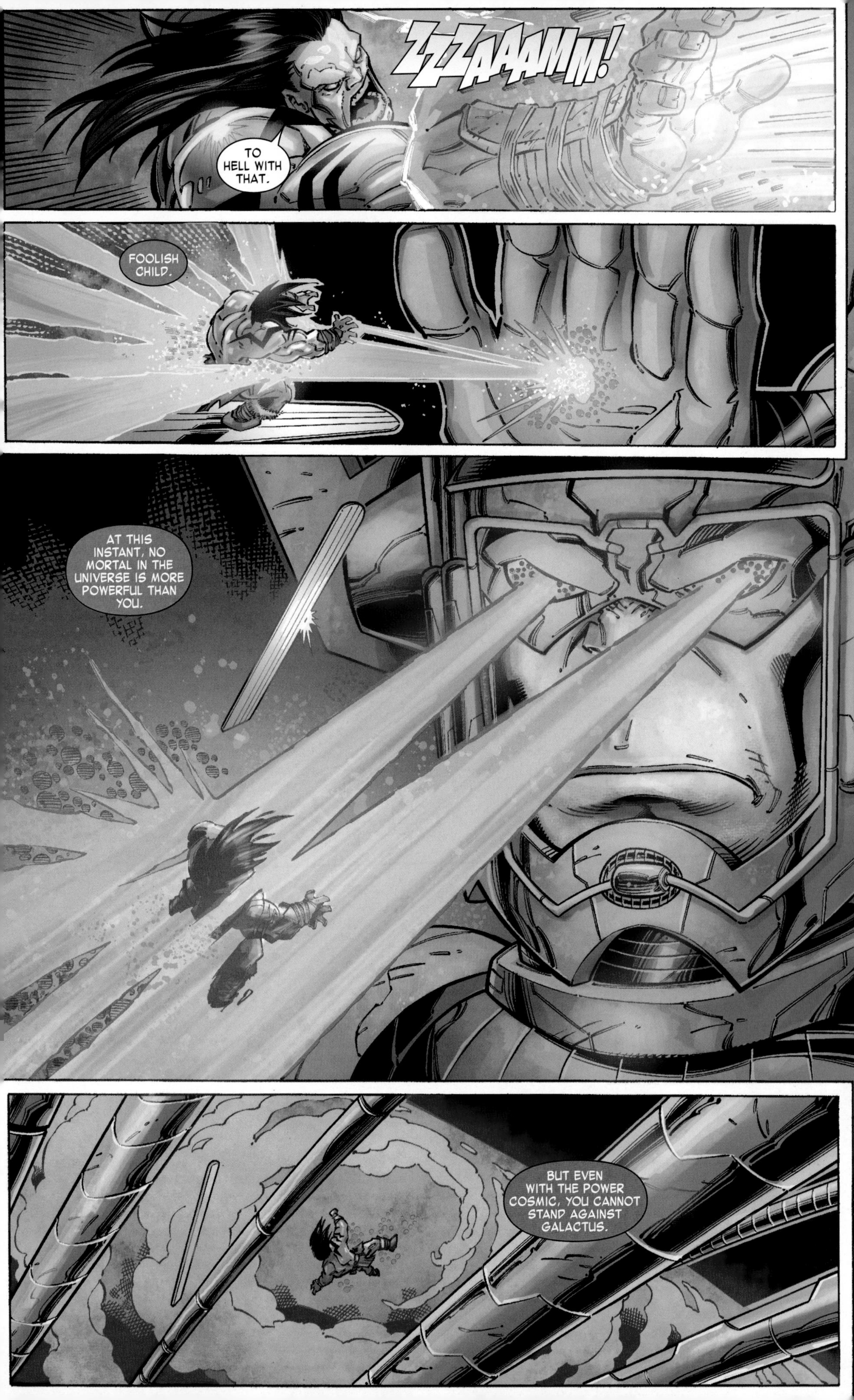
ZZZAAAMM!
TO HELL WITH THAT.
FOOLISH CHILD.
AT THIS INSTANT, NO MORTAL IN THE UNIVERSE IS MORE POWERFUL THAN YOU.
BUT EVEN WITH THE POWER COSMIC, YOU CANNOT STAND AGAINST GALACTUS.

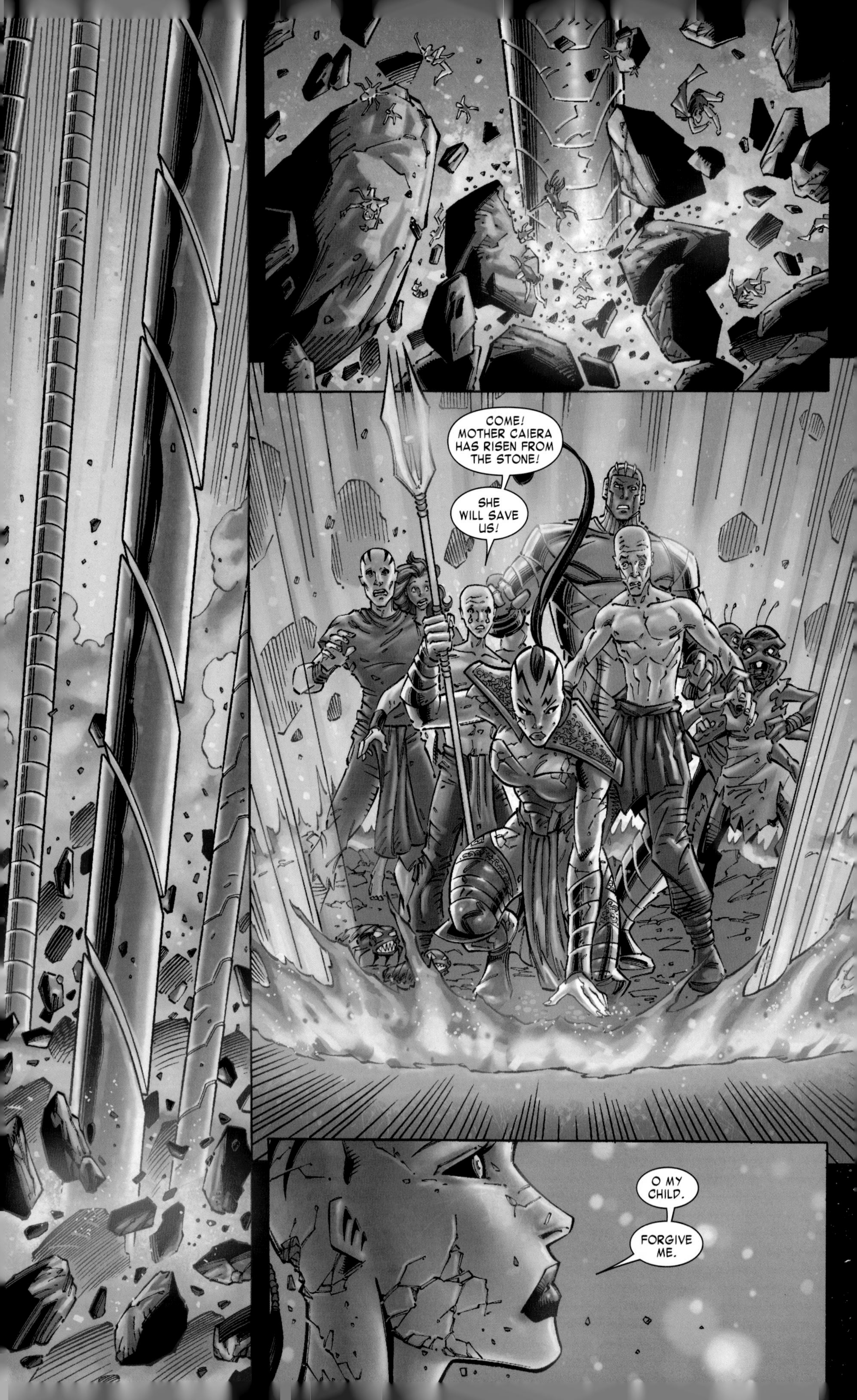
COME! MOTHER CAIERA HAS RISEN FROM THE STONE!
SHE WILL SAVE US!
O MY CHILD.
FORGIVE ME.

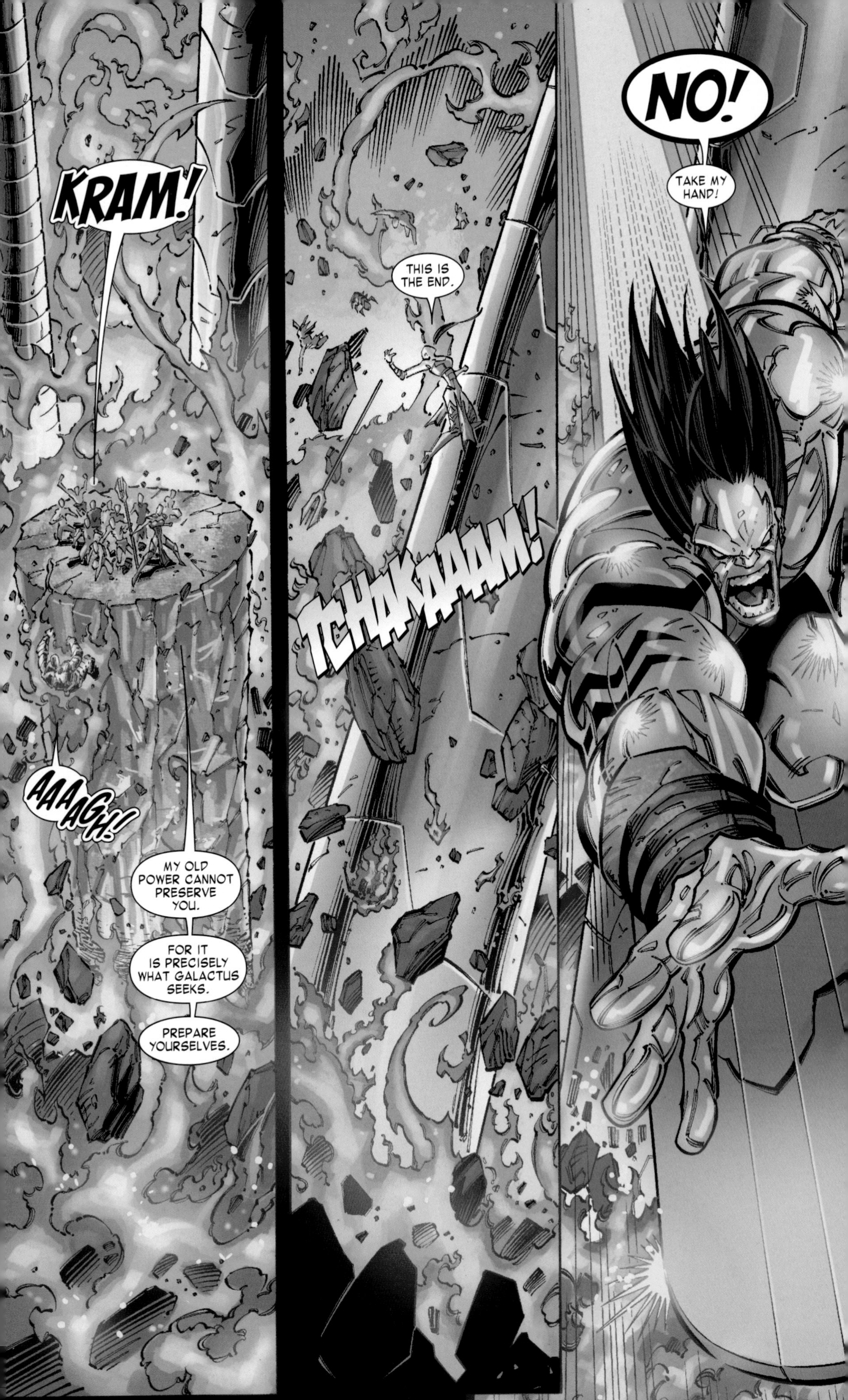
KRAM!
AAAAGH!
MY OLD POWER CANNOT PRESERVE YOU.
FOR IT IS PRECISELY WHAT GALACTUS SEEKS.
PREPARE YOURSELVES.
THIS IS THE END.
TCHAKAAAM!
NO!
TAKE MY HAND!

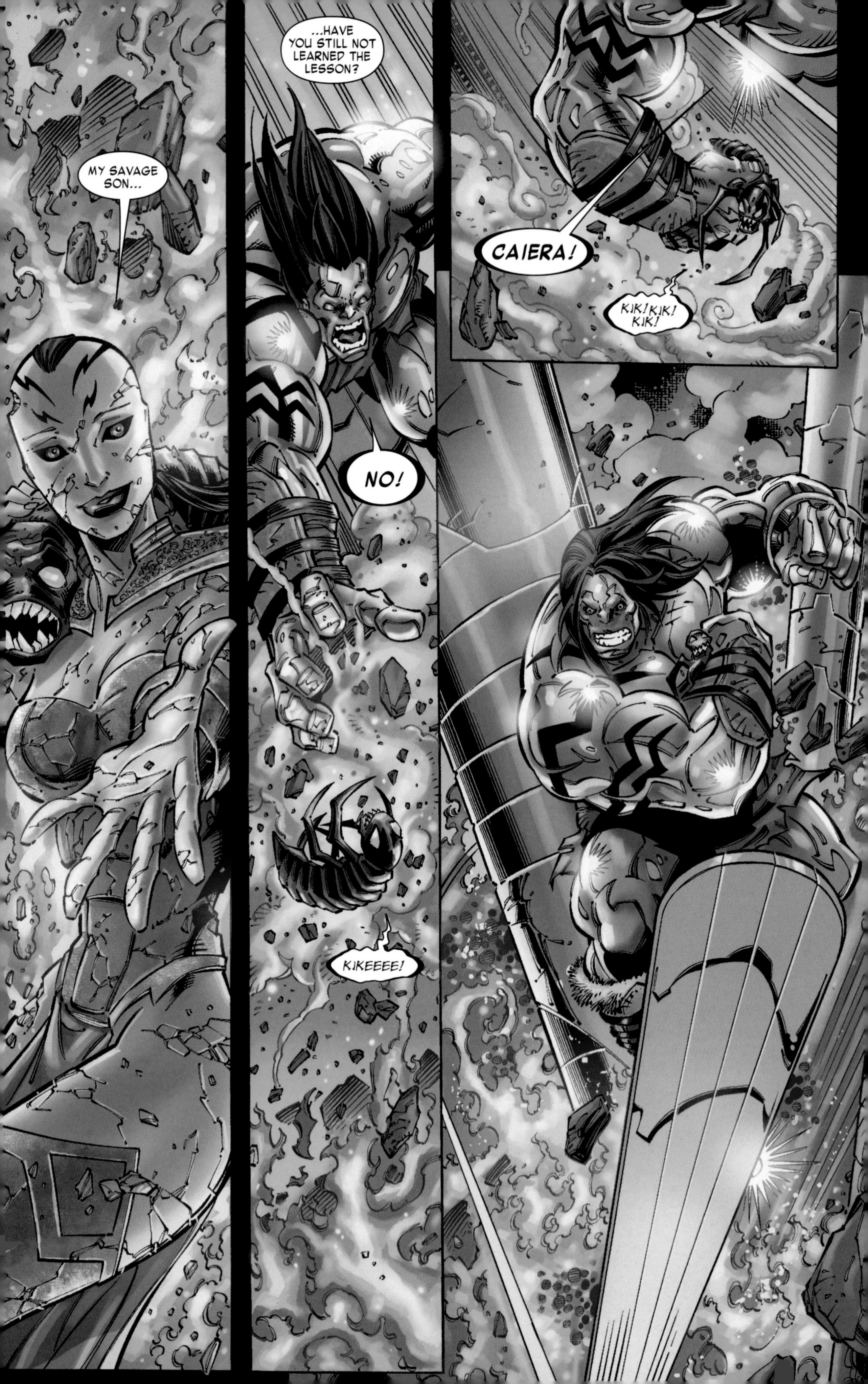
MY SAVAGE SON...
...HAVE YOU STILL NOT LEARNED THE LESSON?
NO!
KIKEEEE!
CAIERA!
KIK! KIK! KIK!

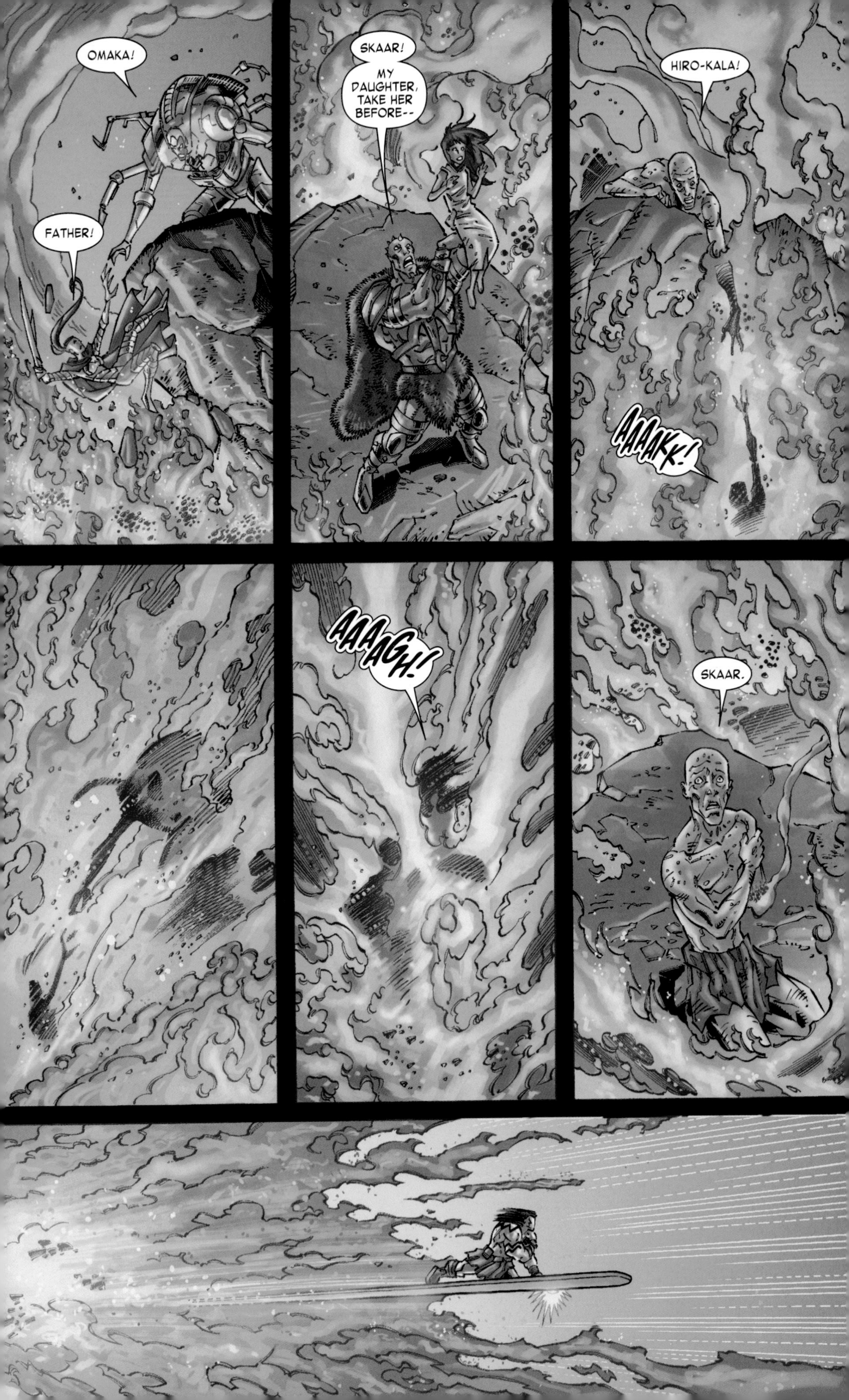
OMAKA!
FATHER!
SKAAR!
MY DAUGHTER, TAKE HER BEFORE--
HIRO-KALA!
AAAAKK!
AAAAGH!
SKAAR.

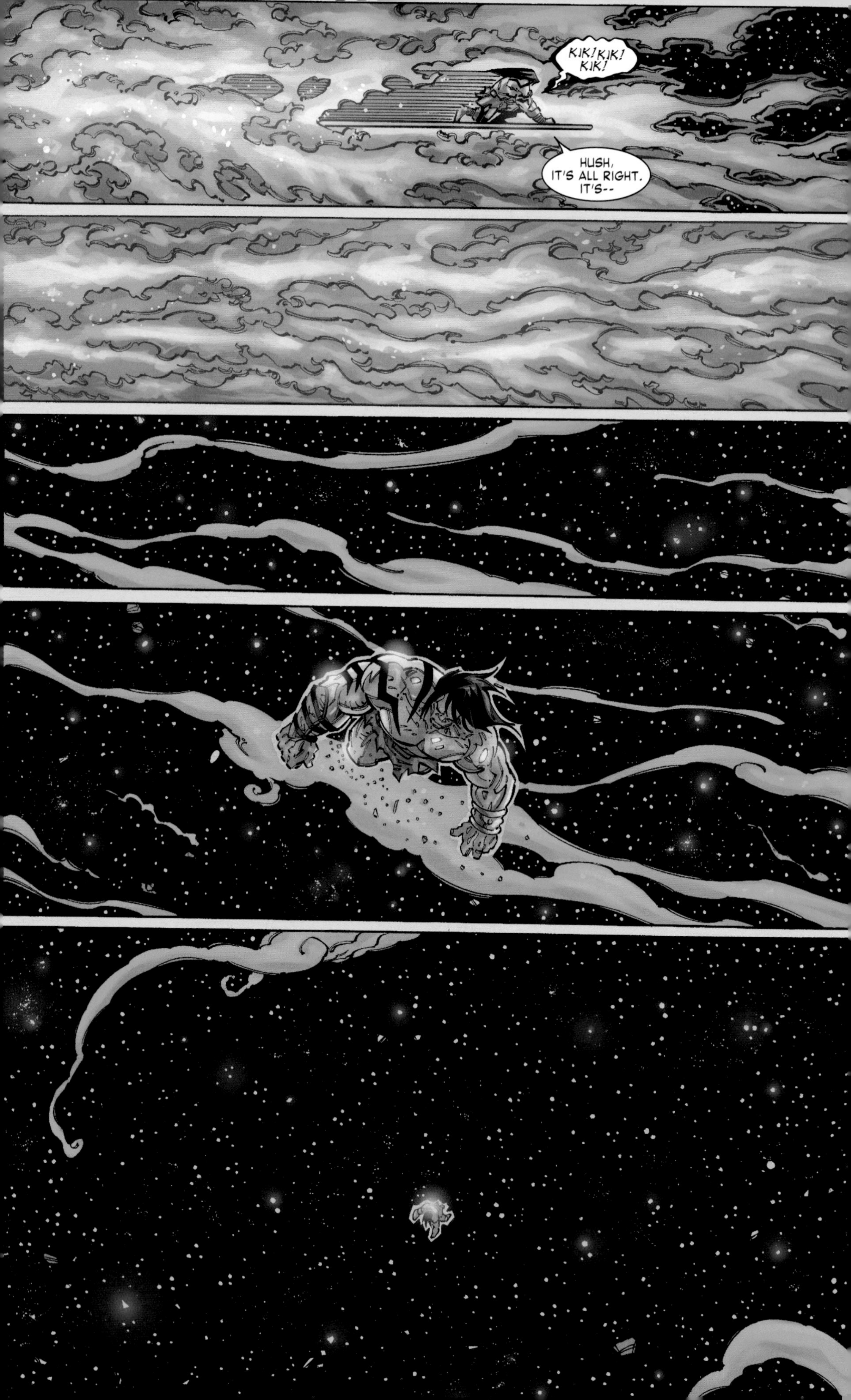
KIK! KIK! KIK!
HUSH, IT'S ALL RIGHT. IT'S--

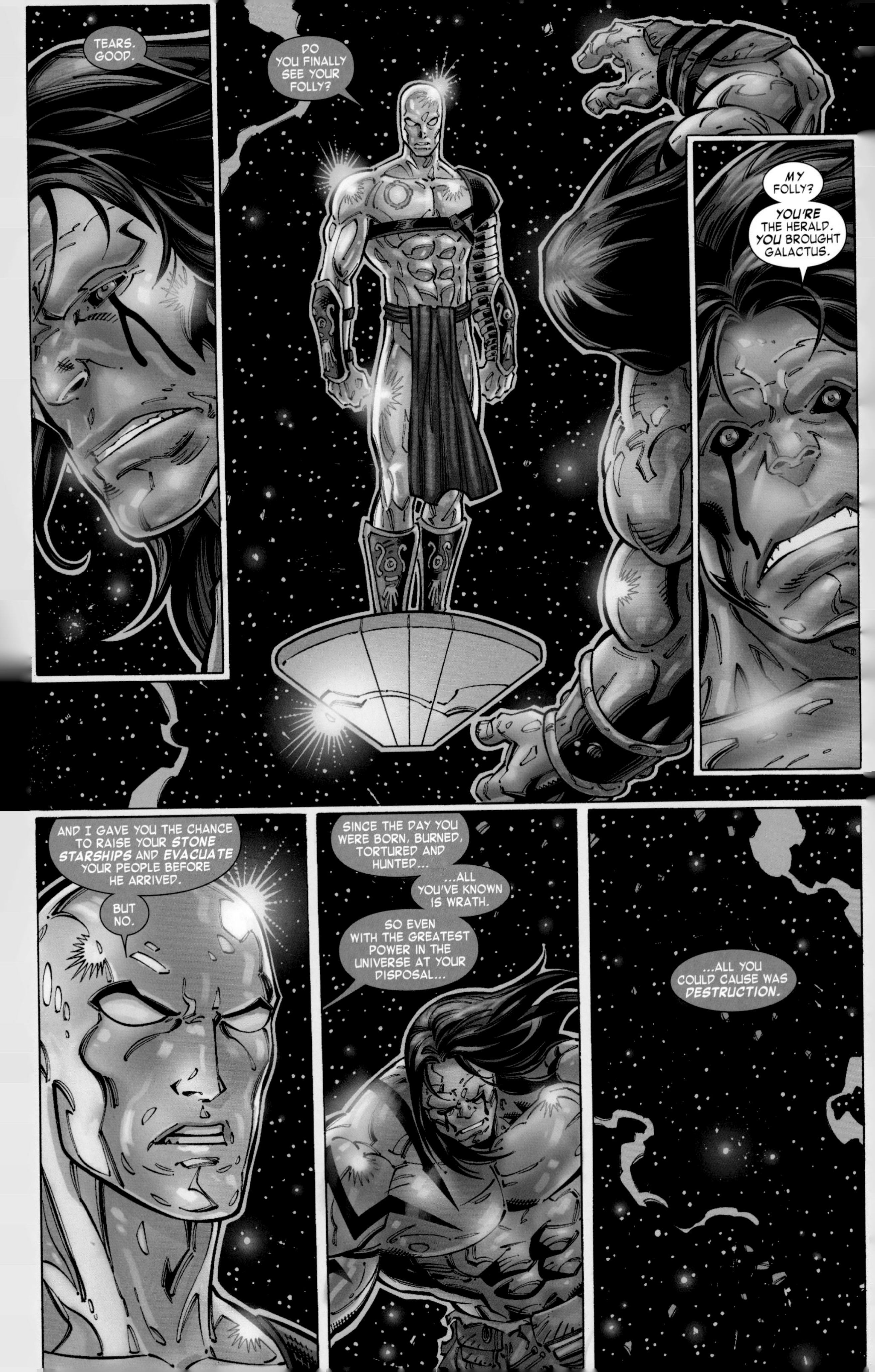
TEARS. GOOD.
DO YOU FINALLY SEE YOUR FOLLY?
MY FOLLY?
YOU'RE THE HERALD. YOU BROUGHT GALACTUS.
AND I GAVE YOU THE CHANCE TO RAISE YOUR STONE STARSHIPS AND EVACUATE YOUR PEOPLE BEFORE HE ARRIVED.
BUT NO.
SINCE THE DAY YOU WERE BORN, BURNED, TORTURED AND HUNTED...
...ALL YOU'VE KNOWN IS WRATH.
SO EVEN WITH THE GREATEST POWER IN THE UNIVERSE AT YOUR DISPOSAL...
...ALL YOU COULD CAUSE WAS DESTRUCTION.

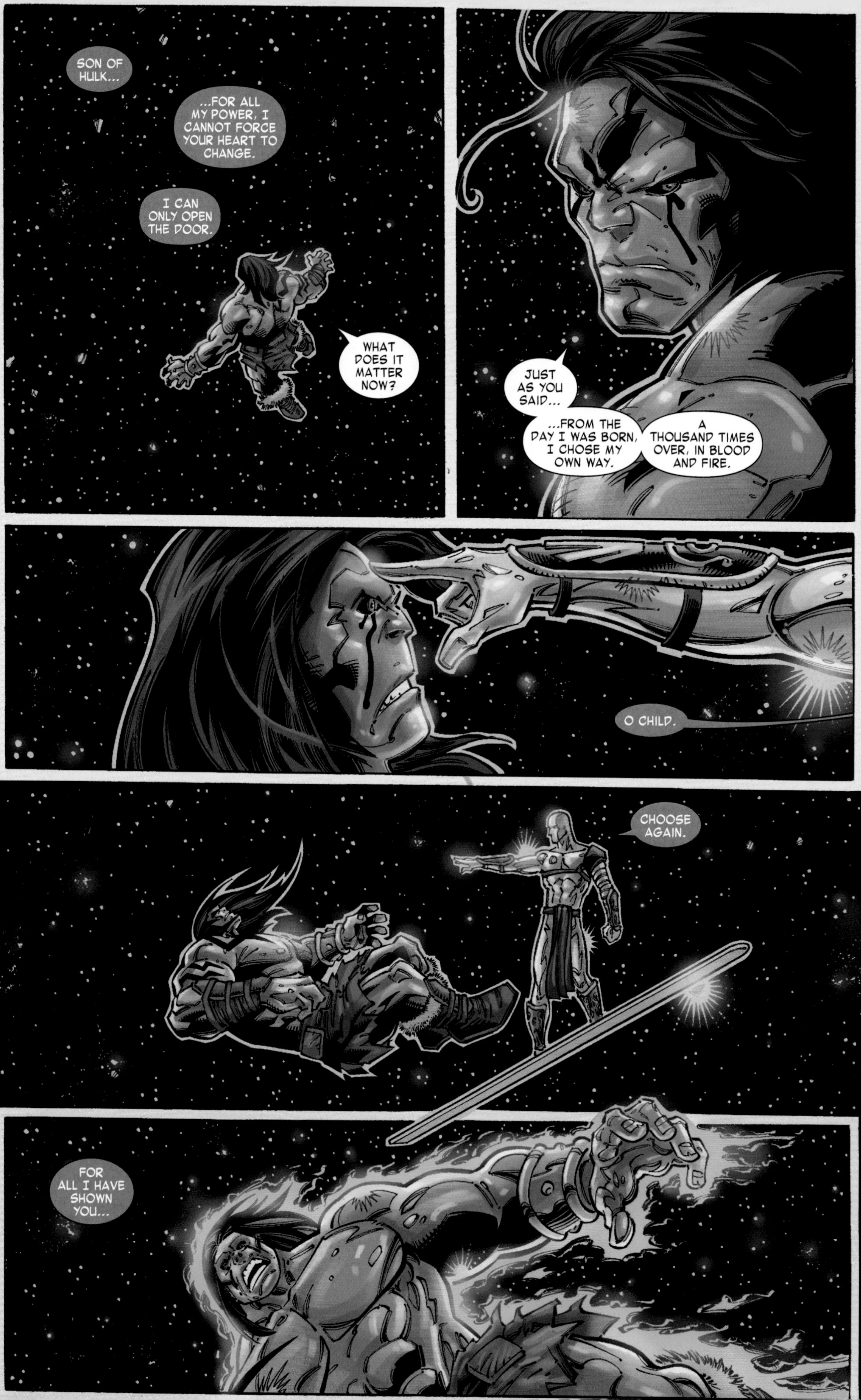
SON OF HULK...
...FOR ALL MY POWER, I CANNOT FORCE YOUR HEART TO CHANGE.
I CAN ONLY OPEN THE DOOR.
WHAT DOES IT MATTER NOW?
JUST AS YOU SAID...
...FROM THE DAY I WAS BORN, I CHOSE MY OWN WAY.
A THOUSAND TIMES OVER, IN BLOOD AND FIRE.
O CHILD.
CHOOSE AGAIN.
FOR ALL I HAVE SHOWN YOU...

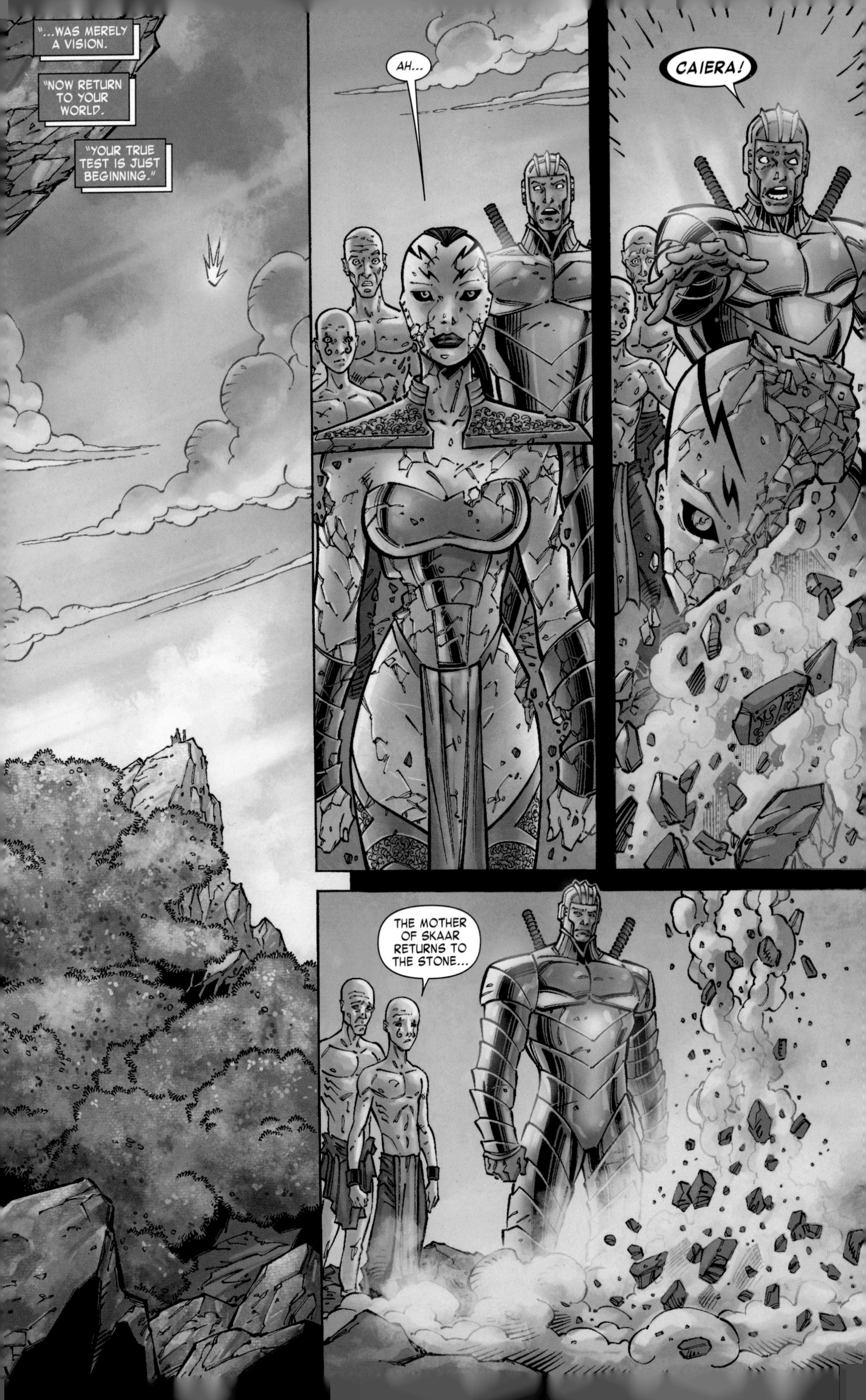
"...WAS MERELY A VISION.
"NOW RETURN TO YOUR WORLD.
"YOUR TRUE TEST IS JUST BEGINNING."
AH...
CAIERA!
THE MOTHER OF SKAAR RETURNS TO THE STONE...

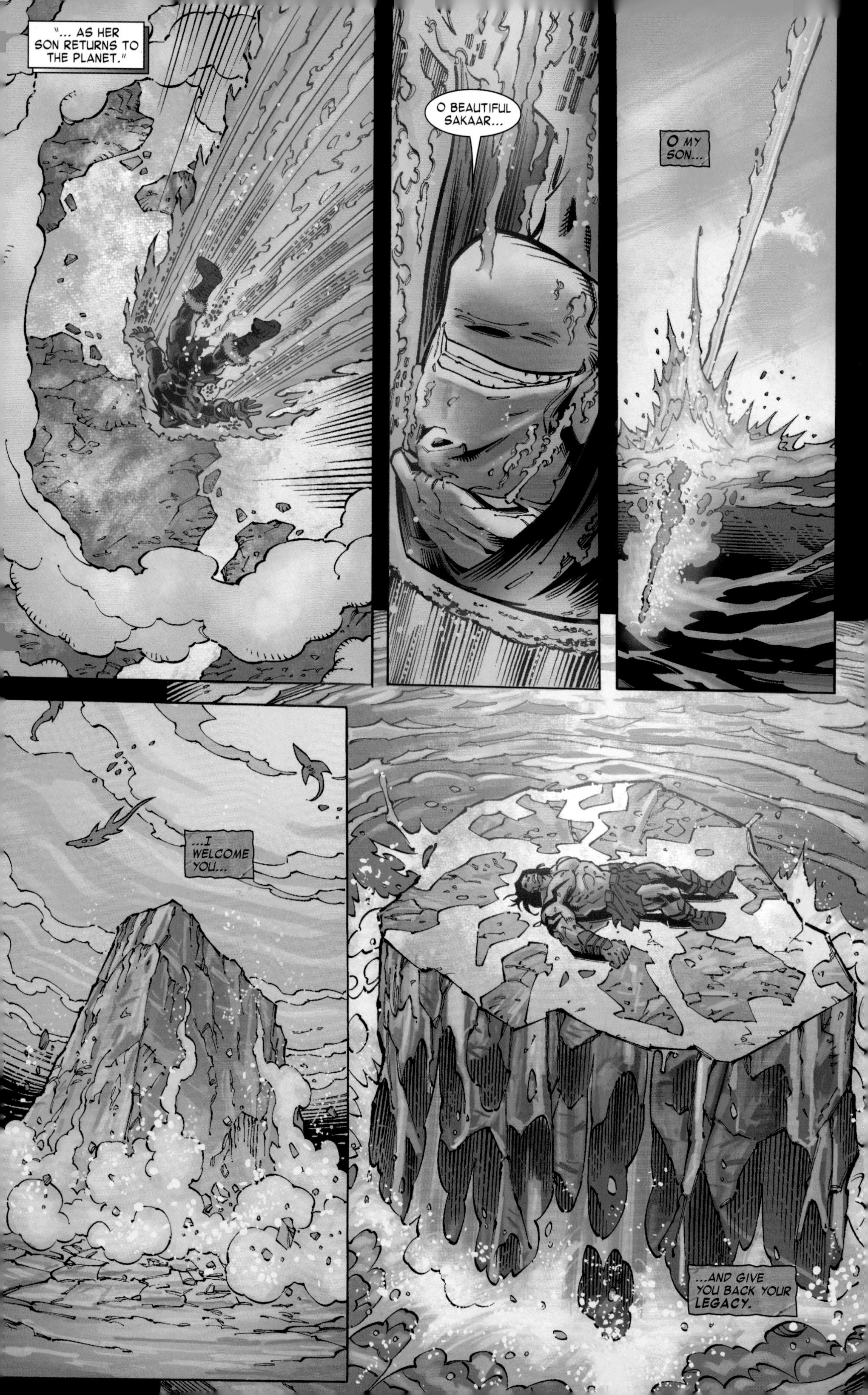
"... AS HER SON RETURNS TO THE PLANET."
O BEAUTIFUL SAKAAR...
O MY SON...
...I WELCOME YOU...
...AND GIVE YOU BACK YOUR LEGACY.

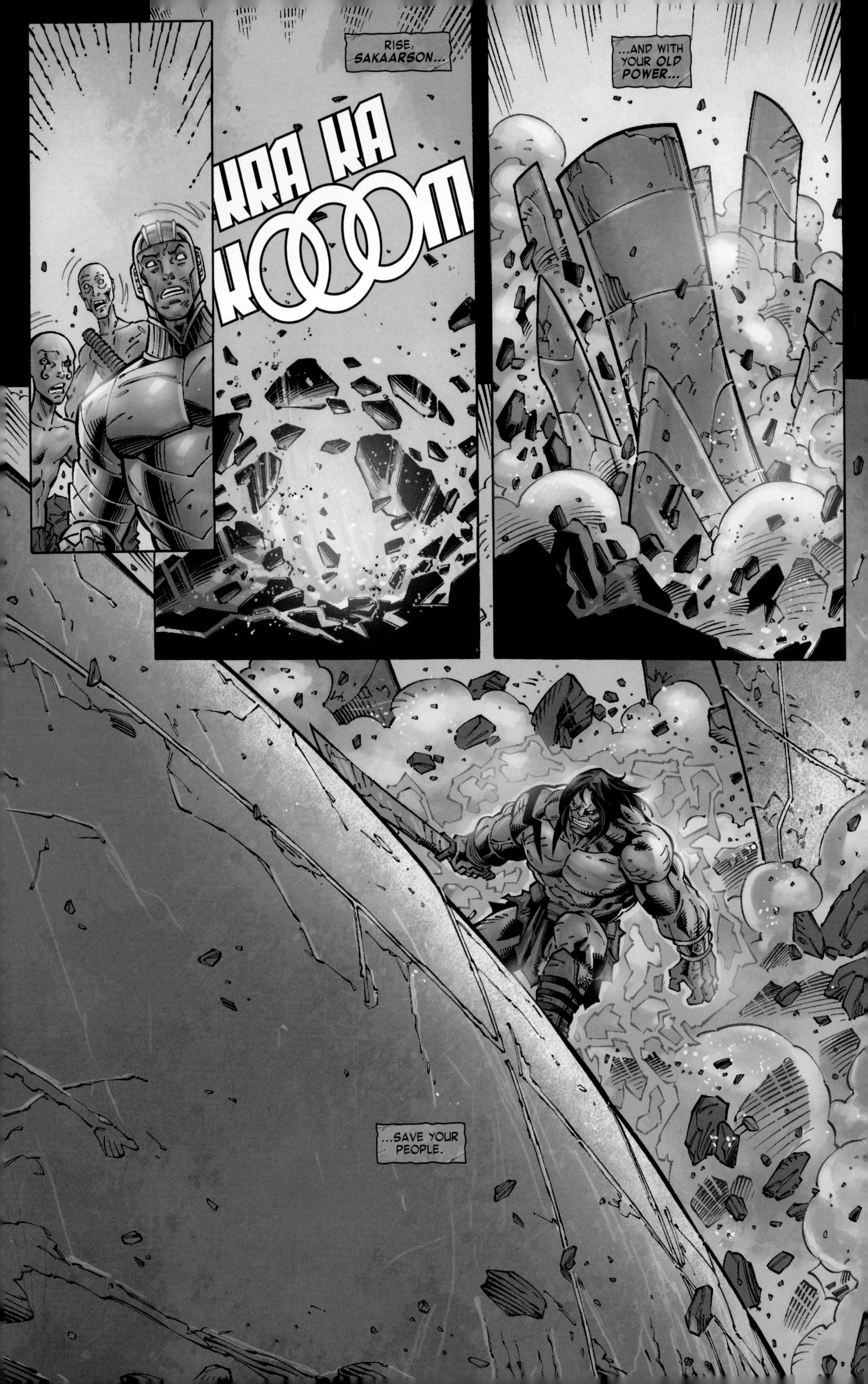
RISE, SAKAARSON...
KRA KA KOOOM
...AND WITH YOUR OLD POWER...
...SAVE YOUR PEOPLE.

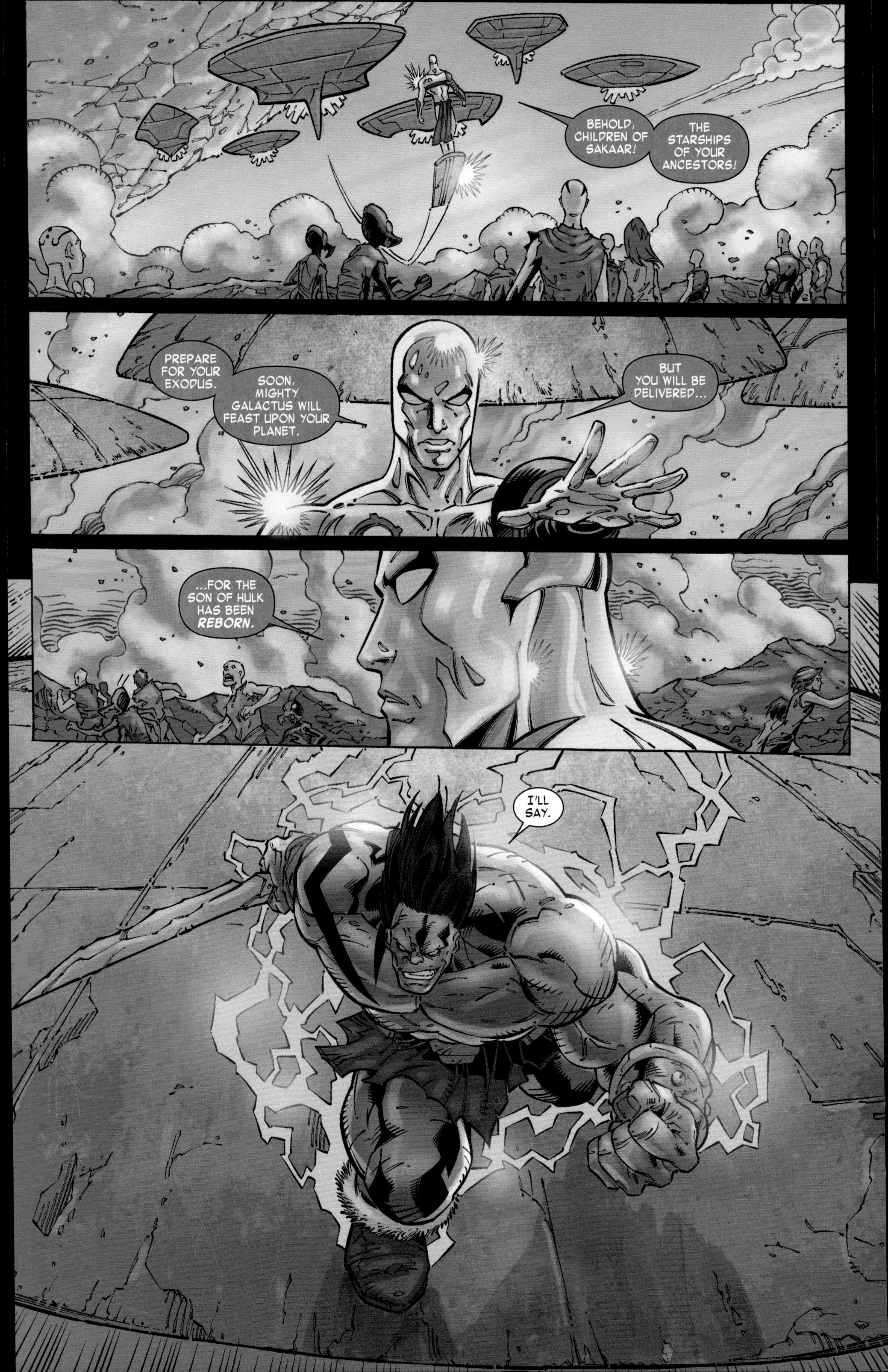
BEHOLD, CHILDREN OF SAKAAR!
THE STARSHIPS OF YOUR ANCESTORS!
PREPARE FOR YOUR EXODUS.
SOON, MIGHTY GALACTUS WILL FEAST UPON YOUR PLANET.
BUT YOU WILL BE DELIVERED...
...FOR THE SON OF HULK HAS BEEN *REBORN.*
I'LL SAY.

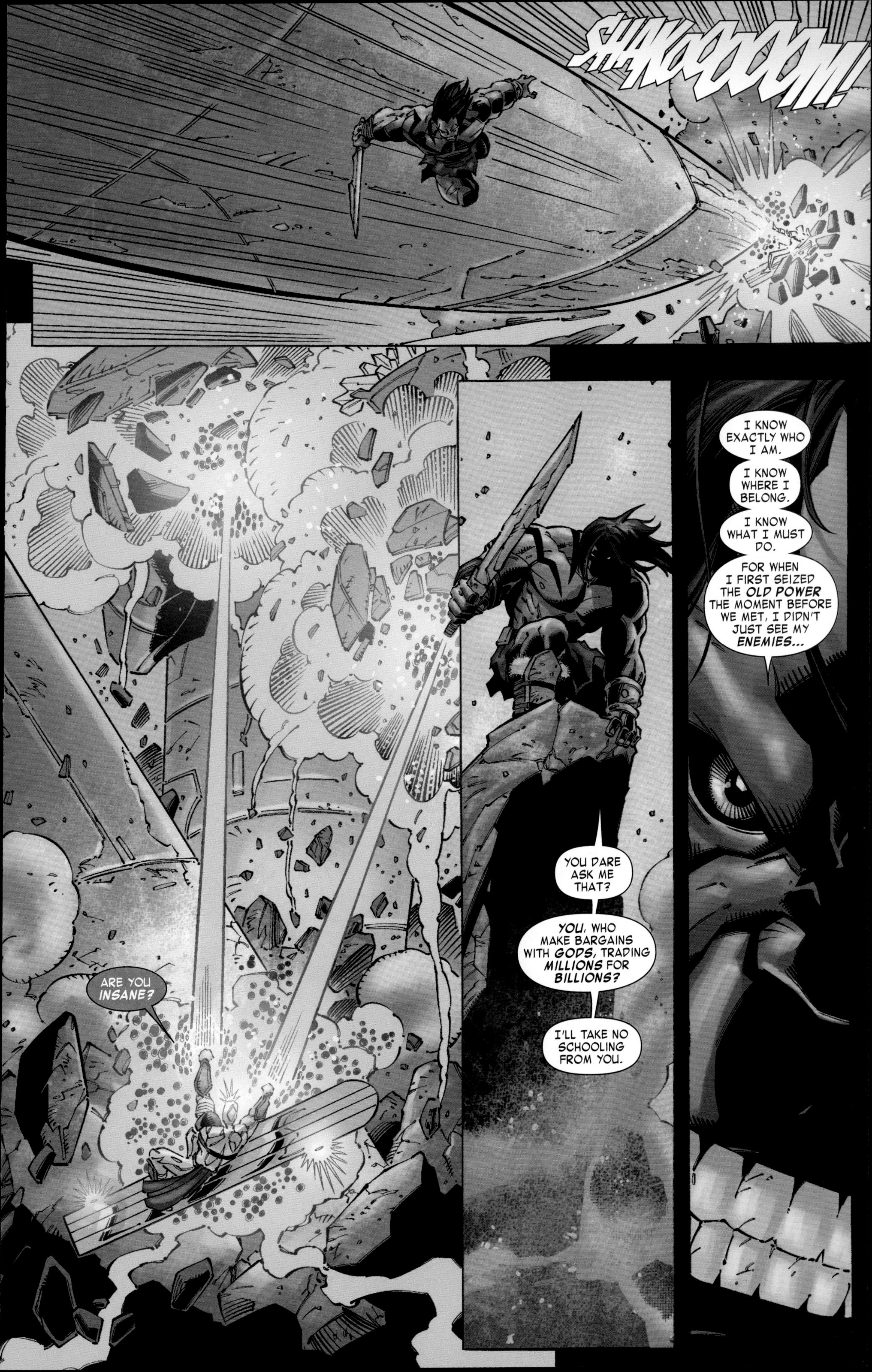
SHAKOOOOOM!
ARE YOU INSANE?
I KNOW EXACTLY WHO I AM.
I KNOW WHERE I BELONG.
I KNOW WHAT I MUST DO.
FOR WHEN I FIRST SEIZED THE OLD POWER THE MOMENT BEFORE WE MET, I DIDN'T JUST SEE MY ENEMIES...
YOU DARE ASK ME THAT?
YOU, WHO MAKE BARGAINS WITH GODS, TRADING MILLIONS FOR BILLIONS?
I'LL TAKE NO SCHOOLING FROM YOU.

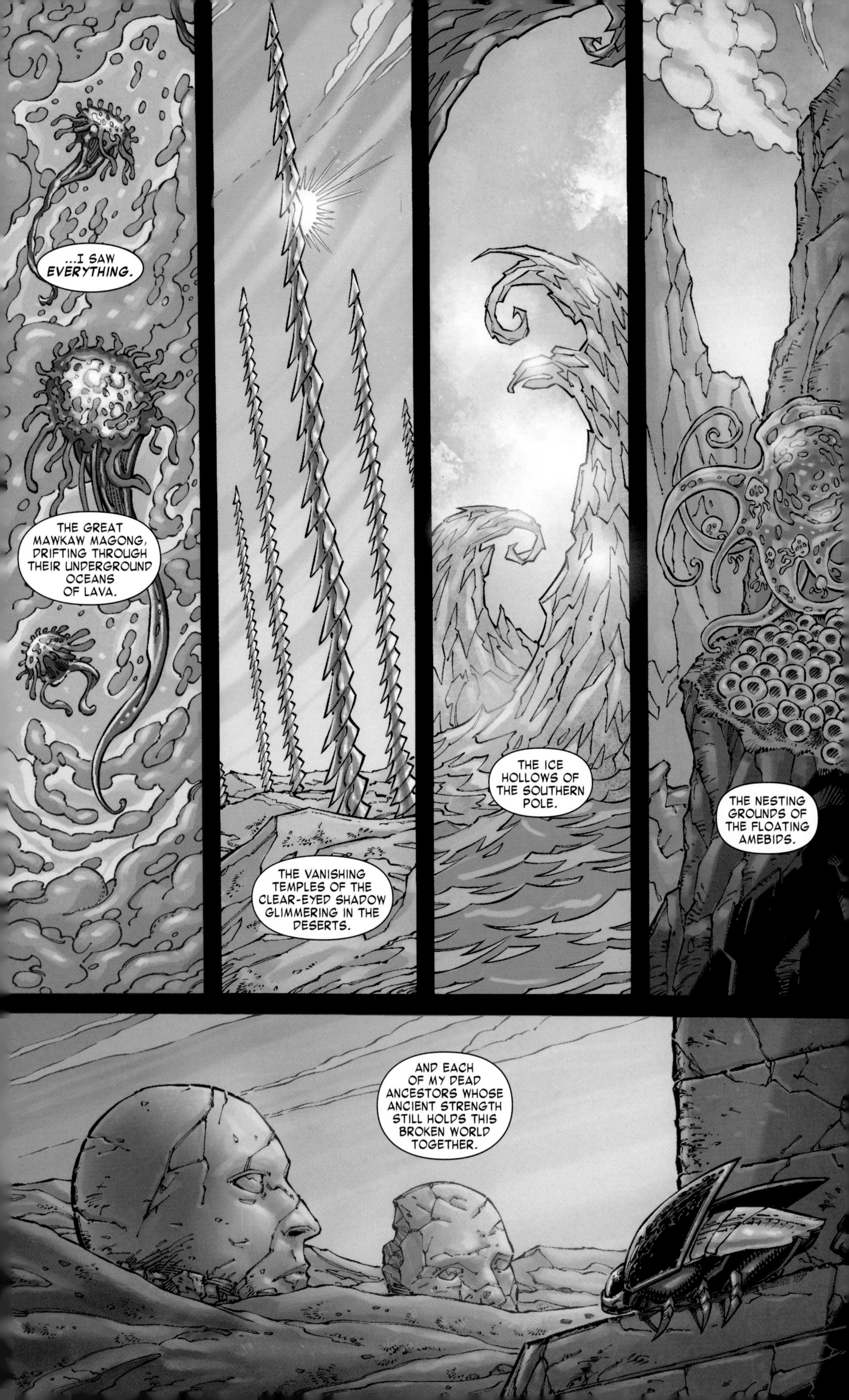

...I SAW EVERYTHING.
THE GREAT MAWKAW MAGONG, DRIFTING THROUGH THEIR UNDERGROUND OCEANS OF LAVA.
THE VANISHING TEMPLES OF THE CLEAR-EYED SHADOW GLIMMERING IN THE DESERTS.
THE ICE HOLLOWS OF THE SOUTHERN POLE.
THE NESTING GROUNDS OF THE FLOATING AMEBIDS.
AND EACH OF MY DEAD ANCESTORS WHOSE ANCIENT STRENGTH STILL HOLDS THIS BROKEN WORLD TOGETHER.

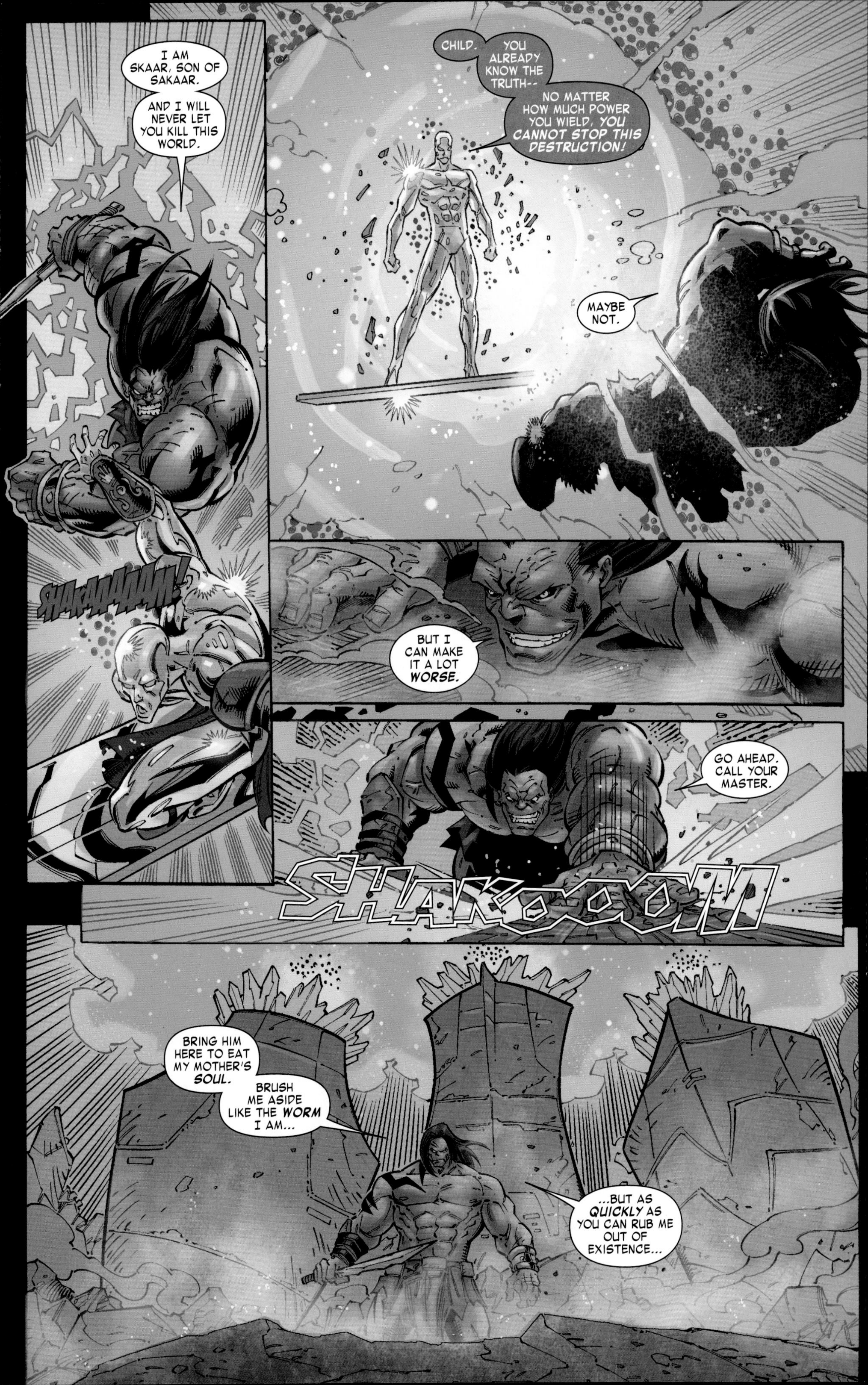
I AM SKAAR, SON OF SAKAAR.
AND I WILL NEVER LET YOU KILL THIS WORLD.
SHAKADADOOM!
CHILD.
YOU ALREADY KNOW THE TRUTH--
NO MATTER HOW MUCH POWER YOU WIELD, YOU CANNOT STOP THIS DESTRUCTION!
MAYBE NOT.
BUT I CAN MAKE IT A LOT WORSE.
GO AHEAD. CALL YOUR MASTER.
SHAKOOOM
BRING HIM HERE TO EAT MY MOTHER'S SOUL.
BRUSH ME ASIDE LIKE THE WORM I AM...
...BUT AS QUICKLY AS YOU CAN RUB ME OUT OF EXISTENCE...

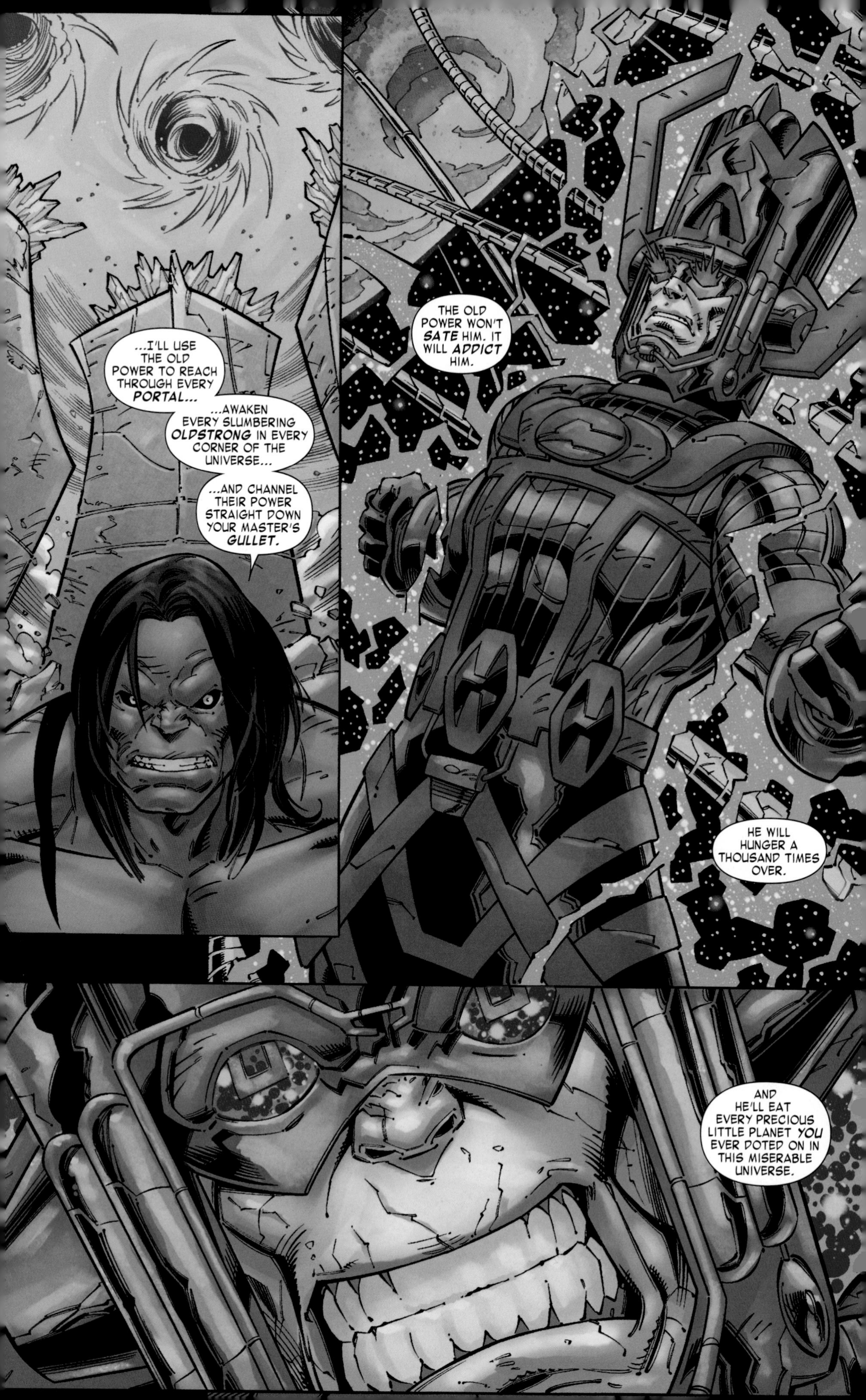
...I'LL USE THE OLD POWER TO REACH THROUGH EVERY PORTAL...
...AWAKEN EVERY SLUMBERING OLDSTRONG IN EVERY CORNER OF THE UNIVERSE...
...AND CHANNEL THEIR POWER STRAIGHT DOWN YOUR MASTER'S GULLET.
THE OLD POWER WON'T SATE HIM. IT WILL ADDICT HIM.
HE WILL HUNGER A THOUSAND TIMES OVER.
AND HE'LL EAT EVERY PRECIOUS LITTLE PLANET YOU EVER DOTED ON IN THIS MISERABLE UNIVERSE.

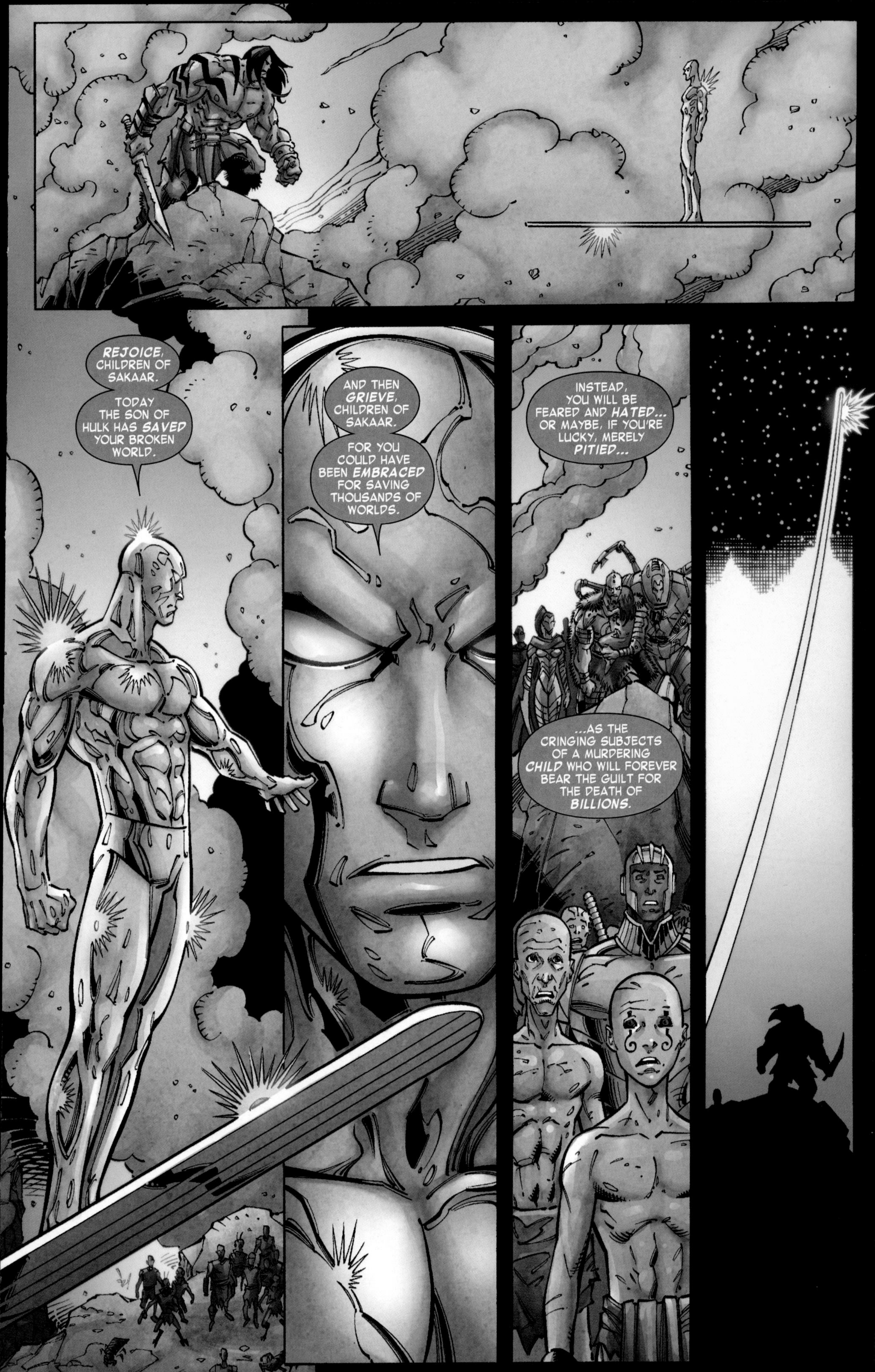
REJOICE, CHILDREN OF SAKAAR.
TODAY THE SON OF HULK HAS SAVED YOUR BROKEN WORLD.
AND THEN GRIEVE, CHILDREN OF SAKAAR.
FOR YOU COULD HAVE BEEN EMBRACED FOR SAVING THOUSANDS OF WORLDS.
INSTEAD, YOU WILL BE FEARED AND HATED... OR MAYBE, IF YOU'RE LUCKY, MERELY PITIED...
...AS THE CRINGING SUBJECTS OF A MURDERING CHILD WHO WILL FOREVER BEAR THE GUILT FOR THE DEATH OF BILLIONS.

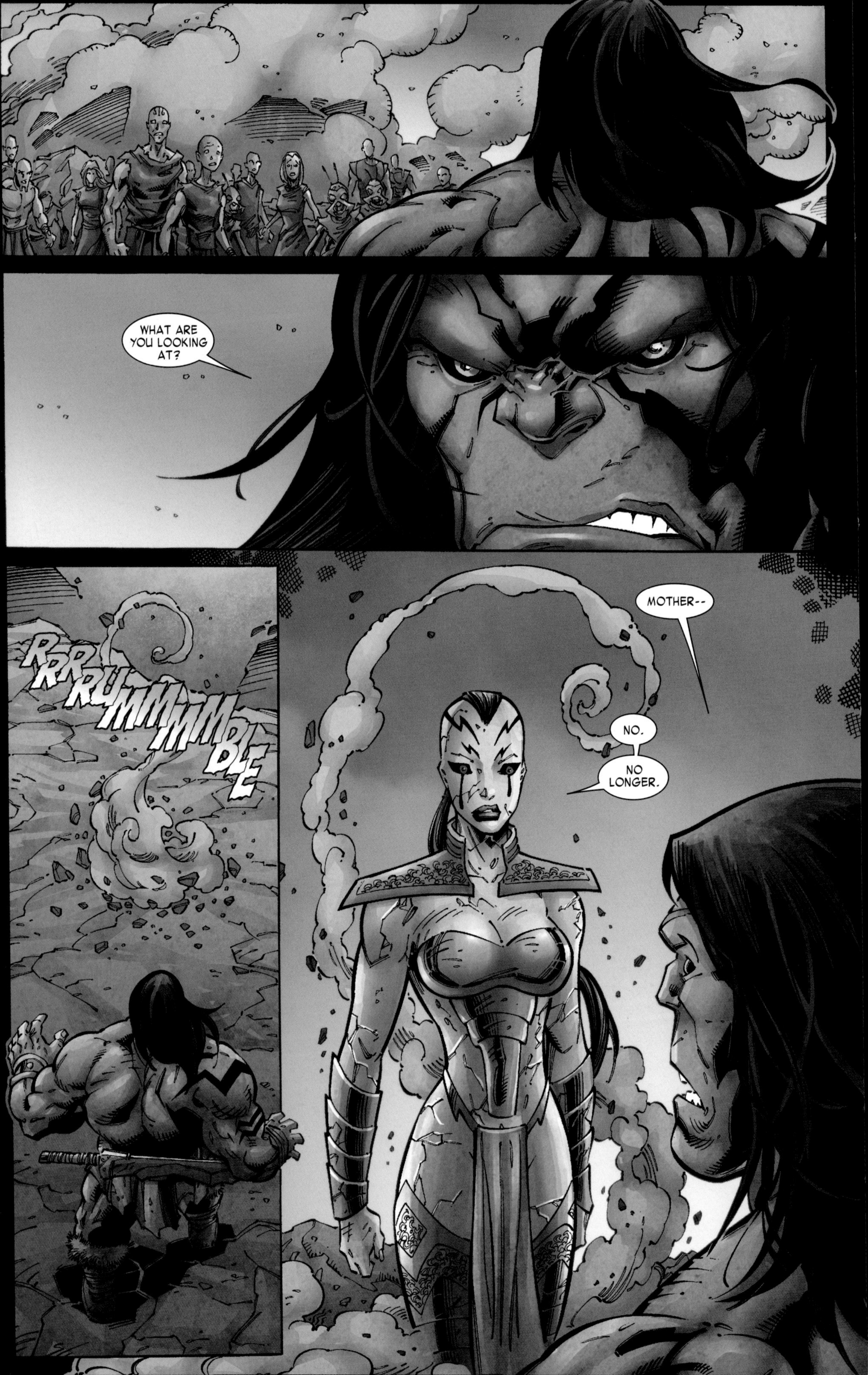
WHAT ARE YOU LOOKING AT?
RRRRUMMMMMBLE
MOTHER--
NO.
NO LONGER.

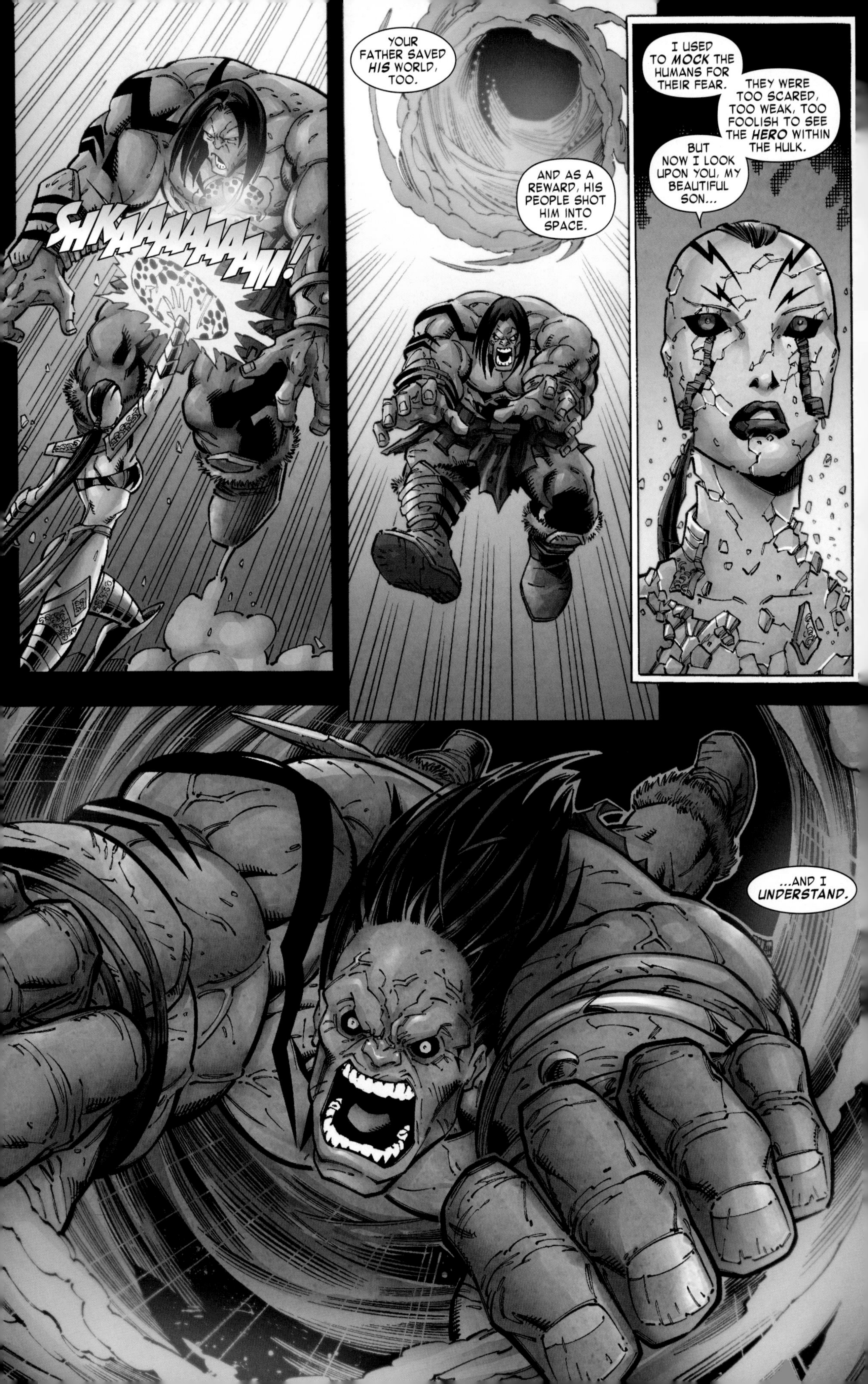
SHKAAAAAAAAM!
YOUR FATHER SAVED *HIS* WORLD, TOO.
AND AS A REWARD, HIS PEOPLE SHOT HIM INTO SPACE.
I USED TO *MOCK* THE HUMANS FOR THEIR FEAR.
THEY WERE TOO SCARED, TOO WEAK, TOO FOOLISH TO SEE THE *HERO* WITHIN THE HULK.
BUT NOW I LOOK UPON YOU, MY BEAUTIFUL SON...
...AND I *UNDERSTAND.*

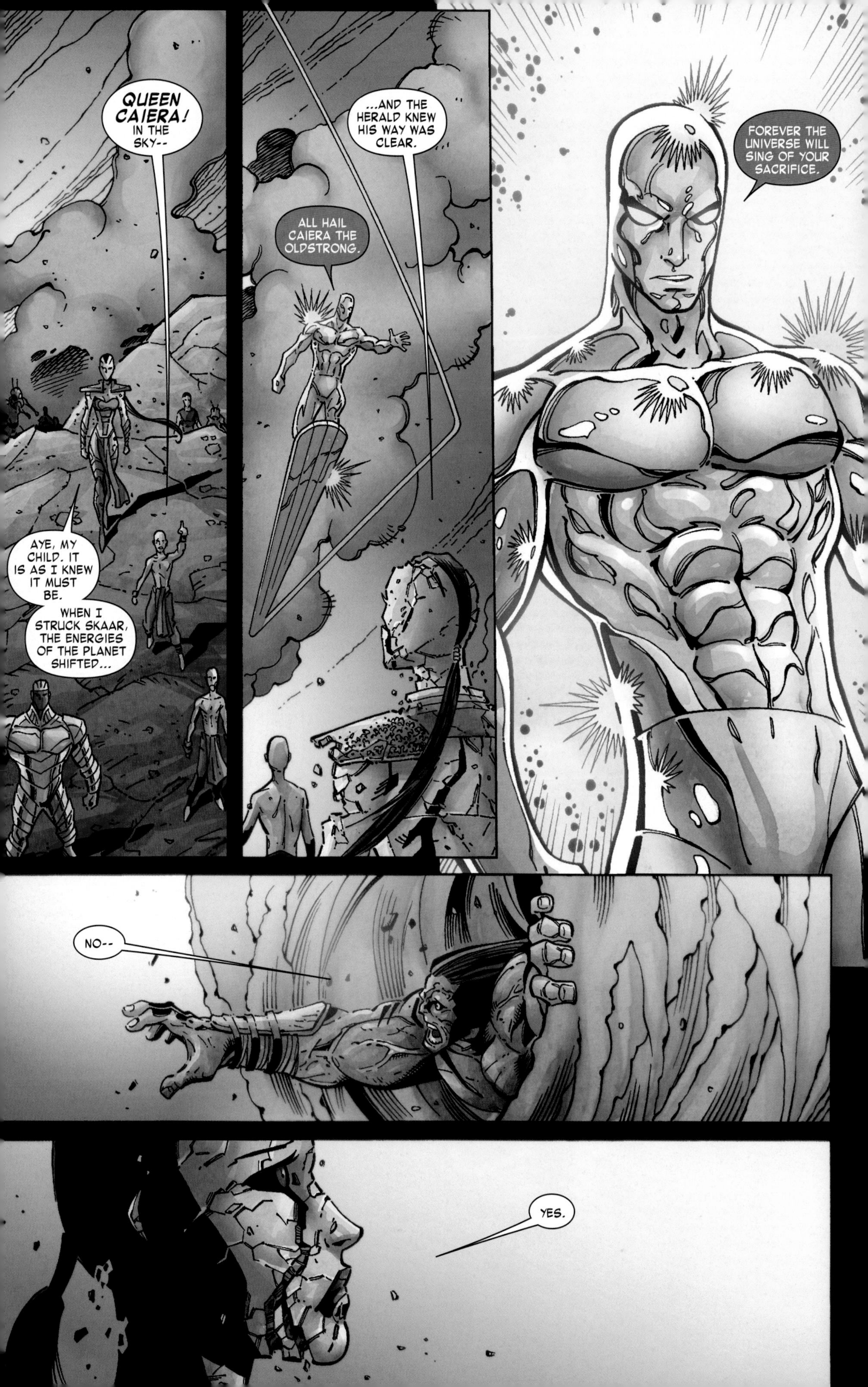
QUEEN CAIERA! IN THE SKY--
AYE, MY CHILD. IT IS AS I KNEW IT MUST BE.
WHEN I STRUCK SKAAR, THE ENERGIES OF THE PLANET SHIFTED...
...AND THE HERALD KNEW HIS WAY WAS CLEAR.
ALL HAIL CAIERA THE OLDSTRONG.
FOREVER THE UNIVERSE WILL SING OF YOUR SACRIFICE.
NO--
YES.

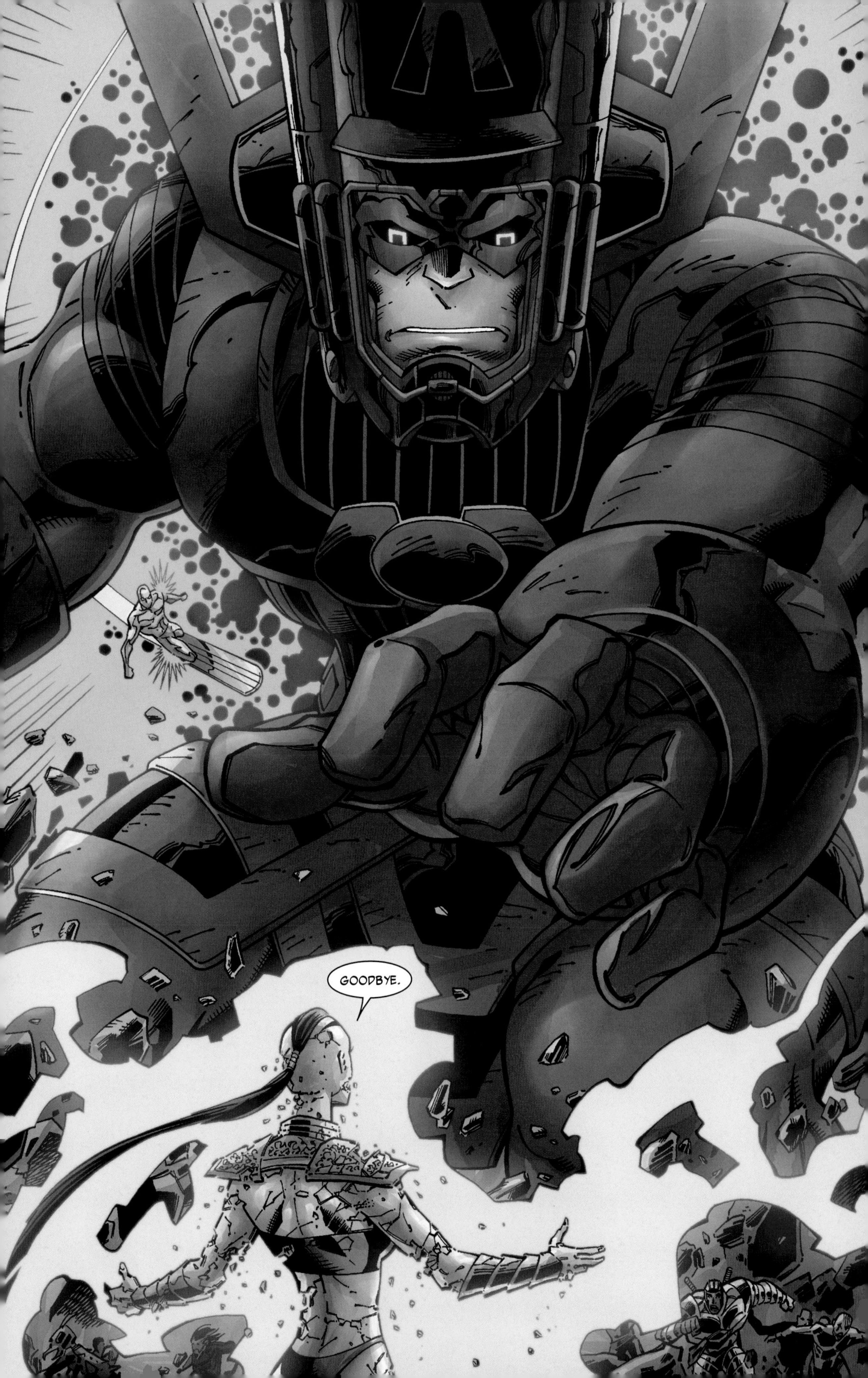
GOODBYE.

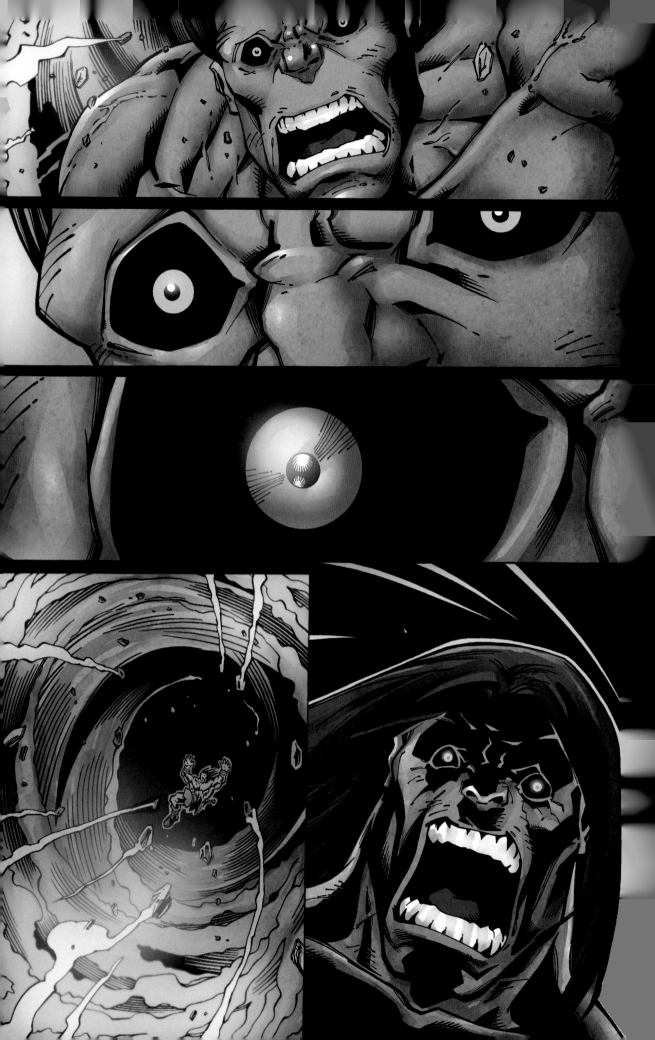

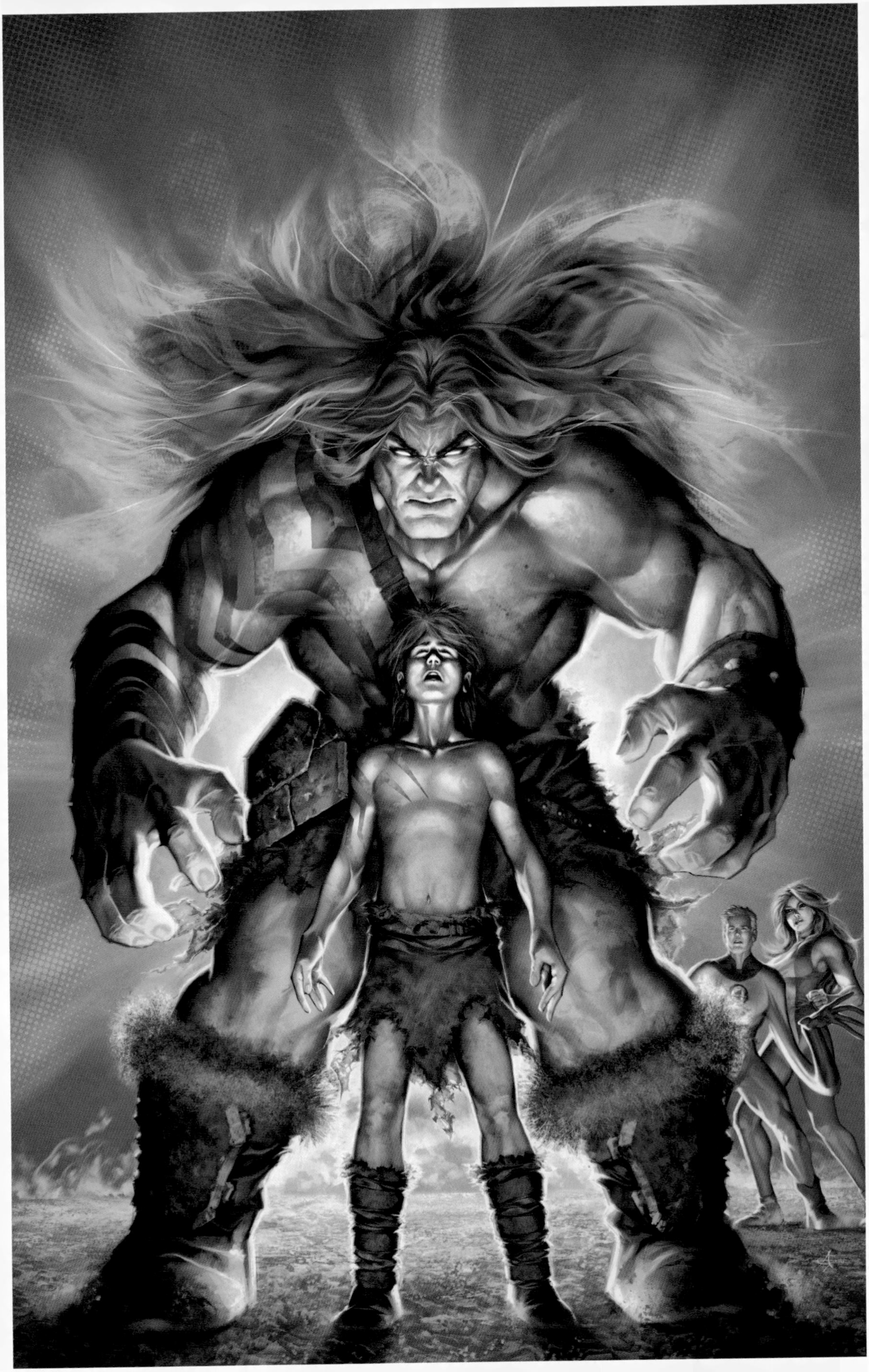

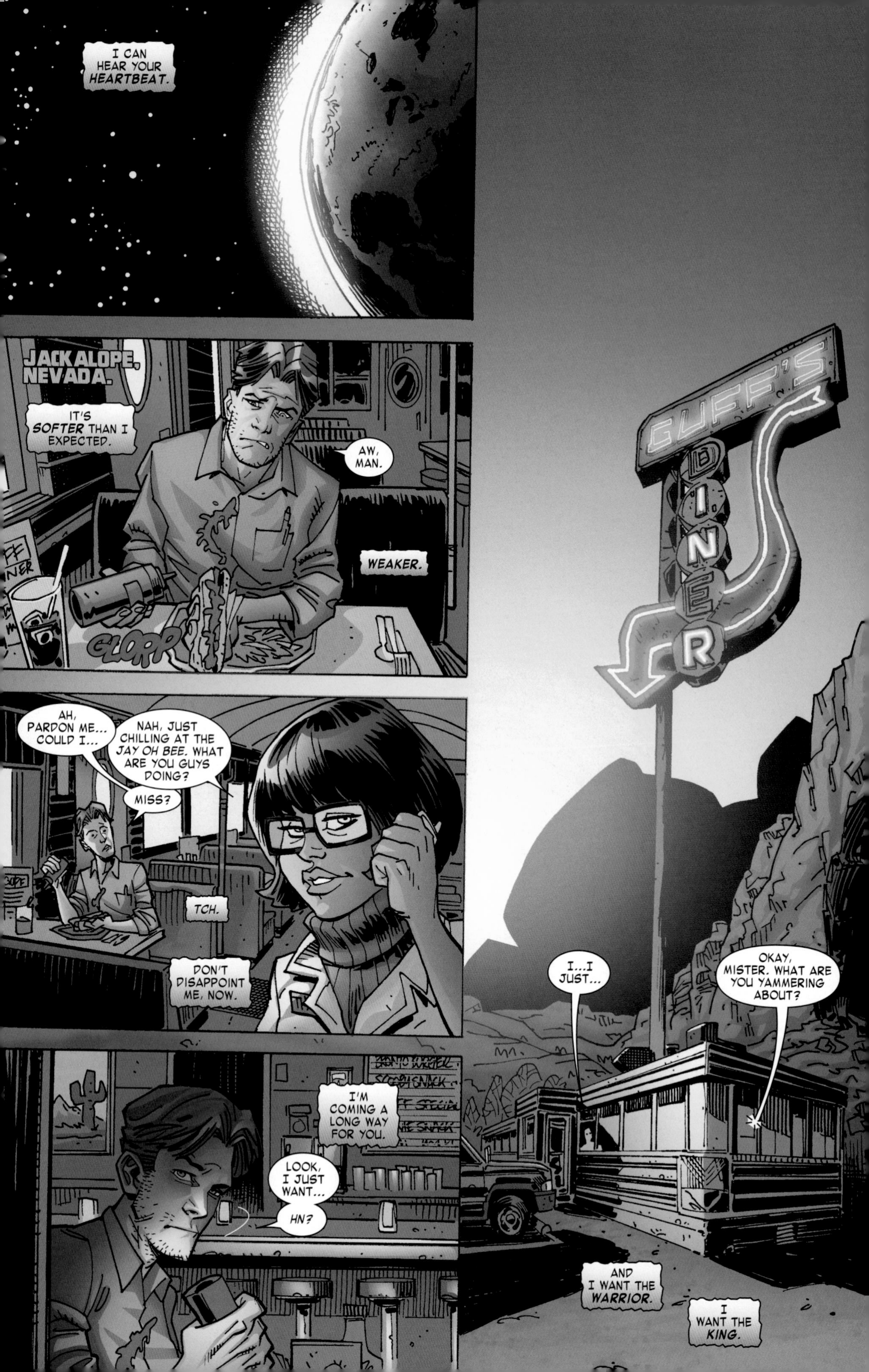
I CAN HEAR YOUR HEARTBEAT.
JACKALOPE, NEVADA.
IT'S SOFTER THAN I EXPECTED.
AW, MAN.
WEAKER.
GLORP
AH, PARDON ME... COULD I...
NAH, JUST CHILLING AT THE JAY OH BEE. WHAT ARE YOU GUYS DOING?
MISS?
TCH.
DON'T DISAPPOINT ME, NOW.
I'M COMING A LONG WAY FOR YOU.
LOOK, I JUST WANT...
HN?
DINER
I...I JUST...
OKAY, MISTER. WHAT ARE YOU YAMMERING ABOUT?
AND I WANT THE WARRIOR.
I WANT THE KING.

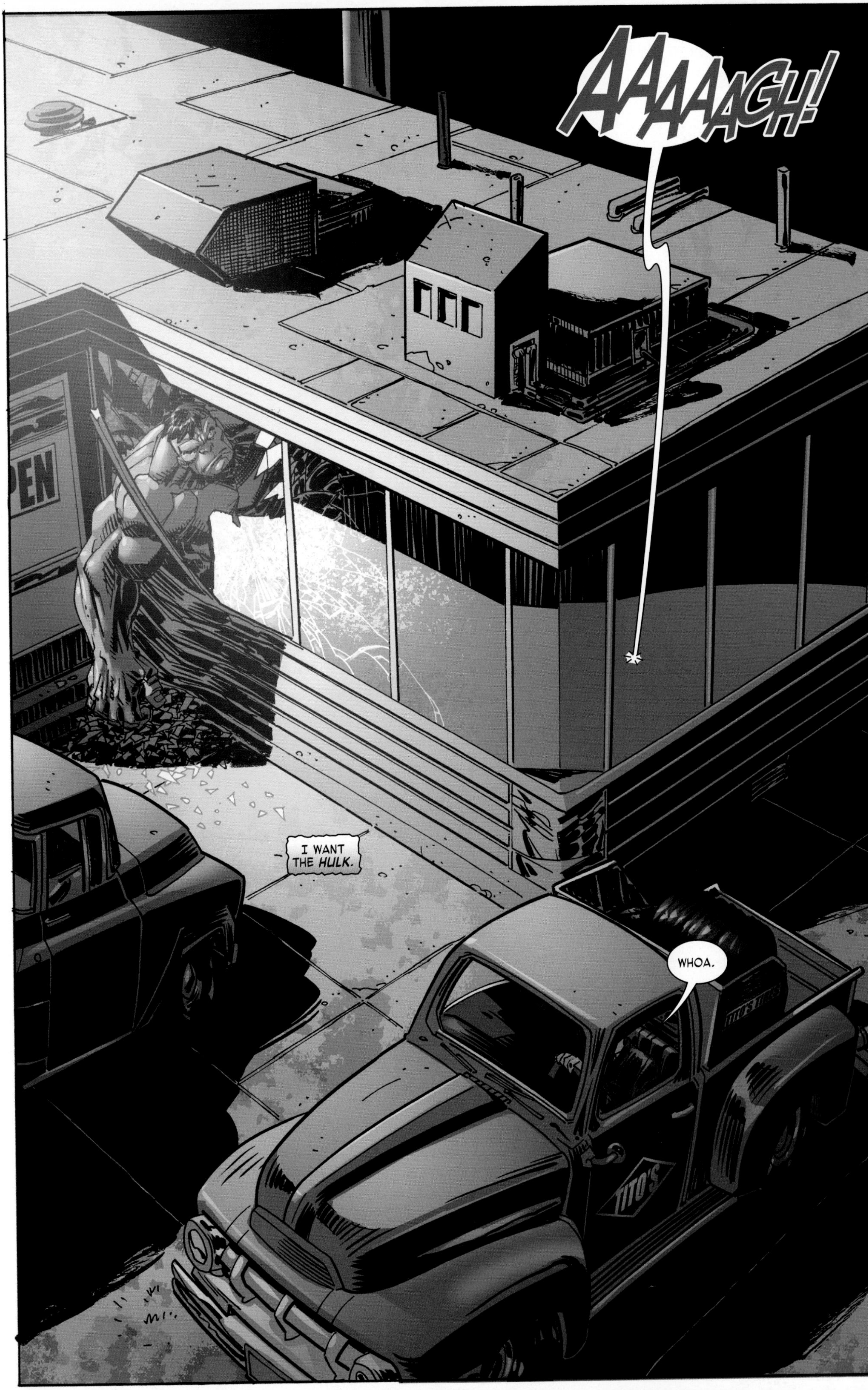
AAAAAGH!
I WANT THE *HULK*.
WHOA.
TITO'S

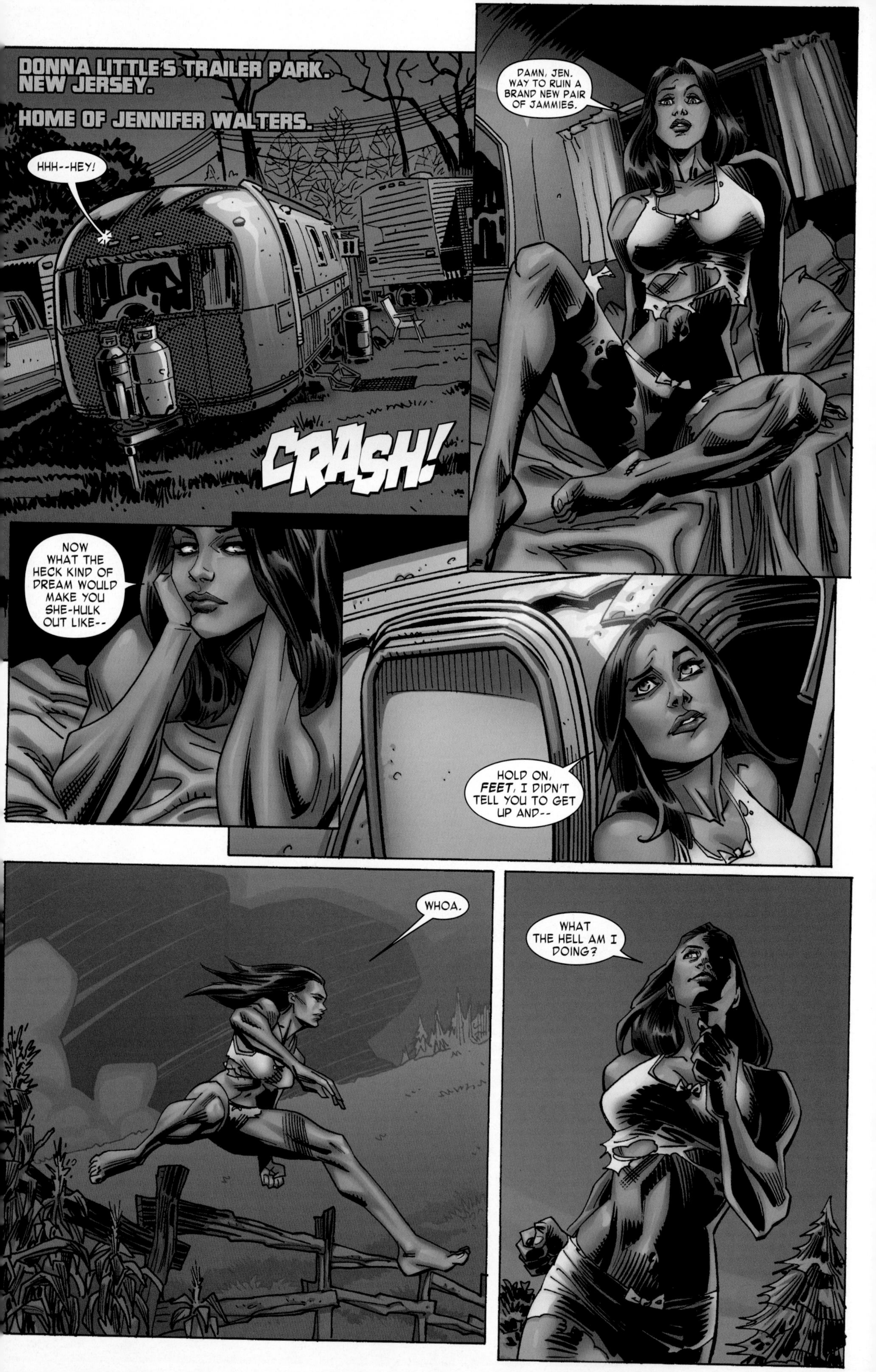
DONNA LITTLE'S TRAILER PARK. NEW JERSEY.
HOME OF JENNIFER WALTERS.
HHH--HEY!
CRASH!
DAMN, JEN. WAY TO RUIN A BRAND NEW PAIR OF JAMMIES.
NOW WHAT THE HECK KIND OF DREAM WOULD MAKE YOU SHE-HULK OUT LIKE--
HOLD ON, FEET, I DIDN'T TELL YOU TO GET UP AND--
WHOA.
WHAT THE HELL AM I DOING?

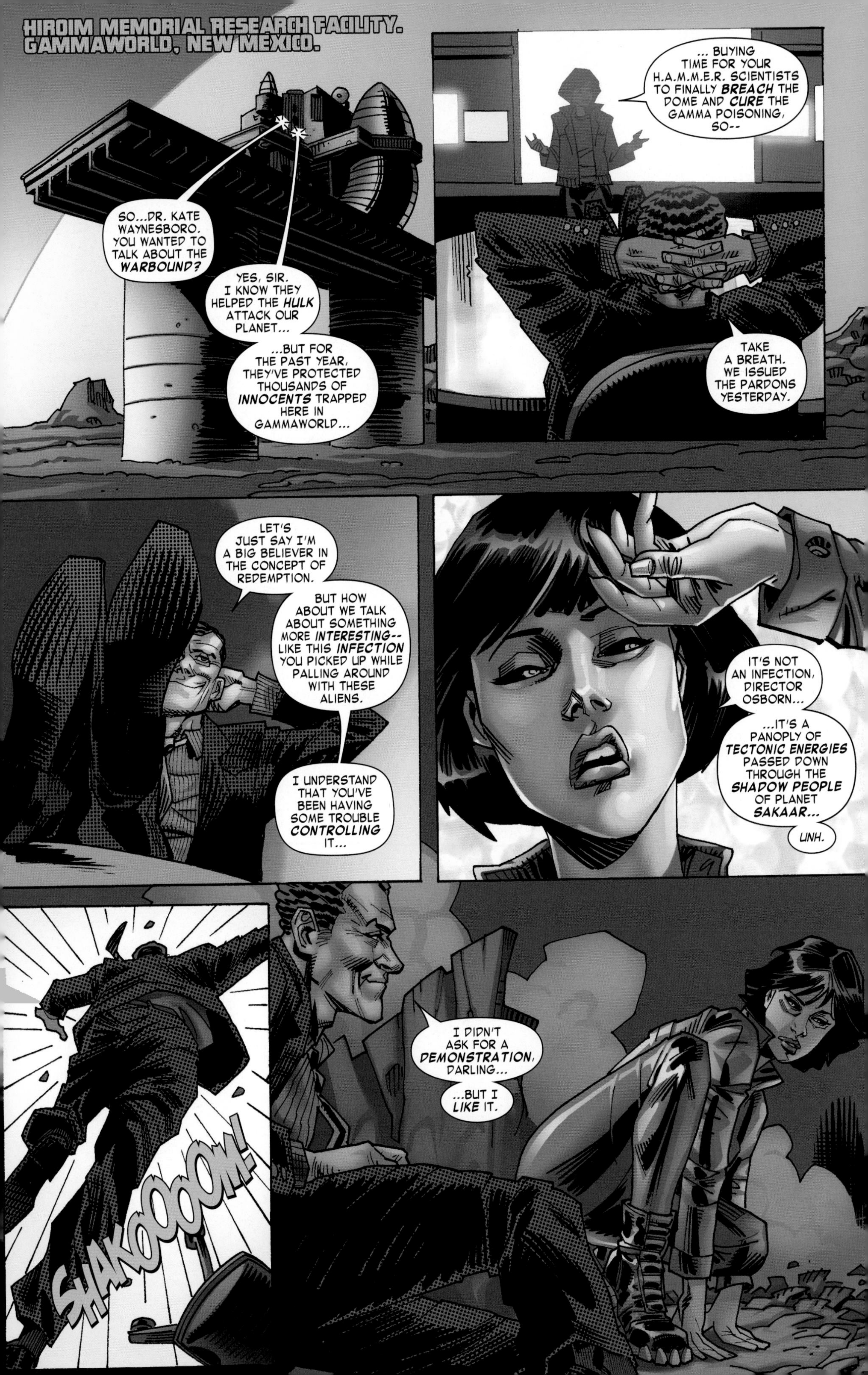
HIROIM MEMORIAL RESEARCH FACILITY. GAMMAWORLD, NEW MEXICO.
SO...DR. KATE WAYNESBORO. YOU WANTED TO TALK ABOUT THE WARBOUND?
YES, SIR. I KNOW THEY HELPED THE HULK ATTACK OUR PLANET...
...BUT FOR THE PAST YEAR, THEY'VE PROTECTED THOUSANDS OF INNOCENTS TRAPPED HERE IN GAMMAWORLD...
... BUYING TIME FOR YOUR H.A.M.M.E.R. SCIENTISTS TO FINALLY BREACH THE DOME AND CURE THE GAMMA POISONING, SO--
TAKE A BREATH. WE ISSUED THE PARDONS YESTERDAY.
LET'S JUST SAY I'M A BIG BELIEVER IN THE CONCEPT OF REDEMPTION.
BUT HOW ABOUT WE TALK ABOUT SOMETHING MORE INTERESTING-- LIKE THIS INFECTION YOU PICKED UP WHILE PALLING AROUND WITH THESE ALIENS.
I UNDERSTAND THAT YOU'VE BEEN HAVING SOME TROUBLE CONTROLLING IT...
IT'S NOT AN INFECTION, DIRECTOR OSBORN...
...IT'S A PANOPLY OF TECTONIC ENERGIES PASSED DOWN THROUGH THE SHADOW PEOPLE OF PLANET SAKAAR...
UNH.
SHAKOOOOM!
I DIDN'T ASK FOR A DEMONSTRATION, DARLING...
...BUT I LIKE IT.

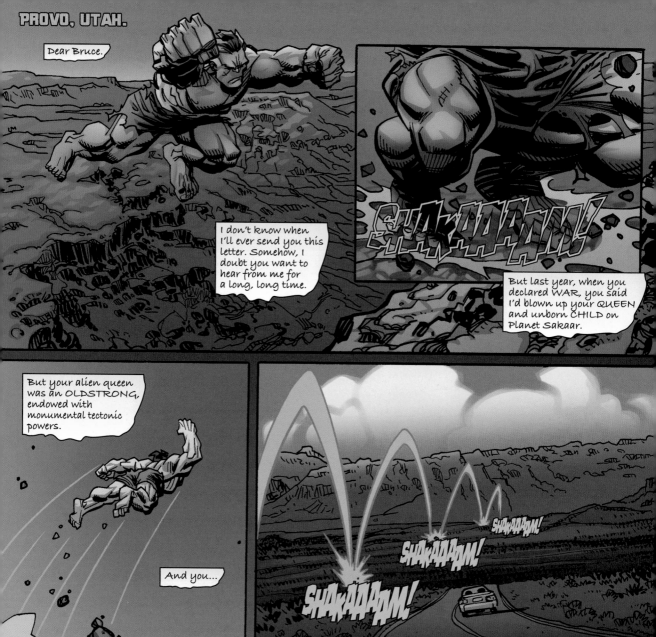

Dear Bruce.

I don't know when I'll ever send you this letter. Somehow, I doubt you want to hear from me for a long, long time.

SHA-AAAAM!

But last year, when you declared WAR, you said I'd blown up your QUEEN and unborn CHILD on Planet Sakaar.

But your alien queen was an OLDSTRONG, endowed with monumental tectonic powers.

And you...

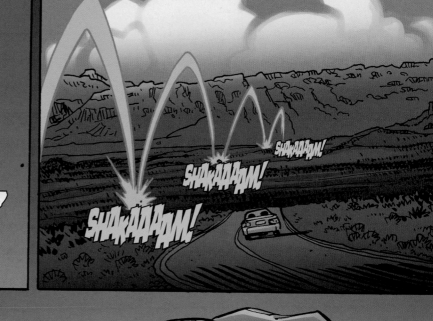

SHAKAAAAM!

SHAKAAAAM!

SHAKAAAAM!

...well, you're the strongest one there is.

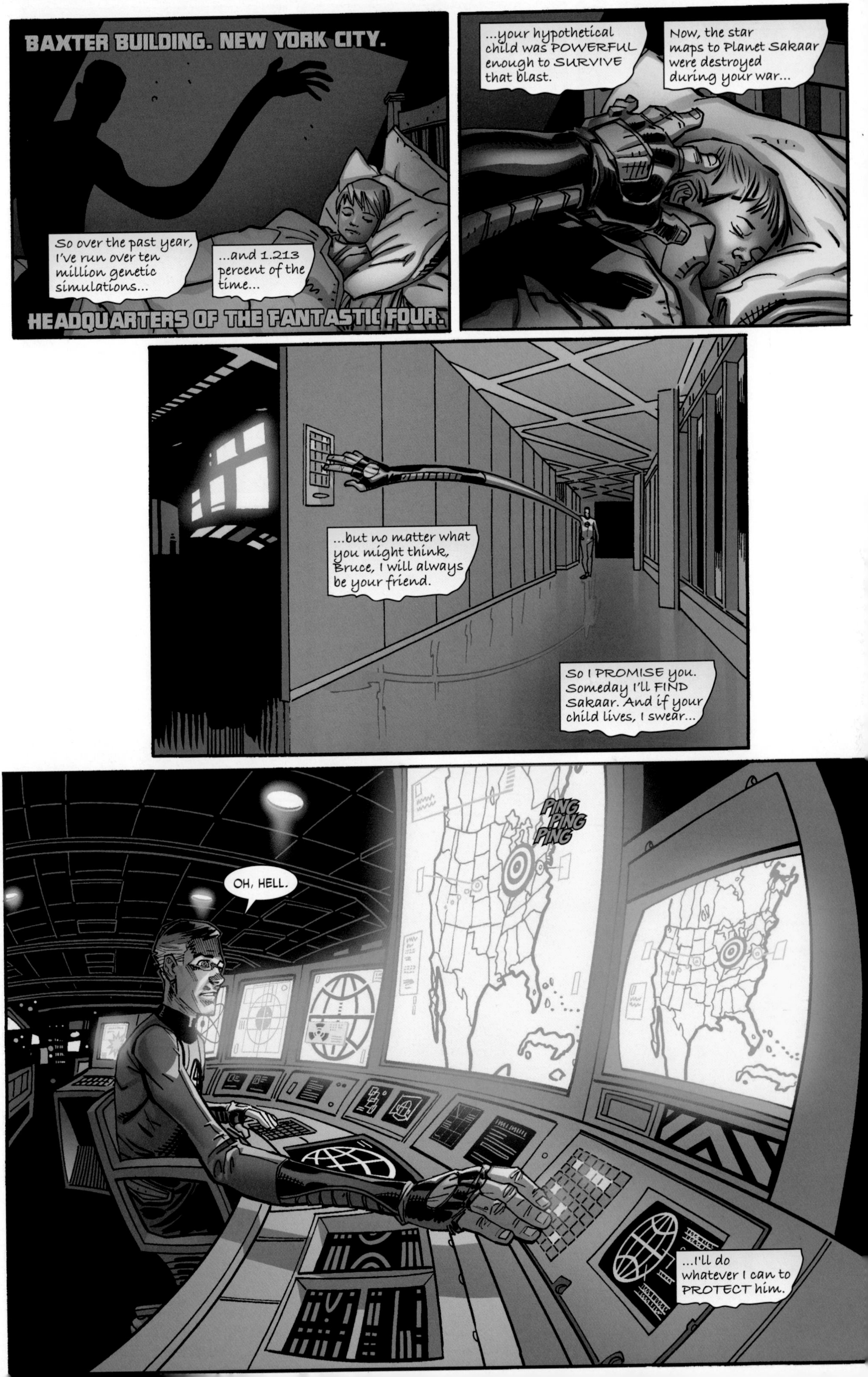

BAXTER BUILDING. NEW YORK CITY.
So over the past year, I've run over ten million genetic simulations...
...and 1.213 percent of the time...
HEADQUARTERS OF THE FANTASTIC FOUR.
...your hypothetical child was POWERFUL enough to SURVIVE that blast.
Now, the star maps to Planet Sakaar were destroyed during your war...
...but no matter what you might think, Bruce, I will always be your friend.
So I PROMISE you. Someday I'll FIND Sakaar. And if your child lives, I swear...
PING PING PING
OH, HELL.
...I'll do whatever I can to PROTECT him.

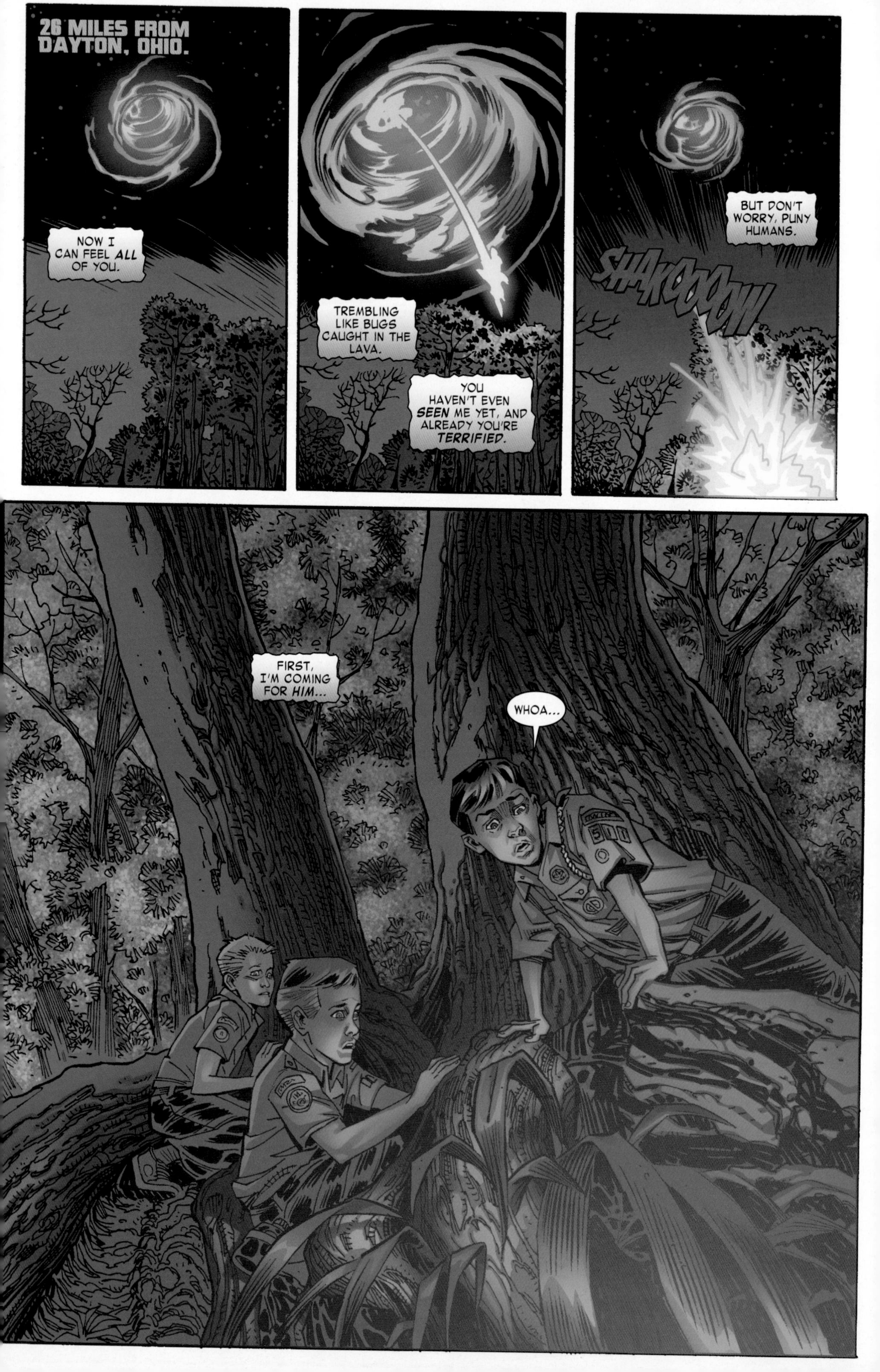
26 MILES FROM DAYTON, OHIO.
NOW I CAN FEEL ALL OF YOU.
TREMBLING LIKE BUGS CAUGHT IN THE LAVA.
YOU HAVEN'T EVEN SEEN ME YET, AND ALREADY YOU'RE TERRIFIED.
BUT DON'T WORRY, PUNY HUMANS.
SHAKOOOOOM
FIRST, I'M COMING FOR HIM...
WHOA...

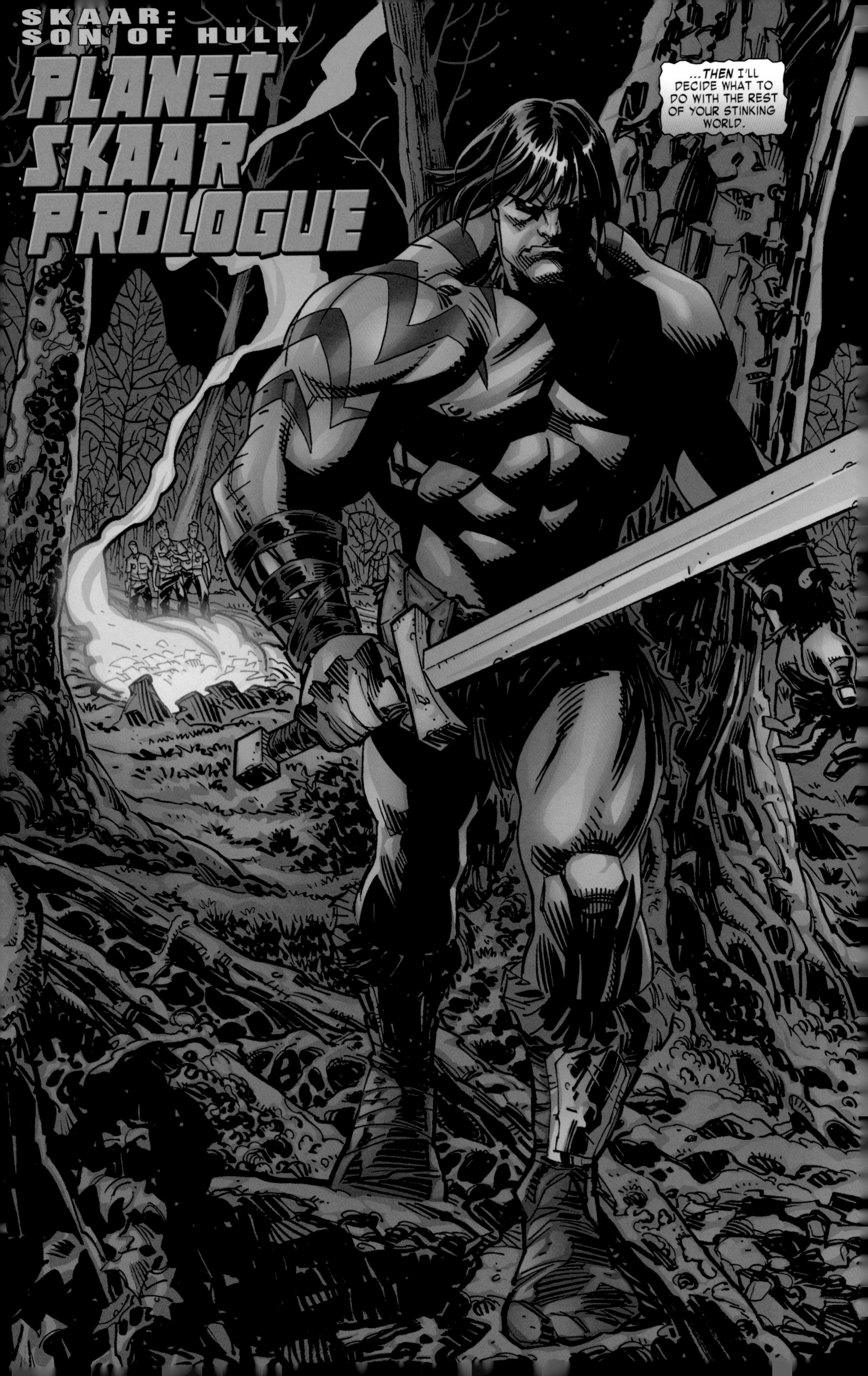
SKAAR:
SON OF HULK
PLANET SKAAR PROLOGUE
...THEN I'LL DECIDE WHAT TO DO WITH THE REST OF YOUR STINKING WORLD.

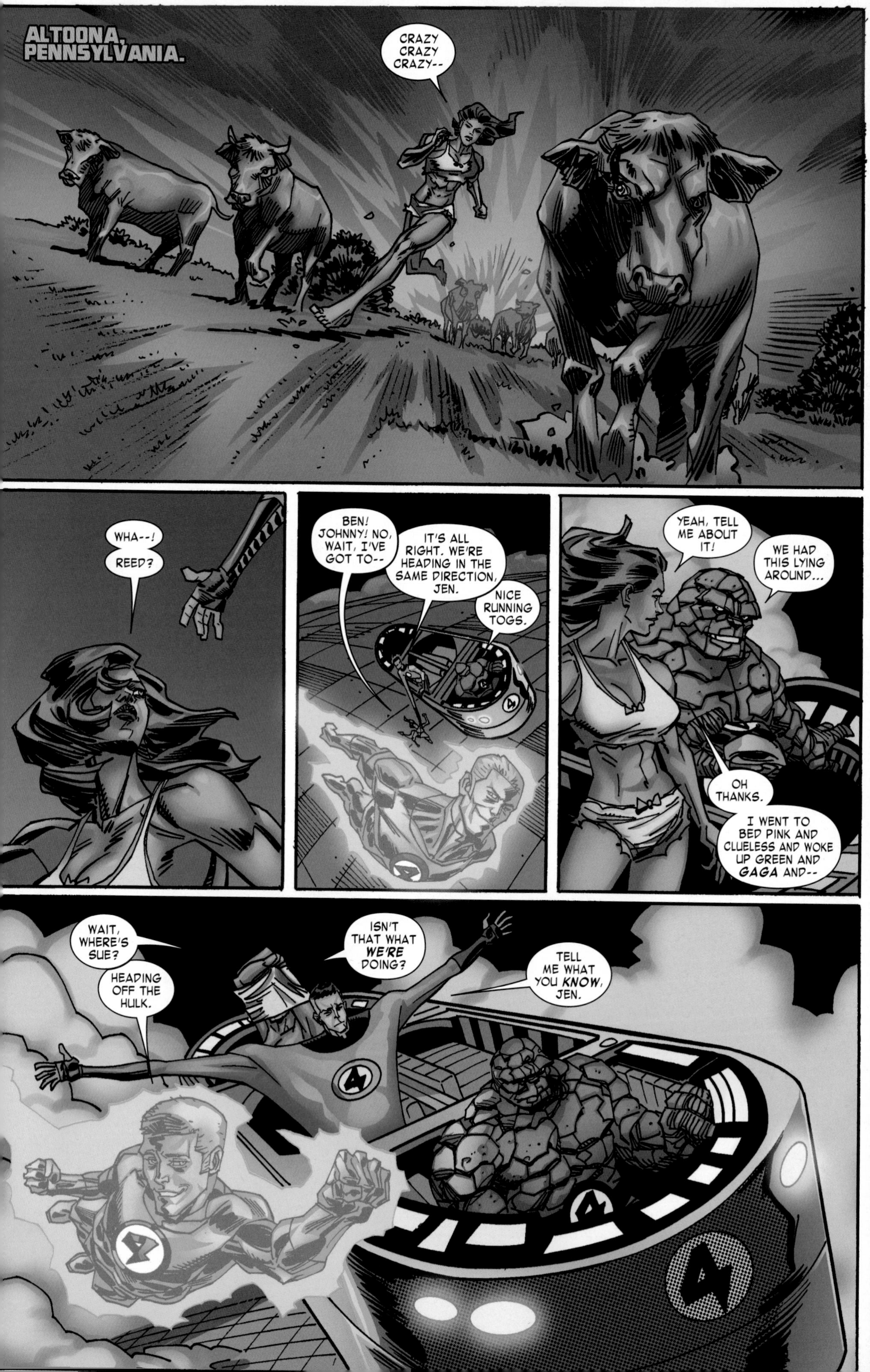
ALTOONA, PENNSYLVANIA.
CRAZY CRAZY CRAZY--
WHA--!
REED?
BEN! JOHNNY! NO, WAIT, I'VE GOT TO--
IT'S ALL RIGHT. WE'RE HEADING IN THE SAME DIRECTION, JEN.
NICE RUNNING TOGS.
YEAH, TELL ME ABOUT IT!
WE HAD THIS LYING AROUND...
OH THANKS.
I WENT TO BED PINK AND CLUELESS GREEN AND WOKE UP GREEN AND GAGA AND--
WAIT, WHERE'S SUE?
HEADING OFF THE HULK.
ISN'T THAT WHAT WE'RE DOING?
TELL ME WHAT YOU KNOW, JEN.

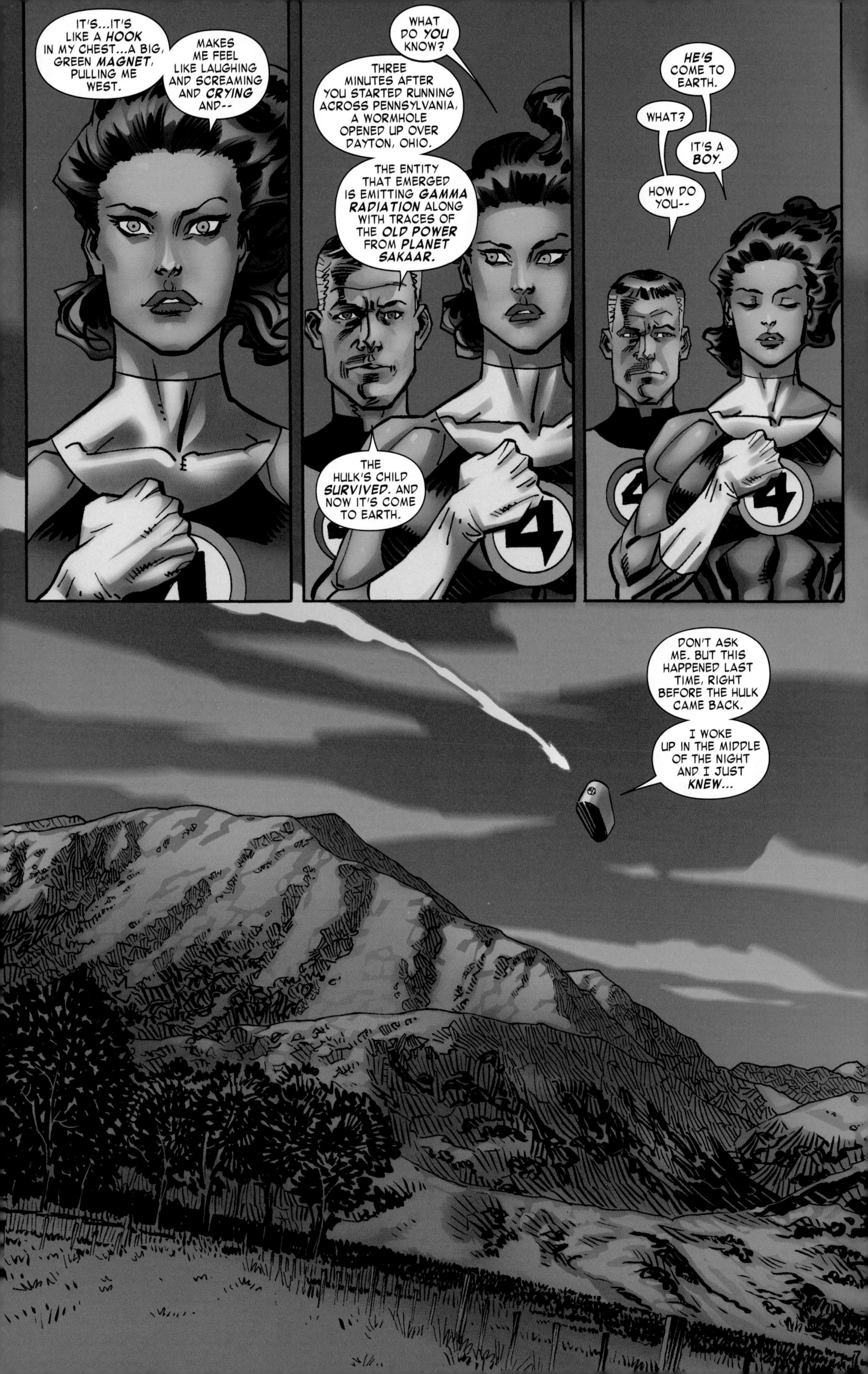
IT'S...IT'S LIKE A HOOK IN MY CHEST...A BIG, GREEN MAGNET, PULLING ME WEST.
MAKES ME FEEL LIKE LAUGHING AND SCREAMING AND CRYING AND--
WHAT DO YOU KNOW?
THREE MINUTES AFTER YOU STARTED RUNNING ACROSS PENNSYLVANIA, A WORMHOLE OPENED UP OVER DAYTON, OHIO.
THE ENTITY THAT EMERGED IS EMITTING GAMMA RADIATION ALONG WITH TRACES OF THE OLD POWER FROM PLANET SAKAAR.
THE HULK'S CHILD SURVIVED. AND NOW IT'S COME TO EARTH.
HE'S COME TO EARTH.
WHAT?
IT'S A BOY.
HOW DO YOU--
DON'T ASK ME. BUT THIS HAPPENED LAST TIME, RIGHT BEFORE THE HULK CAME BACK.
I WOKE UP IN THE MIDDLE OF THE NIGHT AND I JUST KNEW...

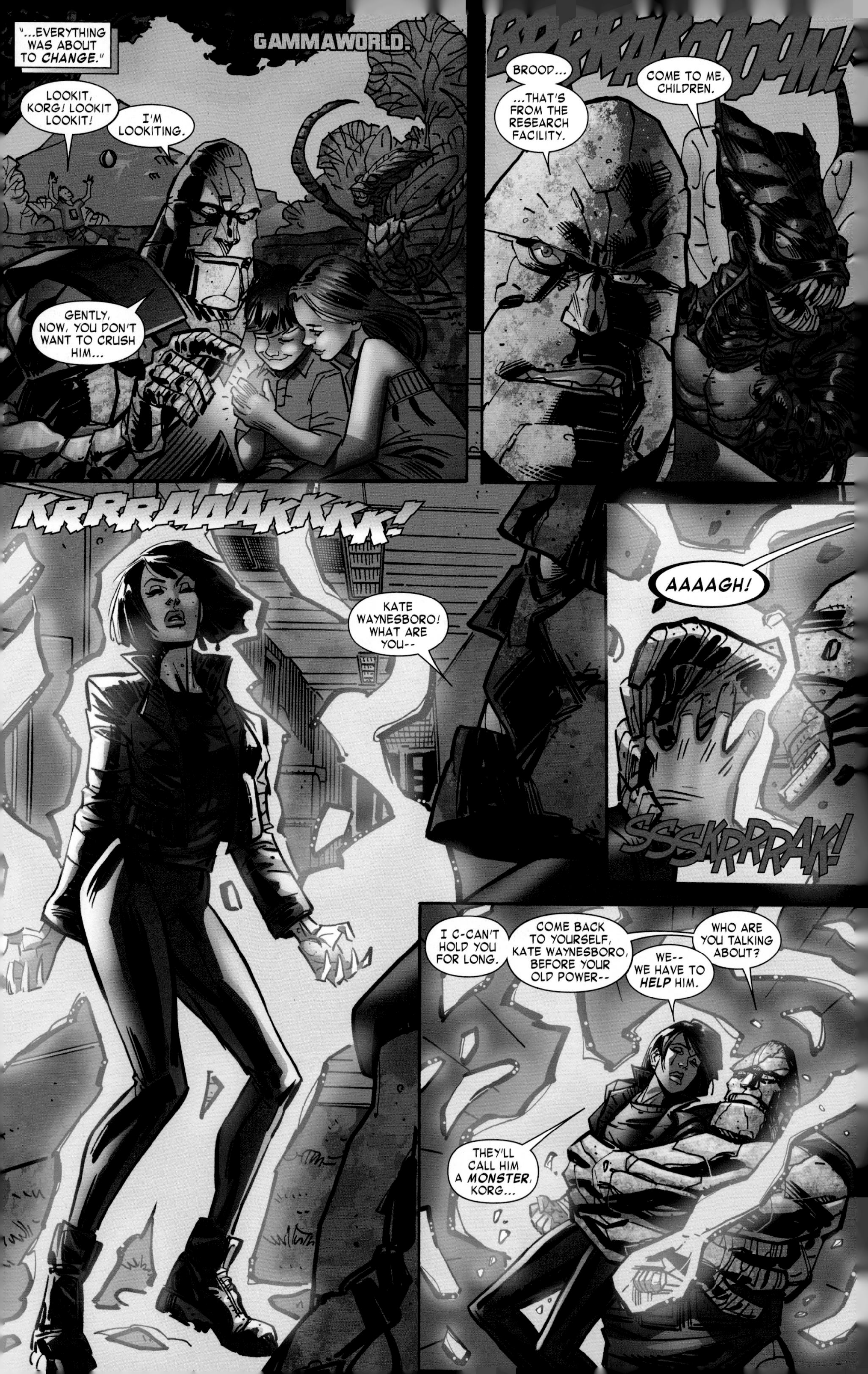
"...EVERYTHING WAS ABOUT TO CHANGE."
GAMMAWORLD.
LOOKIT, KORG! LOOKIT LOOKIT!
I'M LOOKITING.
GENTLY, NOW, YOU DON'T WANT TO CRUSH HIM...
BRROOMKOOOM!
BROOD...
...THAT'S FROM THE RESEARCH FACILITY.
COME TO ME, CHILDREN.
KRRRAAAKKKK!
KATE WAYNESBORO! WHAT ARE YOU--
AAAAGH!
SSSKRRRAK!
I C-CAN'T HOLD YOU FOR LONG.
COME BACK TO YOURSELF, KATE WAYNESBORO, BEFORE YOUR OLD POWER--
WHO ARE YOU TALKING ABOUT?
WE-- WE HAVE TO HELP HIM.
THEY'LL CALL HIM A MONSTER, KORG...

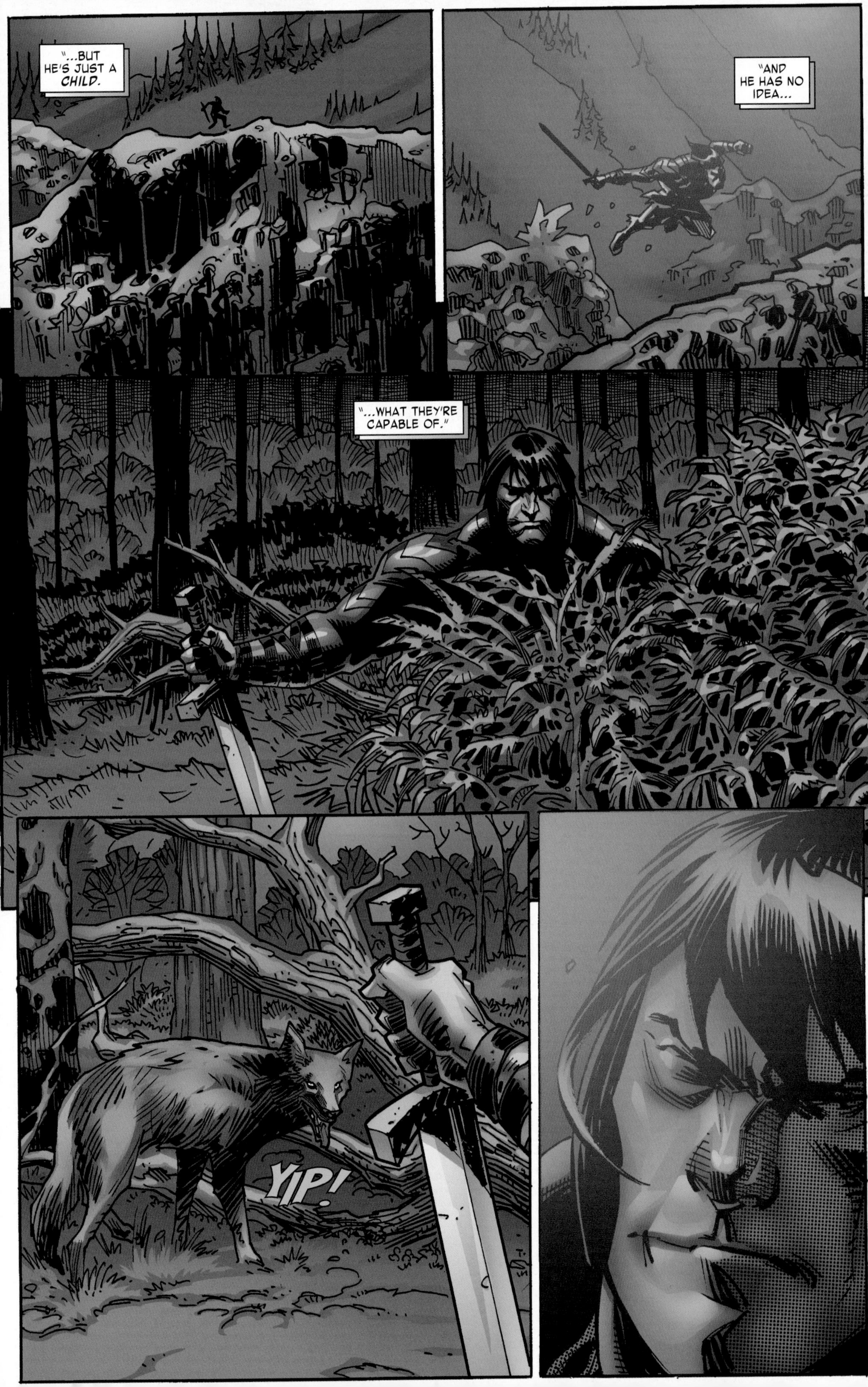
"...BUT HE'S JUST A CHILD.
"AND HE HAS NO IDEA...
"...WHAT THEY'RE CAPABLE OF."
YIP!

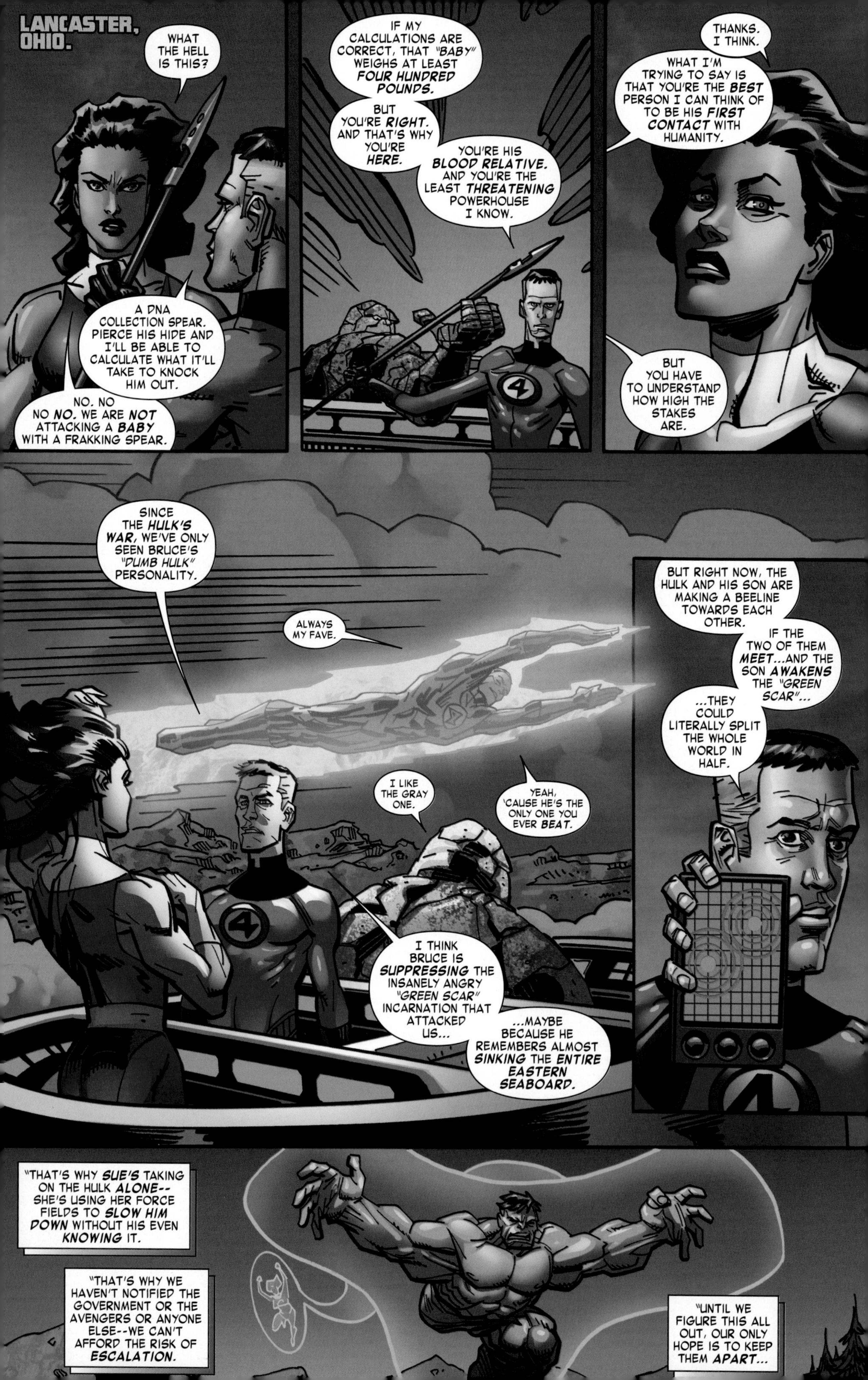
LANCASTER, OHIO.
WHAT THE HELL IS THIS?
A DNA COLLECTION SPEAR. PIERCE HIS HIDE AND I'LL BE ABLE TO CALCULATE WHAT IT'LL TAKE TO KNOCK HIM OUT.
NO. NO NO NO. WE ARE NOT ATTACKING A BABY WITH A FRAKKING SPEAR.
IF MY CALCULATIONS ARE CORRECT, THAT "BABY" WEIGHS AT LEAST FOUR HUNDRED POUNDS.
BUT YOU'RE RIGHT. AND THAT'S WHY YOU'RE HERE.
YOU'RE HIS BLOOD RELATIVE. AND YOU'RE THE LEAST THREATENING POWERHOUSE I KNOW.
THANKS. I THINK.
WHAT I'M TRYING TO SAY IS THAT YOU'RE THE BEST PERSON I CAN THINK OF TO BE HIS FIRST CONTACT WITH HUMANITY.
BUT YOU HAVE TO UNDERSTAND HOW HIGH THE STAKES ARE.
SINCE THE HULK'S WAR, WE'VE ONLY SEEN BRUCE'S "DUMB HULK" PERSONALITY.
ALWAYS MY FAVE.
I LIKE THE GRAY ONE.
YEAH, 'CAUSE HE'S THE ONLY ONE YOU EVER BEAT.
I THINK BRUCE IS SUPPRESSING THE INSANELY ANGRY "GREEN SCAR" INCARNATION THAT ATTACKED US...
...MAYBE BECAUSE HE REMEMBERS ALMOST SINKING THE ENTIRE EASTERN SEABOARD.
BUT RIGHT NOW, THE HULK AND HIS SON ARE MAKING A BEELINE TOWARDS EACH OTHER.
IF THE TWO OF THEM MEET...AND THE SON AWAKENS THE "GREEN SCAR"...
...THEY COULD LITERALLY SPLIT THE WHOLE WORLD IN HALF.
"THAT'S WHY SUE'S TAKING ON THE HULK ALONE--SHE'S USING HER FORCE FIELDS TO SLOW HIM DOWN WITHOUT HIS EVEN KNOWING IT.
"THAT'S WHY WE HAVEN'T NOTIFIED THE GOVERNMENT OR THE AVENGERS OR ANYONE ELSE--WE CAN'T AFFORD THE RISK OF ESCALATION.
"UNTIL WE FIGURE THIS ALL OUT, OUR ONLY HOPE IS TO KEEP THEM APART...

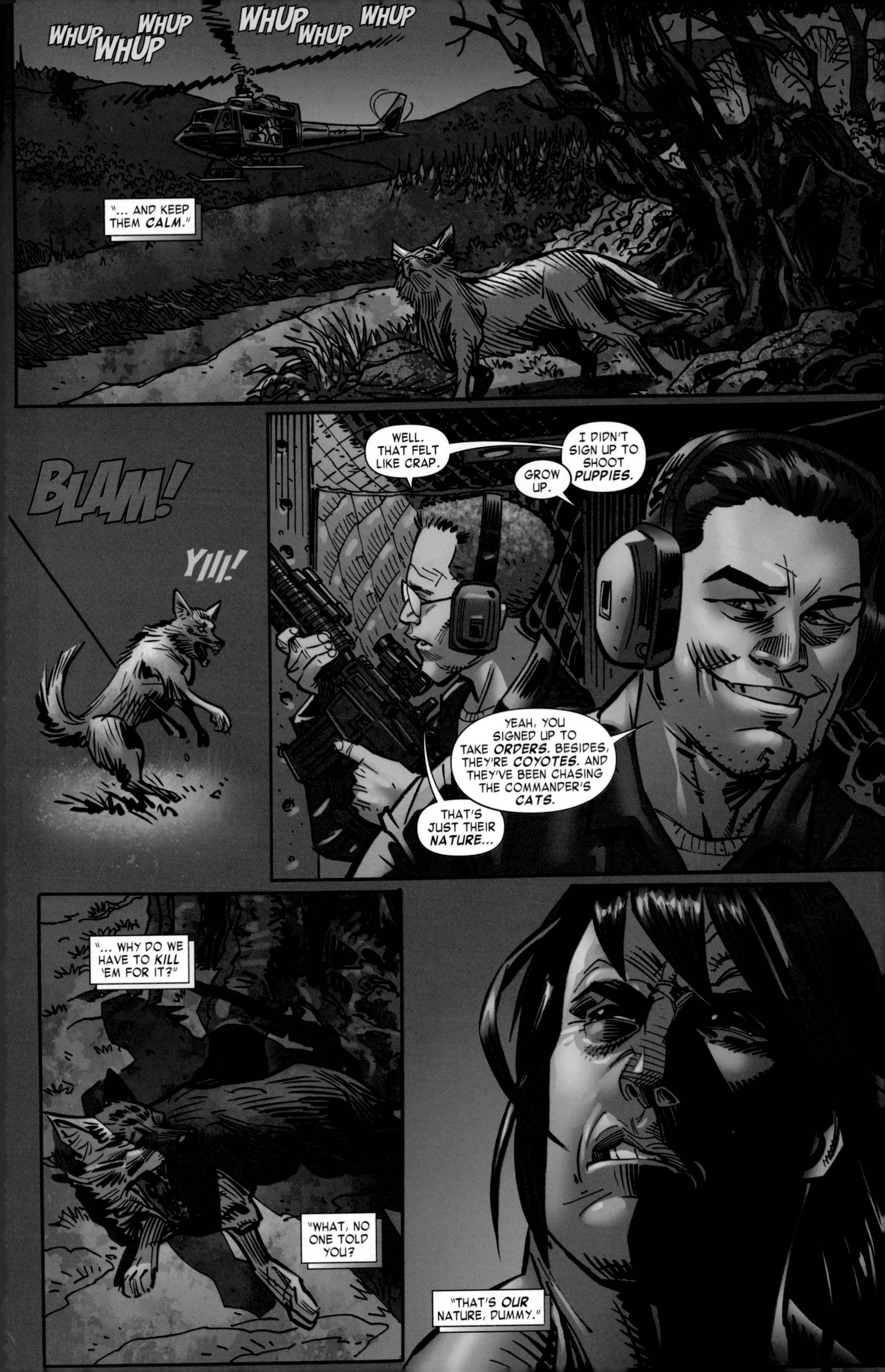
WHUP WHUP WHUP WHUP WHUP WHUP
"... AND KEEP THEM CALM."
BLAM!
YIII!
WELL. THAT FELT LIKE CRAP.
I DIDN'T SIGN UP TO SHOOT PUPPIES.
GROW UP.
YEAH, YOU SIGNED UP TO TAKE ORDERS. BESIDES, THEY'RE COYOTES. AND THEY'VE BEEN CHASING THE COMMANDER'S CATS.
THAT'S JUST THEIR NATURE...
"... WHY DO WE HAVE TO KILL 'EM FOR IT?"
"WHAT, NO ONE TOLD YOU?
"THAT'S OUR NATURE, DUMMY."

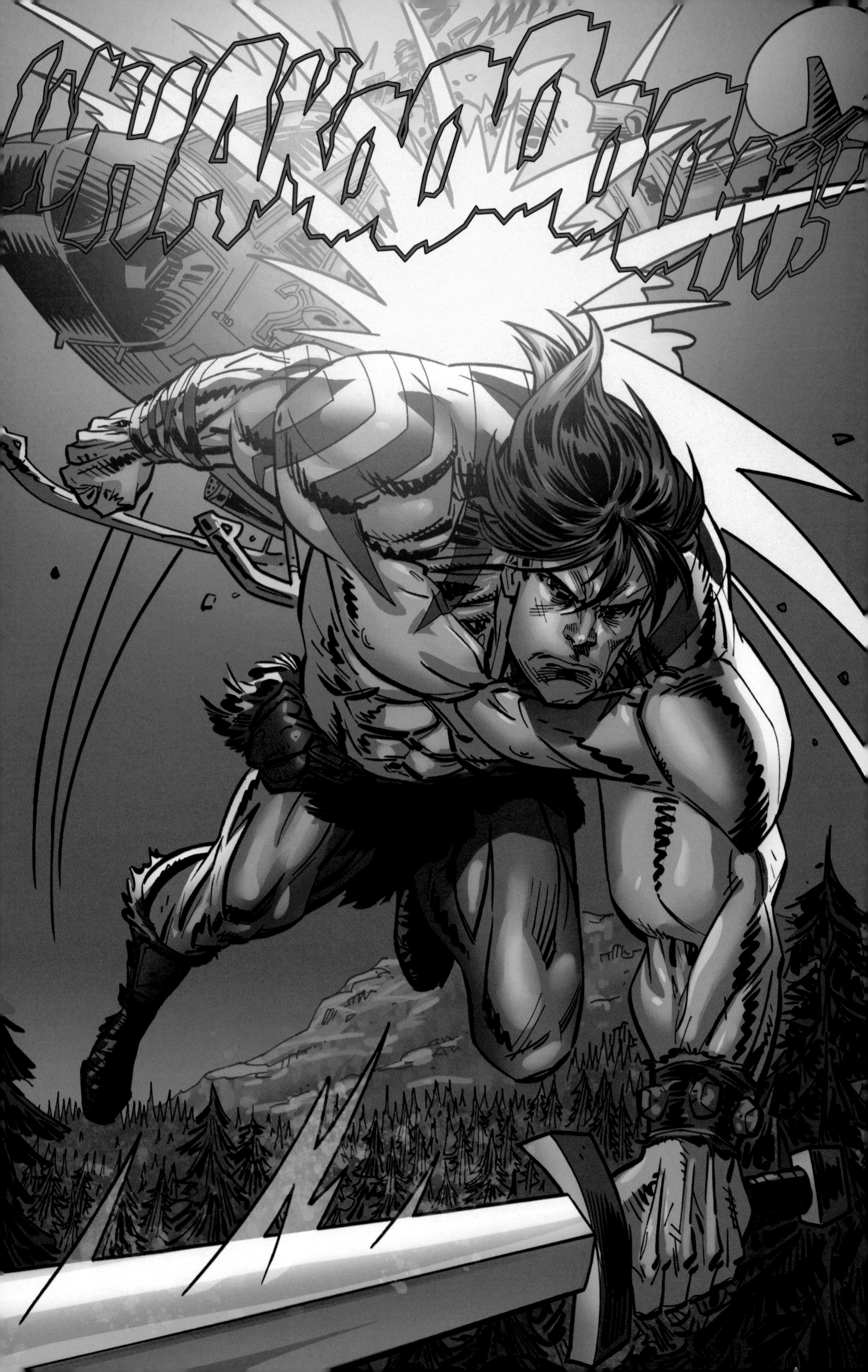

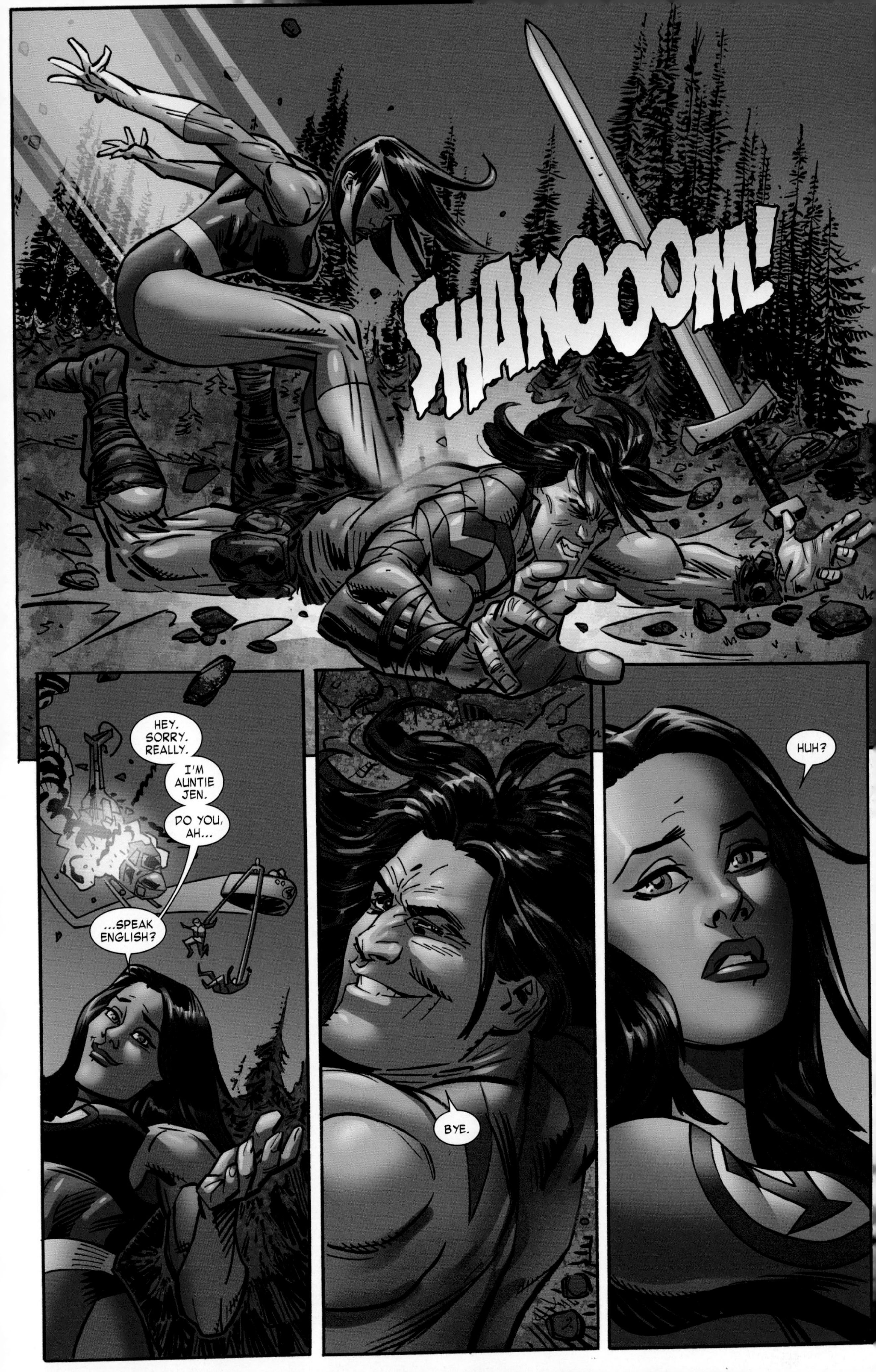
SHAKOOOM!
HEY. SORRY. REALLY.
I'M AUNTIE JEN.
DO YOU, AH...
...SPEAK ENGLISH?
BYE.
HUH?

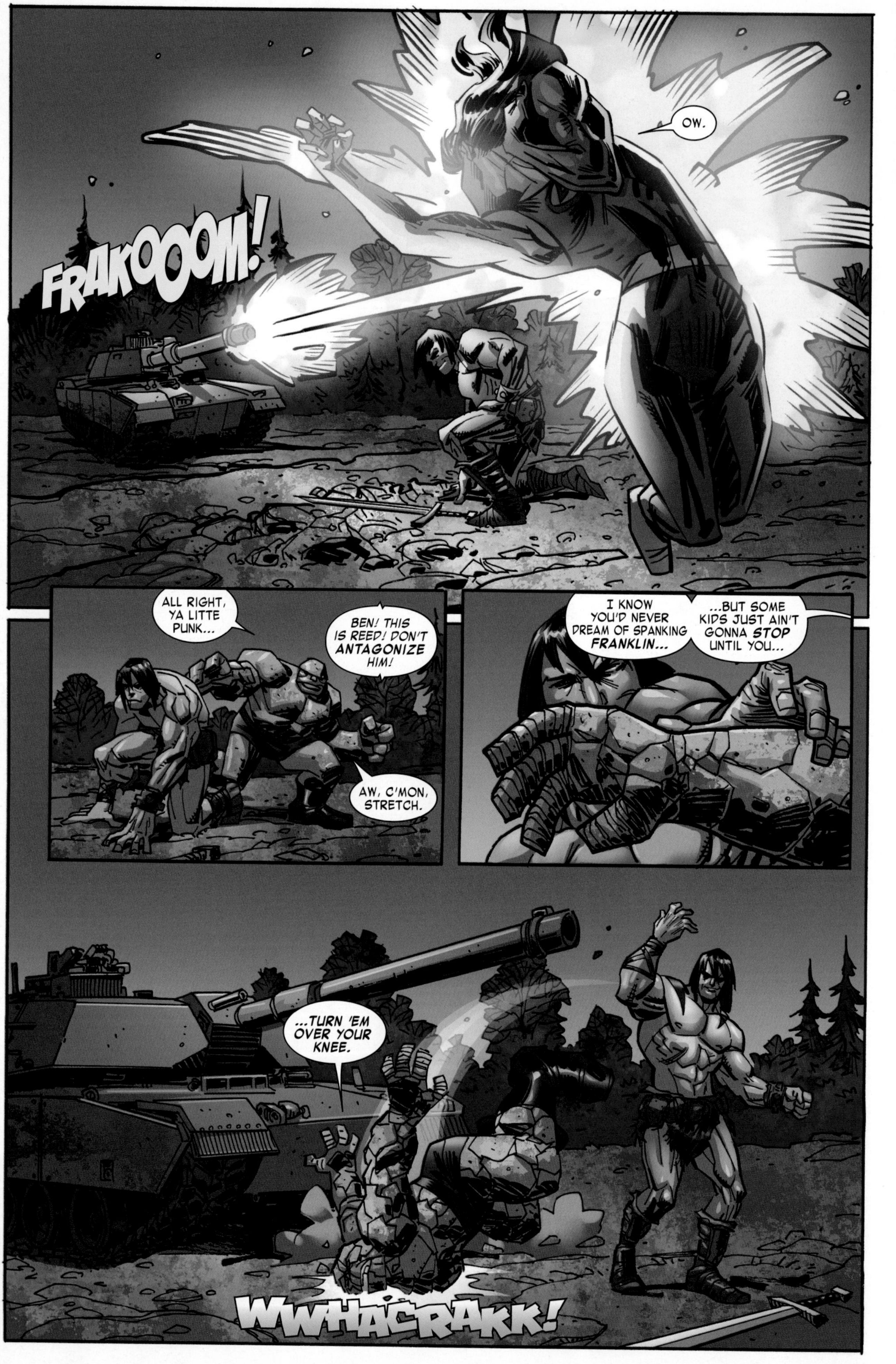
OW.
FRAKOOOM!
ALL RIGHT, YA LITTE PUNK...
BEN! THIS IS REED! DON'T ANTAGONIZE HIM!
AW, C'MON, STRETCH.
I KNOW YOU'D NEVER DREAM OF SPANKING FRANKLIN...
...BUT SOME KIDS JUST AIN'T GONNA STOP UNTIL YOU...
...TURN 'EM OVER YOUR KNEE.
WWHACRAKK!

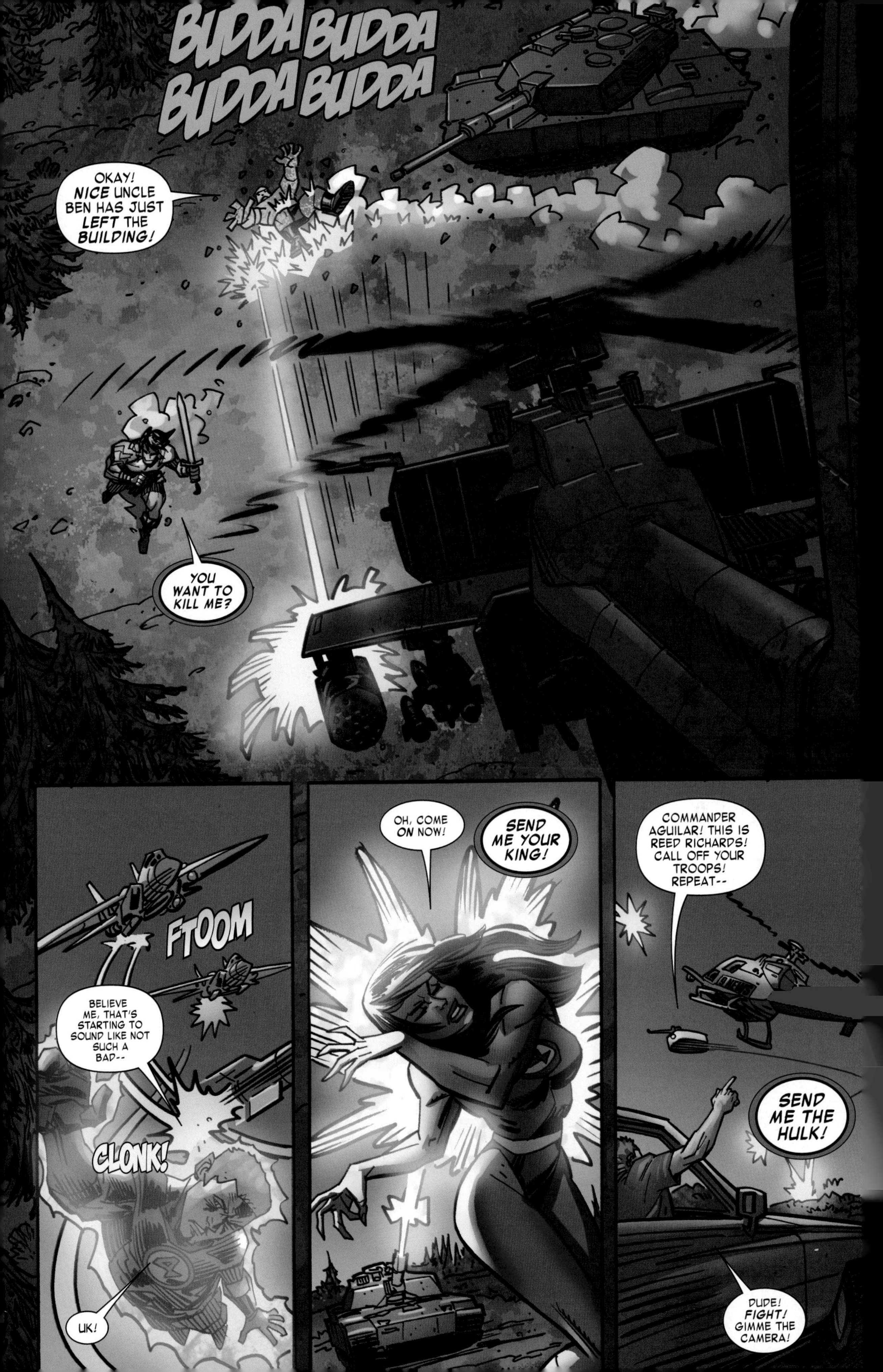
BUDDA BUDDA
BUDDA BUDDA
OKAY! NICE UNCLE BEN HAS JUST LEFT THE BUILDING!
YOU WANT TO KILL ME?
FTOOM
BELIEVE ME, THAT'S STARTING TO SOUND LIKE NOT SUCH A BAD--
CLONK!
UK!
OH, COME ON NOW!
SEND ME YOUR KING!
COMMANDER AGUILAR! THIS IS REED RICHARDS! CALL OFF YOUR TROOPS! REPEAT--
SEND ME THE HULK!
DUDE! FIGHT! GIMME THE CAMERA!

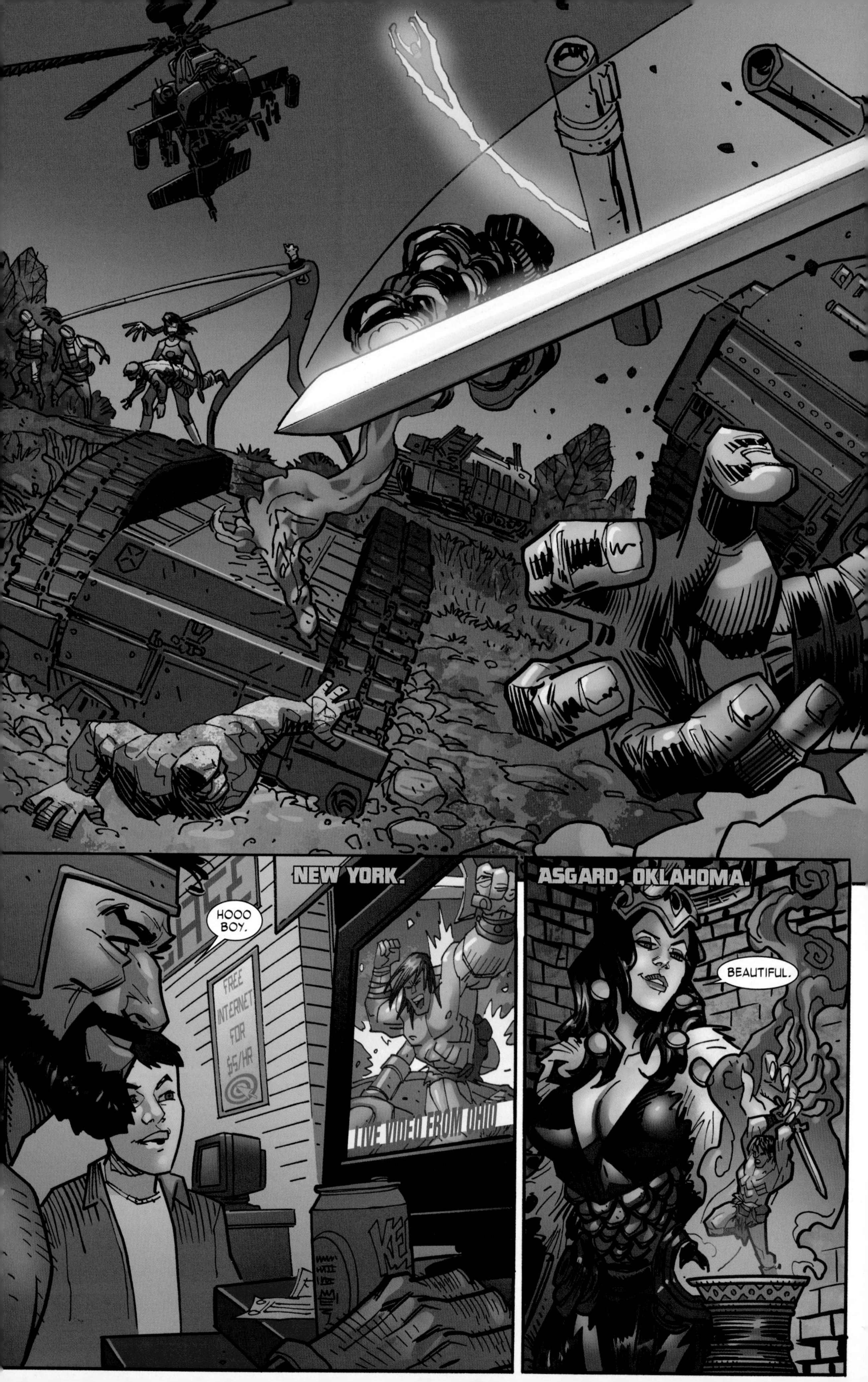
NEW YORK.
HOOO BOY.
FREE INTERNET FOR $5/HR
LIVE VIDEO FROM OHIO
ASGARD, OKLAHOMA.
BEAUTIFUL.

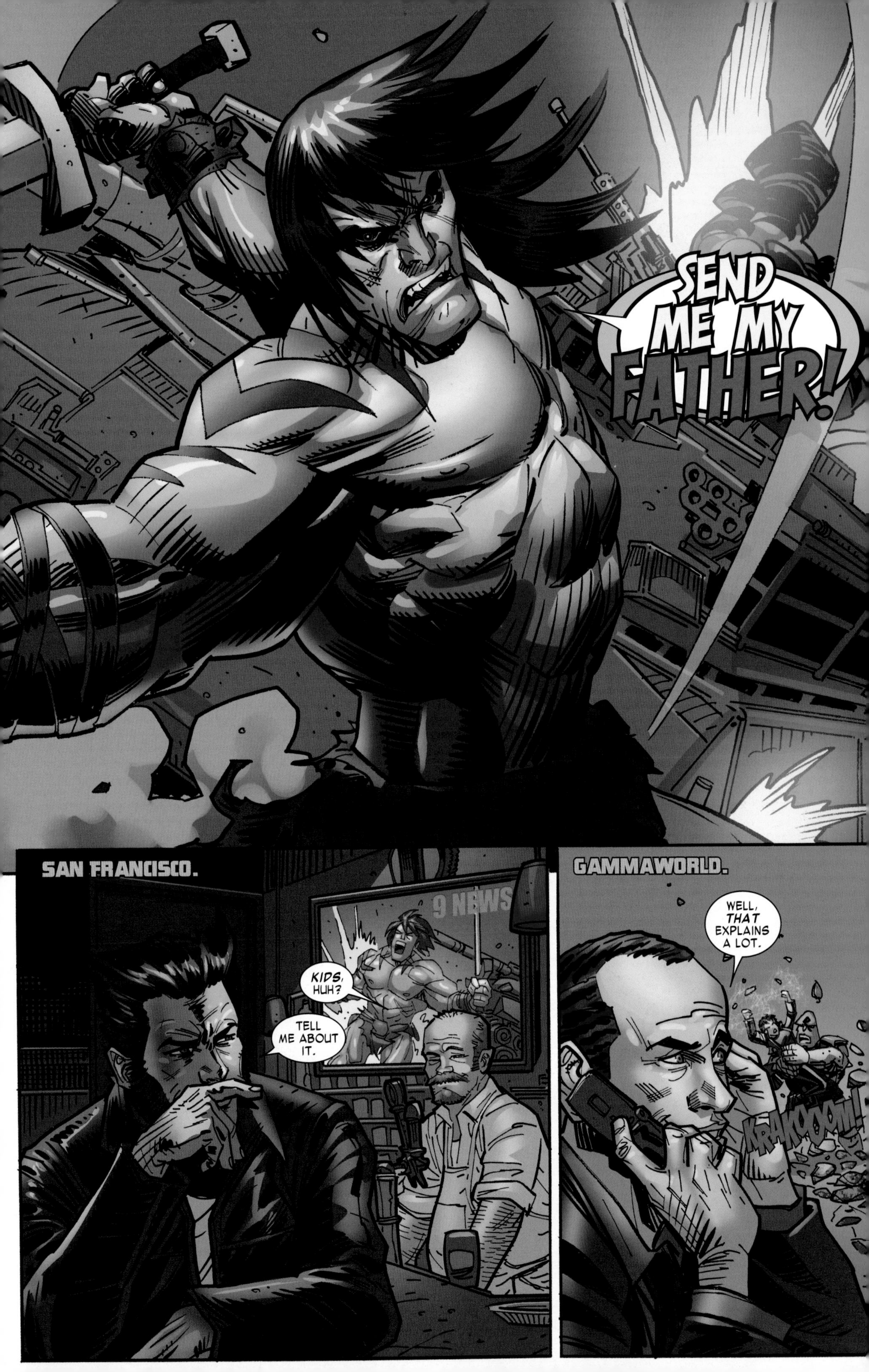
SEND ME MY FATHER!
SAN FRANCISCO.
9 NEWS
KIDS, HUH?
TELL ME ABOUT IT.
GAMMAWORLD.
WELL, THAT EXPLAINS A LOT.
KRAKOOOM!

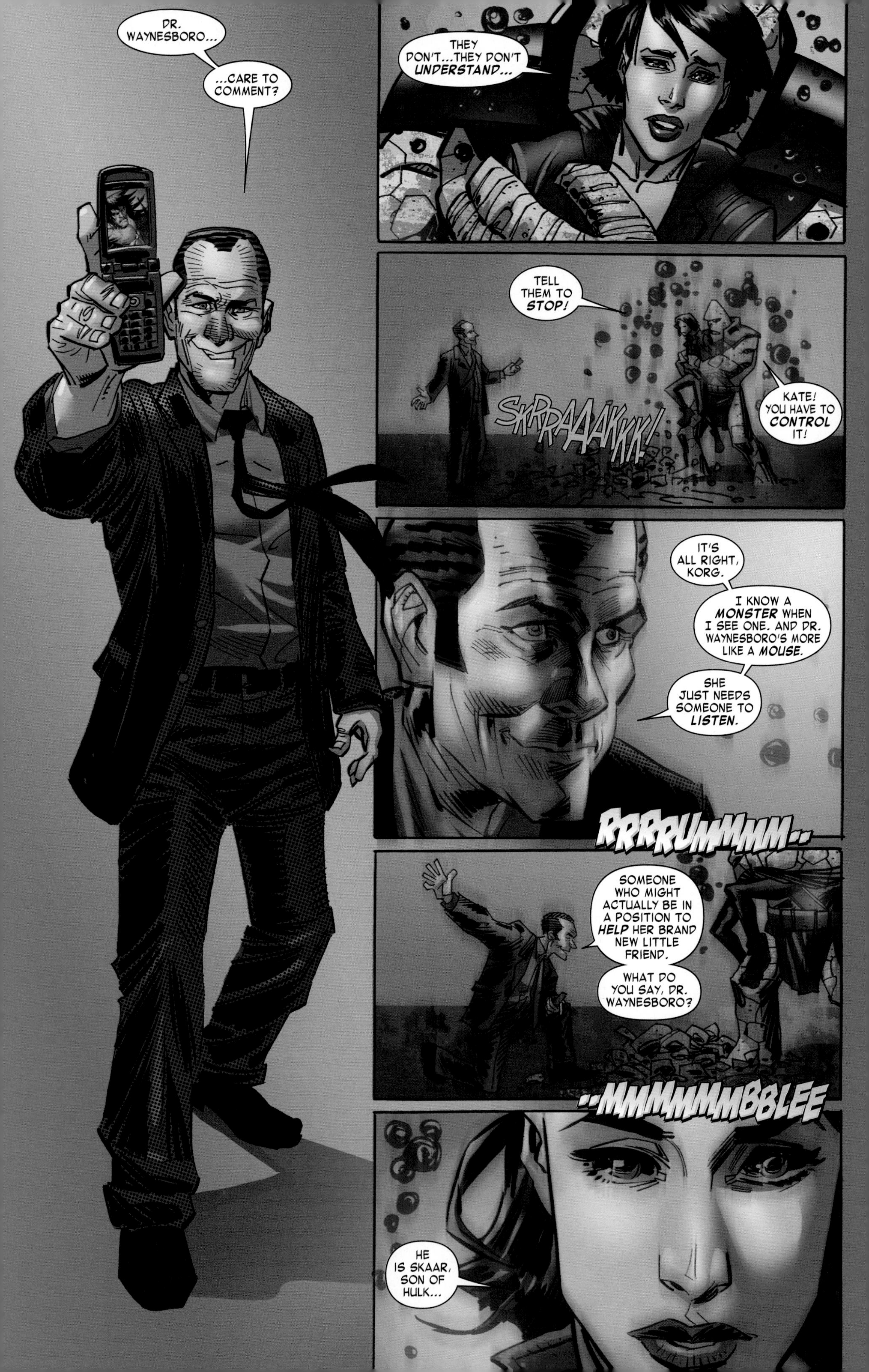
DR. WAYNESBORO...
...CARE TO COMMENT?
THEY DON'T...THEY DON'T UNDERSTAND...
TELL THEM TO STOP!
SKRRAAAKKK!
KATE! YOU HAVE TO CONTROL IT!
IT'S ALL RIGHT, KORG.
I KNOW A MONSTER WHEN I SEE ONE. AND DR. WAYNESBORO'S MORE LIKE A MOUSE.
SHE JUST NEEDS SOMEONE TO LISTEN.
RRRRUMMMM..
SOMEONE WHO MIGHT ACTUALLY BE IN A POSITION TO HELP HER BRAND NEW LITTLE FRIEND.
WHAT DO YOU SAY, DR. WAYNESBORO?
..MMMMMMBBLEE
HE IS SKAAR, SON OF HULK...

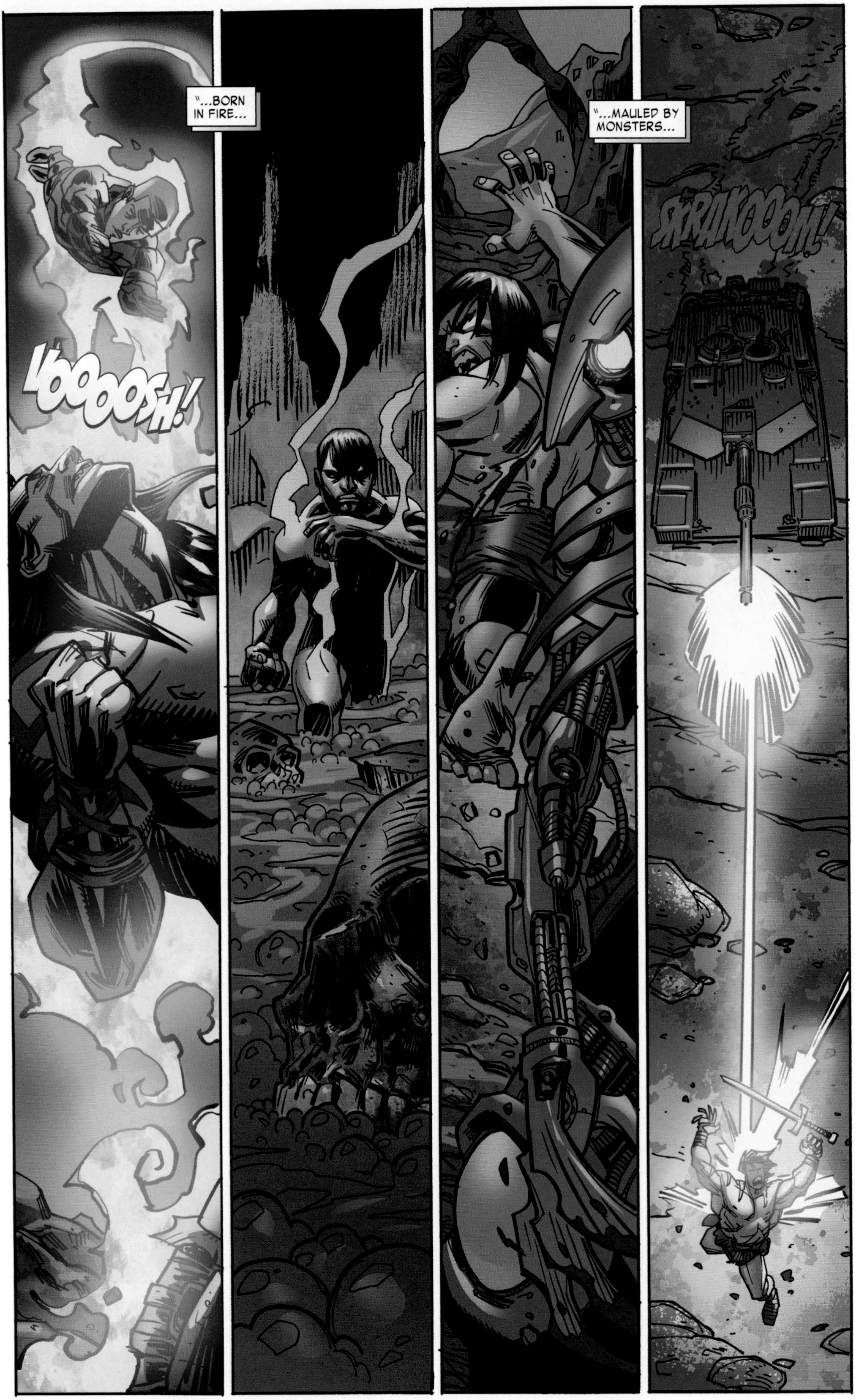

"...BORN IN FIRE...
VOOOOSH!
"...MAULED BY MONSTERS...
SKRANOOOM!

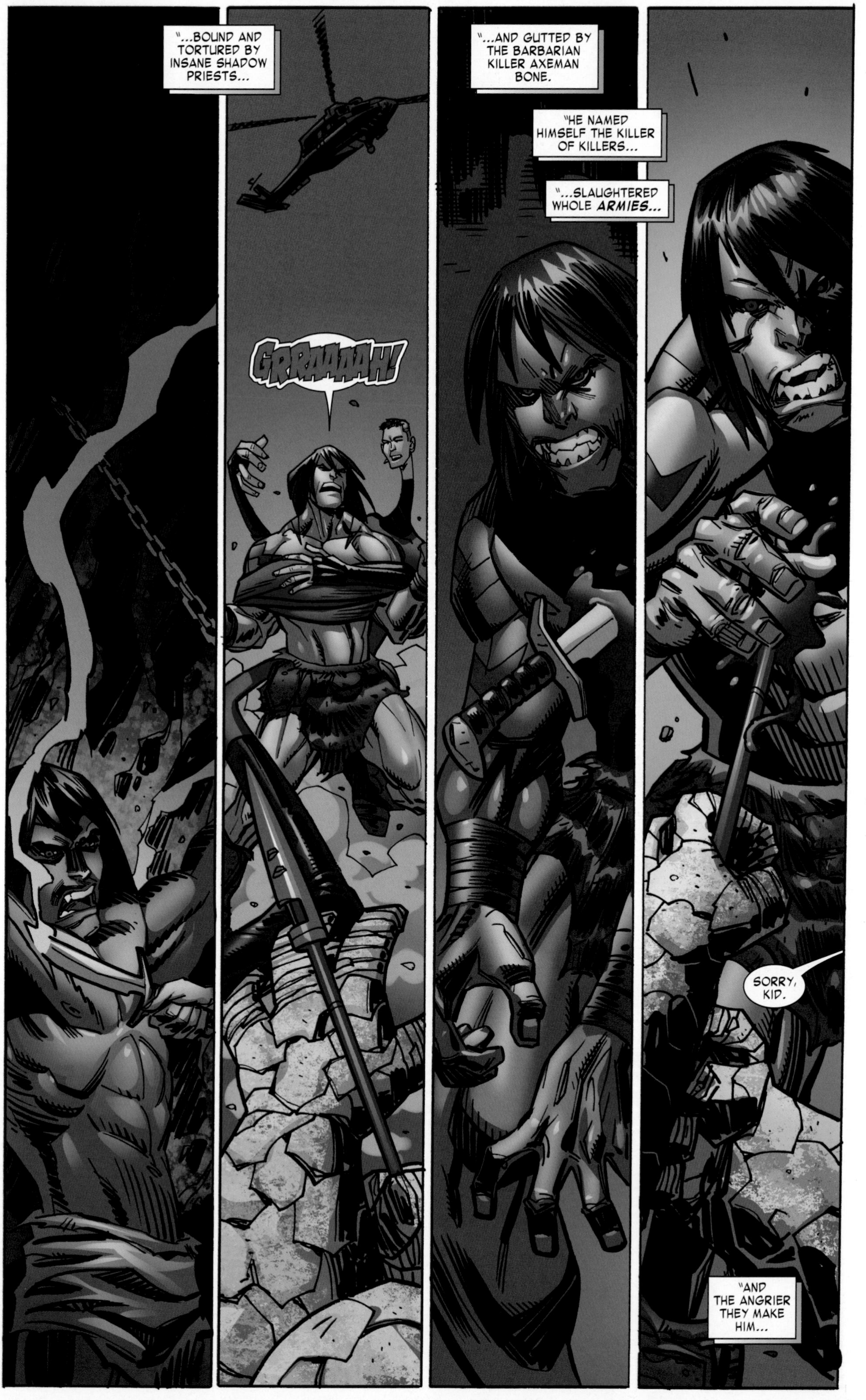
"...BOUND AND TORTURED BY INSANE SHADOW PRIESTS...
GRRAAAAAH!
"...AND GUTTED BY THE BARBARIAN KILLER AXEMAN BONE.
"HE NAMED HIMSELF THE KILLER OF KILLERS...
"...SLAUGHTERED WHOLE ARMIES...
SORRY, KID.
"AND THE ANGRIER THEY MAKE HIM...

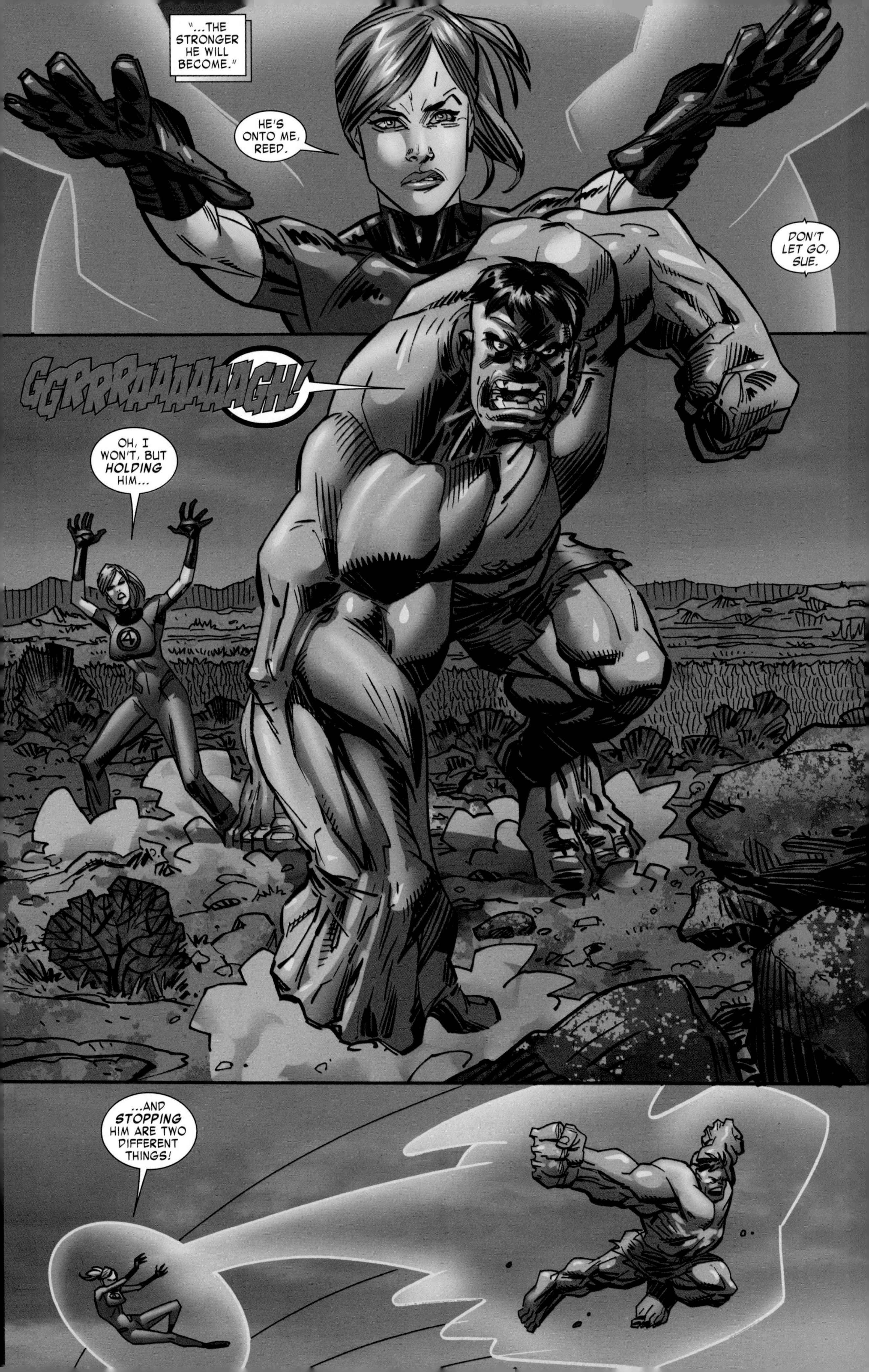
"...THE STRONGER HE WILL BECOME."
HE'S ONTO ME, REED.
DON'T LET GO, SUE.
GGRRRAAAAAAAGH!
OH, I WON'T, BUT HOLDING HIM...
...AND STOPPING HIM ARE TWO DIFFERENT THINGS!

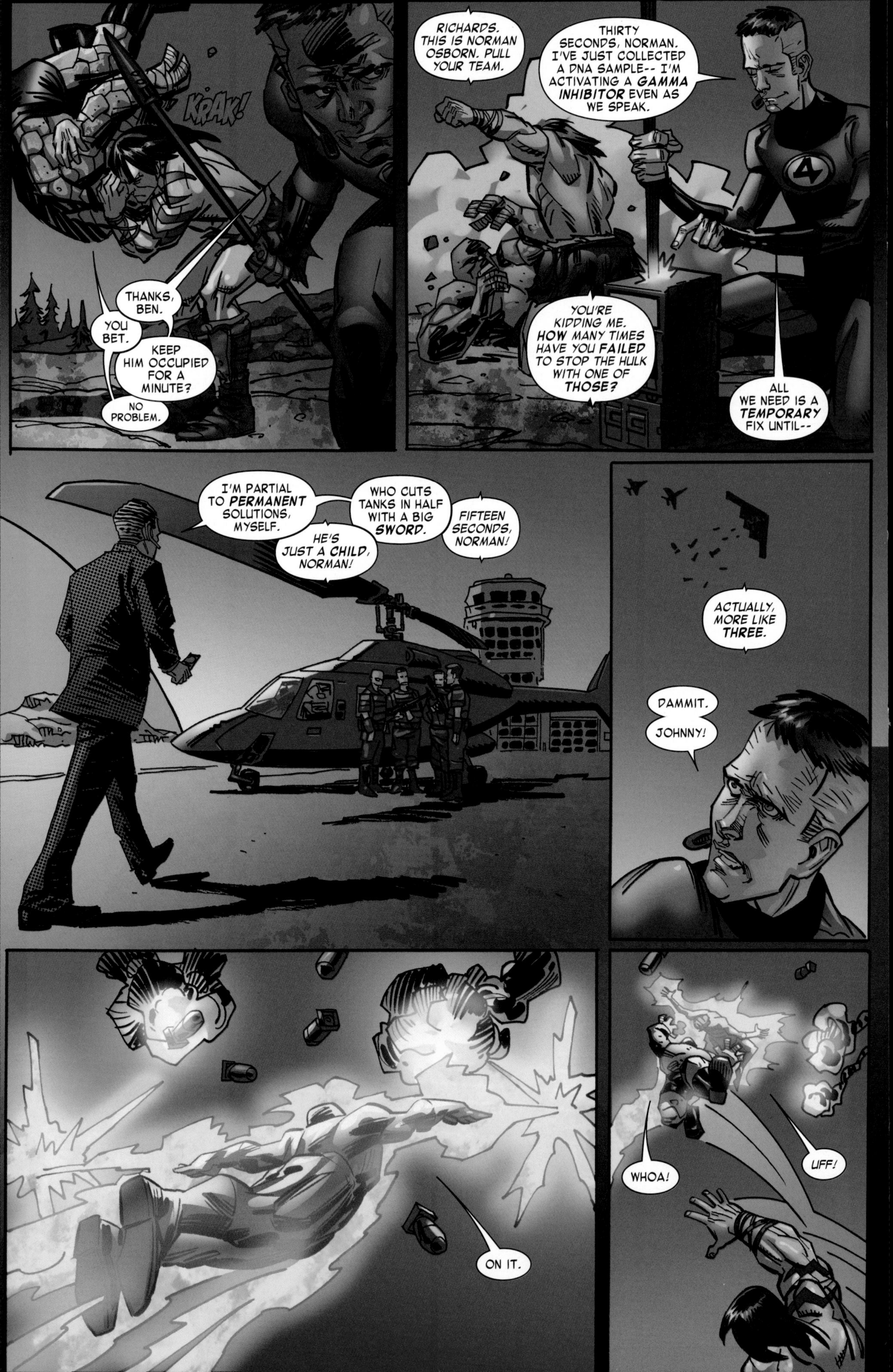
KRAK!
THANKS, BEN.
YOU BET.
KEEP HIM OCCUPIED FOR A MINUTE?
NO PROBLEM.
RICHARDS. THIS IS NORMAN OSBORN. PULL YOUR TEAM.
THIRTY SECONDS, NORMAN. I'VE JUST COLLECTED A DNA SAMPLE-- I'M ACTIVATING A GAMMA INHIBITOR EVEN AS WE SPEAK.
YOU'RE KIDDING ME. HOW MANY TIMES HAVE YOU FAILED TO STOP THE HULK WITH ONE OF THOSE?
ALL WE NEED IS A TEMPORARY FIX UNTIL--
I'M PARTIAL TO PERMANENT SOLUTIONS, MYSELF.
HE'S JUST A CHILD, NORMAN!
WHO CUTS TANKS IN HALF WITH A BIG SWORD.
FIFTEEN SECONDS, NORMAN!
ACTUALLY, MORE LIKE THREE.
DAMMIT.
JOHNNY!
ON IT.
WHOA!
UFF!

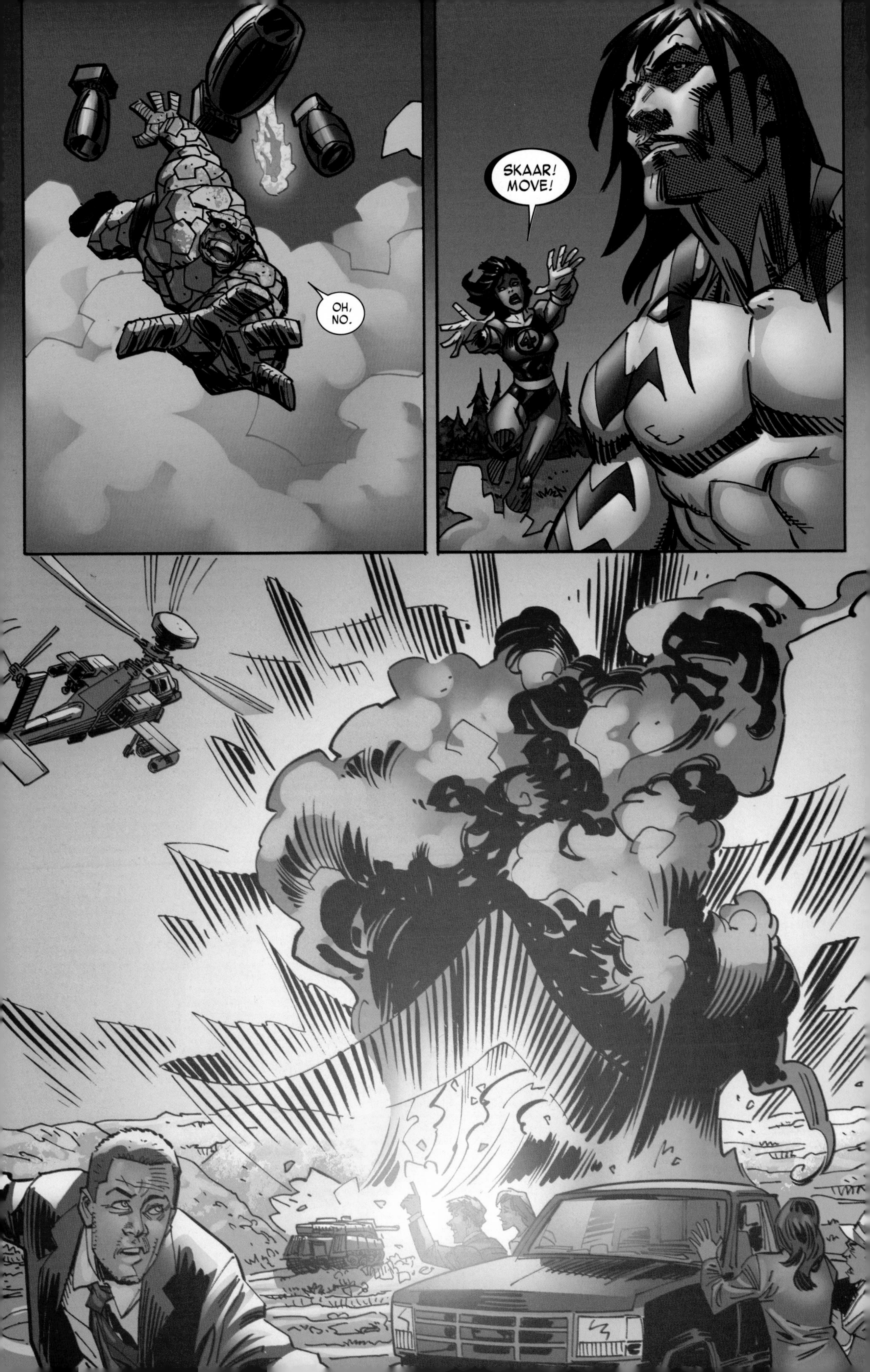
OH, NO.
SKAAR! MOVE!

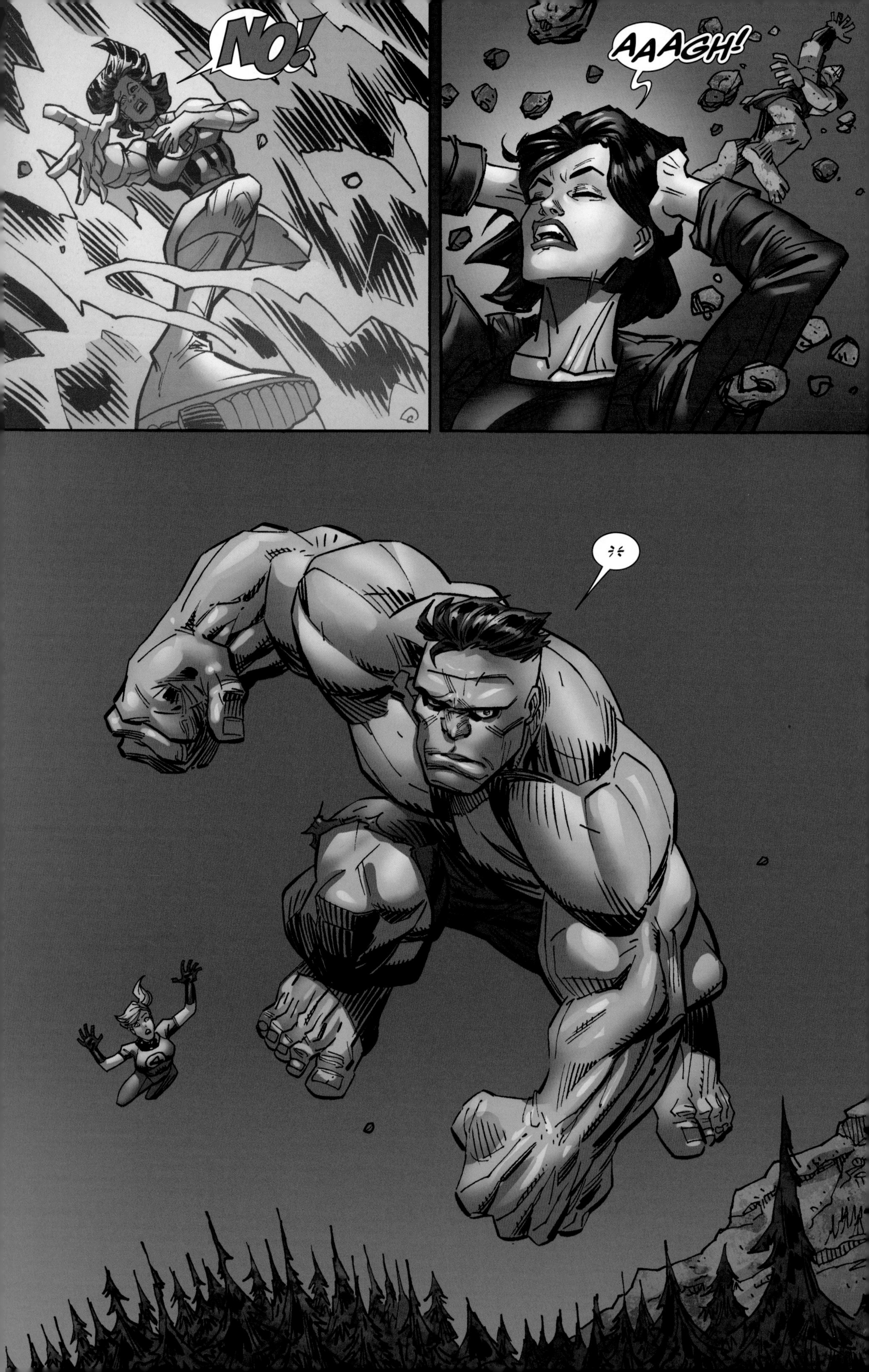
NO!
AAAGH!

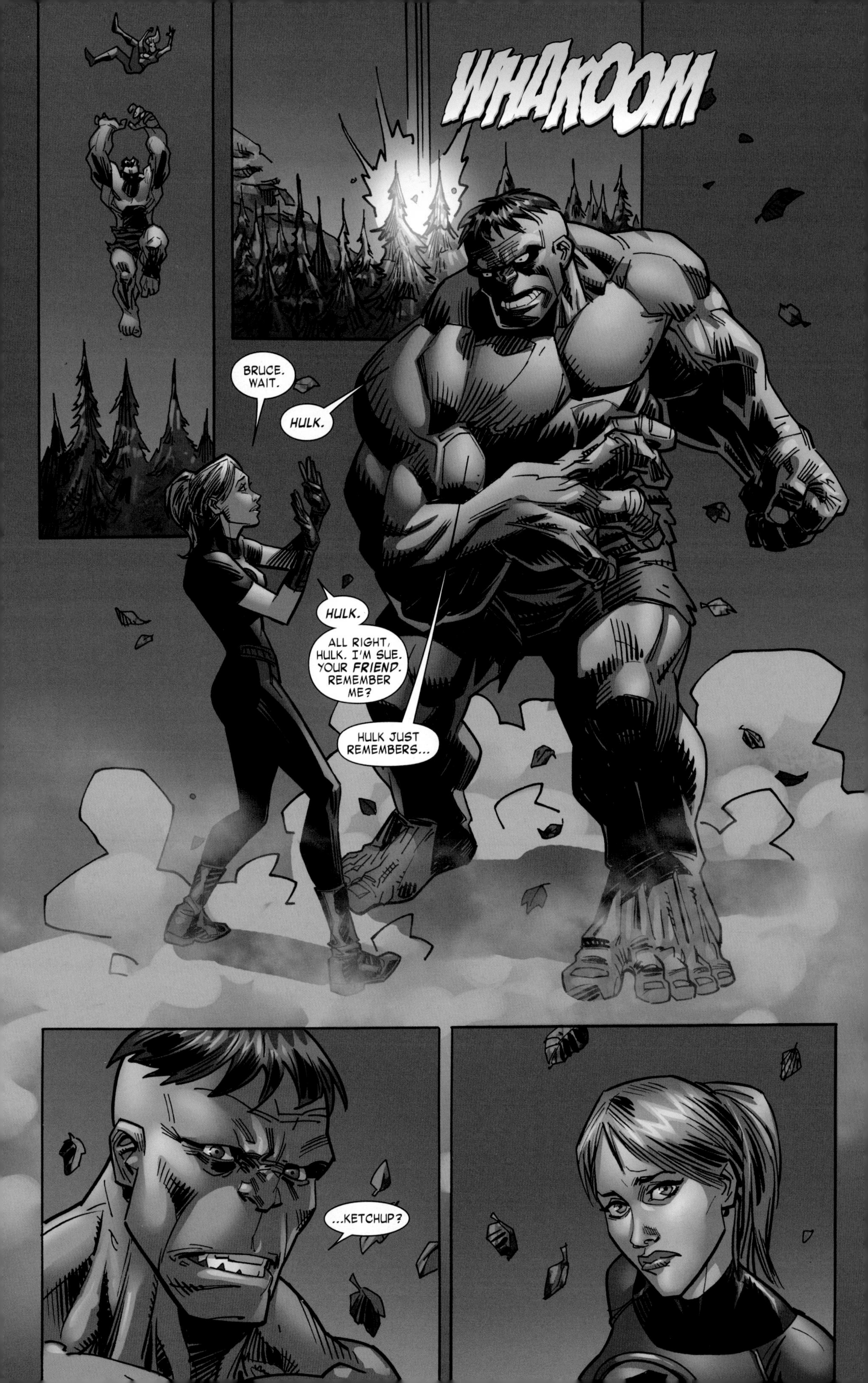
WHAKOOM
BRUCE. WAIT.
HULK.
HULK.
ALL RIGHT, HULK. I'M SUE. YOUR FRIEND. REMEMBER ME?
HULK JUST REMEMBERS...
...KETCHUP?

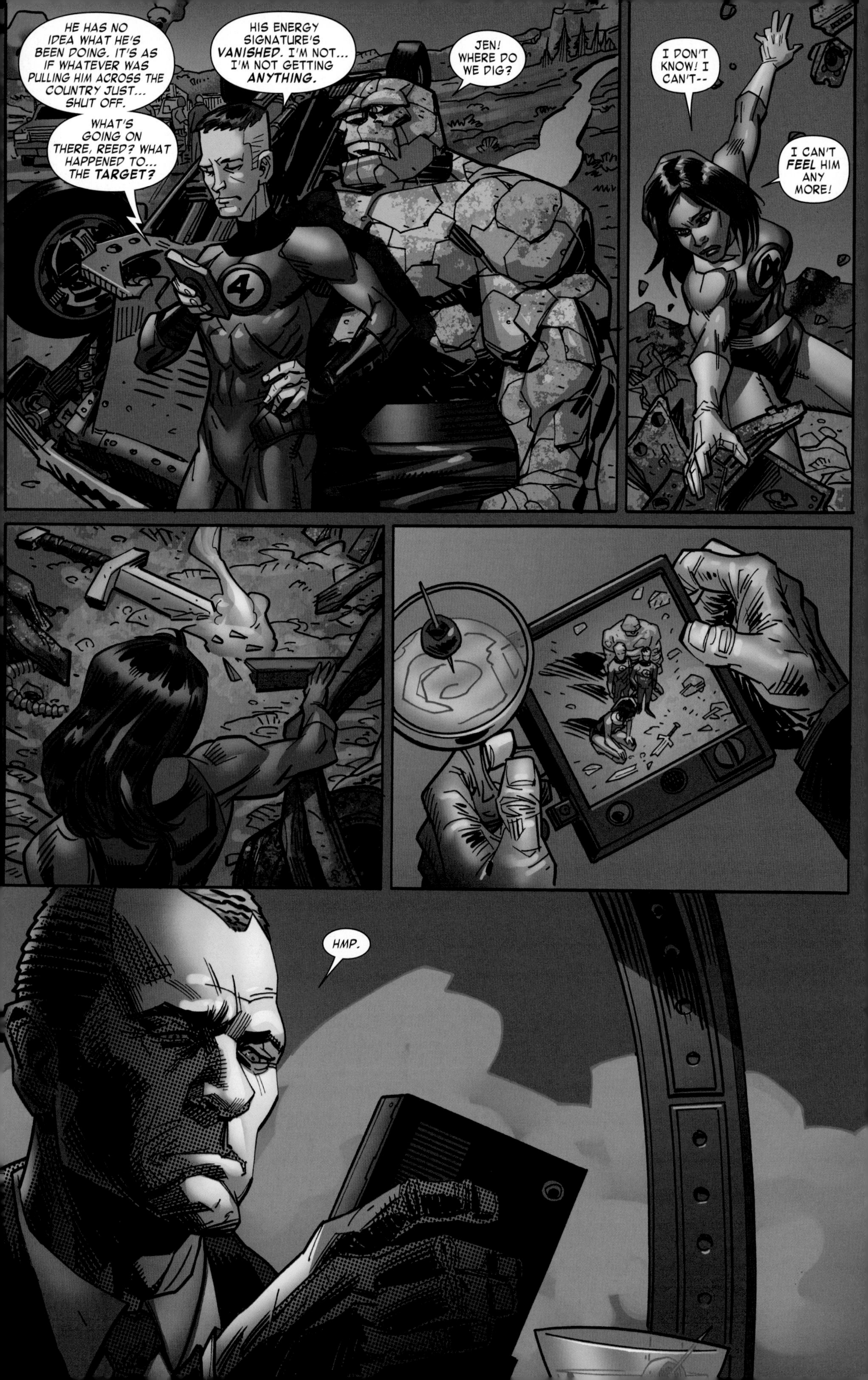
HE HAS NO IDEA WHAT HE'S BEEN DOING. IT'S AS IF WHATEVER WAS PULLING HIM ACROSS THE COUNTRY JUST... SHUT OFF.
WHAT'S GOING ON THERE, REED? WHAT HAPPENED TO... THE TARGET?
HIS ENERGY SIGNATURE'S VANISHED. I'M NOT... I'M NOT GETTING ANYTHING.
JEN! WHERE DO WE DIG?
I DON'T KNOW! I CAN'T--
I CAN'T FEEL HIM ANY MORE!
HMP.

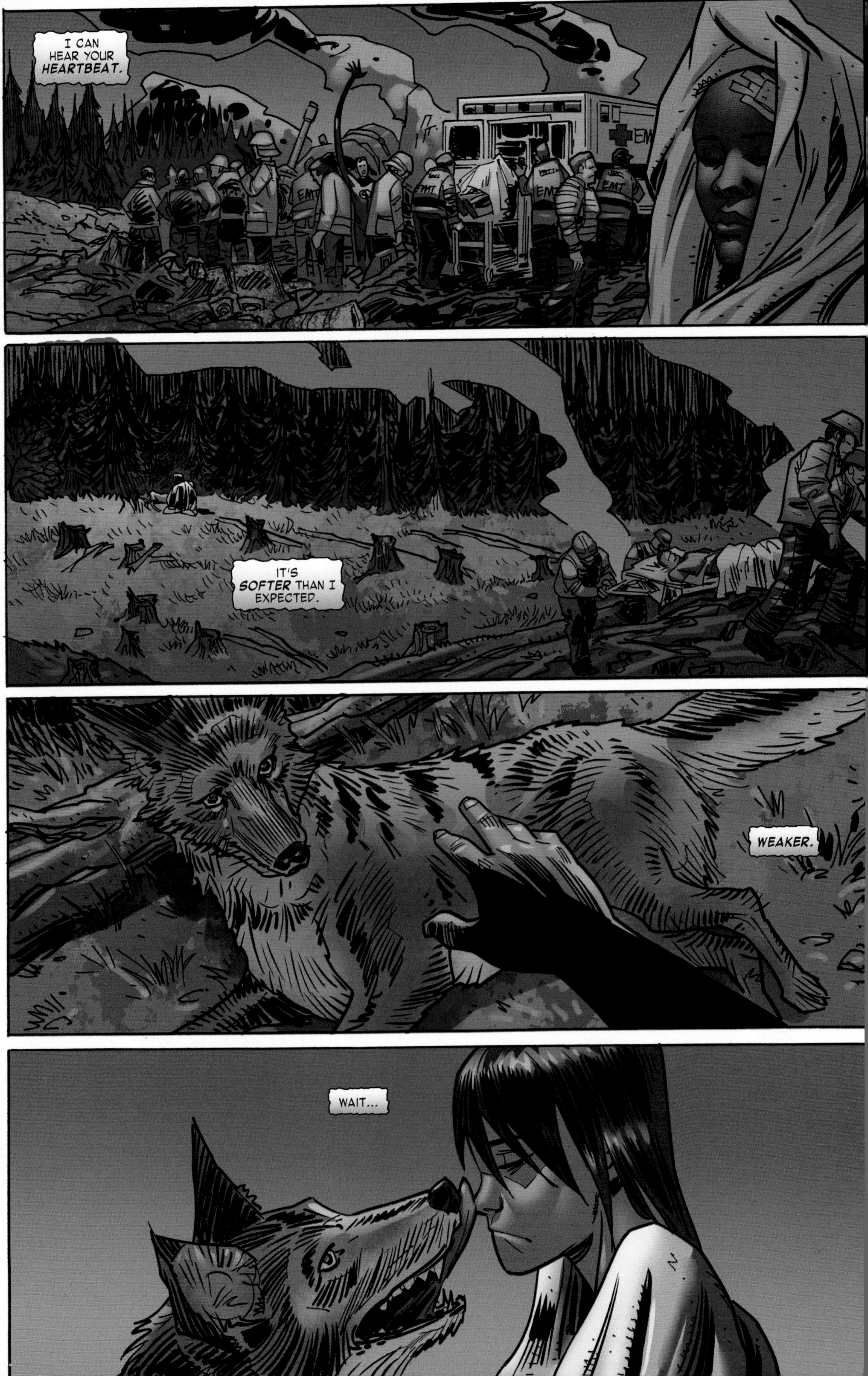
I CAN HEAR YOUR HEARTBEAT.
IT'S SOFTER THAN I EXPECTED.
WEAKER.
WAIT...

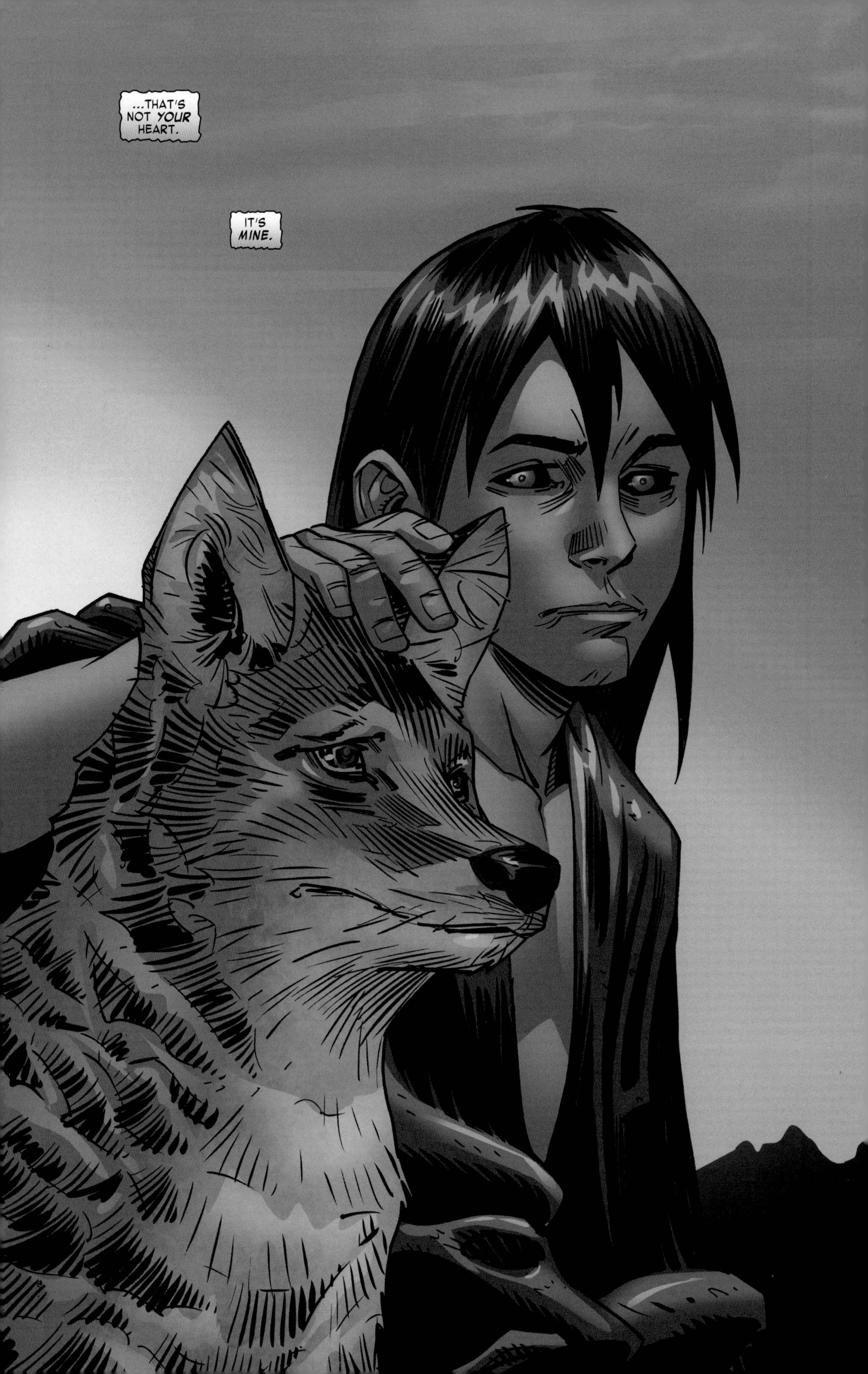
...THAT'S NOT YOUR HEART.
IT'S MINE.

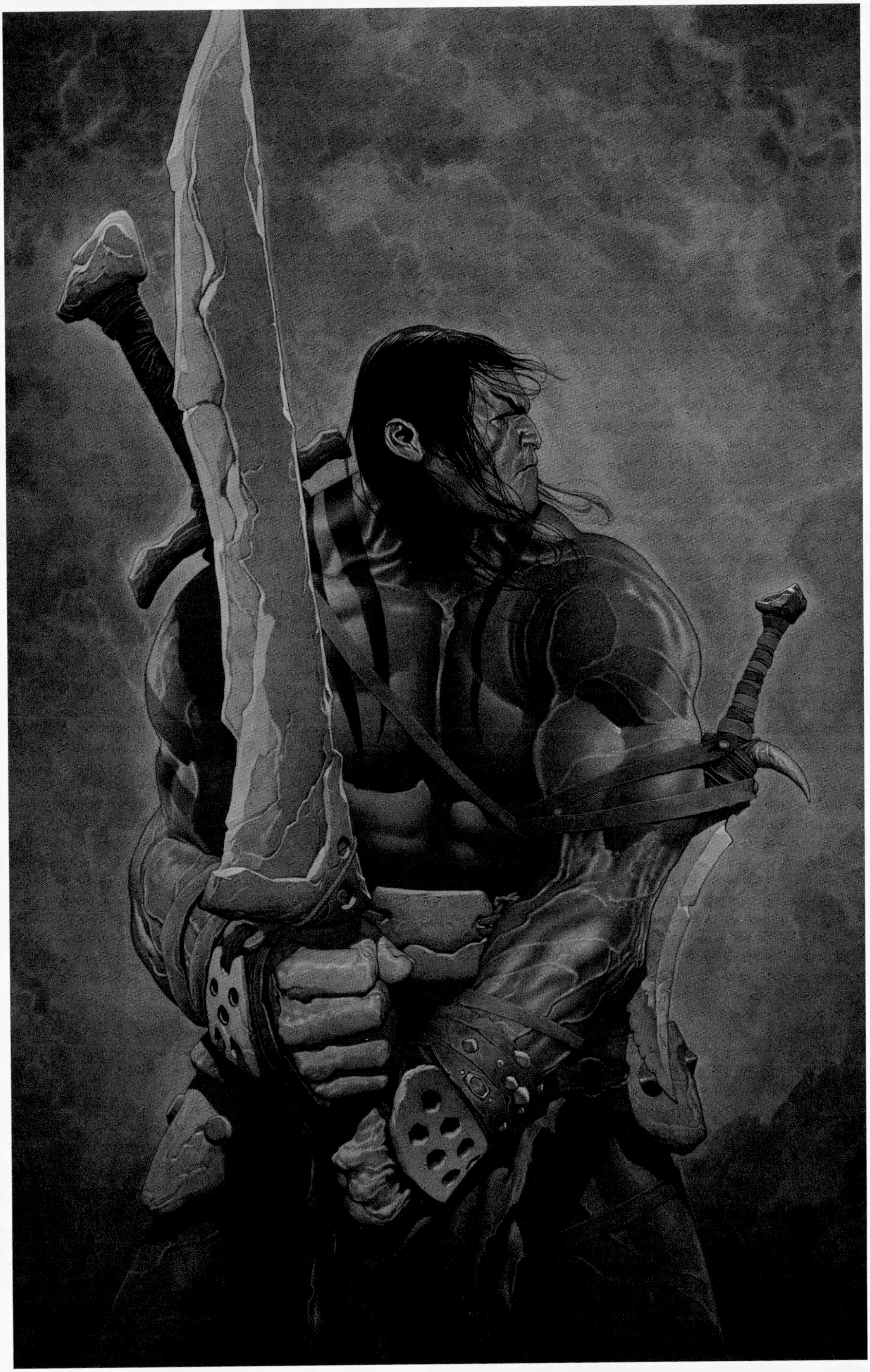

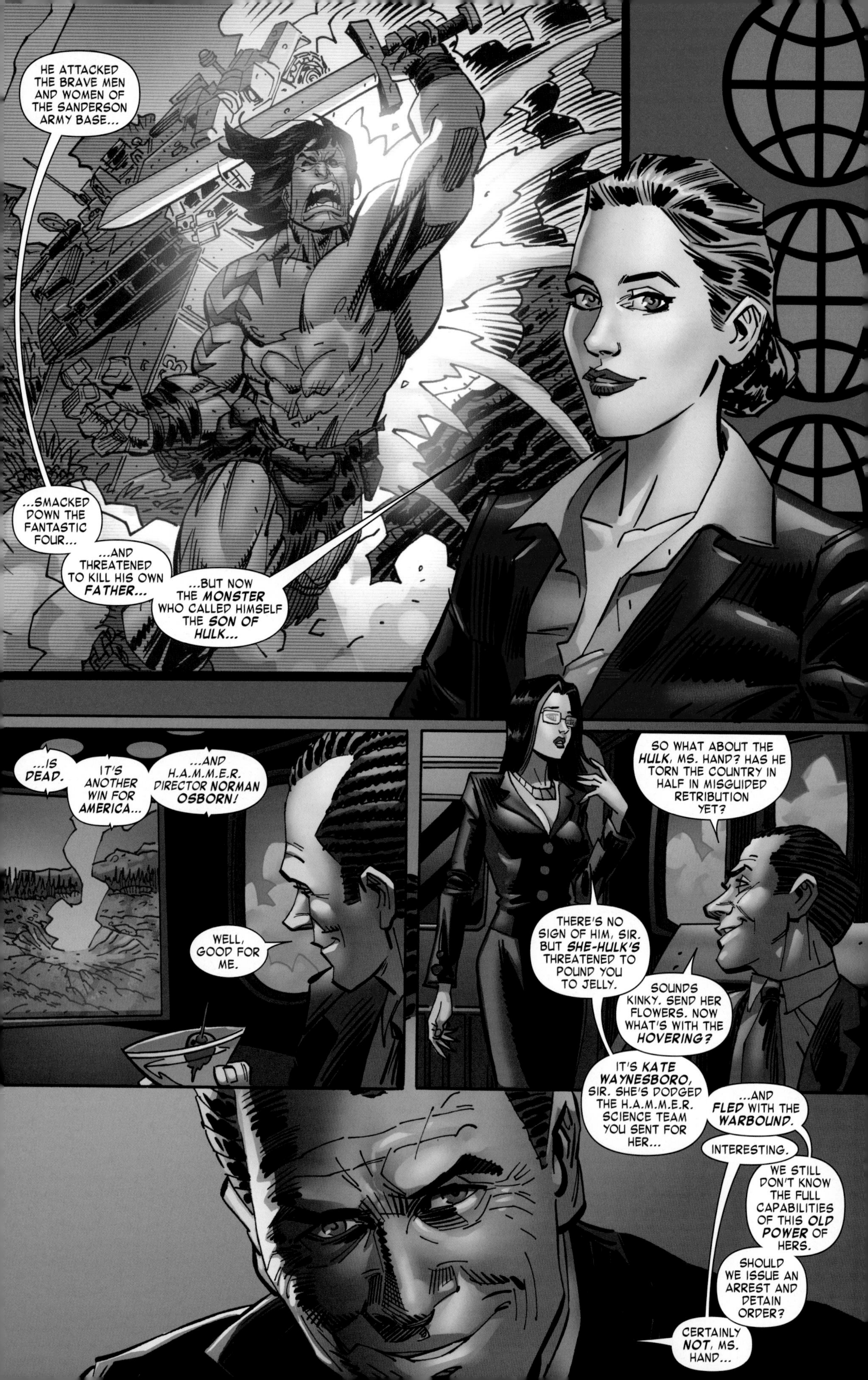
HE ATTACKED THE BRAVE MEN AND WOMEN OF THE SANDERSON ARMY BASE...
...SMACKED DOWN THE FANTASTIC FOUR...
...AND THREATENED TO KILL HIS OWN FATHER...
...BUT NOW THE MONSTER WHO CALLED HIMSELF THE SON OF HULK...
...IS DEAD.
IT'S ANOTHER WIN FOR AMERICA...
...AND H.A.M.M.E.R. DIRECTOR NORMAN OSBORN!
WELL, GOOD FOR ME.
SO WHAT ABOUT THE HULK, MS. HAND? HAS HE TORN THE COUNTRY IN HALF IN MISGUIDED RETRIBUTION YET?
THERE'S NO SIGN OF HIM, SIR. BUT SHE-HULK'S THREATENED TO POUND YOU TO JELLY.
SOUNDS KINKY. SEND HER FLOWERS. NOW WHAT'S WITH THE HOVERING?
IT'S KATE WAYNESBORO, SIR. SHE'S DODGED THE H.A.M.M.E.R. SCIENCE TEAM YOU SENT FOR HER...
...AND FLED WITH THE WARBOUND.
INTERESTING.
WE STILL DON'T KNOW THE FULL CAPABILITIES OF THIS OLD POWER OF HERS.
SHOULD WE ISSUE AN ARREST AND DETAIN ORDER?
CERTAINLY NOT, MS. HAND...

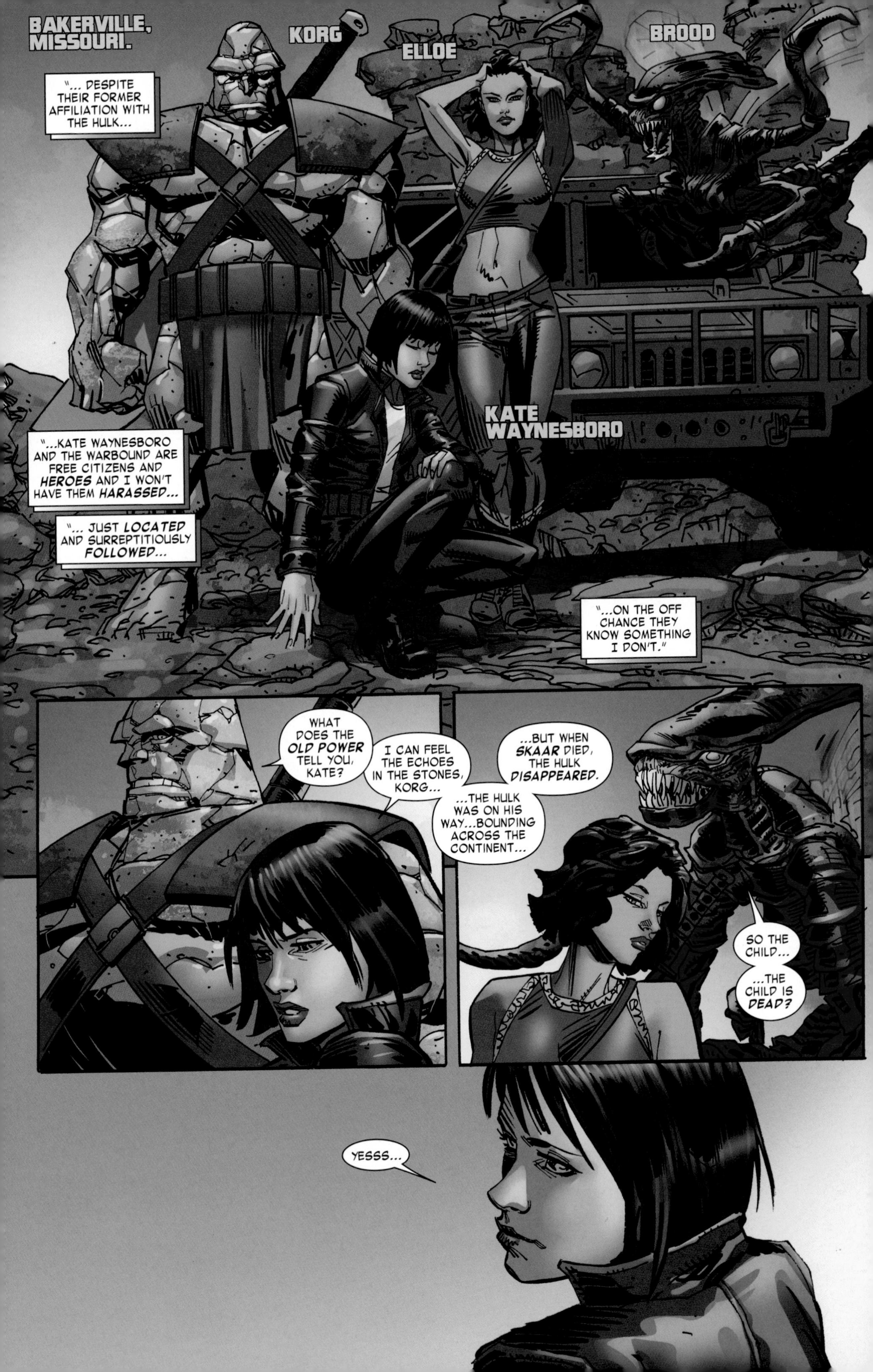
BAKERVILLE, MISSOURI.
KORG
ELLOE
BROOD
"... DESPITE THEIR FORMER AFFILIATION WITH THE HULK...
"...KATE WAYNESBORO AND THE WARBOUND ARE FREE CITIZENS AND HEROES AND I WON'T HAVE THEM HARASSED...
"... JUST LOCATED AND SURREPTITIOUSLY FOLLOWED...
KATE WAYNESBORO
"...ON THE OFF CHANCE THEY KNOW SOMETHING I DON'T."
WHAT DOES THE OLD POWER TELL YOU, KATE?
I CAN FEEL THE ECHOES IN THE STONES, KORG...
...THE HULK WAS ON HIS WAY...BOUNDING ACROSS THE CONTINENT...
...BUT WHEN SKAAR DIED, THE HULK DISAPPEARED.
SO THE CHILD...
...THE CHILD IS DEAD?
YESSS...

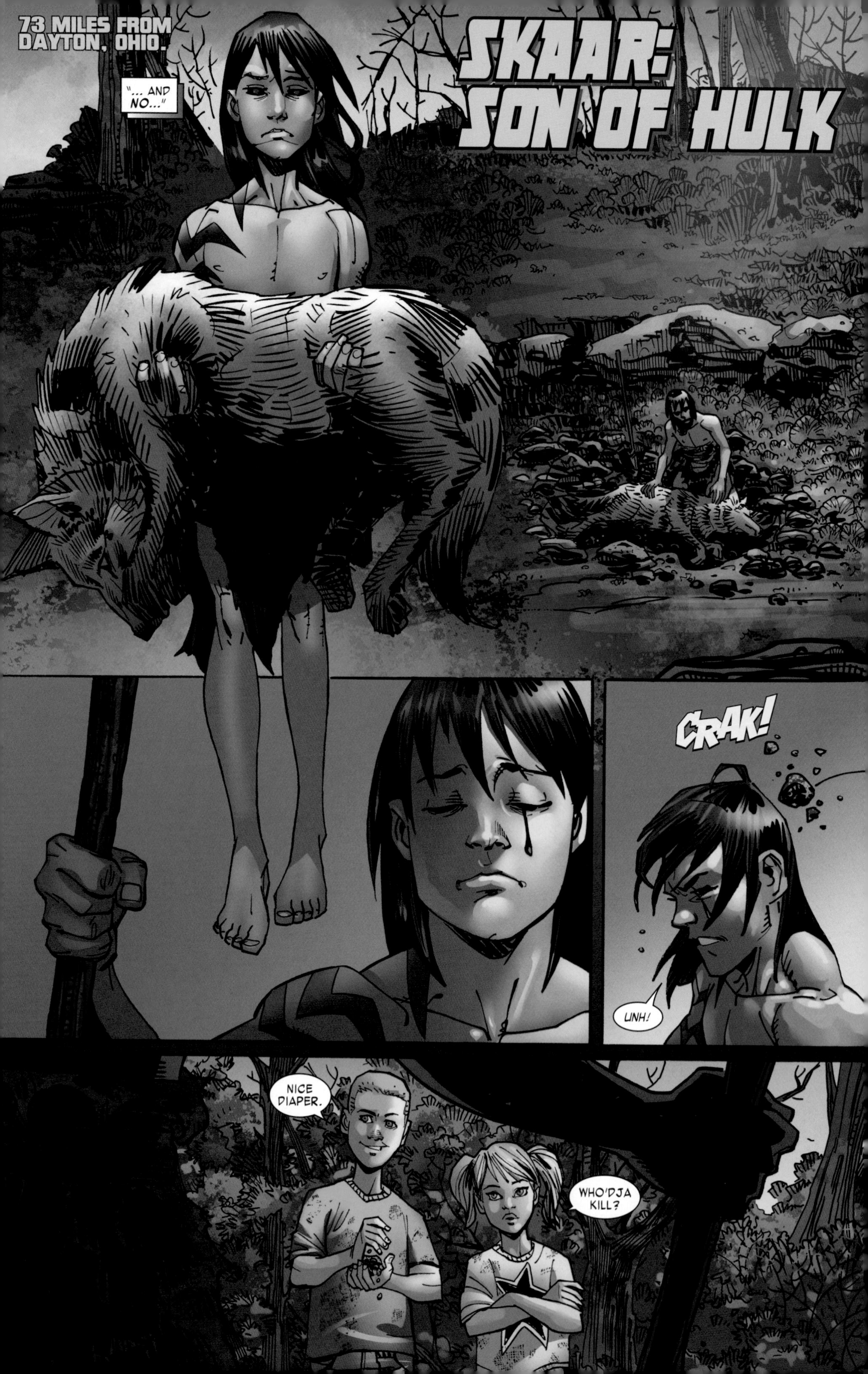
73 MILES FROM DAYTON, OHIO.
SKAAR: SON OF HULK
"... AND NO..."
CRAK!
UNH!
NICE DIAPER.
WHO'DJA KILL?

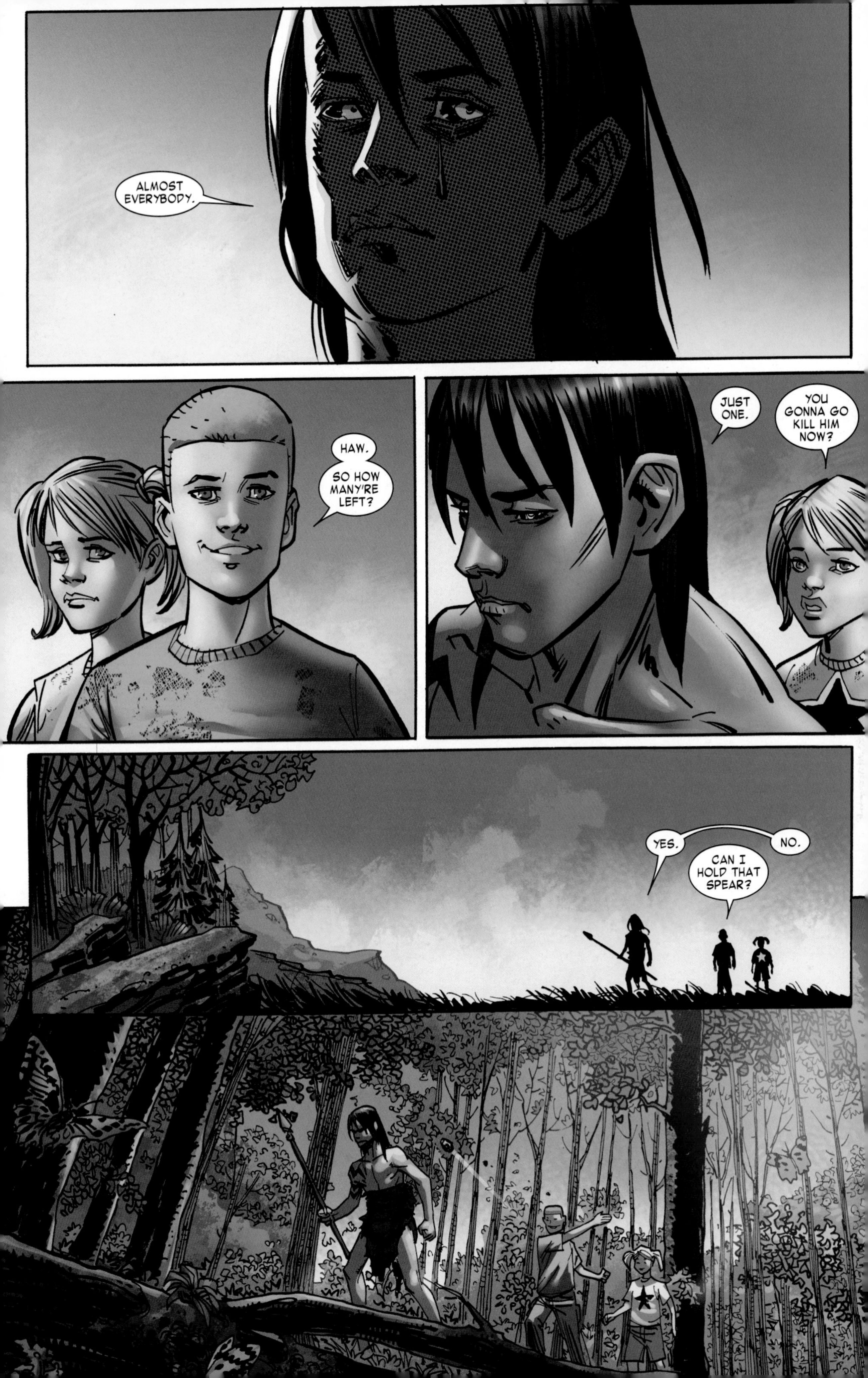
ALMOST EVERYBODY.
HAW.
SO HOW MANY'RE LEFT?
JUST ONE.
YOU GONNA GO KILL HIM NOW?
YES.
NO.
CAN I HOLD THAT SPEAR?

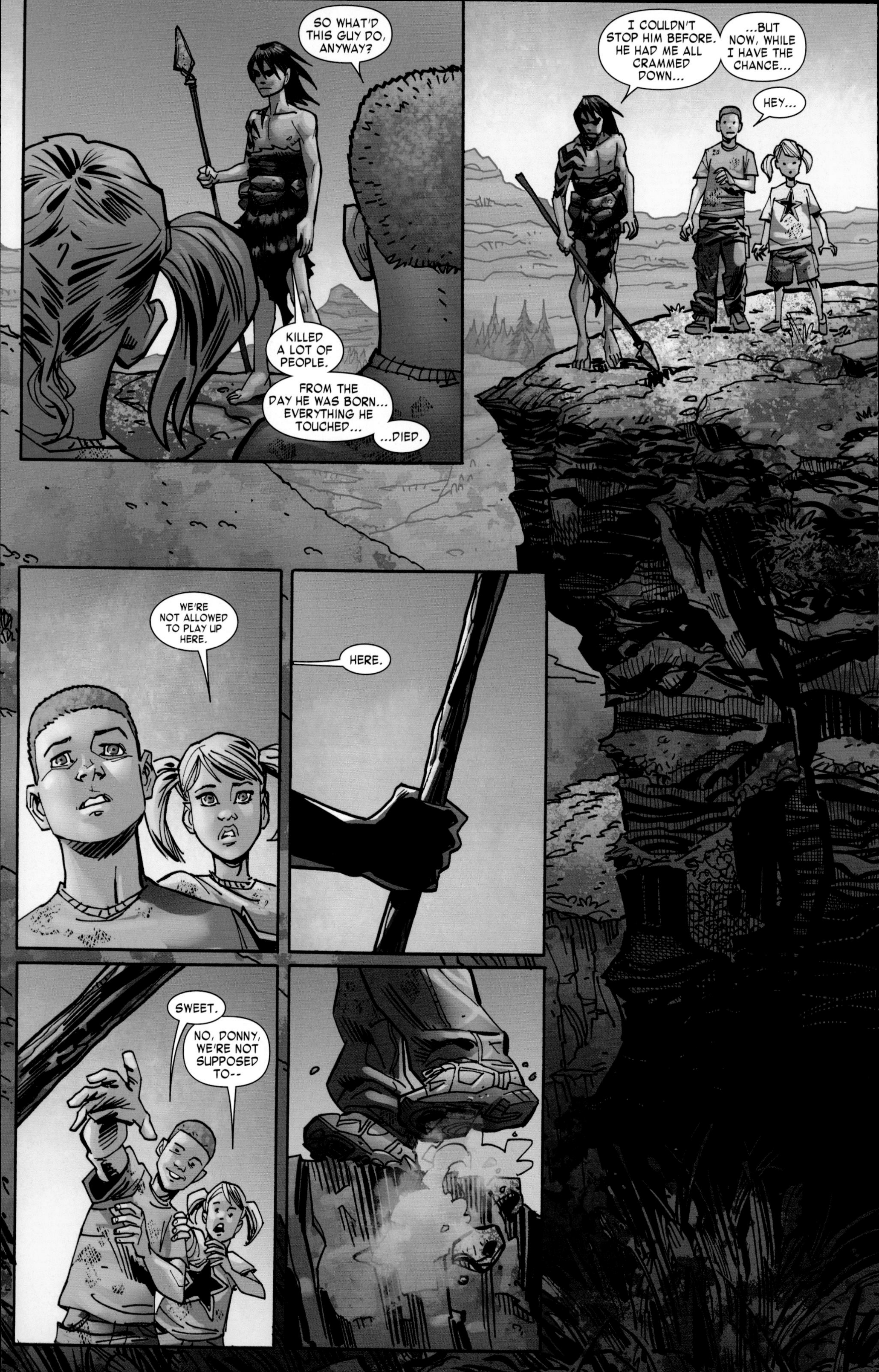
SO WHAT'D THIS GUY DO, ANYWAY?
KILLED A LOT OF PEOPLE.
FROM THE DAY HE WAS BORN... EVERYTHING HE TOUCHED...
...DIED.
I COULDN'T STOP HIM BEFORE. HE HAD ME ALL CRAMMED DOWN...
...BUT NOW, WHILE I HAVE THE CHANCE...
HEY...
WE'RE NOT ALLOWED TO PLAY UP HERE.
HERE.
SWEET.
NO, DONNY, WE'RE NOT SUPPOSED TO--

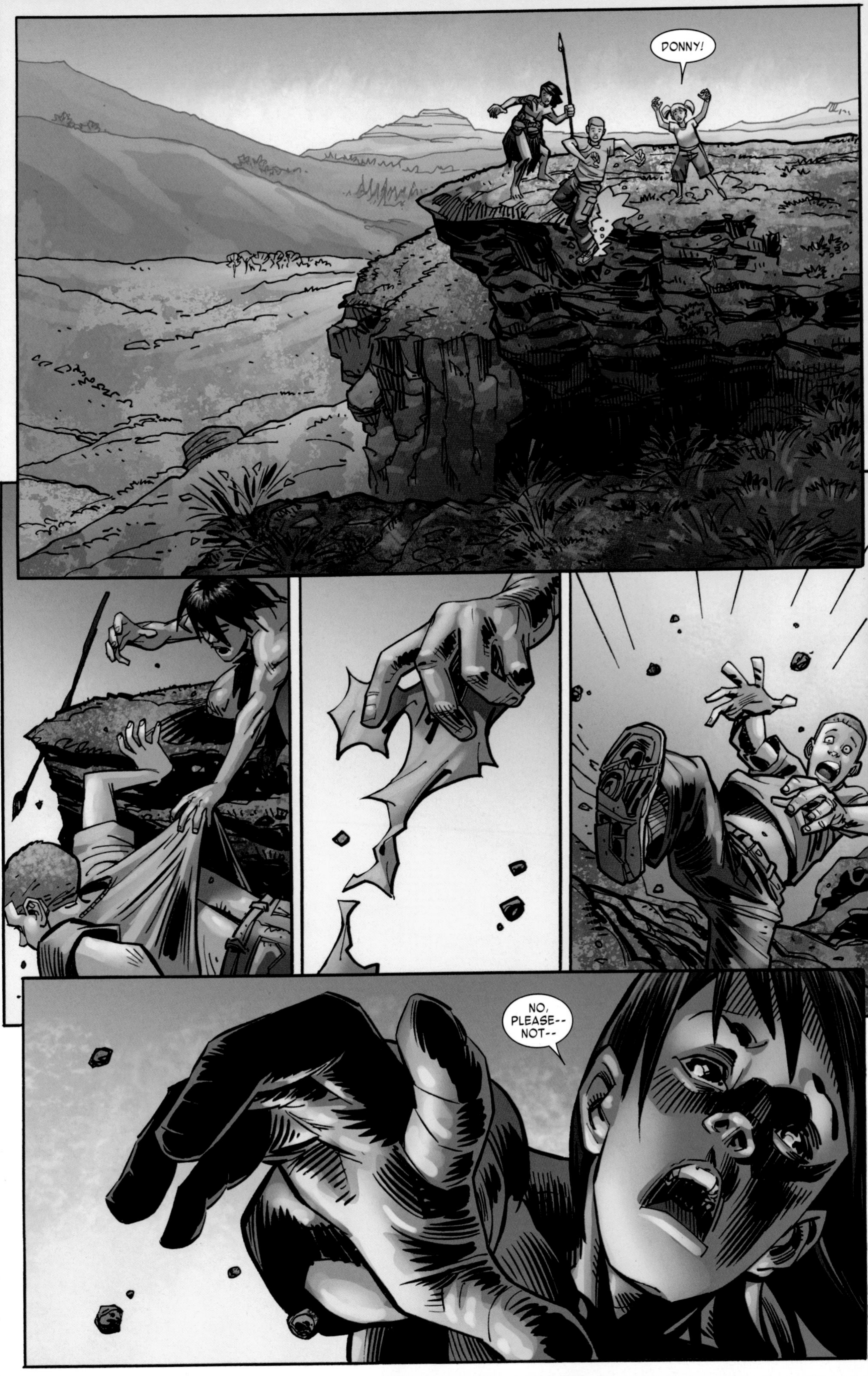
DONNY!
NO, PLEASE-- NOT--

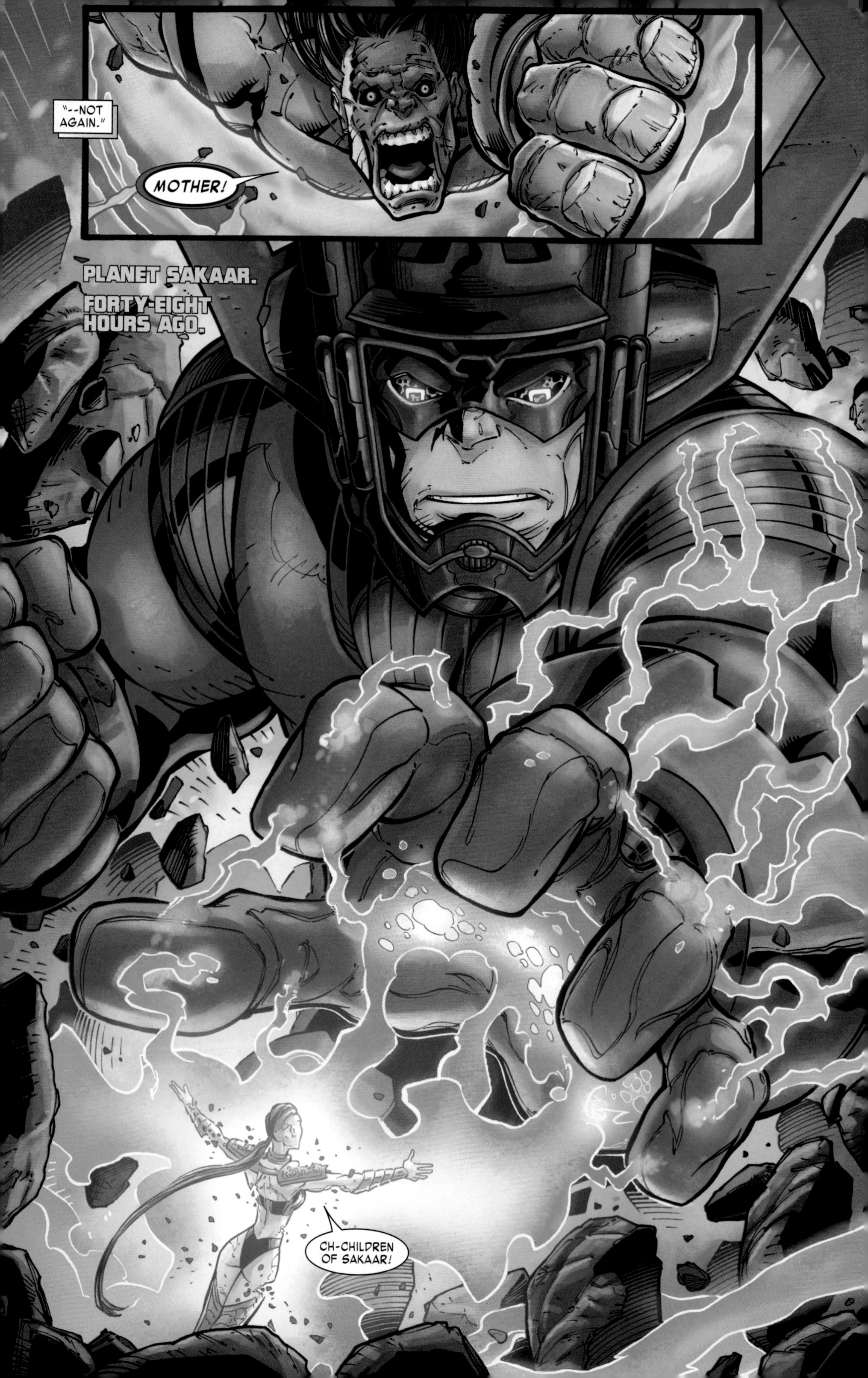
"--NOT AGAIN."
MOTHER!
PLANET SAKAAR.
FORTY-EIGHT HOURS AGO.
CH-CHILDREN OF SAKAAR!

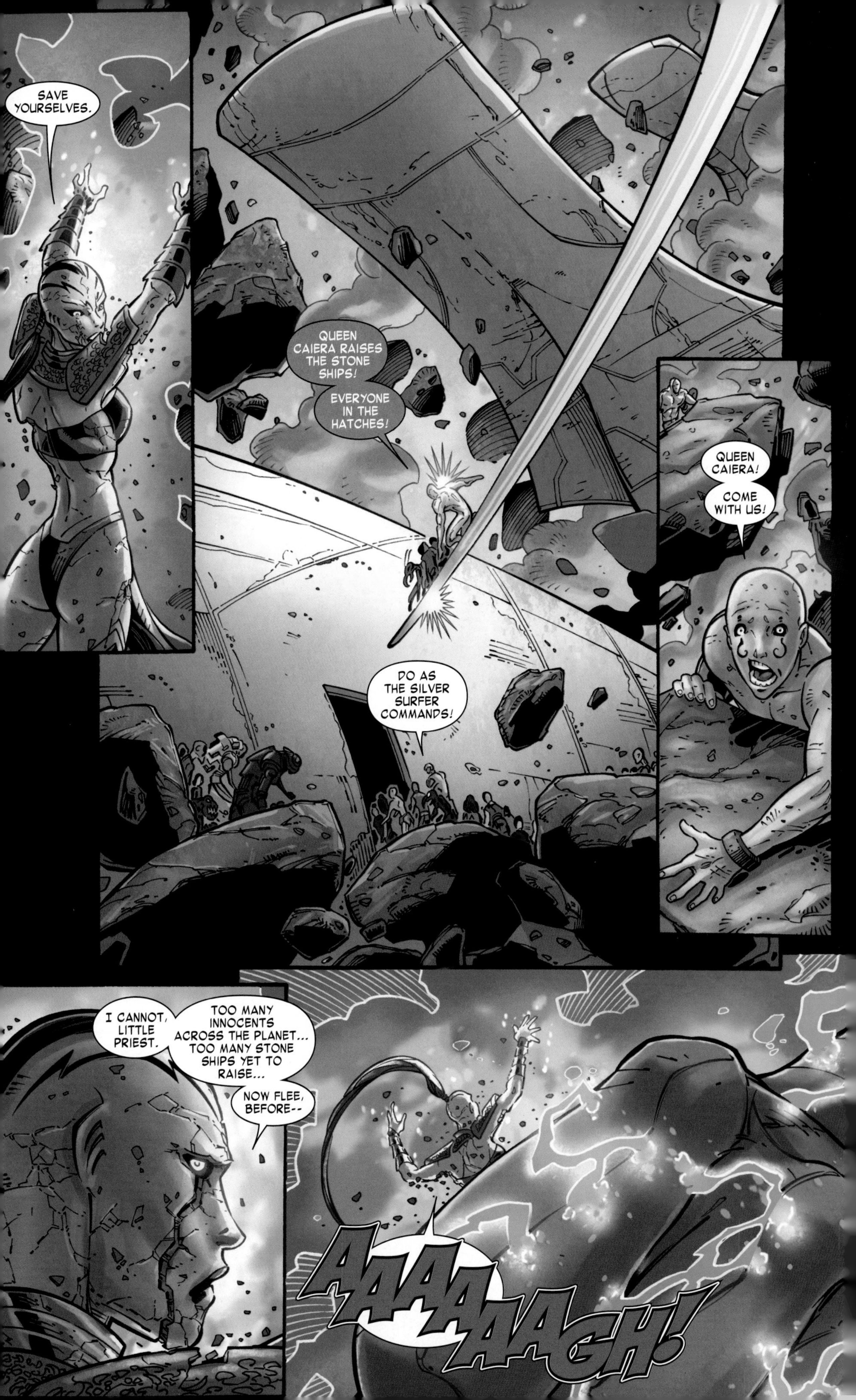
SAVE YOURSELVES.
QUEEN CAIERA RAISES THE STONE SHIPS!
EVERYONE IN THE HATCHES!
QUEEN CAIERA!
COME WITH US!
DO AS THE SILVER SURFER COMMANDS!
I CANNOT, LITTLE PRIEST.
TOO MANY INNOCENTS ACROSS THE PLANET... TOO MANY STONE SHIPS YET TO RAISE...
NOW FLEE, BEFORE--
AAAAAAGH!

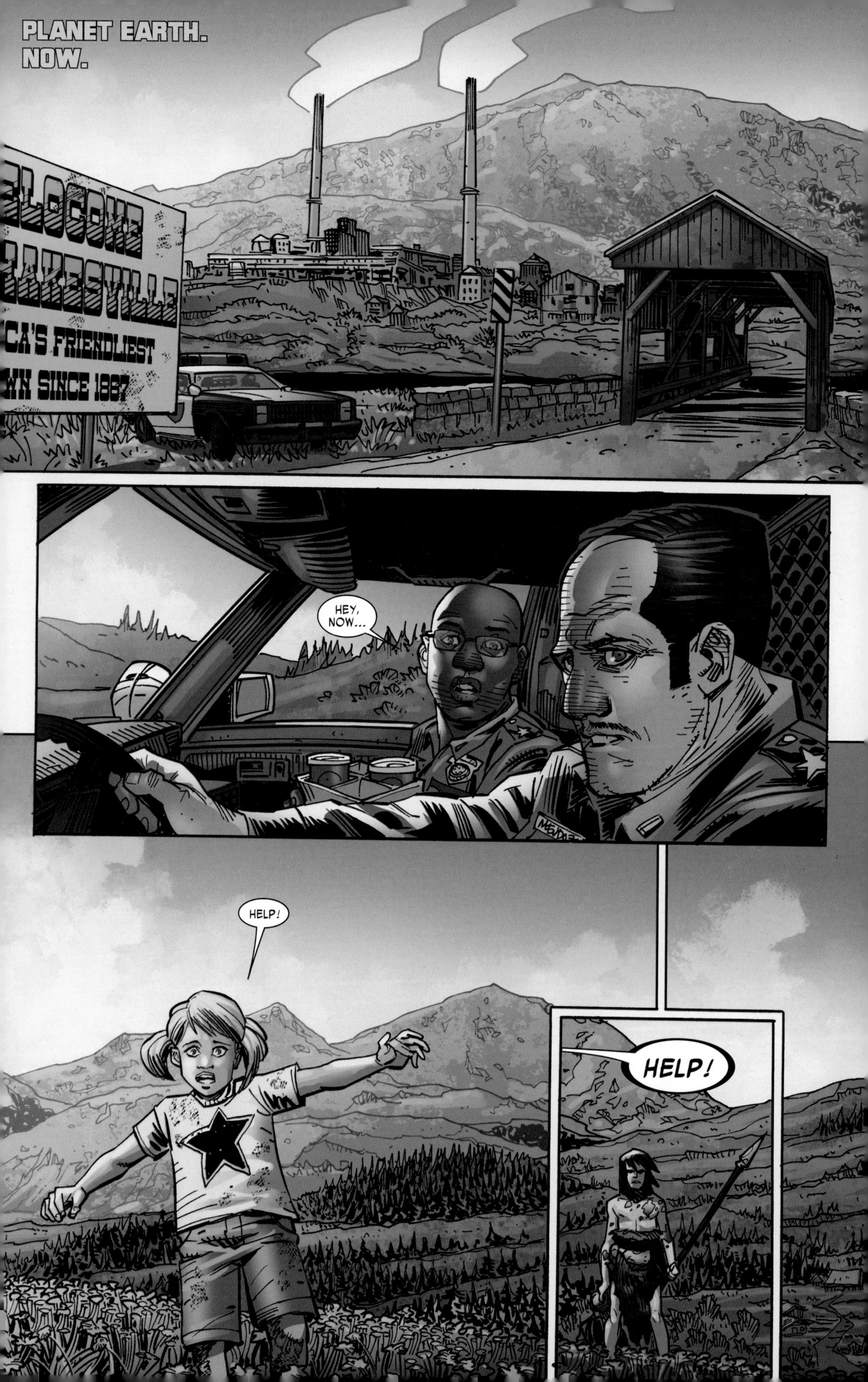
PLANET EARTH.
NOW.
HEY, NOW...
HELP!
HELP!

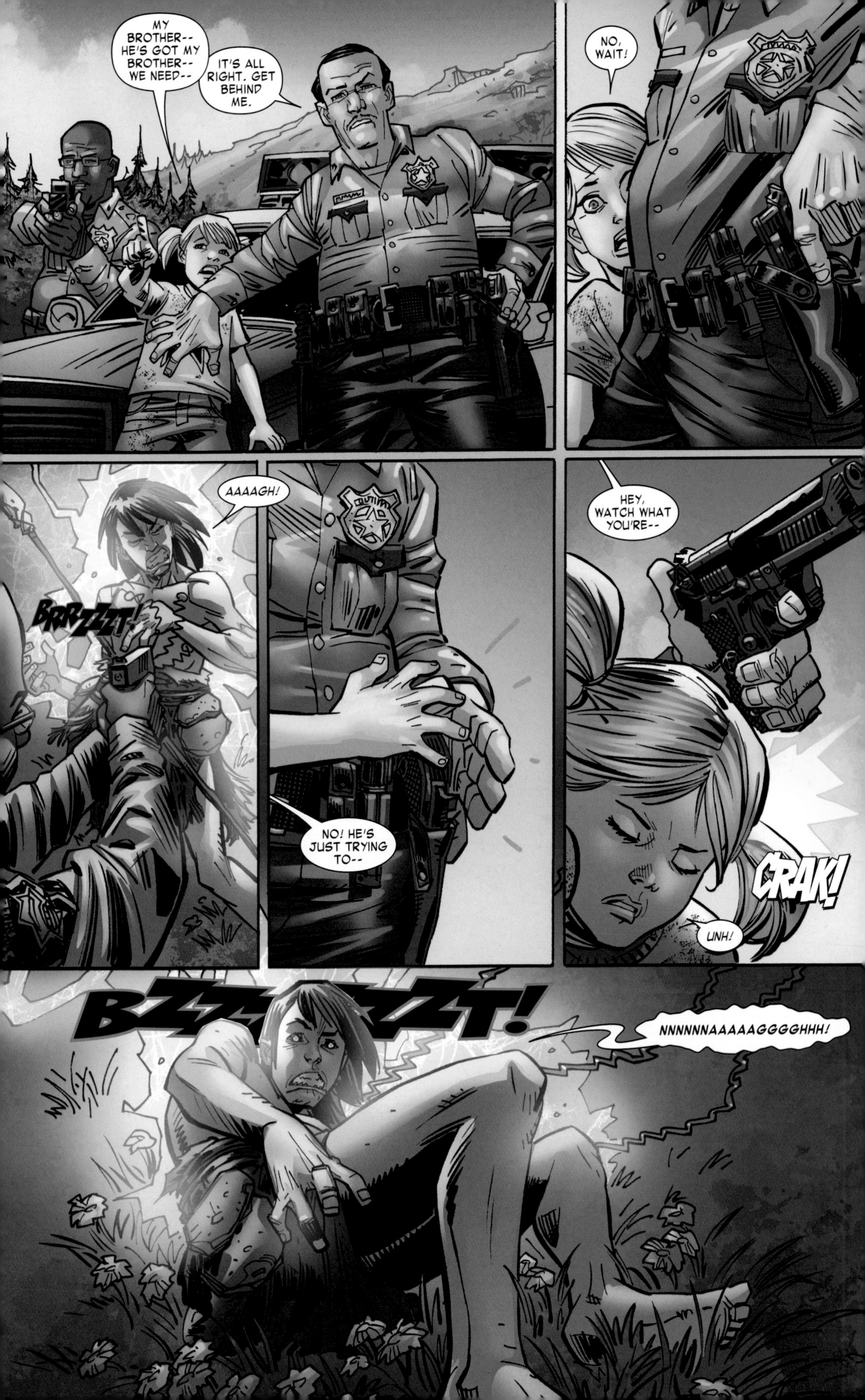
MY BROTHER-- HE'S GOT MY BROTHER-- WE NEED--
IT'S ALL RIGHT. GET BEHIND ME.
NO, WAIT!
AAAAGH!
BRRZZZT!
NO! HE'S JUST TRYING TO--
HEY, WATCH WHAT YOU'RE--
CRAK!
UNH!
BZZZZZZT!
NNNNNNAAAAAGGGGHHH!

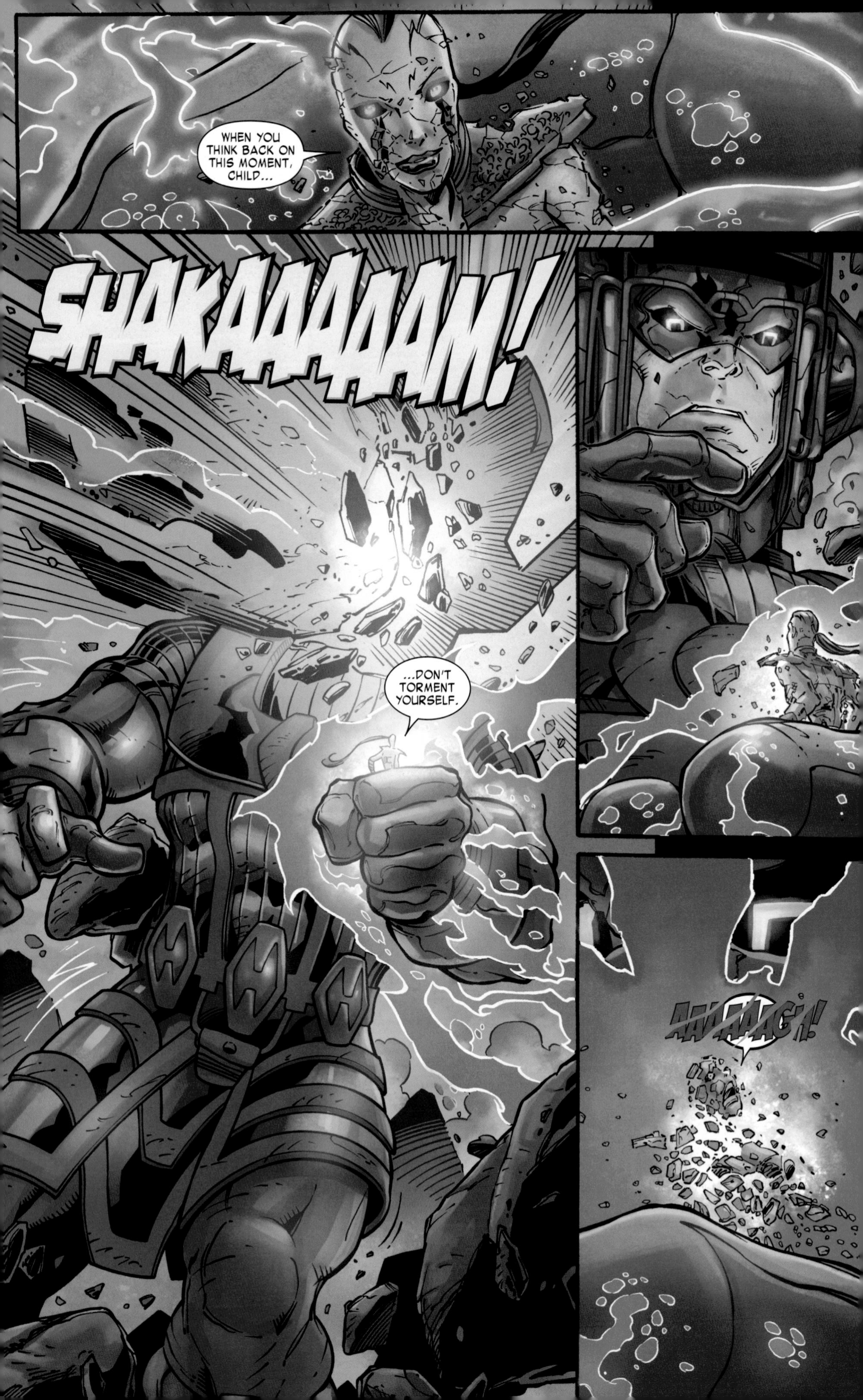
WHEN YOU THINK BACK ON THIS MOMENT, CHILD...
SHAKAAAAAAM!
...DON'T TORMENT YOURSELF.
AAAAAGH!

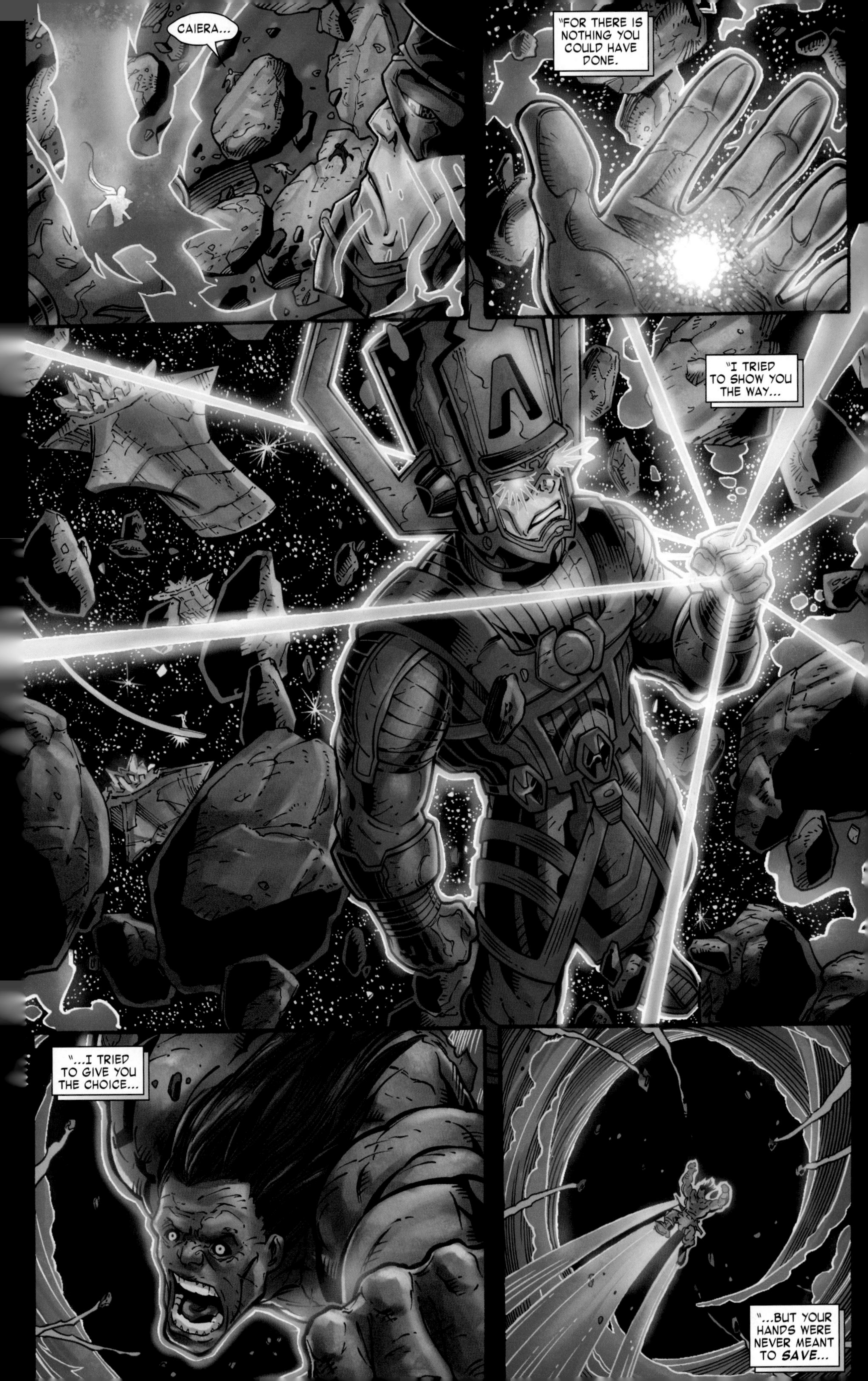
CAIERA...
"FOR THERE IS NOTHING YOU COULD HAVE DONE.
"I TRIED TO SHOW YOU THE WAY...
"...I TRIED TO GIVE YOU THE CHOICE...
"...BUT YOUR HANDS WERE NEVER MEANT TO SAVE...

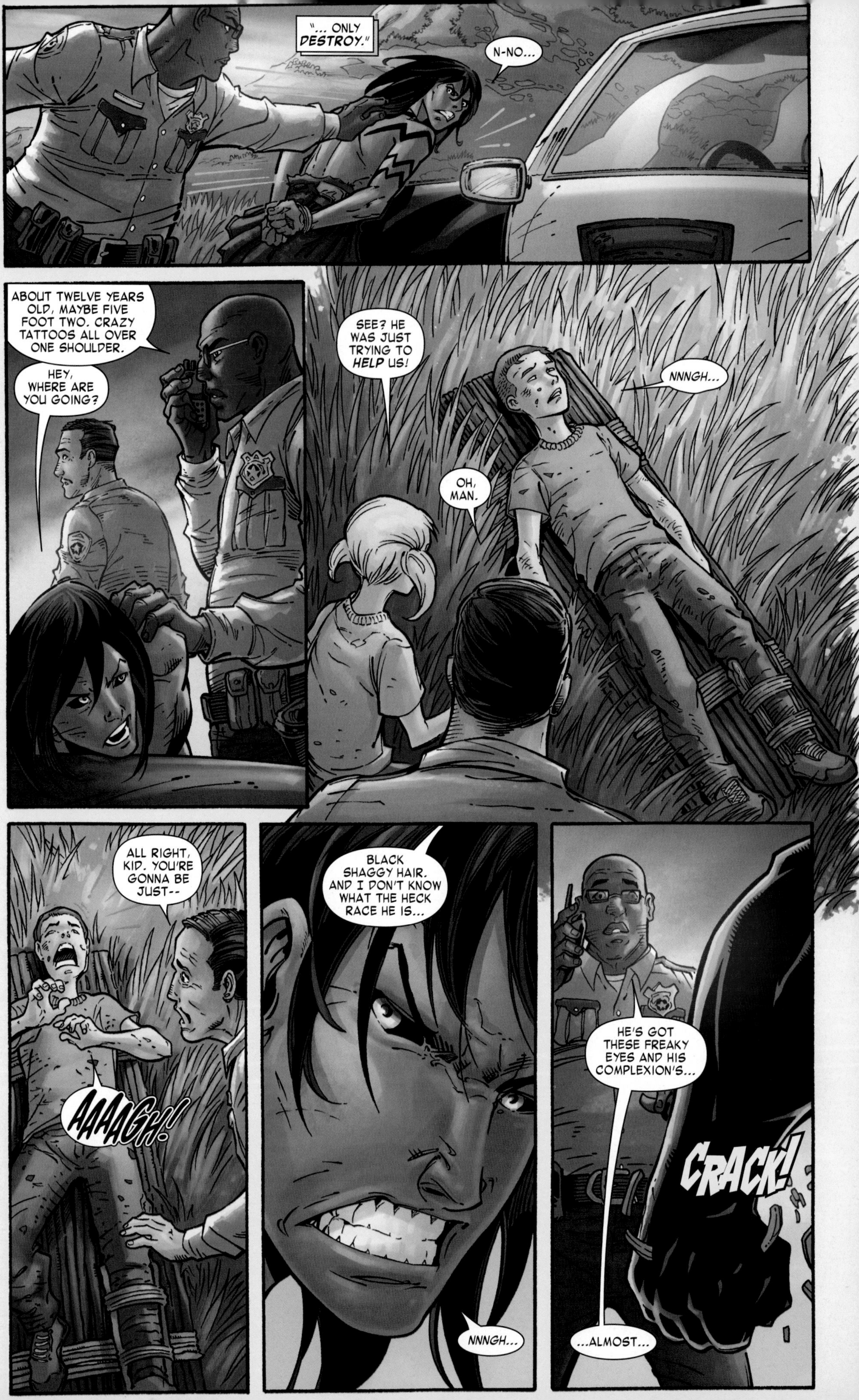
"... ONLY DESTROY."
N-NO...
ABOUT TWELVE YEARS OLD, MAYBE FIVE FOOT TWO. CRAZY TATTOOS ALL OVER ONE SHOULDER.
HEY, WHERE ARE YOU GOING?
SEE? HE WAS JUST TRYING TO HELP US!
NNNGH...
OH, MAN.
ALL RIGHT, KID. YOU'RE GONNA BE JUST--
AAAAGH!
BLACK SHAGGY HAIR. AND I DON'T KNOW WHAT THE HECK RACE HE IS...
NNNGH...
HE'S GOT THESE FREAKY EYES AND HIS COMPLEXION'S...
...ALMOST...
CRACK!

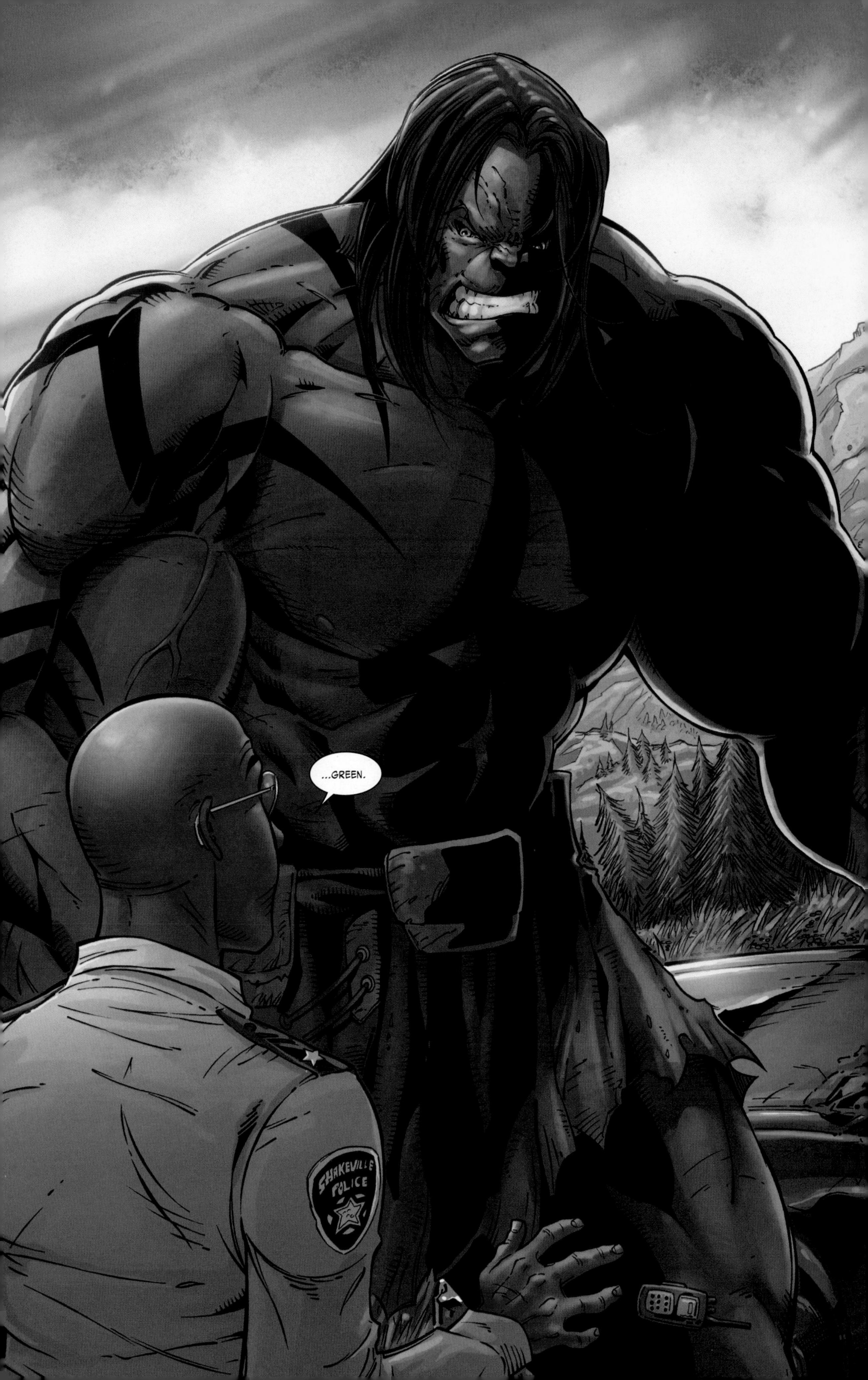
...GREEN.
SHAKEVILLE POLICE

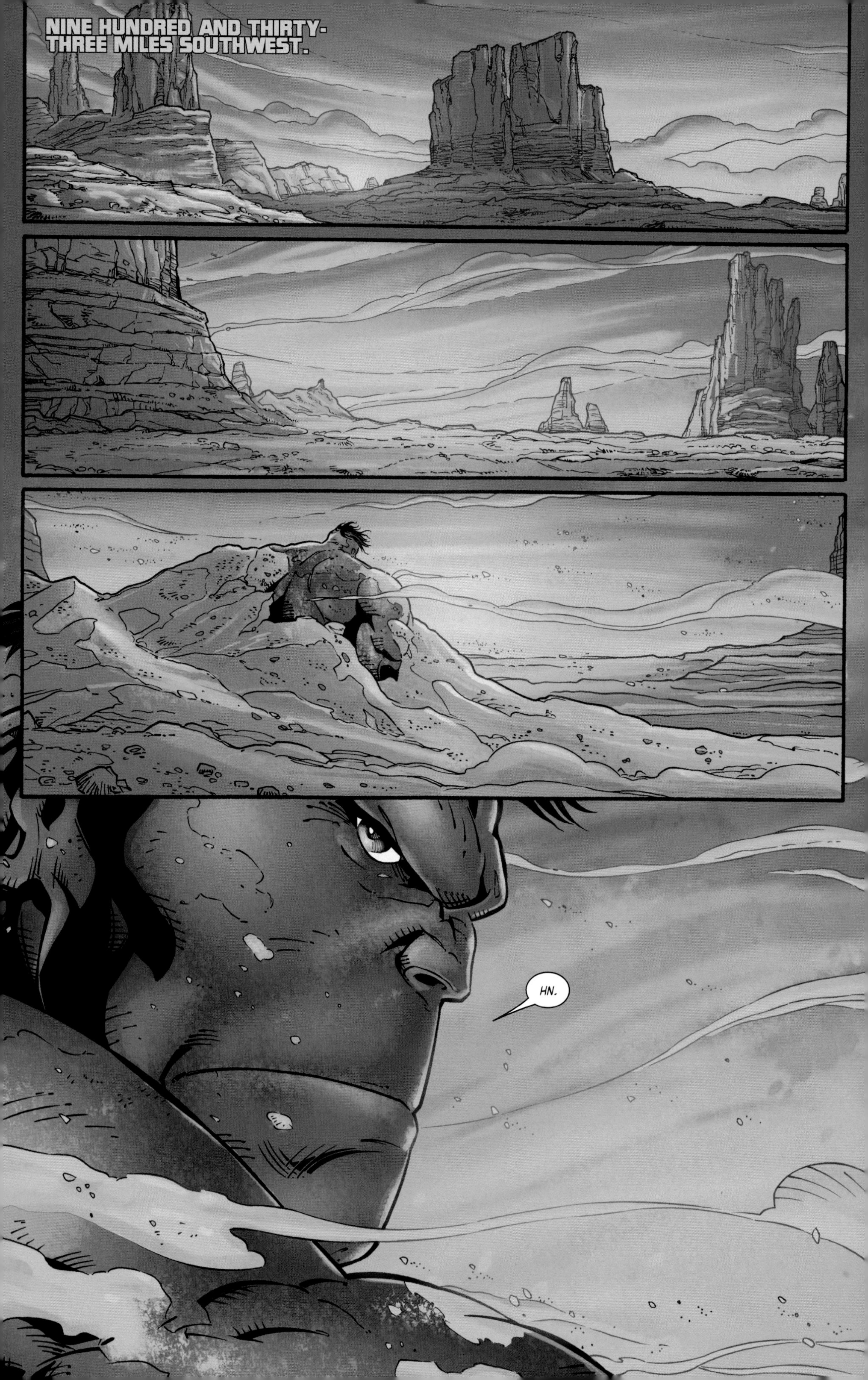
NINE HUNDRED AND THIRTY-THREE MILES SOUTHWEST.
HN.

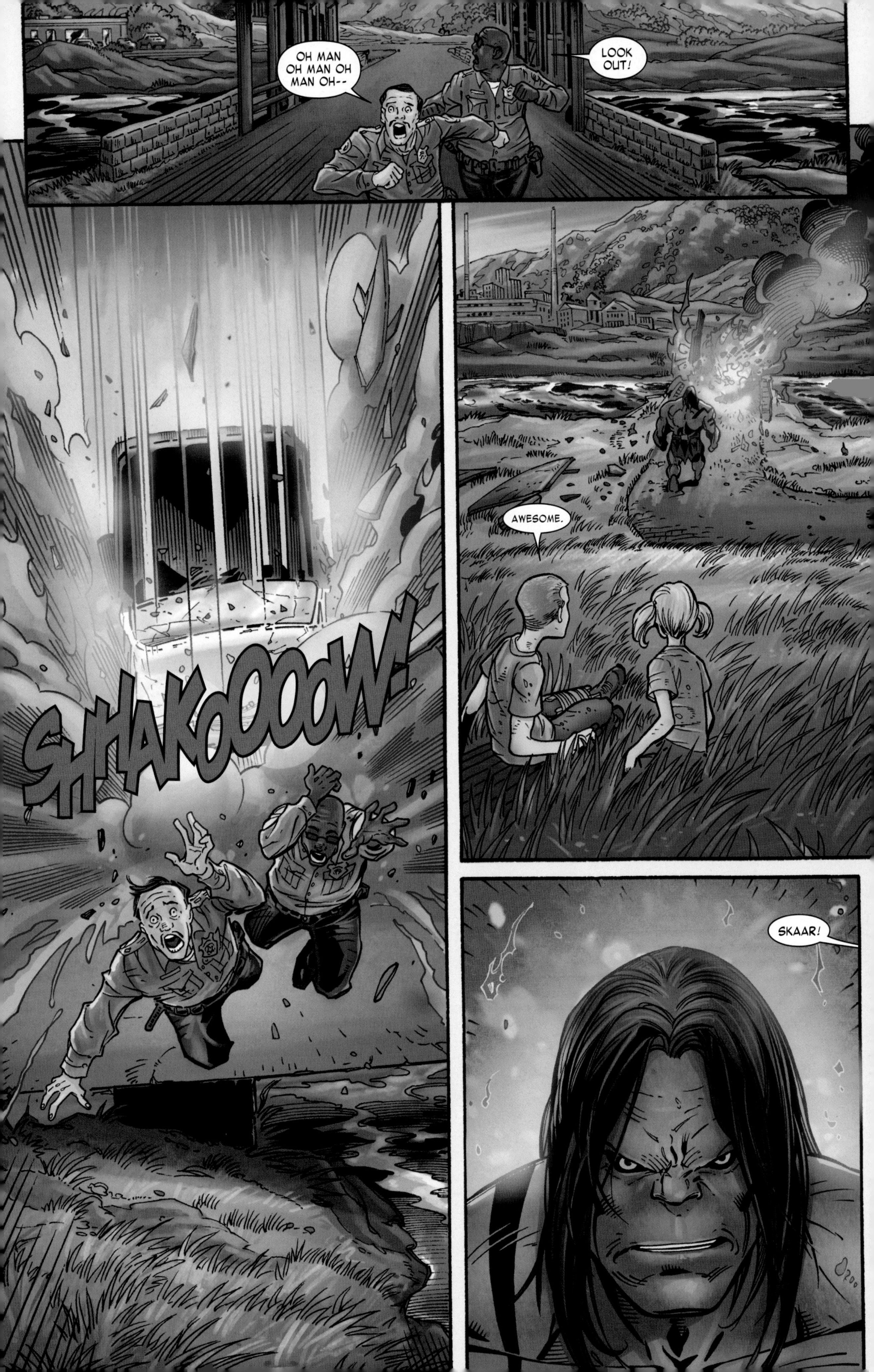
OH MAN OH MAN OH MAN OH--
LOOK OUT!
SHAKOOOOW!
AWESOME.
SKAAR!

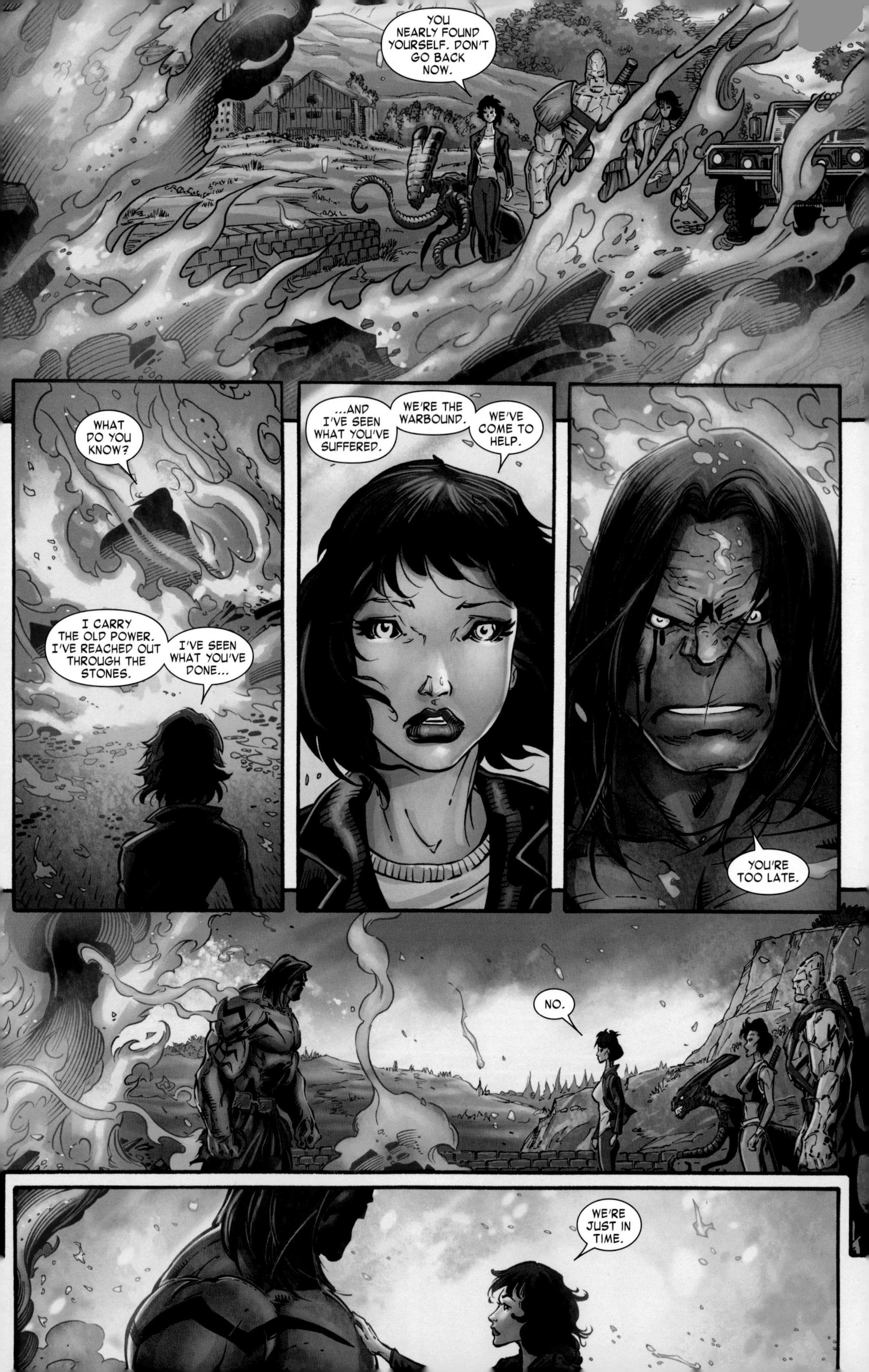
YOU NEARLY FOUND YOURSELF. DON'T GO BACK NOW.
WHAT DO YOU KNOW?
I CARRY THE OLD POWER. I'VE REACHED OUT THROUGH THE STONES.
I'VE SEEN WHAT YOU'VE DONE...
...AND I'VE SEEN WHAT YOU'VE SUFFERED.
WE'RE THE WARBOUND.
WE'VE COME TO HELP.
YOU'RE TOO LATE.
NO.
WE'RE JUST IN TIME.

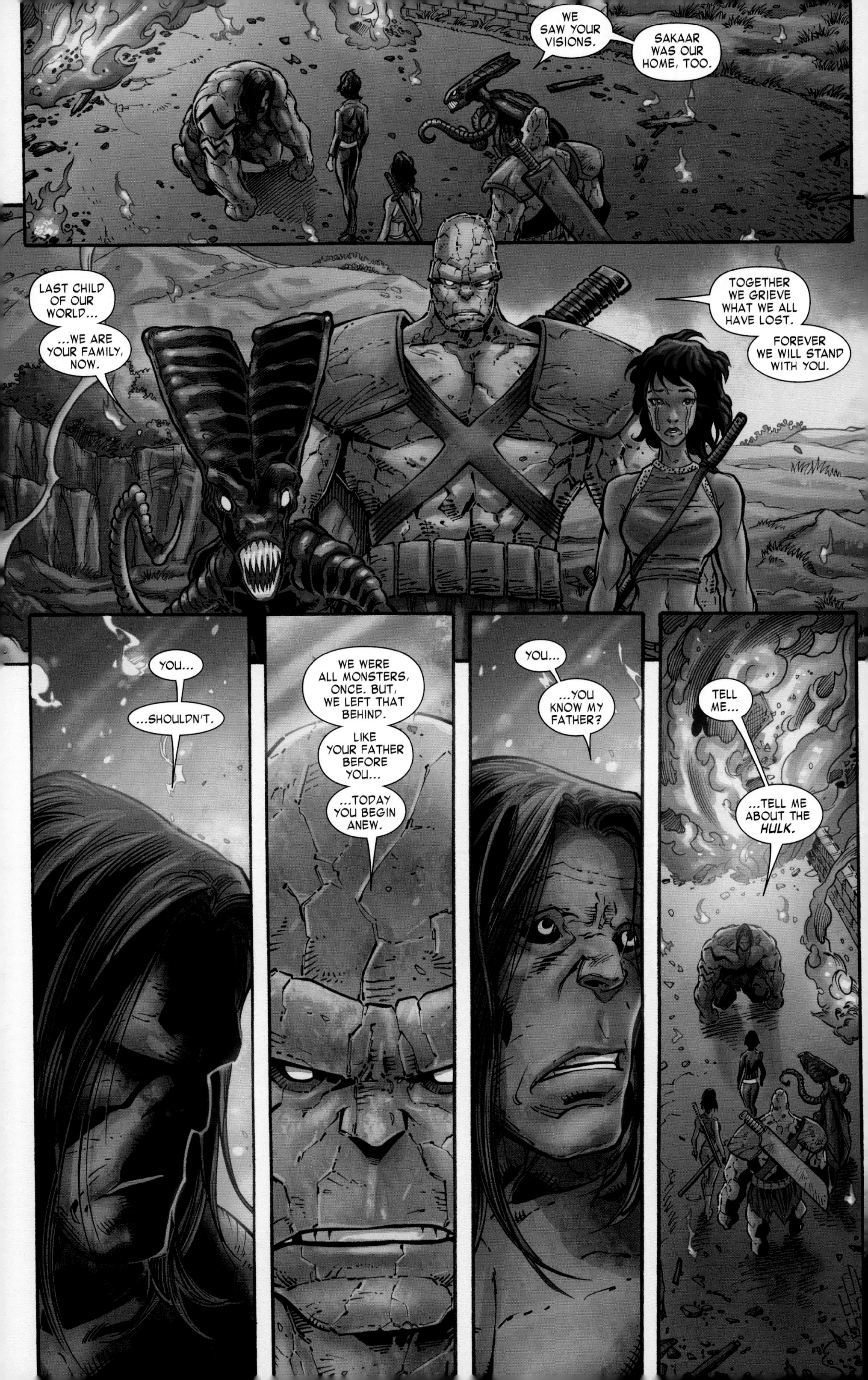
WE SAW YOUR VISIONS.
SAKAAR WAS OUR HOME, TOO.
LAST CHILD OF OUR WORLD...
...WE ARE YOUR FAMILY, NOW.
TOGETHER WE GRIEVE WHAT WE ALL HAVE LOST.
FOREVER WE WILL STAND WITH YOU.
YOU...
...SHOULDN'T.
WE WERE ALL MONSTERS, ONCE. BUT, WE LEFT THAT BEHIND.
LIKE YOUR FATHER BEFORE YOU...
...TODAY YOU BEGIN ANEW.
YOU...
...YOU KNOW MY FATHER?
TELL ME...
...TELL ME ABOUT THE HULK.

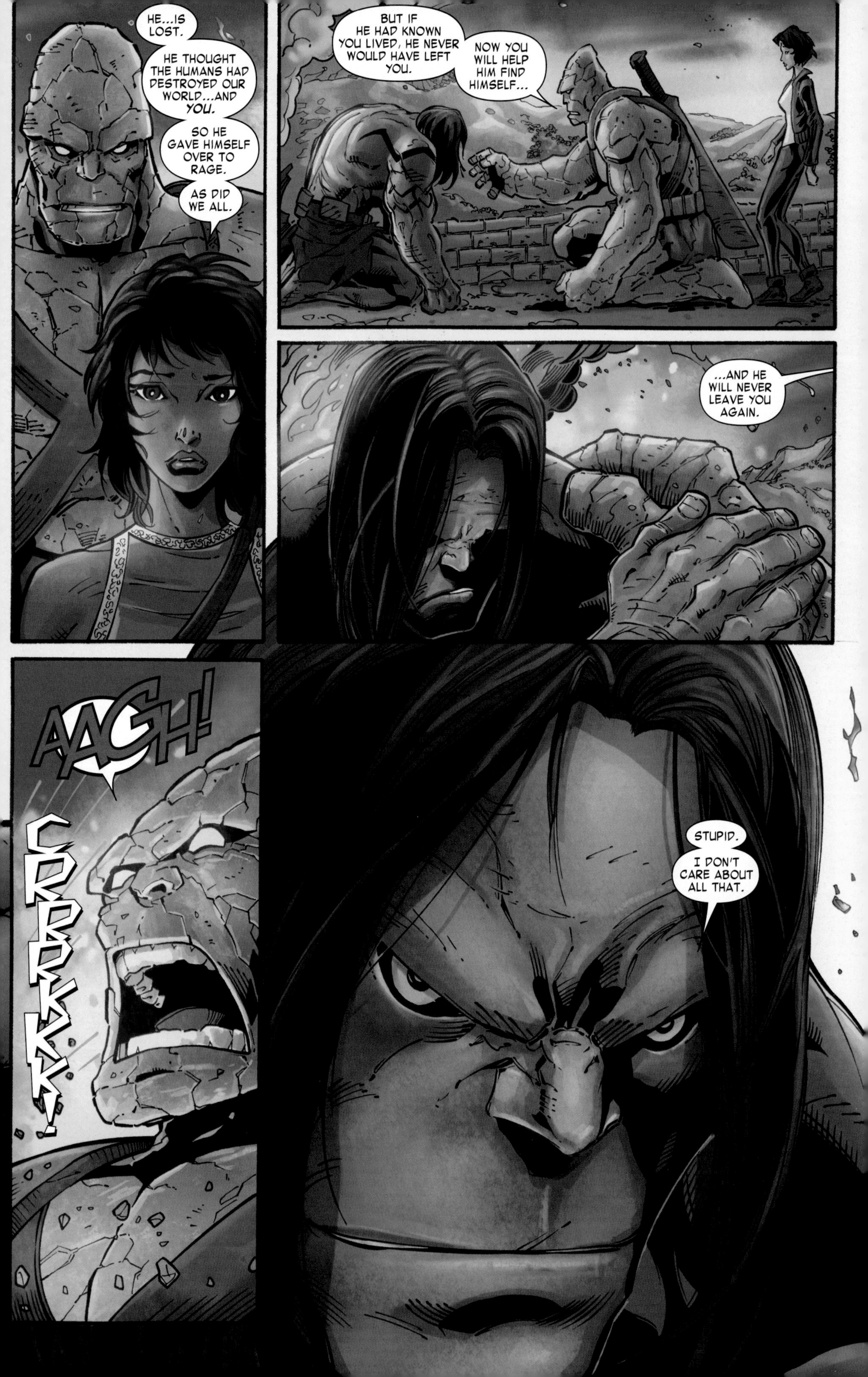
HE...IS LOST.
HE THOUGHT THE HUMANS HAD DESTROYED OUR WORLD...AND YOU.
SO HE GAVE HIMSELF OVER TO RAGE.
AS DID WE ALL.
BUT IF HE HAD KNOWN YOU LIVED, HE NEVER WOULD HAVE LEFT YOU.
NOW YOU WILL HELP HIM FIND HIMSELF...
...AND HE WILL NEVER LEAVE YOU AGAIN.
AAGH!
CRRRKKK!
STUPID.
I DON'T CARE ABOUT ALL THAT.

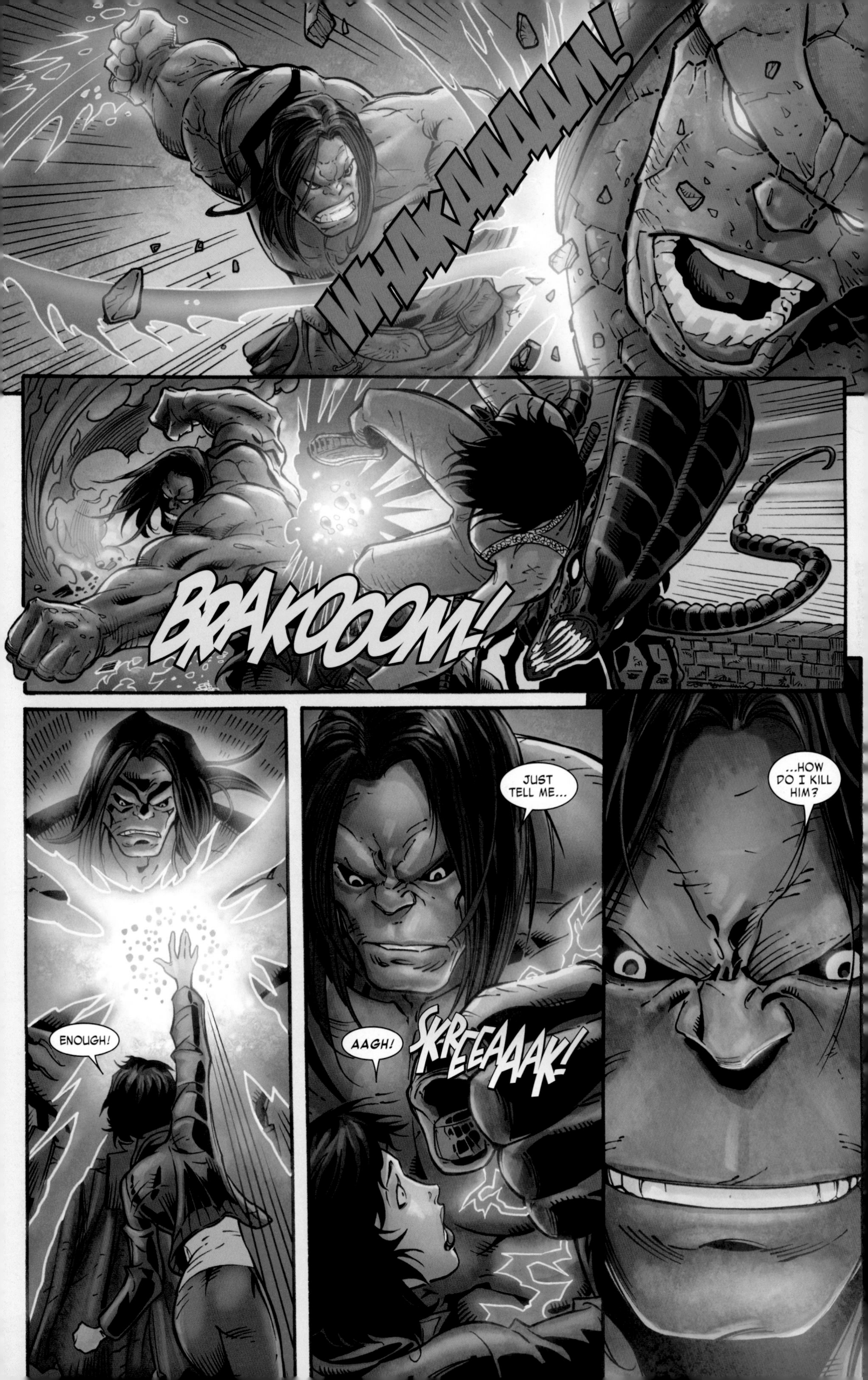
WHAKAAAAAM!
BRAKOOOOM!
ENOUGH!
JUST TELL ME...
AAGH!
SKREEEAAAK!
...HOW DO I KILL HIM?

SHAKOOOOOM!

SHAKOOOOOOM!

SHAKOOOOOOOOOM!

SIMPLE...

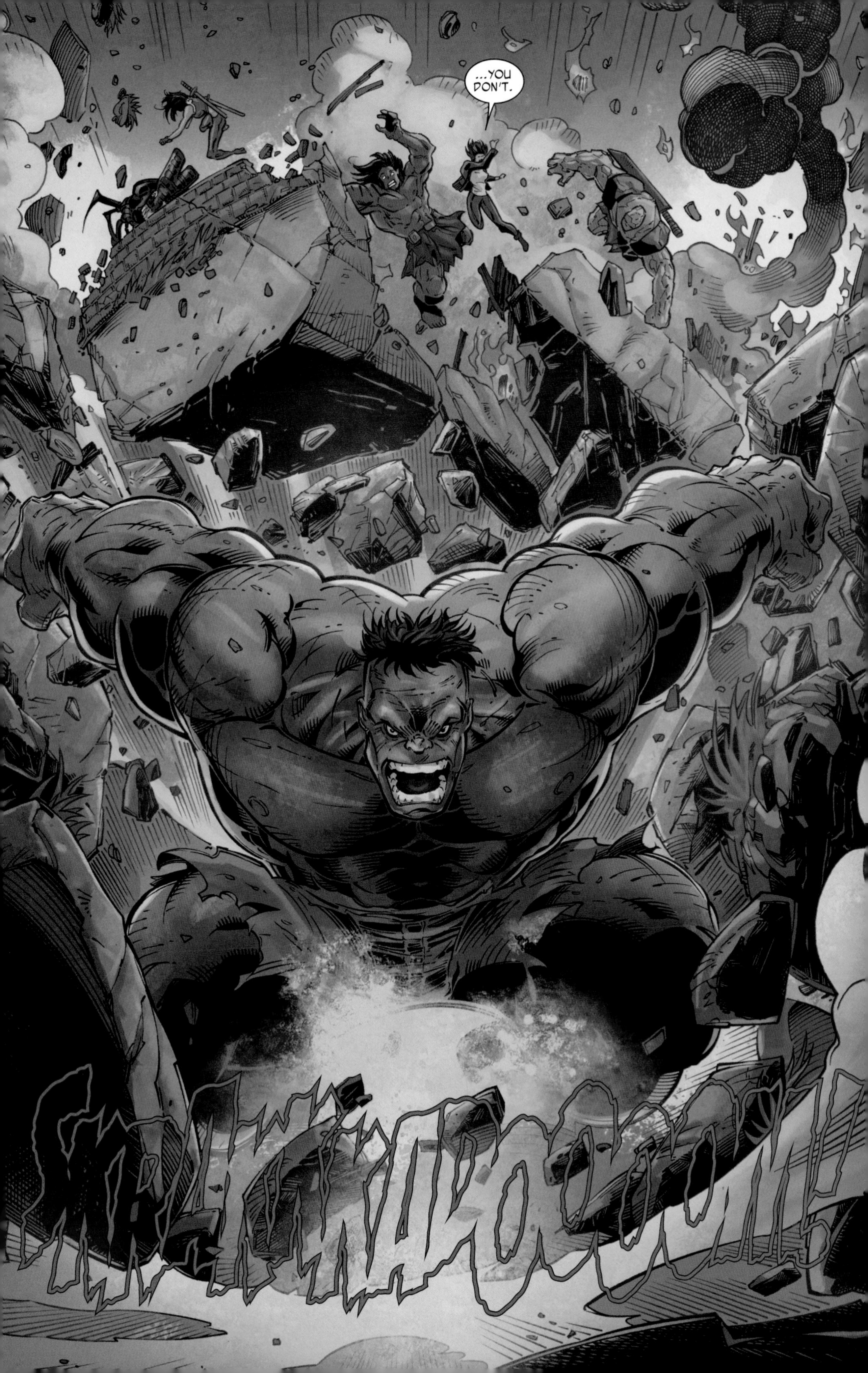
...YOU DON'T.

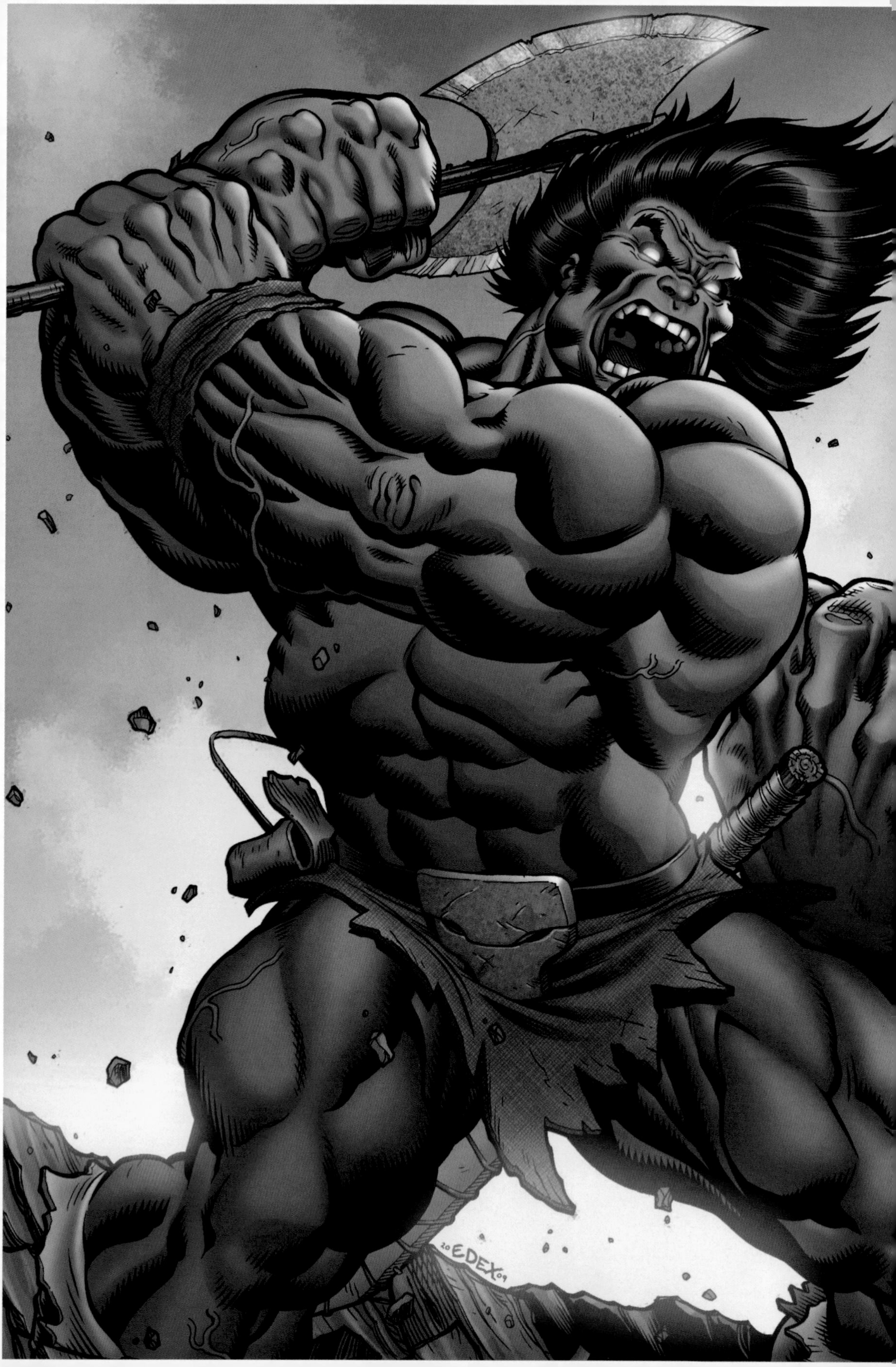
EDEX

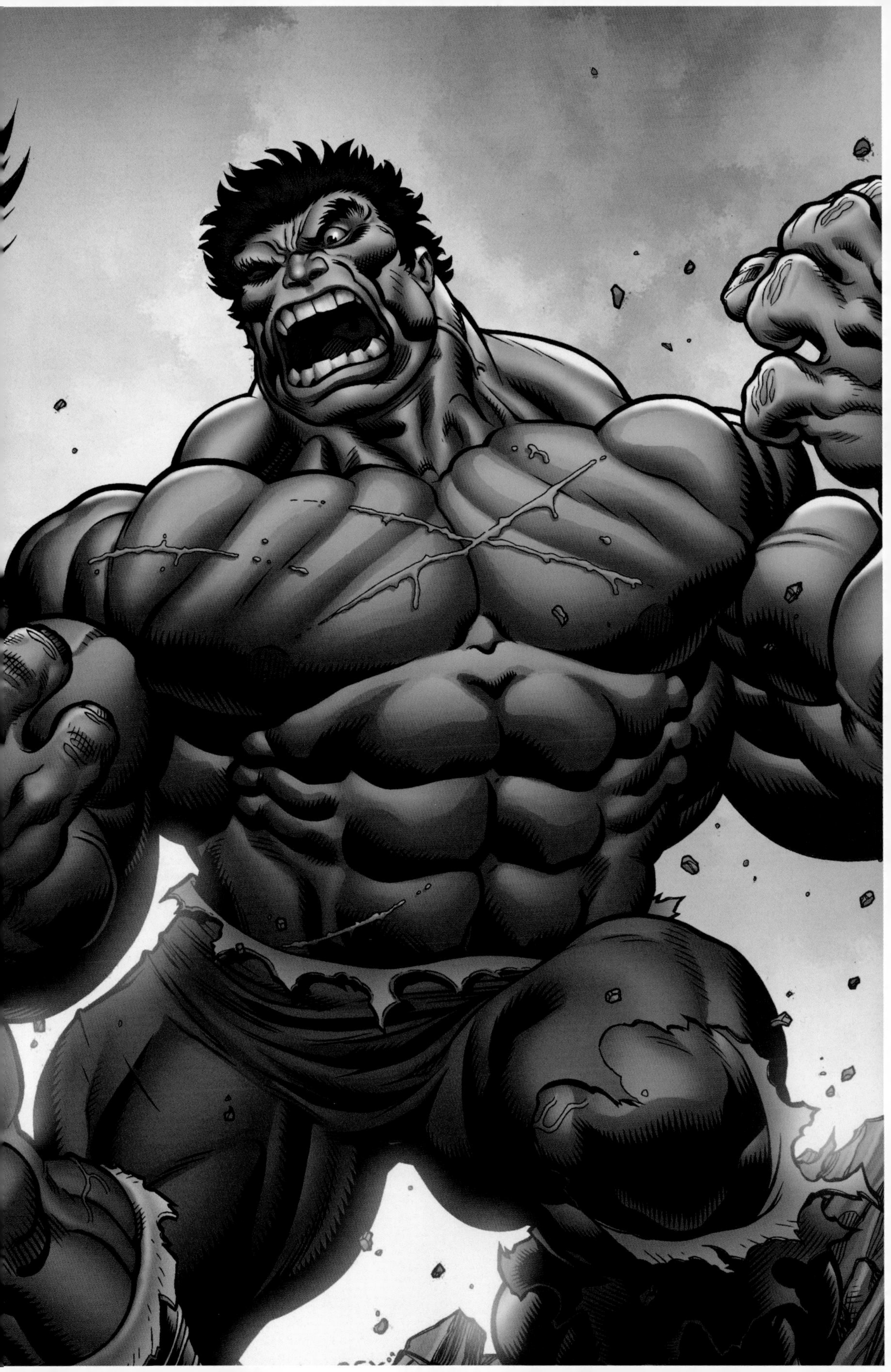

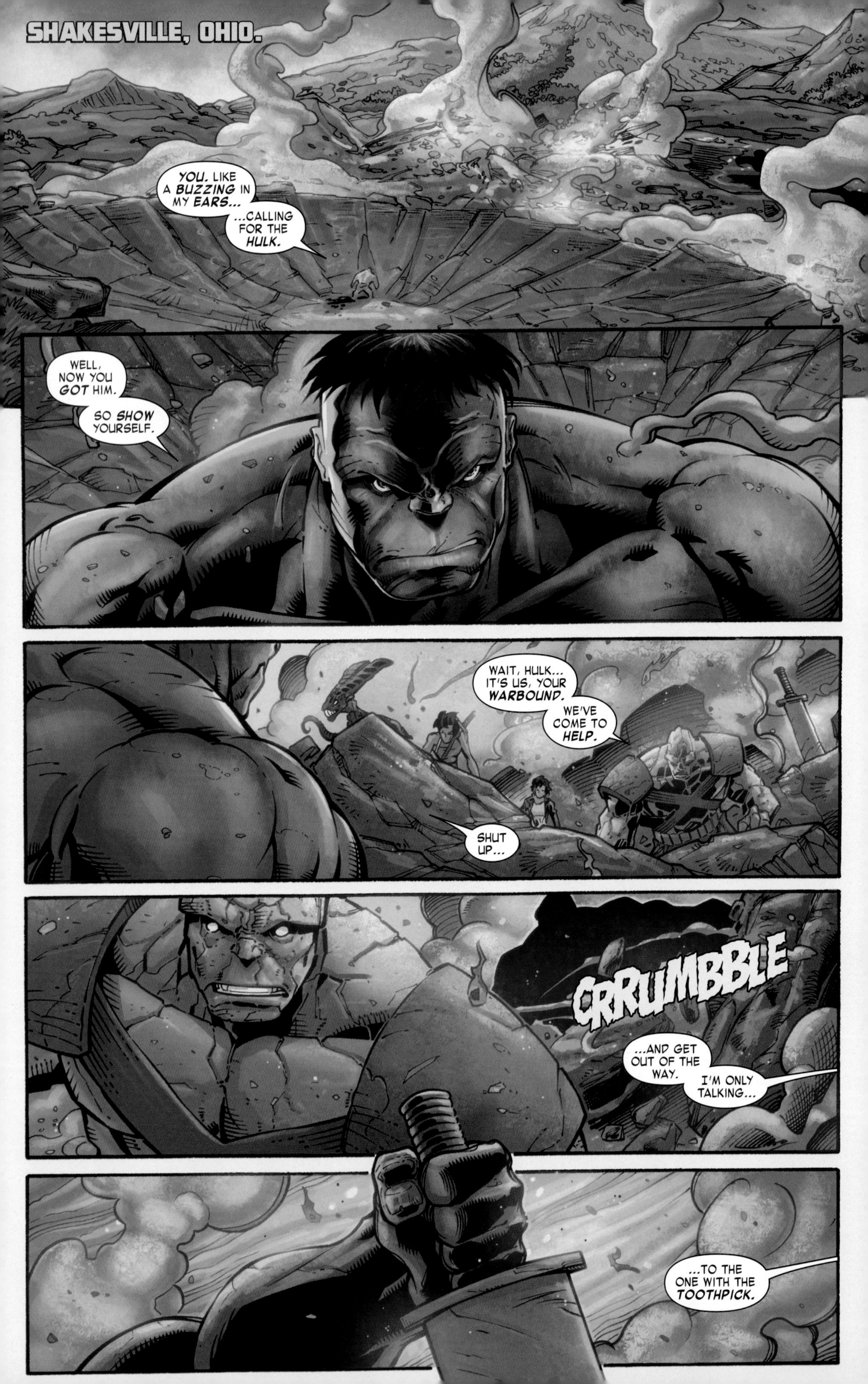
SHAKESVILLE, OHIO.
YOU. LIKE A BUZZING IN MY EARS...
...CALLING FOR THE HULK.
WELL, NOW YOU GOT HIM.
SO SHOW YOURSELF.
WAIT, HULK... IT'S US, YOUR WARBOUND.
WE'VE COME TO HELP.
SHUT UP...
CRRUMBBLE
...AND GET OUT OF THE WAY.
I'M ONLY TALKING...
...TO THE ONE WITH THE TOOTHPICK.

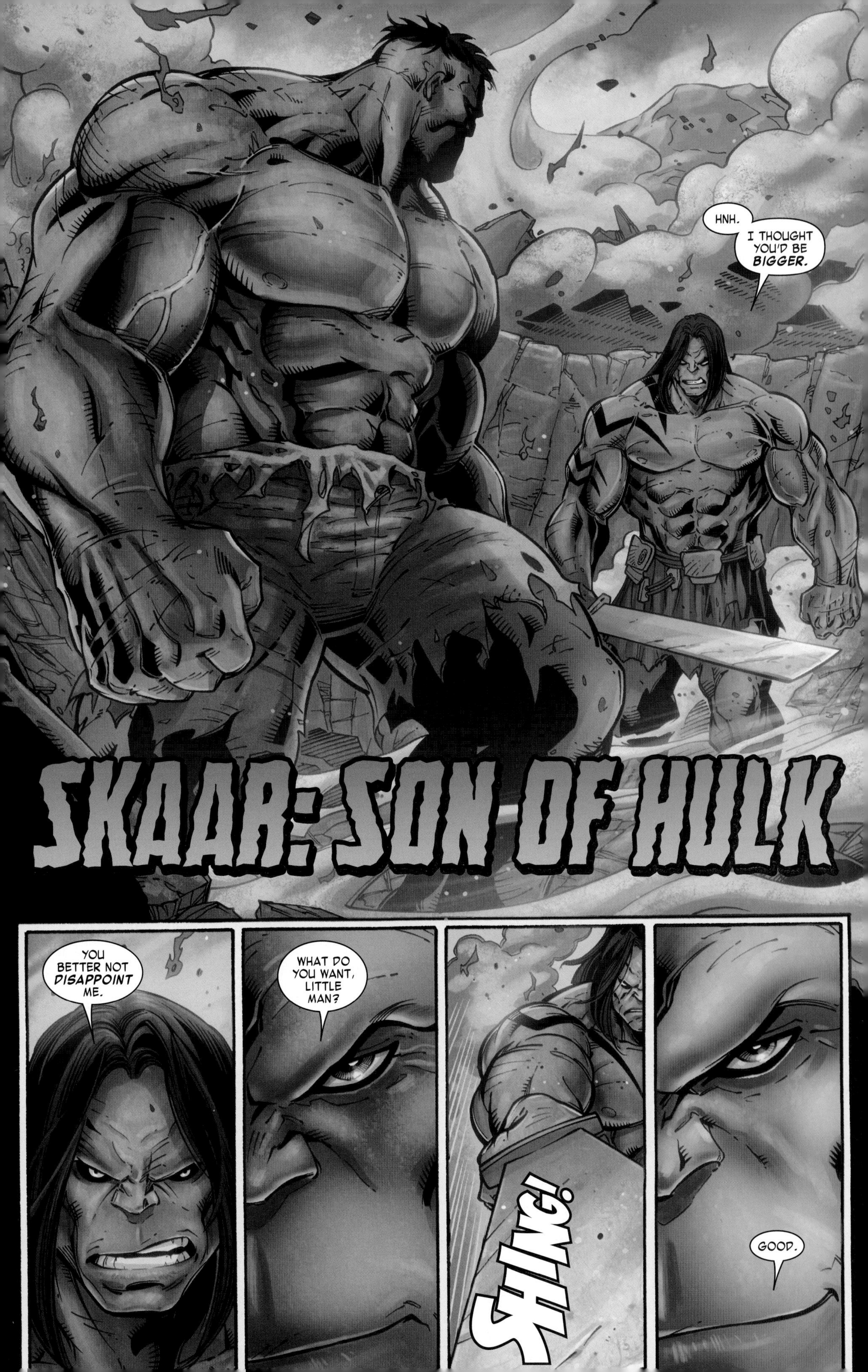
HNH. I THOUGHT YOU'D BE BIGGER.
SKAAR: SON OF HULK
YOU BETTER NOT DISAPPOINT ME.
WHAT DO YOU WANT, LITTLE MAN?
SHING!
GOOD.

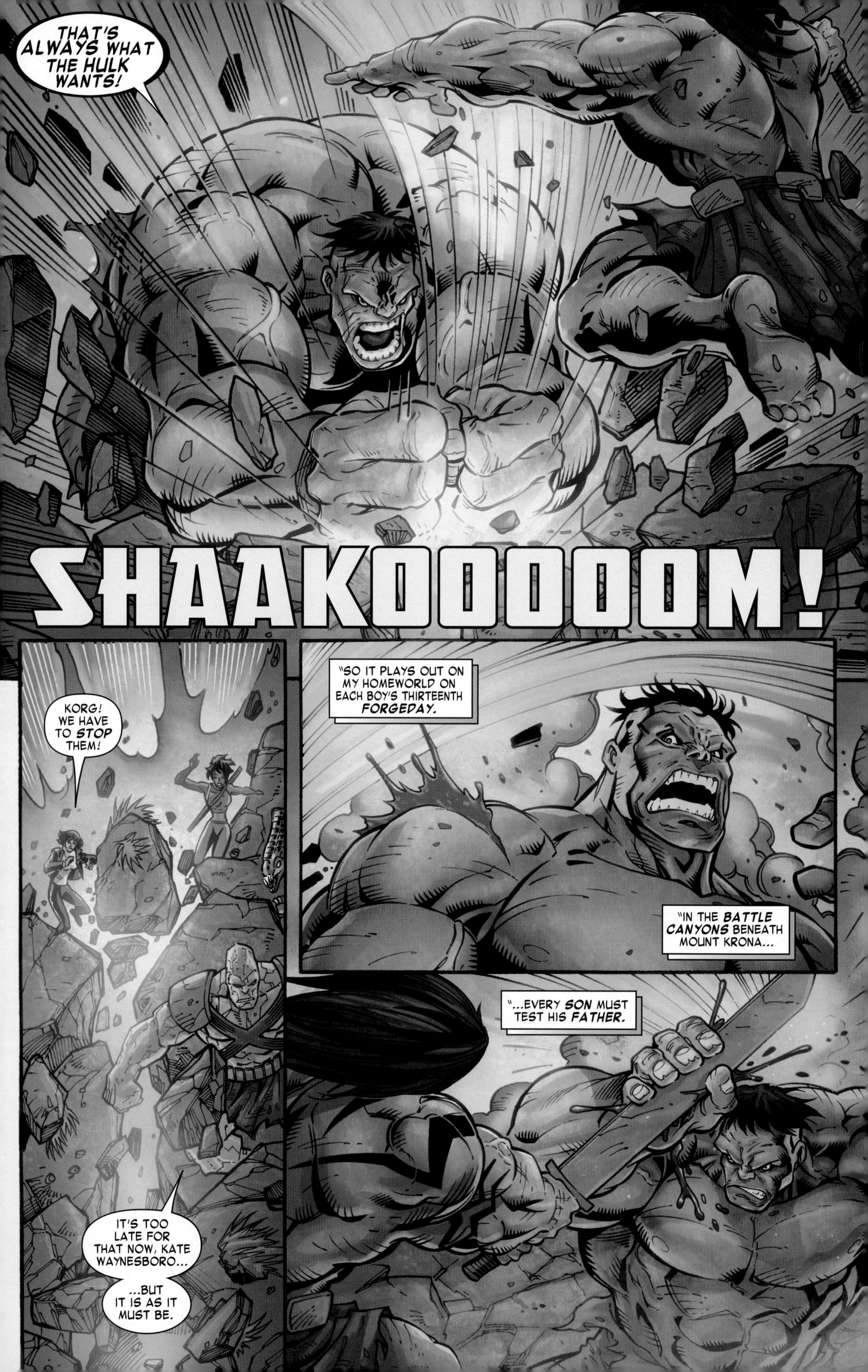
THAT'S ALWAYS WHAT THE HULK WANTS!
SHAAKOOOOOM!
KORG! WE HAVE TO STOP THEM!
"SO IT PLAYS OUT ON MY HOMEWORLD ON EACH BOY'S THIRTEENTH FORGEDAY.
"IN THE BATTLE CANYONS BENEATH MOUNT KRONA...
"...EVERY SON MUST TEST HIS FATHER.
IT'S TOO LATE FOR THAT NOW, KATE WAYNESBORO...
...BUT IT IS AS IT MUST BE.

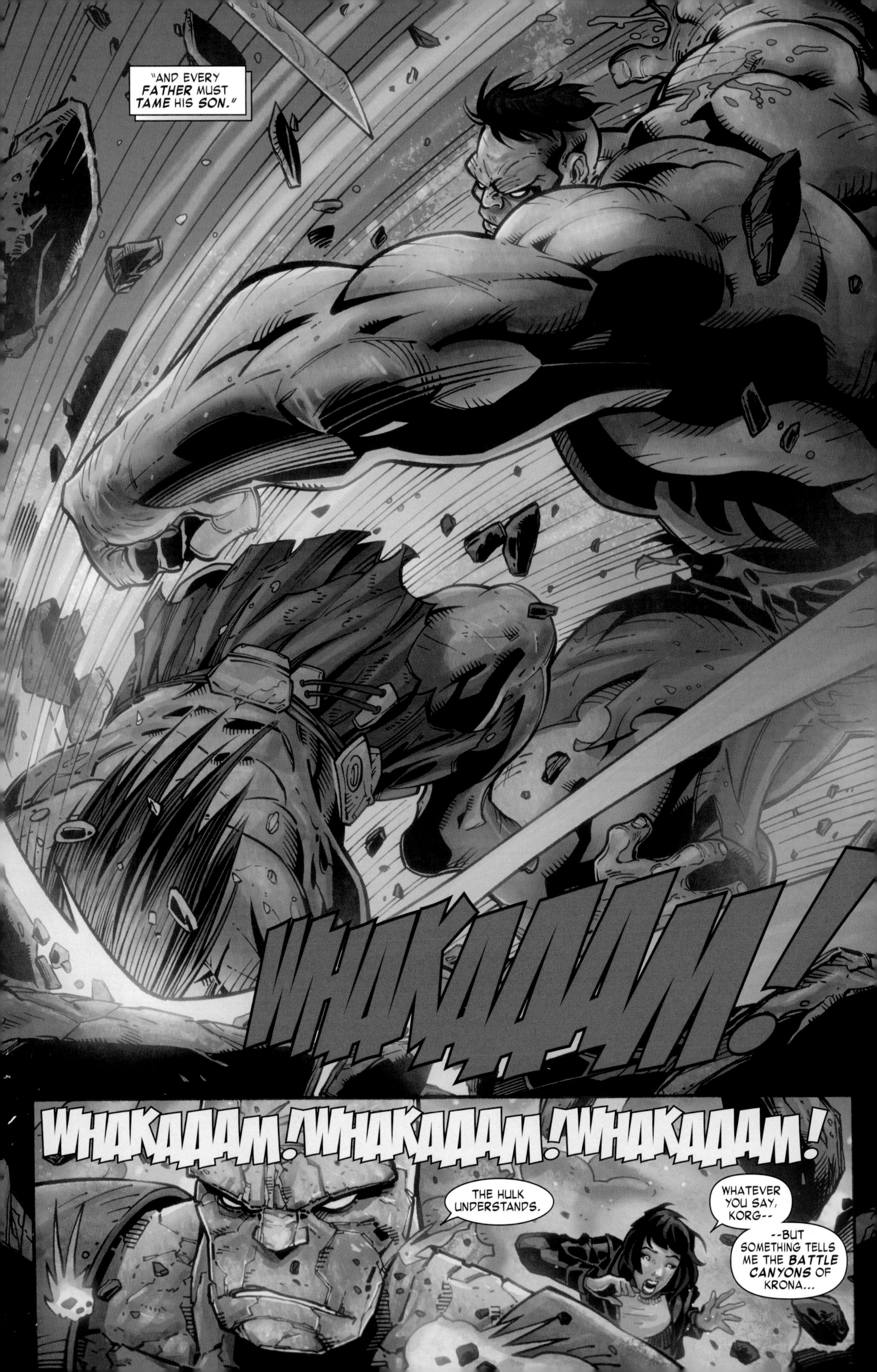
"AND EVERY FATHER MUST TAME HIS SON."
WHAKAAAM!
WHAKAAAM! WHAKAAAM! WHAKAAAM!
THE HULK UNDERSTANDS.
WHATEVER YOU SAY, KORG--
--BUT SOMETHING TELLS ME THE BATTLE CANYONS OF KRONA...

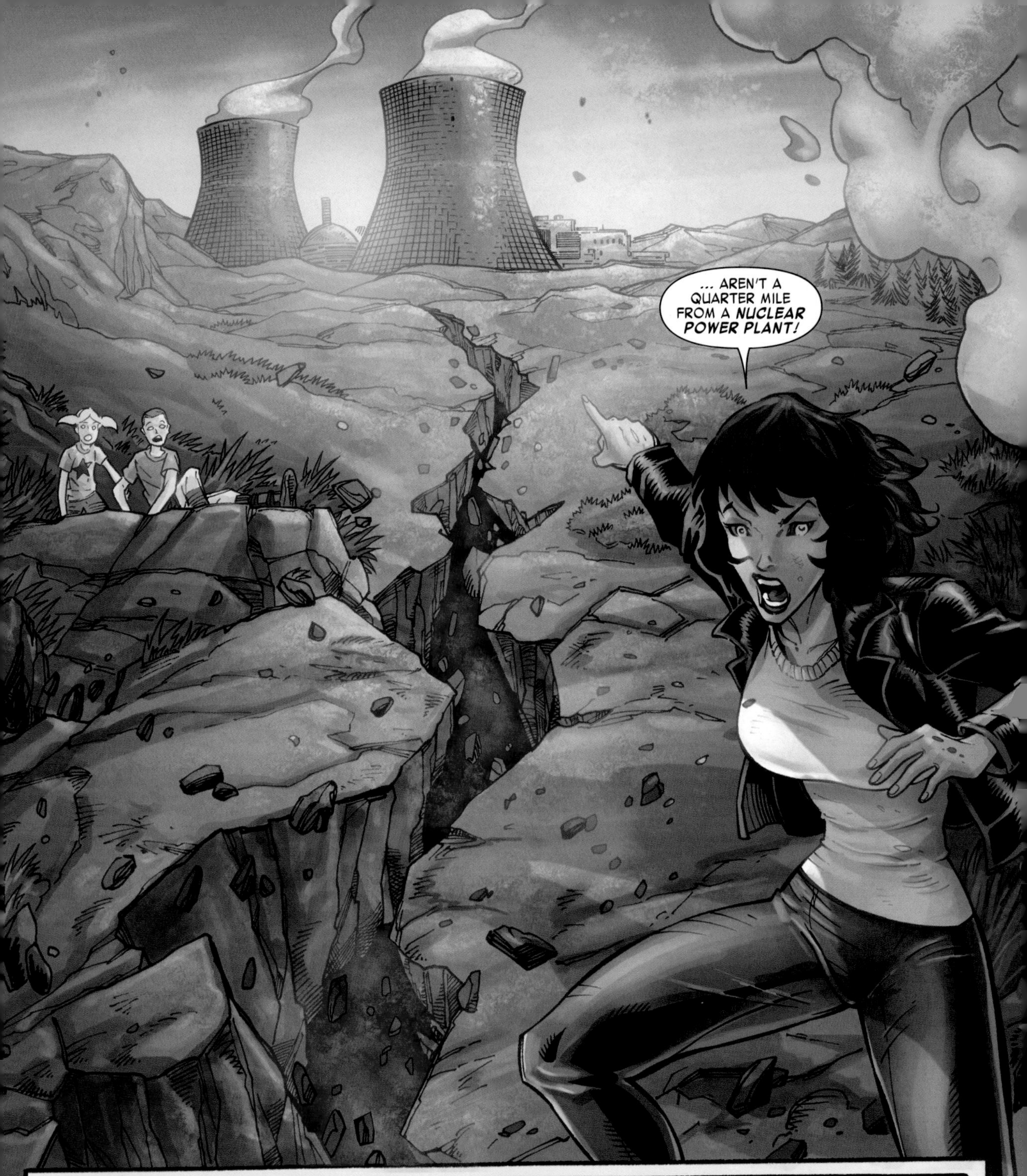
... AREN'T A QUARTER MILE FROM A NUCLEAR POWER PLANT!

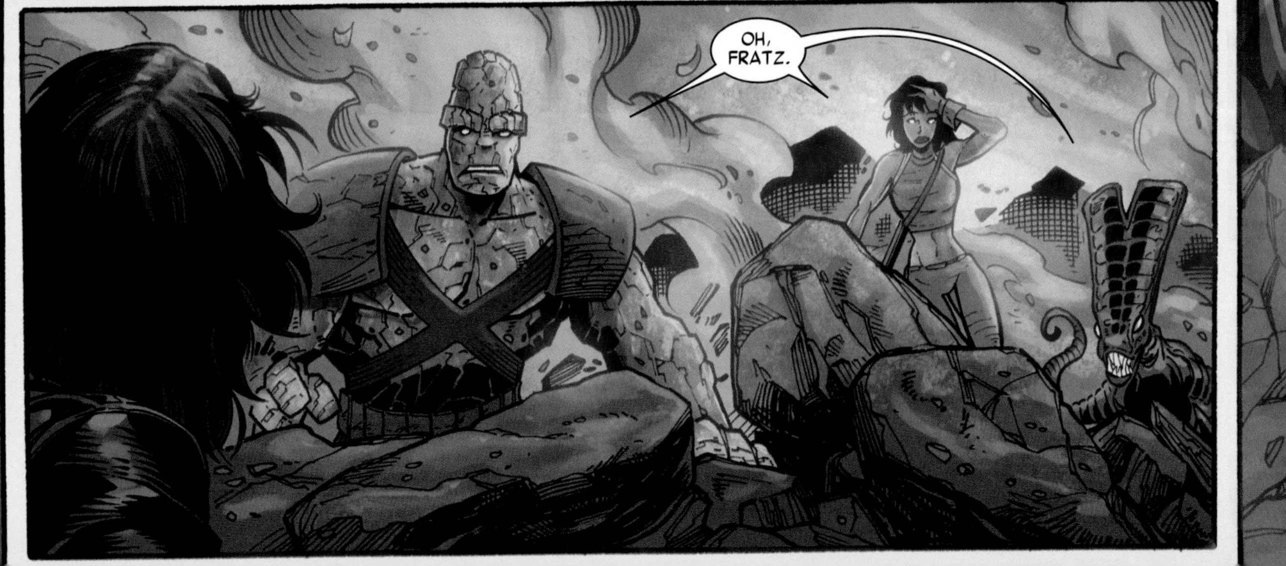
OH, FRATZ.

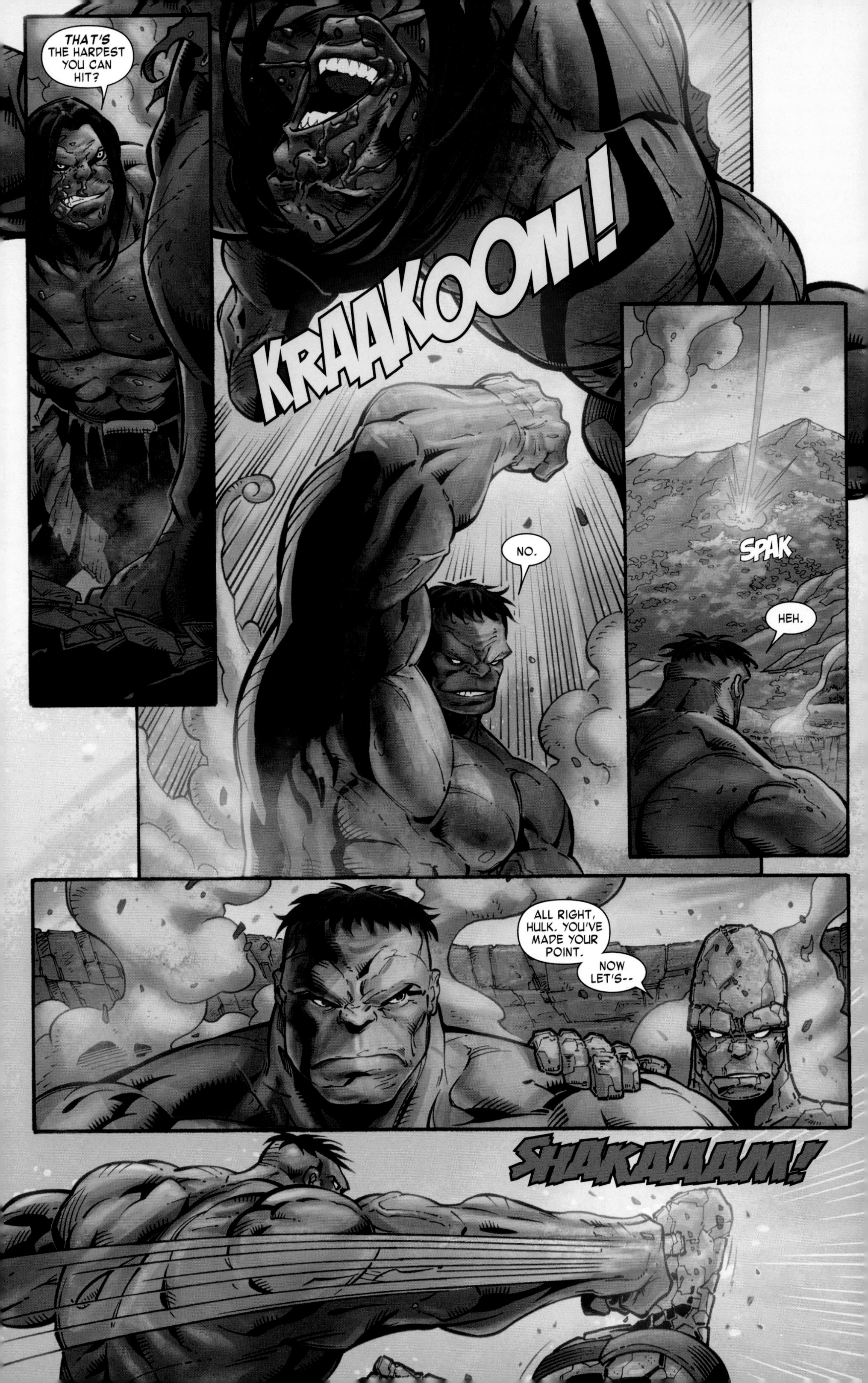
THAT'S THE HARDEST YOU CAN HIT?
KRAAKOOM!
NO.
SPAK
HEH.
ALL RIGHT, HULK. YOU'VE MADE YOUR POINT.
NOW LET'S--
SHAKAAAAM!

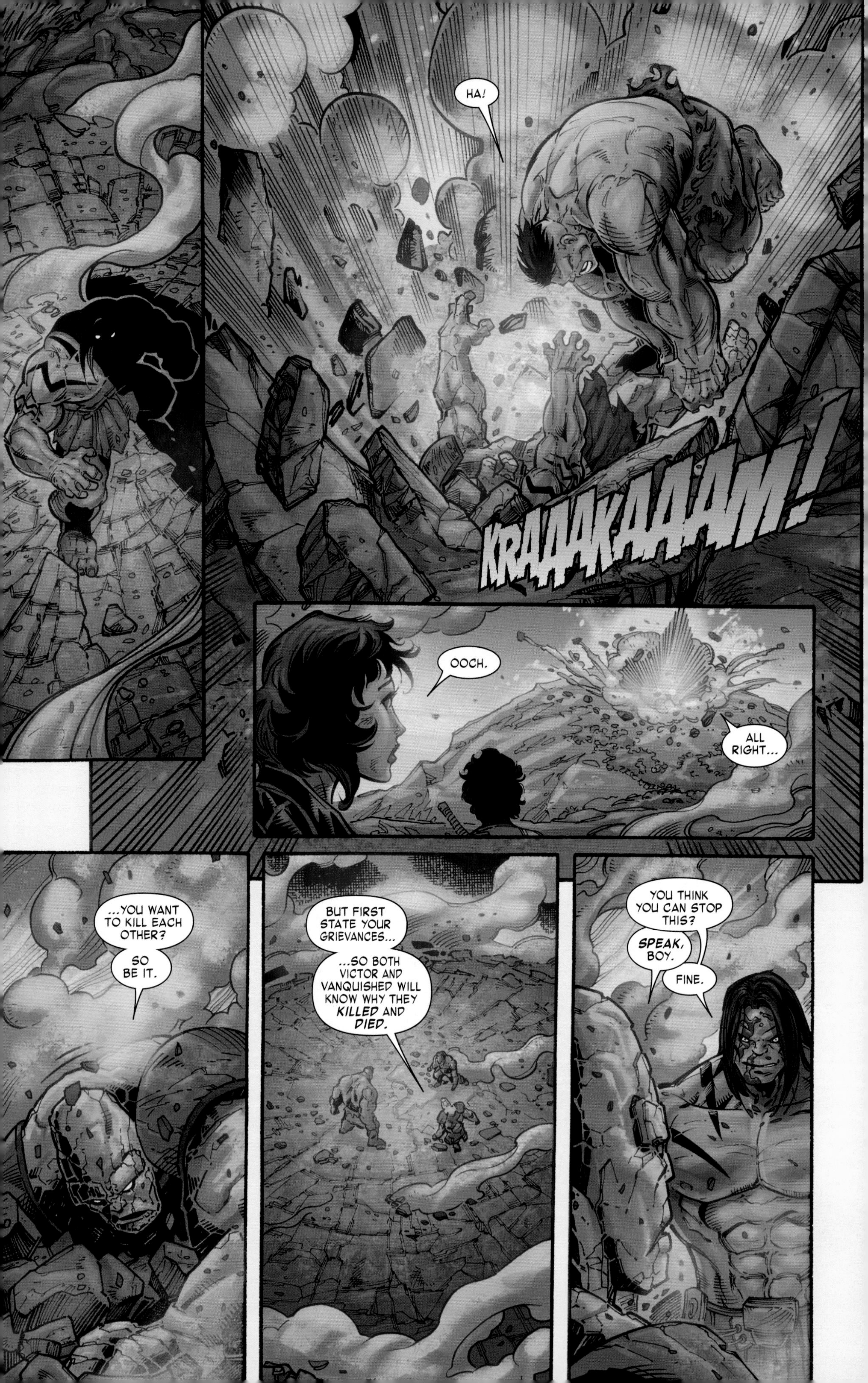
HA!
KRAAAKAAAM!
OOCH.
ALL RIGHT...
...YOU WANT TO KILL EACH OTHER?
SO BE IT.
BUT FIRST STATE YOUR GRIEVANCES...
...SO BOTH VICTOR AND VANQUISHED WILL KNOW WHY THEY KILLED AND DIED.
YOU THINK YOU CAN STOP THIS?
SPEAK, BOY.
FINE.

MY MOTHER SAID YOU WERE A HERO.

EVERYTHING I NEVER WAS.

BUT I NEVER GOT TO ASK HER...

"...WHAT KIND OF HERO LEAVES HIS SON TO BURN...

"...HIS PEOPLE TO BLEED...

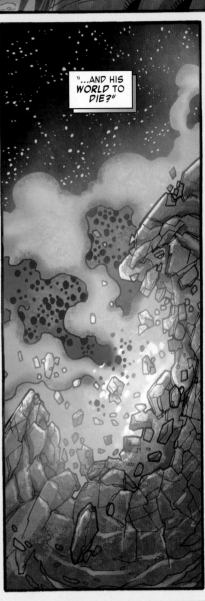

"...AND HIS WORLD TO DIE?"

CRAZY LONGHAIR! WHY'RE YOU BOTHERING HULK WITH YOUR STUPID STORIES?

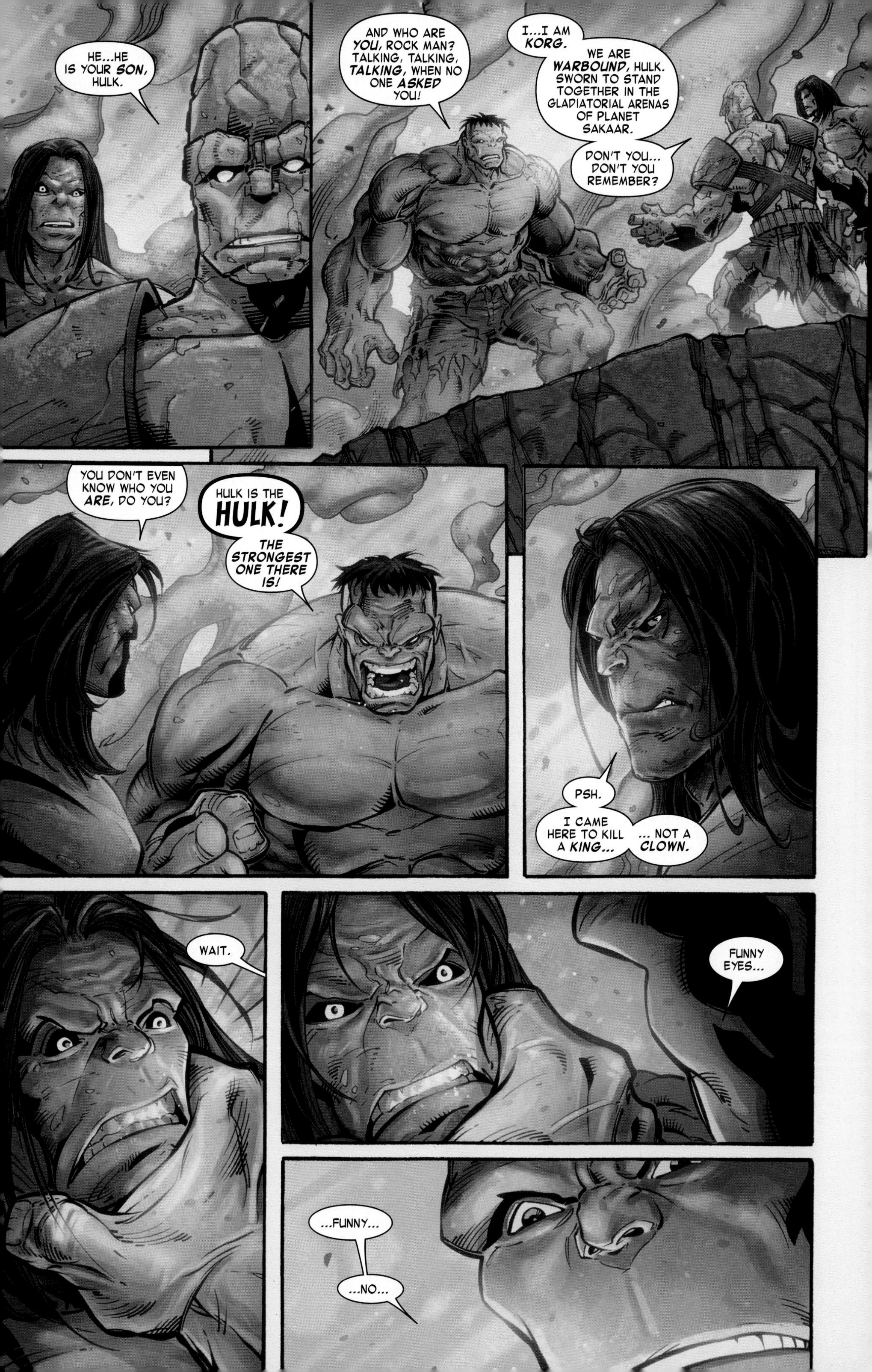
HE...HE IS YOUR SON, HULK.
AND WHO ARE YOU, ROCK MAN? TALKING, TALKING, TALKING, WHEN NO ONE ASKED YOU!
I...I AM KORG.
WE ARE WARBOUND, HULK. SWORN TO STAND TOGETHER IN THE GLADIATORIAL ARENAS OF PLANET SAKAAR.
DON'T YOU... DON'T YOU REMEMBER?
YOU DON'T EVEN KNOW WHO YOU ARE, DO YOU?
HULK IS THE HULK!
THE STRONGEST ONE THERE IS!
PSH.
I CAME HERE TO KILL A KING...
... NOT A CLOWN.
WAIT.
FUNNY EYES...
...FUNNY...
...NO...

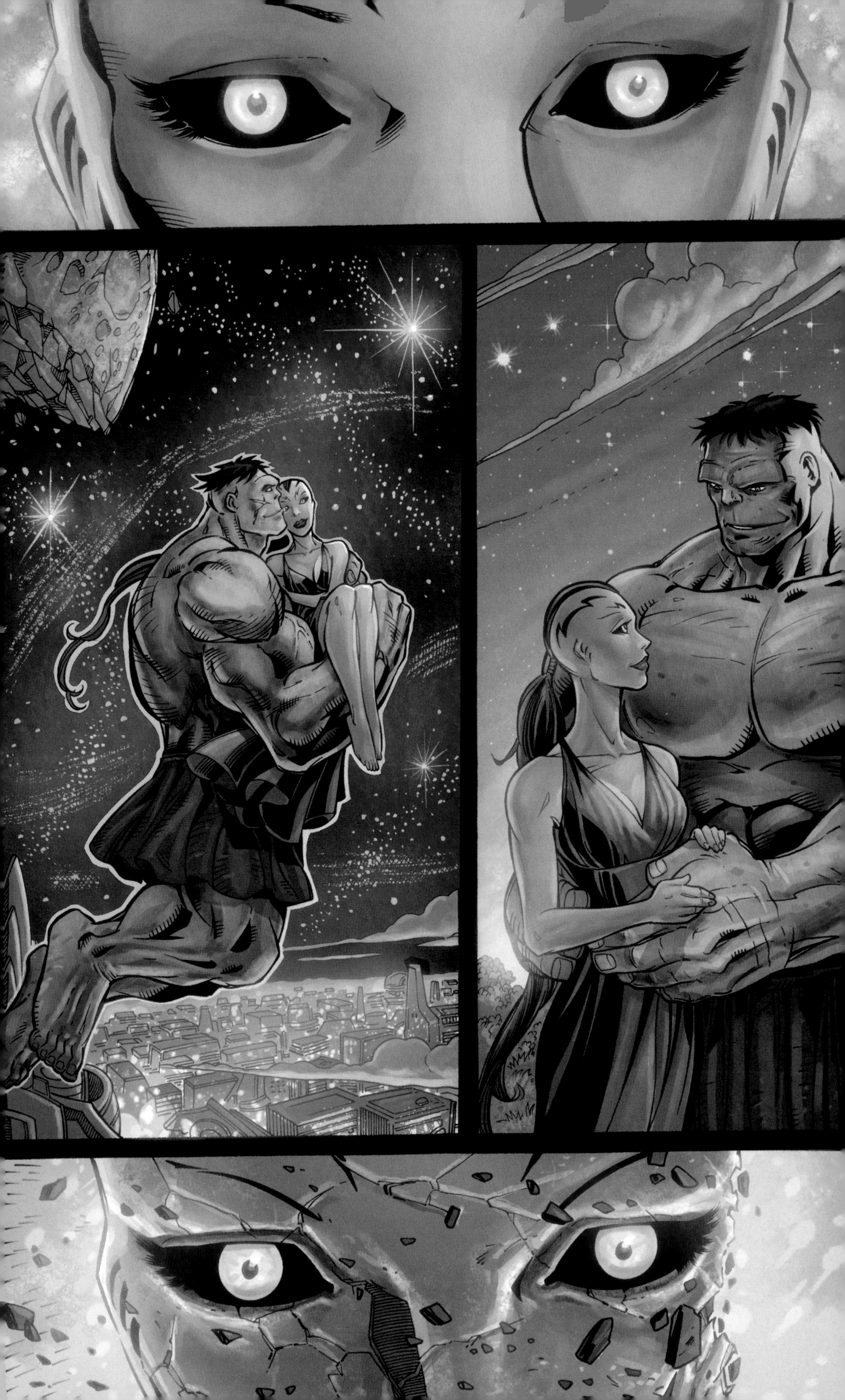

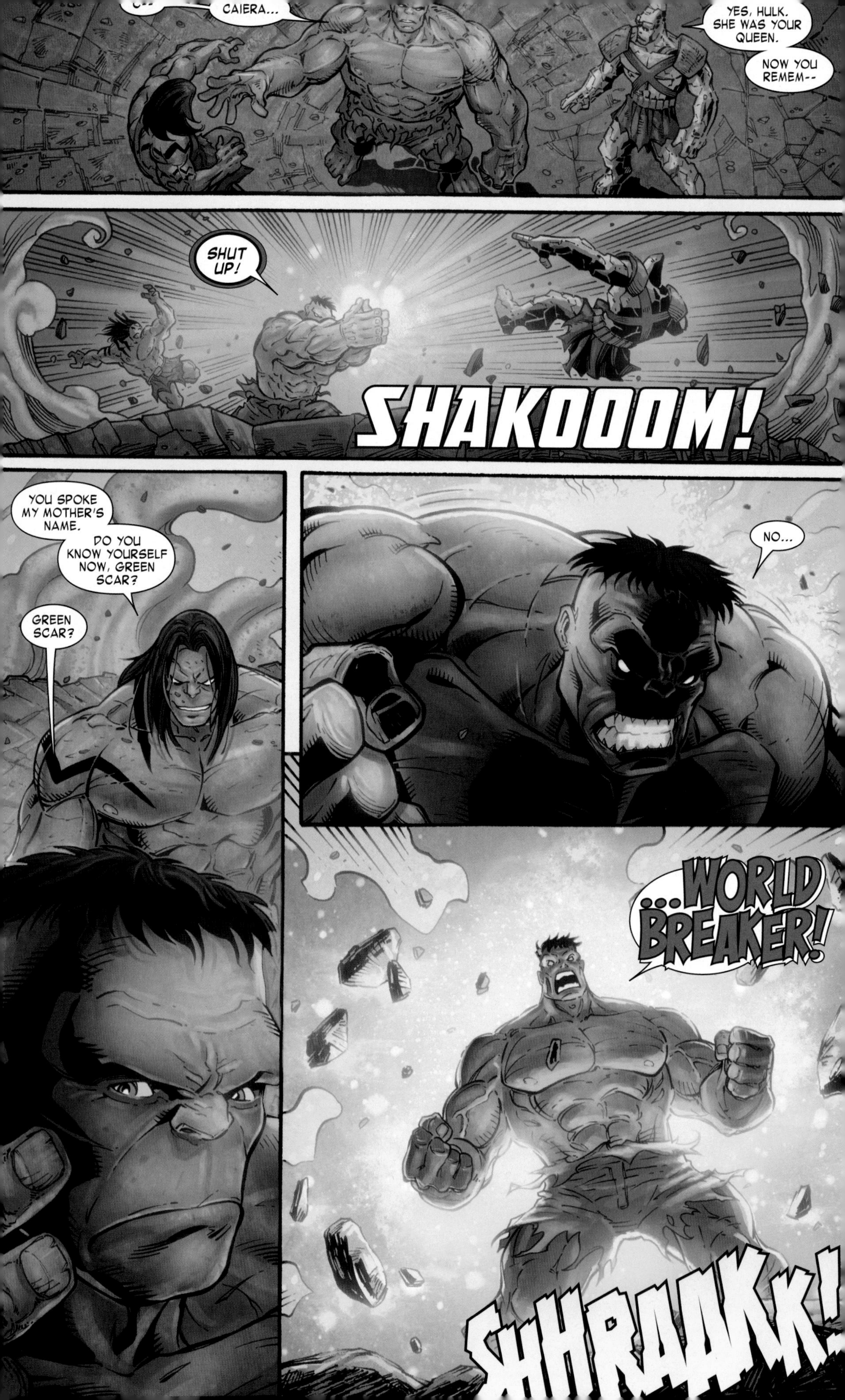
CAIERA...
YES, HULK. SHE WAS YOUR QUEEN.
NOW YOU REMEM--
SHUT UP!
SHAKOOOM!
YOU SPOKE MY MOTHER'S NAME.
DO YOU KNOW YOURSELF NOW, GREEN SCAR?
GREEN SCAR?
NO...
...WORLD BREAKER!
SHHRAAKK!

NO. NO.

NNNEVER...

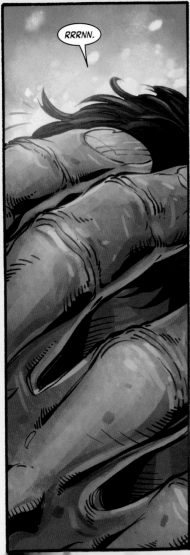

RRRNN.

HNH.

HULK BORED NOW.

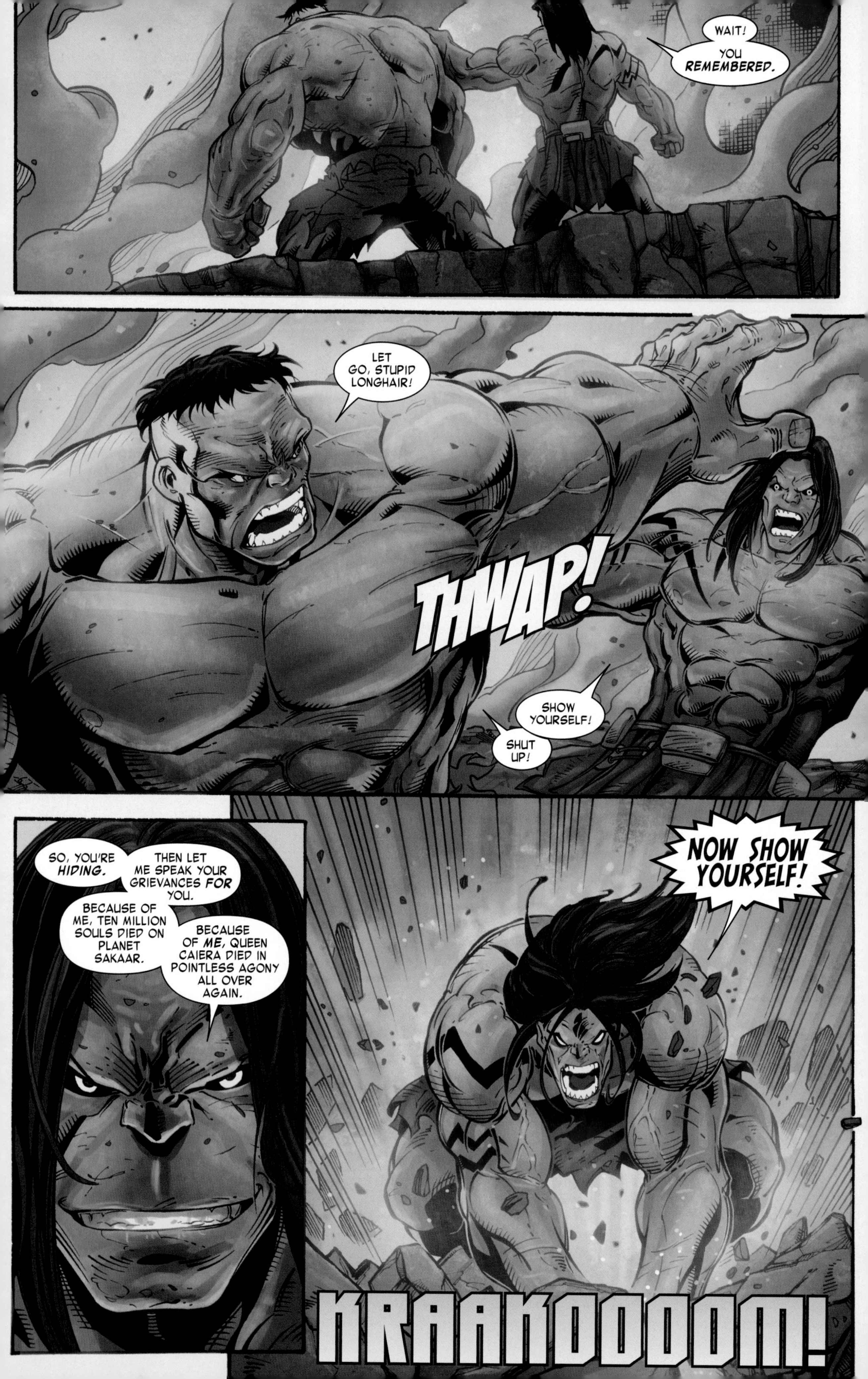
WAIT!
YOU REMEMBERED.
LET GO, STUPID LONGHAIR!
THWAP!
SHOW YOURSELF!
SHUT UP!
SO, YOU'RE HIDING.
THEN LET ME SPEAK YOUR GRIEVANCES FOR YOU.
BECAUSE OF ME, TEN MILLION SOULS DIED ON PLANET SAKAAR.
BECAUSE OF ME, QUEEN CAIERA DIED IN POINTLESS AGONY ALL OVER AGAIN.
NOW SHOW YOURSELF!
KRAAKOOOOM!

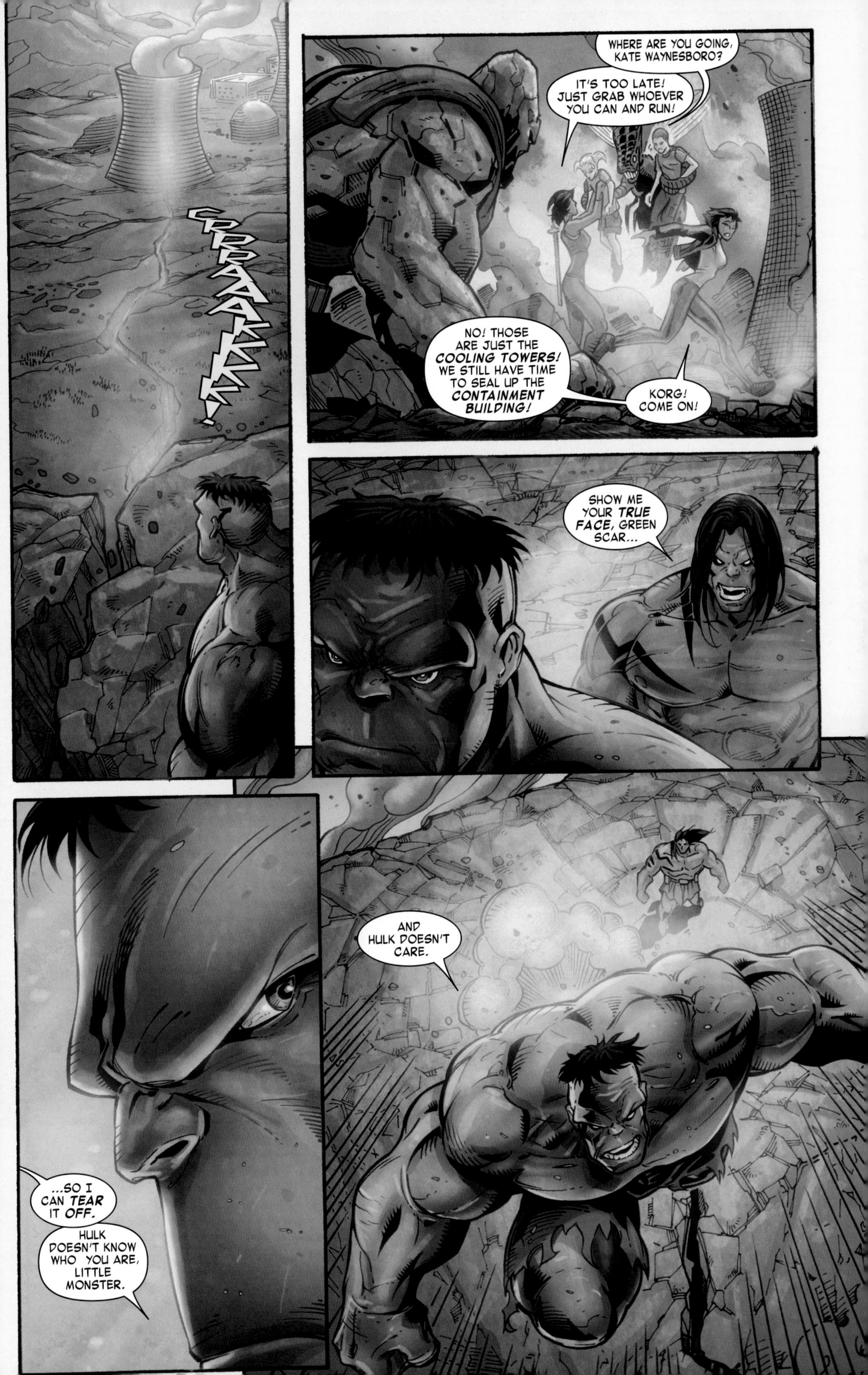
CRRRAAAKKKK!
WHERE ARE YOU GOING, KATE WAYNESBORO?
IT'S TOO LATE! JUST GRAB WHOEVER YOU CAN AND RUN!
NO! THOSE ARE JUST THE COOLING TOWERS! WE STILL HAVE TIME TO SEAL UP THE CONTAINMENT BUILDING!
KORG! COME ON!
SHOW ME YOUR TRUE FACE, GREEN SCAR...
...SO I CAN TEAR IT OFF.
HULK DOESN'T KNOW WHO YOU ARE, LITTLE MONSTER.
AND HULK DOESN'T CARE.

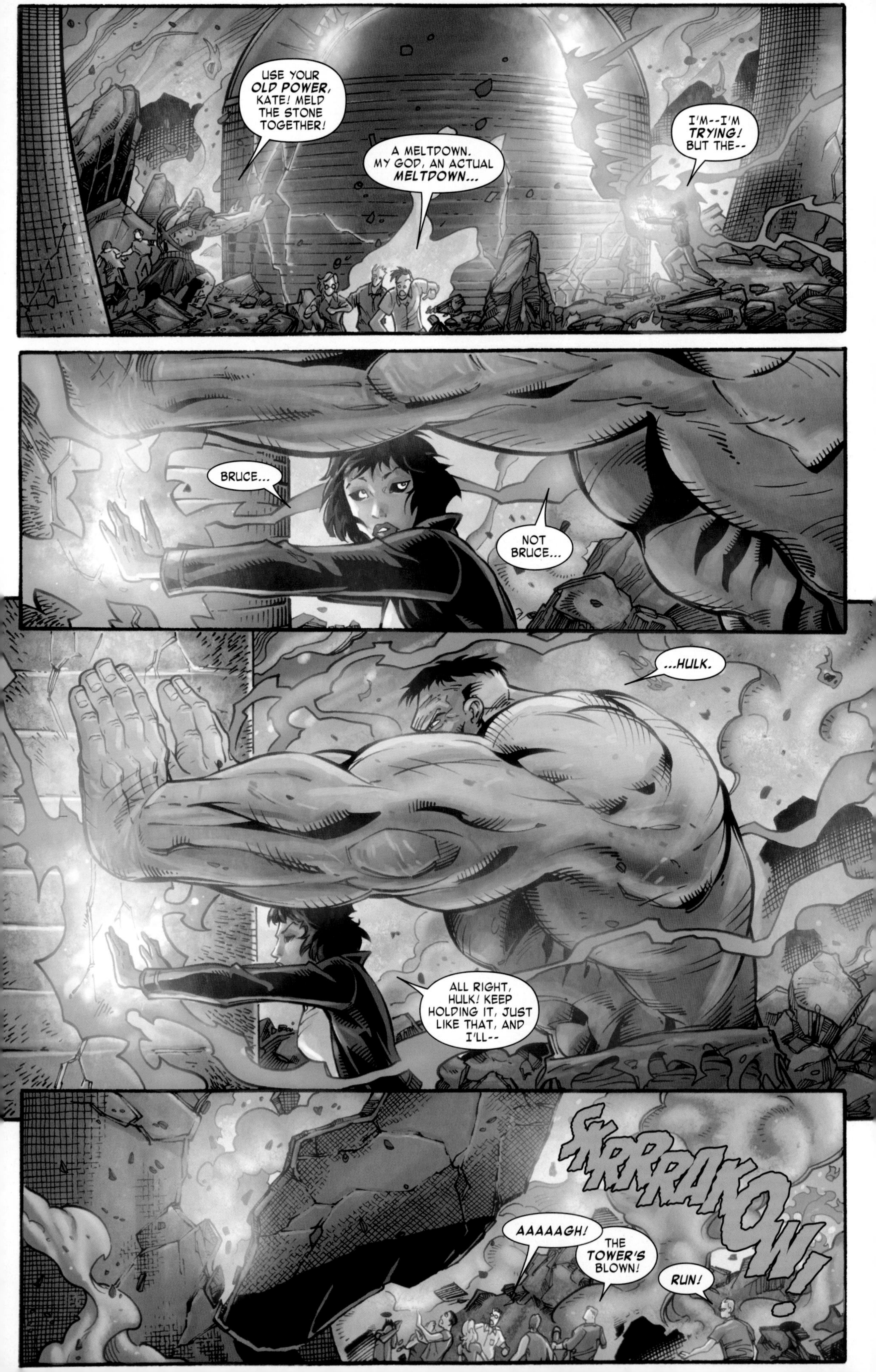

USE YOUR OLD POWER, KATE! MELD THE STONE TOGETHER!
A MELTDOWN. MY GOD, AN ACTUAL MELTDOWN...
I'M--I'M TRYING! BUT THE--
BRUCE...
NOT BRUCE...
...HULK.
ALL RIGHT, HULK! KEEP HOLDING IT, JUST LIKE THAT, AND I'LL--
SKRRAKOW!
AAAAAGH!
THE TOWER'S BLOWN!
RUN!

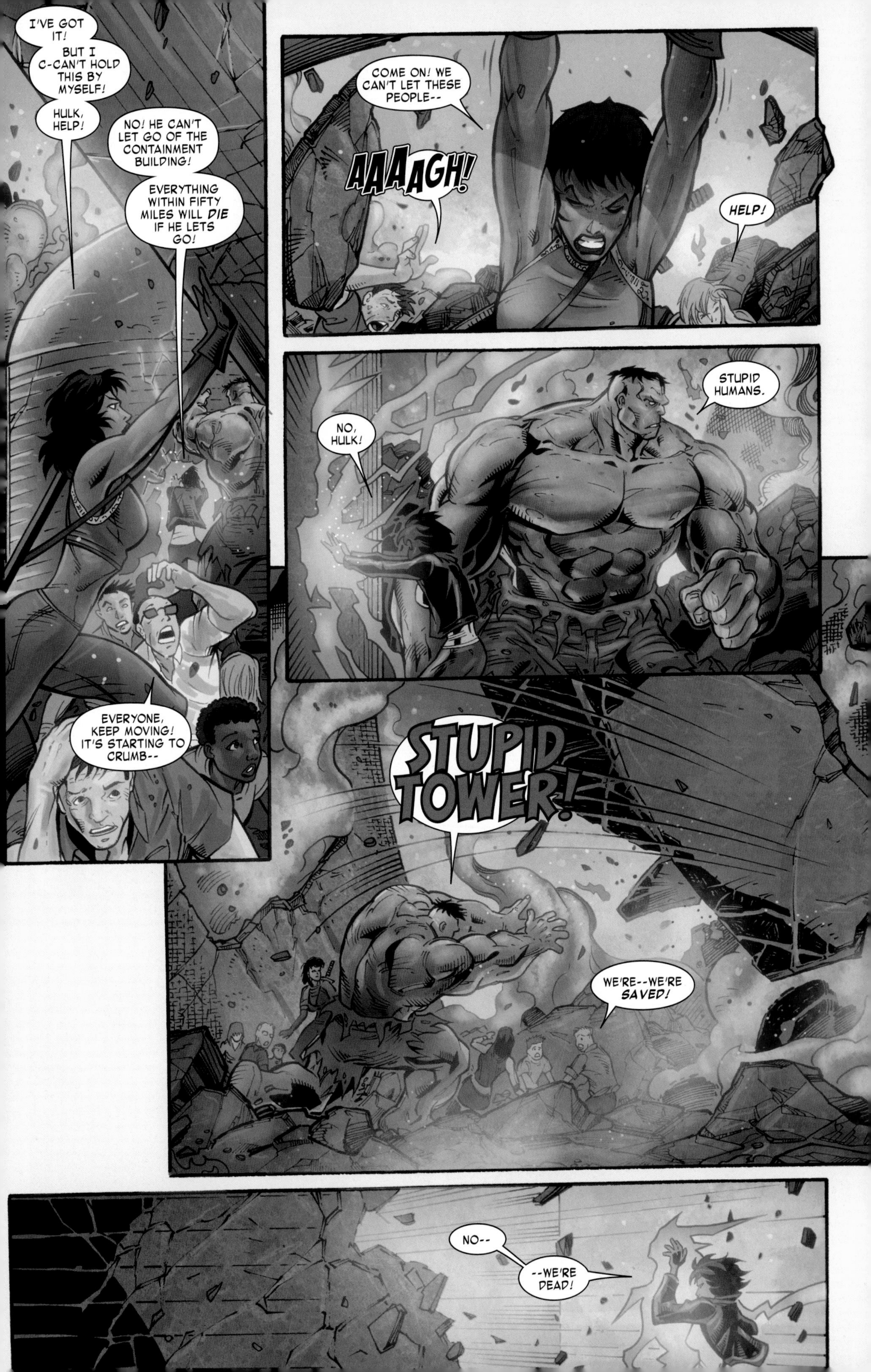
I'VE GOT IT!
BUT I C-CAN'T HOLD THIS BY MYSELF!
HULK, HELP!
NO! HE CAN'T LET GO OF THE CONTAINMENT BUILDING!
EVERYTHING WITHIN FIFTY MILES WILL *DIE* IF HE LETS GO!
EVERYONE, KEEP MOVING! IT'S STARTING TO CRUMB--
COME ON! WE CAN'T LET THESE PEOPLE--
AAAAGH!
HELP!
NO, HULK!
STUPID HUMANS.
STUPID TOWER!
WE'RE--WE'RE *SAVED!*
NO--
--WE'RE DEAD!

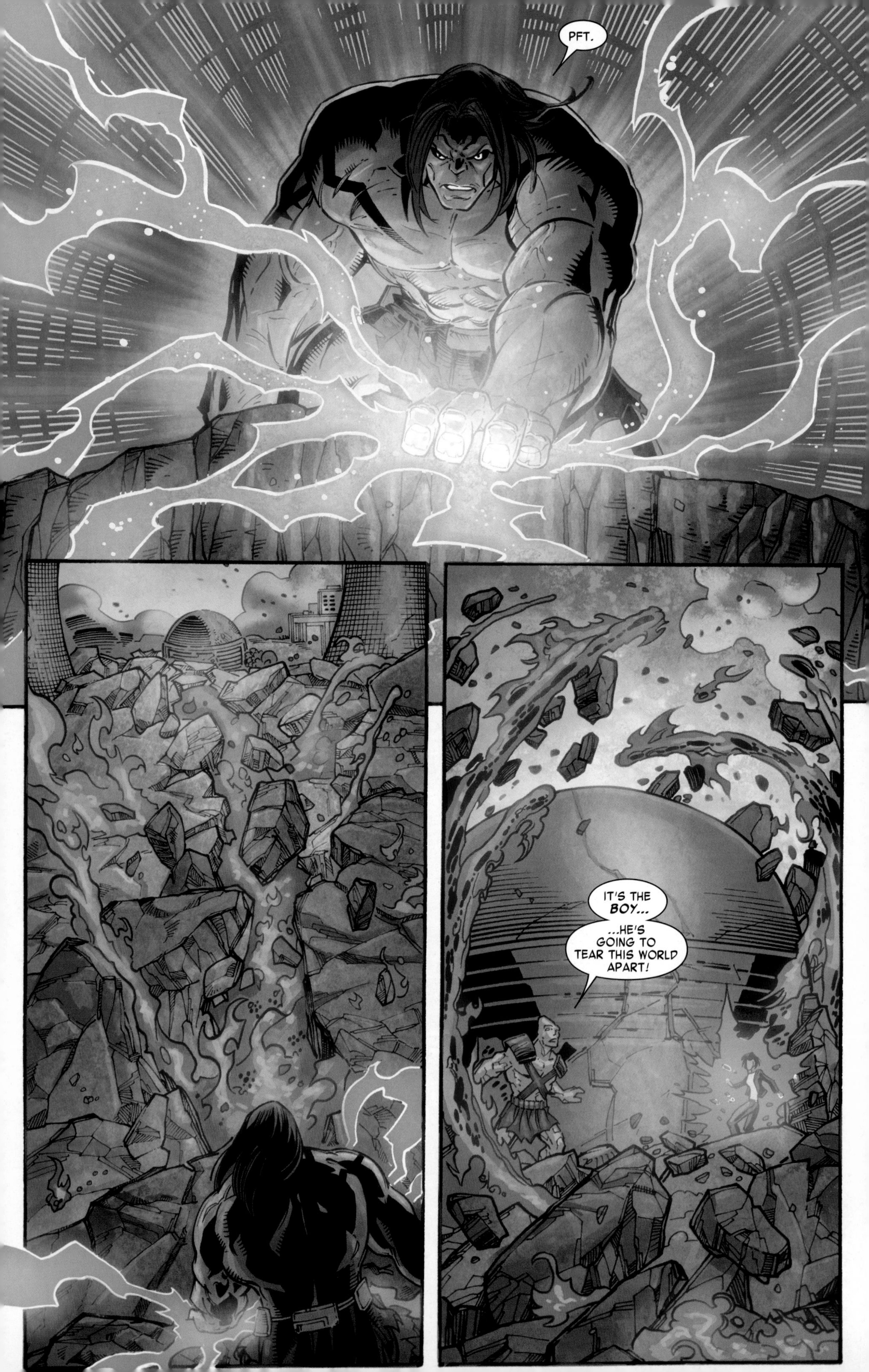
PFT.
IT'S THE BOY...
...HE'S GOING TO TEAR THIS WORLD APART!

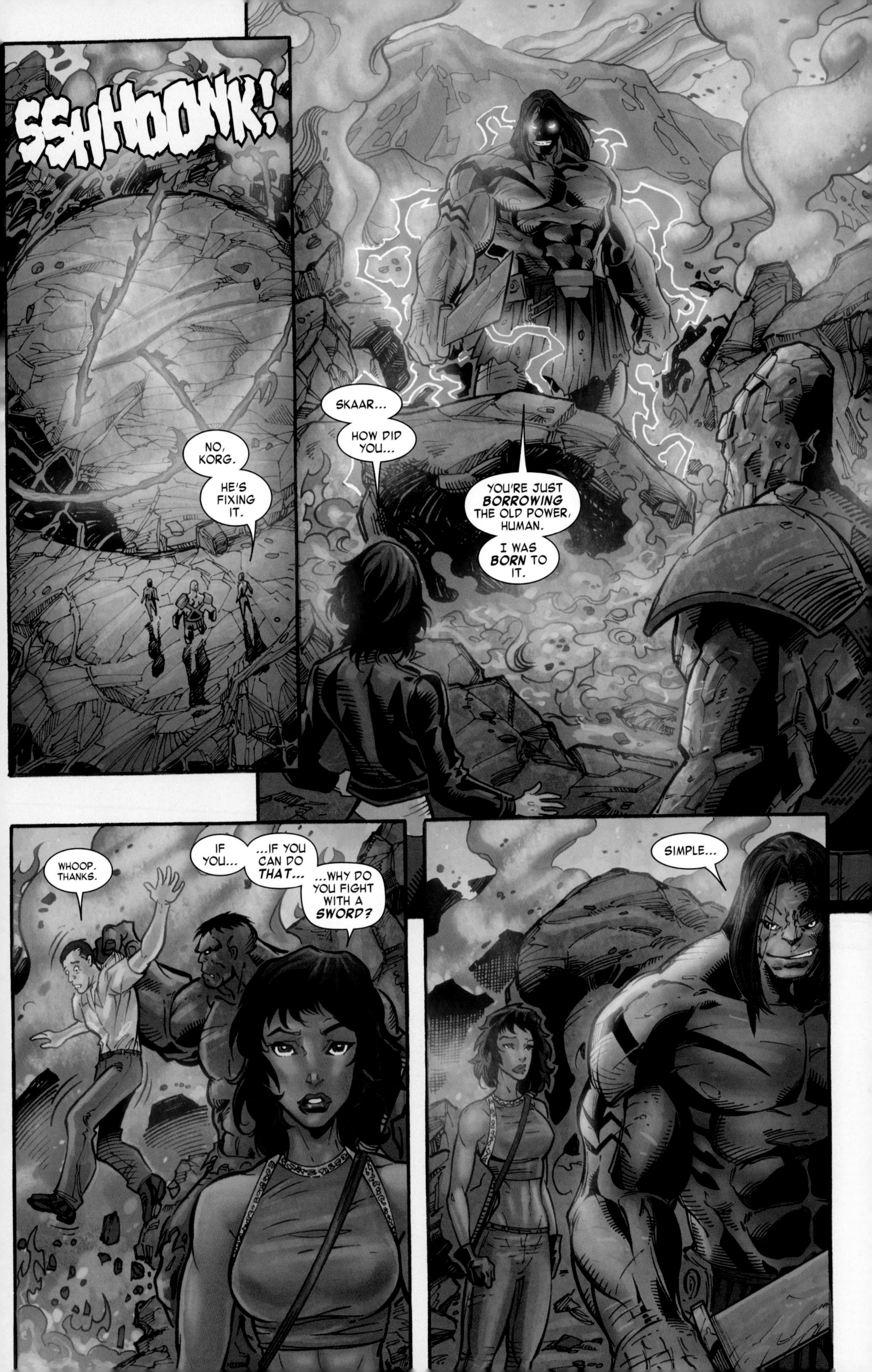
SSHHOONK!
NO, KORG.
HE'S FIXING IT.
SKAAR...
HOW DID YOU...
YOU'RE JUST BORROWING THE OLD POWER, HUMAN.
I WAS BORN TO IT.
WHOOP. THANKS.
IF YOU...
...IF YOU CAN DO THAT...
...WHY DO YOU FIGHT WITH A SWORD?
SIMPLE...

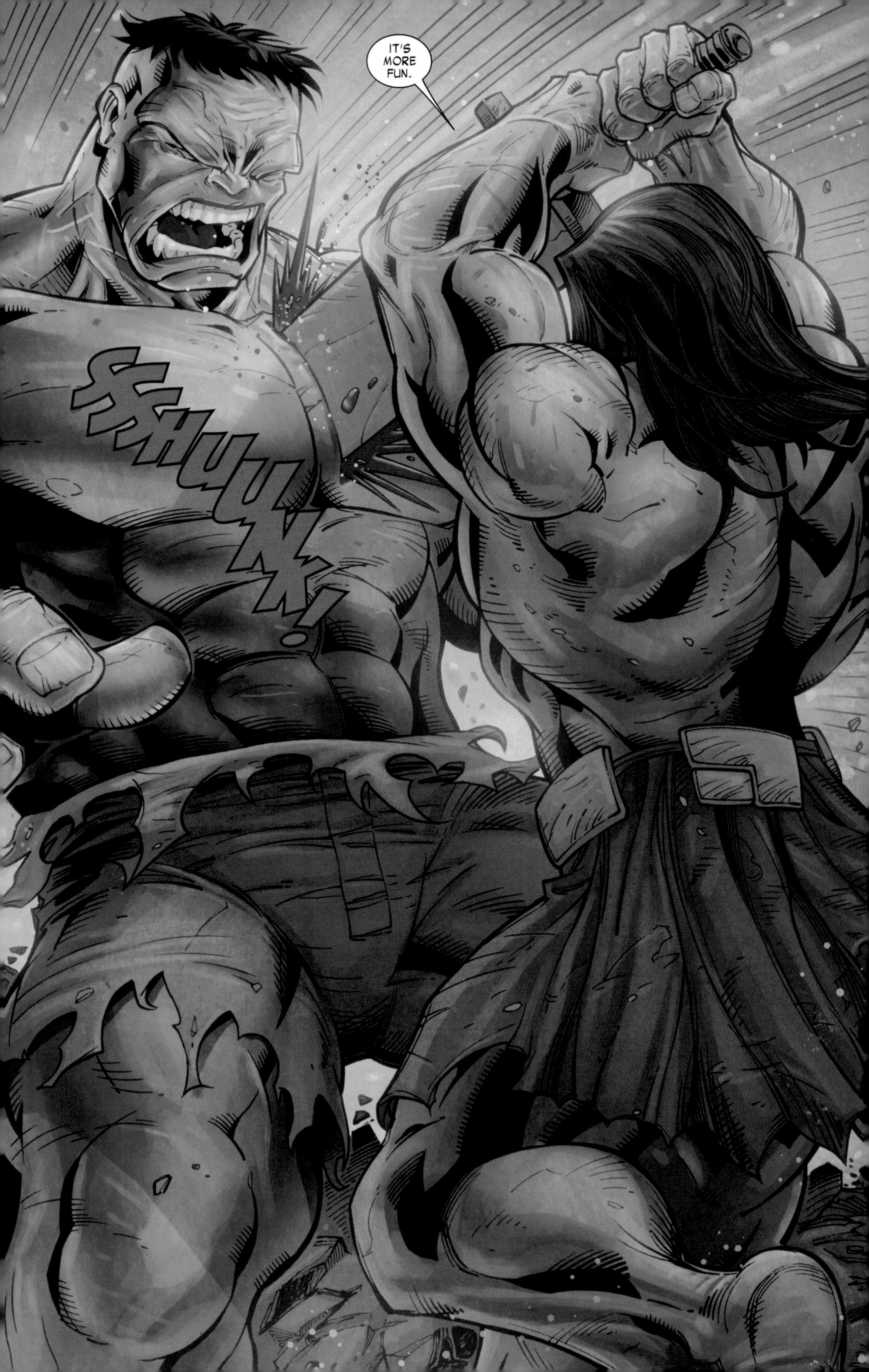
IT'S MORE FUN.
SSHUUK!

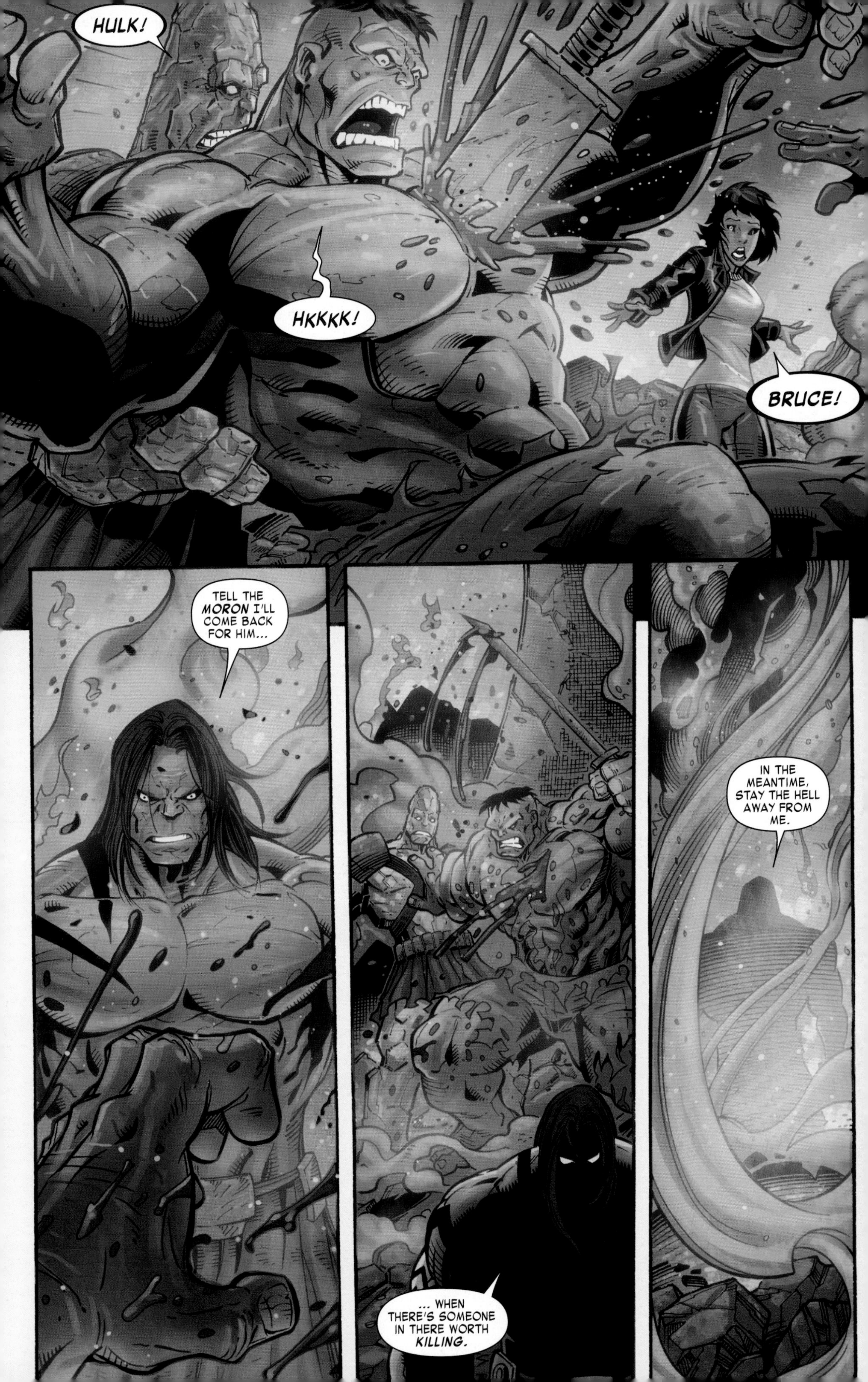
HULK!
HKKKK!
BRUCE!
TELL THE MORON I'LL COME BACK FOR HIM...
... WHEN THERE'S SOMEONE IN THERE WORTH KILLING.
IN THE MEANTIME, STAY THE HELL AWAY FROM ME.

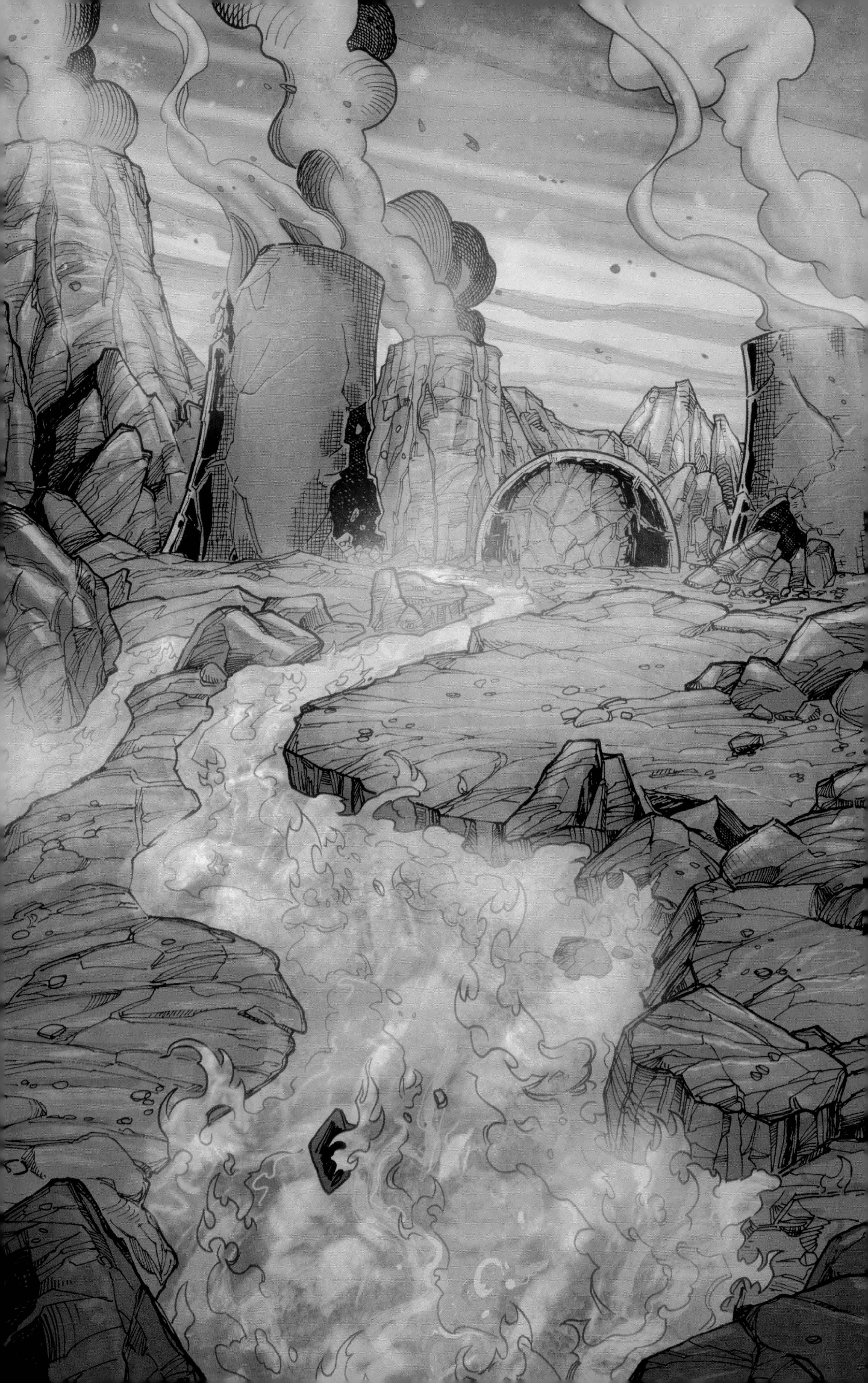

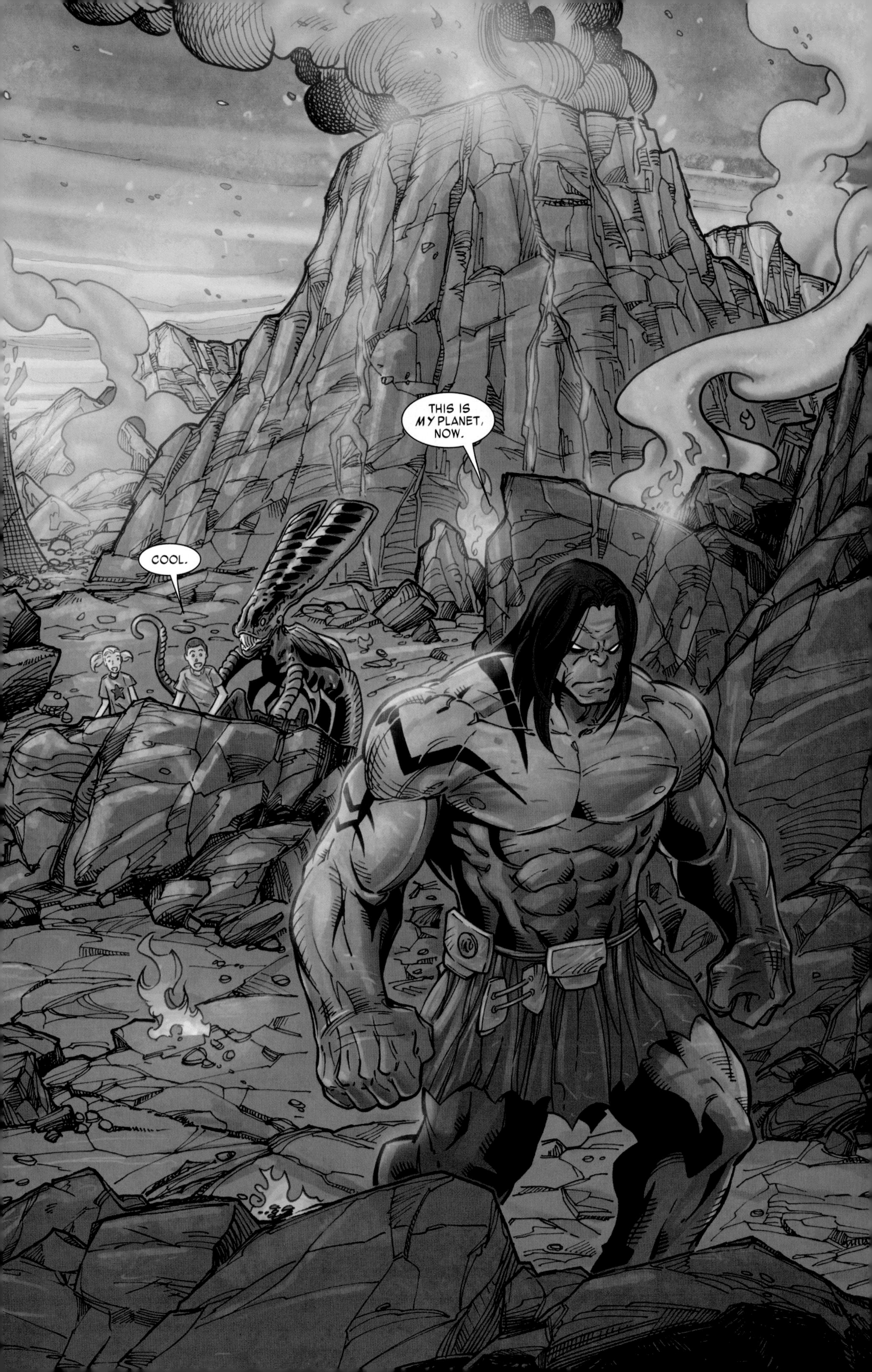
THIS IS MY PLANET, NOW.
COOL.

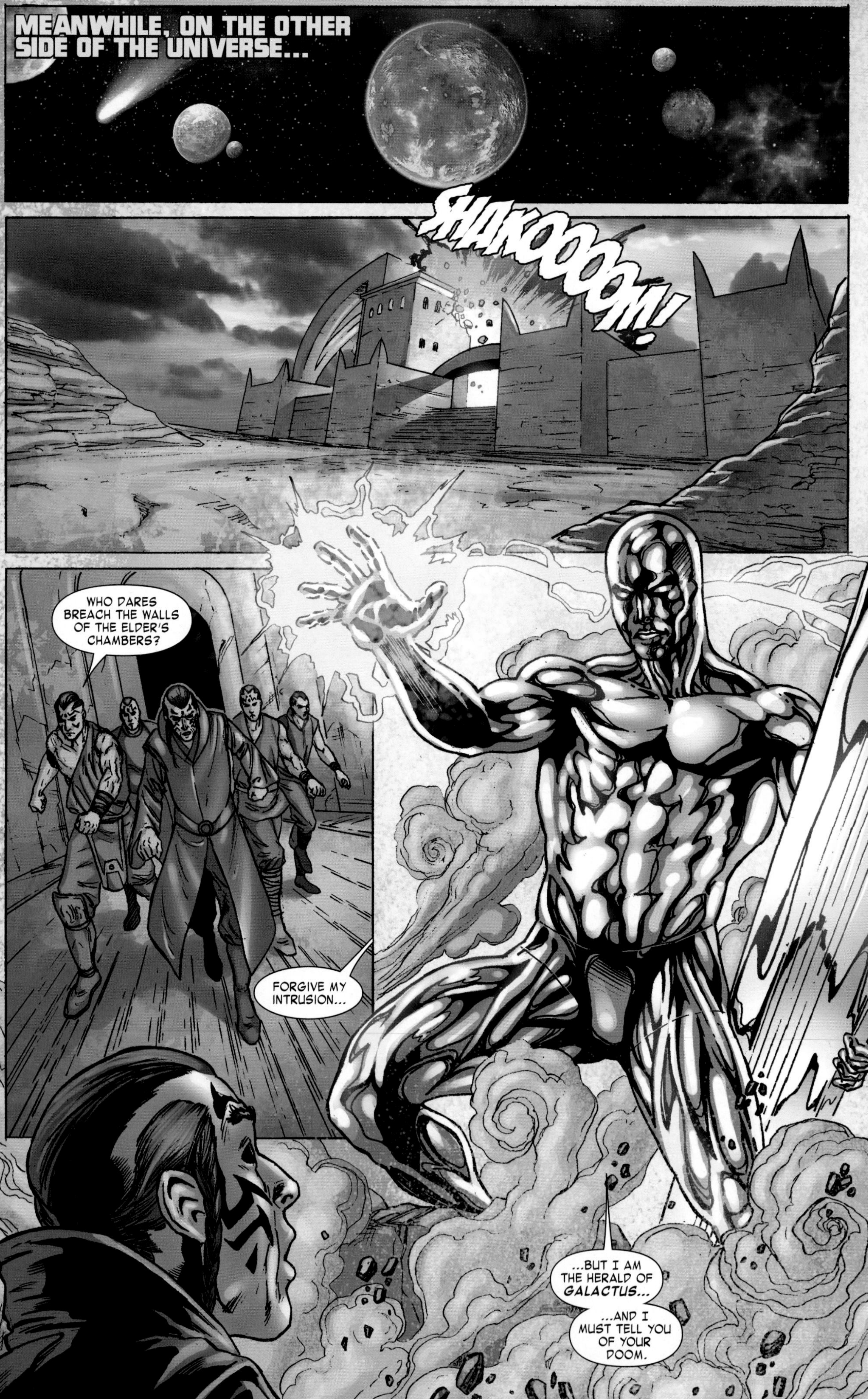
MEANWHILE, ON THE OTHER SIDE OF THE UNIVERSE...
SHAKOOOOOM!
WHO DARES BREACH THE WALLS OF THE ELDER'S CHAMBERS?
FORGIVE MY INTRUSION...
...BUT I AM THE HERALD OF GALACTUS...
...AND I MUST TELL YOU OF YOUR DOOM.

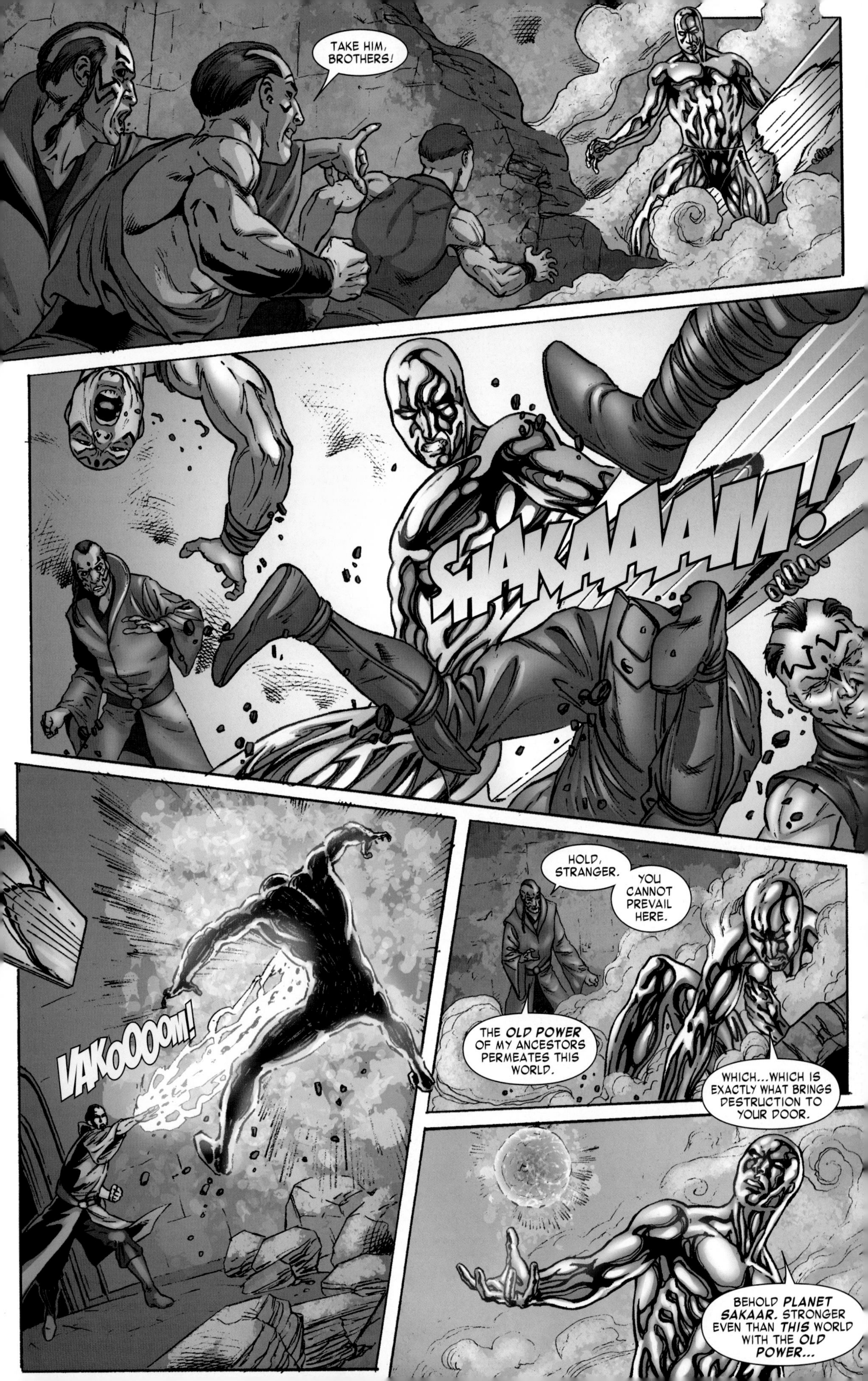
TAKE HIM, BROTHERS!
SHAKAAAAM!
VAKOOOOM!
HOLD, STRANGER.
YOU CANNOT PREVAIL HERE.
THE OLD POWER OF MY ANCESTORS PERMEATES THIS WORLD.
WHICH...WHICH IS EXACTLY WHAT BRINGS DESTRUCTION TO YOUR DOOR.
BEHOLD PLANET SAKAAR. STRONGER EVEN THAN THIS WORLD WITH THE OLD POWER...

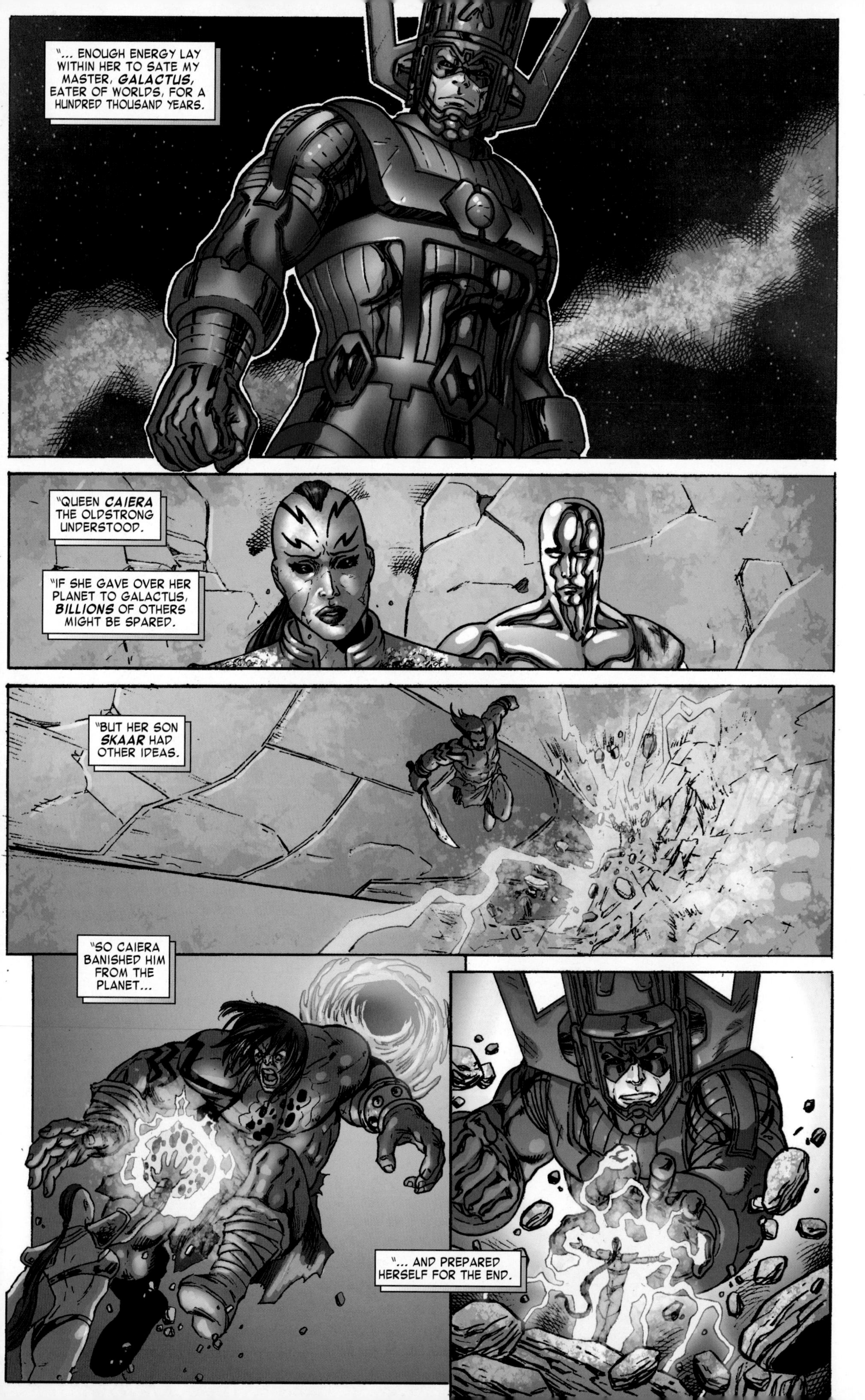
"... ENOUGH ENERGY LAY WITHIN HER TO SATE MY MASTER, GALACTUS, EATER OF WORLDS, FOR A HUNDRED THOUSAND YEARS.
"QUEEN CAIERA THE OLDSTRONG UNDERSTOOD.
"IF SHE GAVE OVER HER PLANET TO GALACTUS, BILLIONS OF OTHERS MIGHT BE SPARED.
"BUT HER SON SKAAR HAD OTHER IDEAS.
"SO CAIERA BANISHED HIM FROM THE PLANET...
"... AND PREPARED HERSELF FOR THE END.

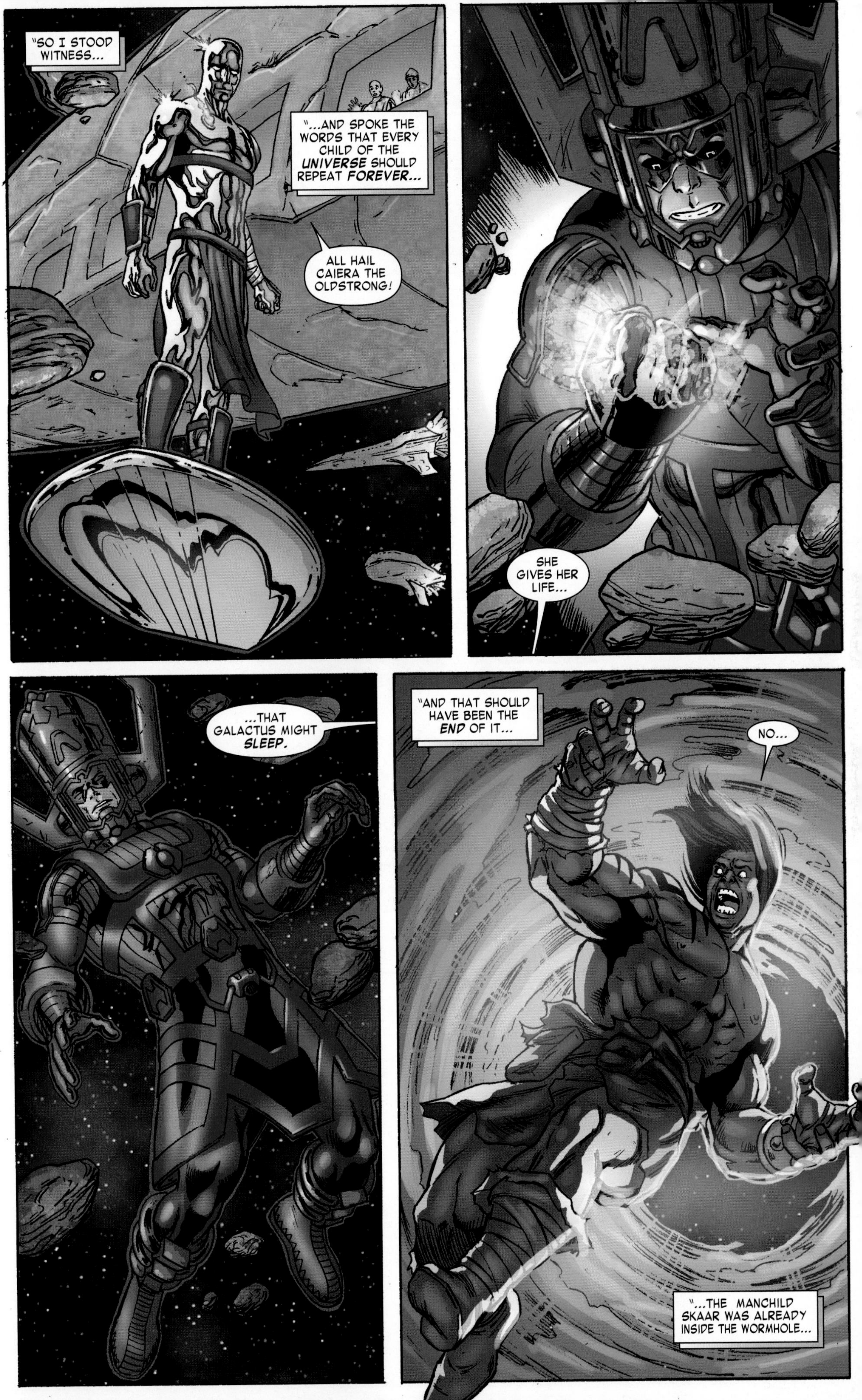

"SO I STOOD WITNESS...
"...AND SPOKE THE WORDS THAT EVERY CHILD OF THE UNIVERSE SHOULD REPEAT FOREVER...
ALL HAIL CAIERA THE OLDSTRONG!
SHE GIVES HER LIFE...
...THAT GALACTUS MIGHT SLEEP.
"AND THAT SHOULD HAVE BEEN THE END OF IT...
NO...
"...THE MANCHILD SKAAR WAS ALREADY INSIDE THE WORMHOLE...

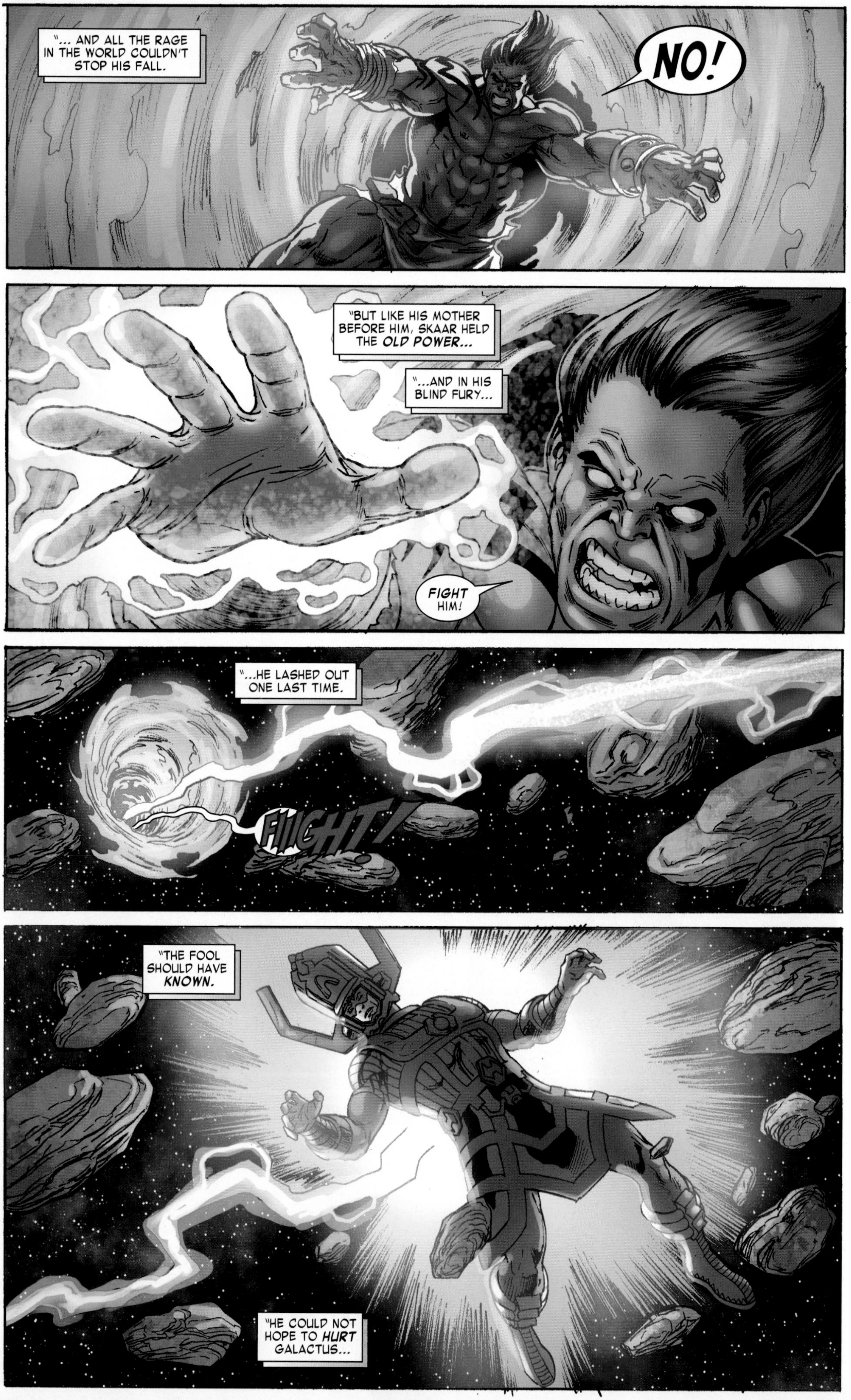
"... AND ALL THE RAGE IN THE WORLD COULDN'T STOP HIS FALL.
NO!
"BUT LIKE HIS MOTHER BEFORE HIM, SKAAR HELD THE OLD POWER...
"...AND IN HIS BLIND FURY...
FIGHT HIM!
"...HE LASHED OUT ONE LAST TIME.
FIIIGHT!
"THE FOOL SHOULD HAVE KNOWN.
"HE COULD NOT HOPE TO HURT GALACTUS...

... ONLY *AWAKEN HIM.*

HRRN...

...NNMM...

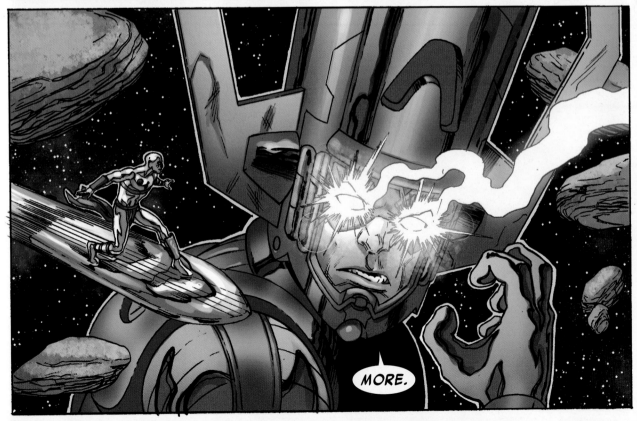

MORE.

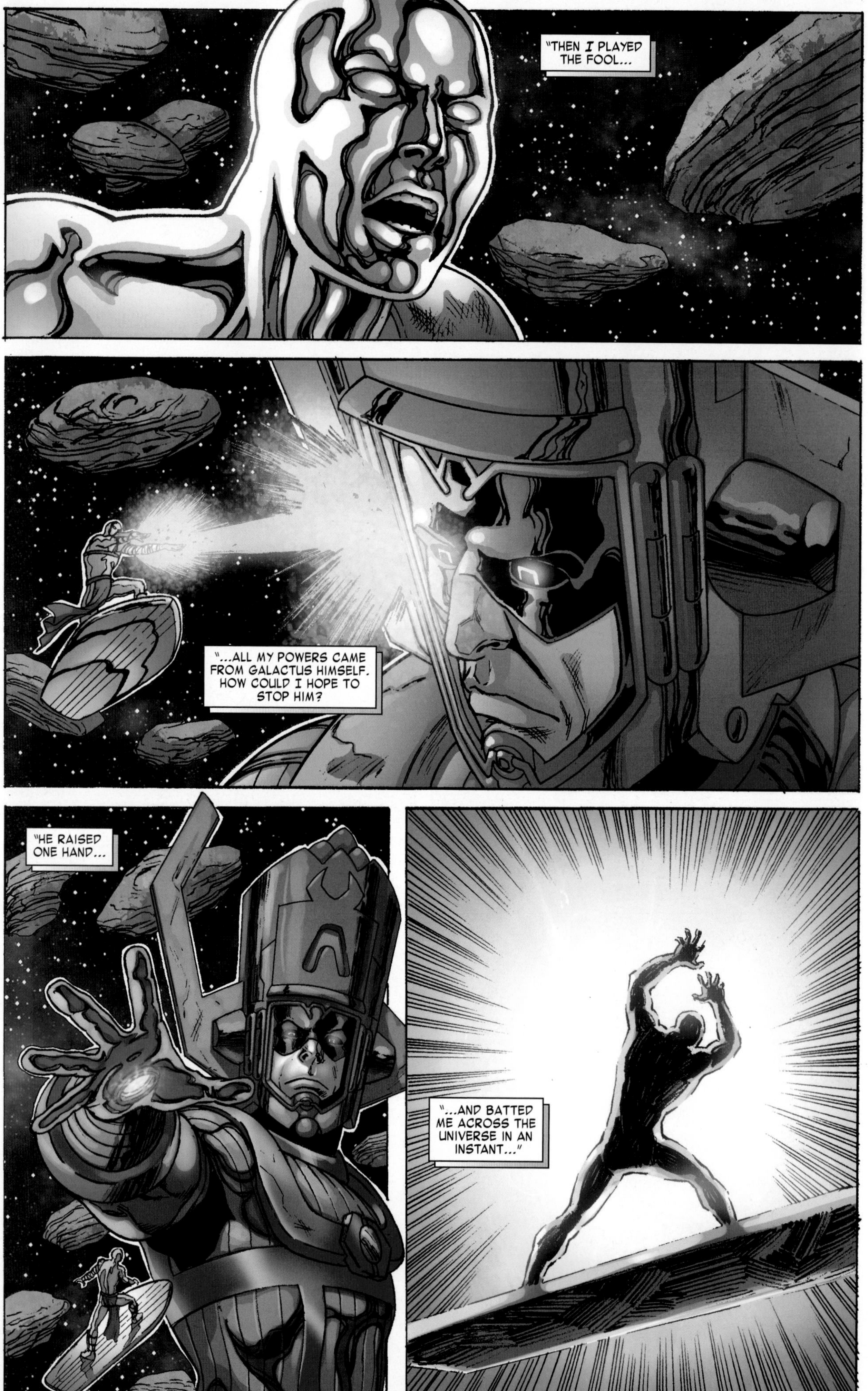
"THEN *I* PLAYED THE FOOL...
"...ALL MY POWERS CAME FROM GALACTUS HIMSELF. HOW COULD I HOPE TO STOP HIM?
"HE RAISED ONE HAND...
"...AND BATTED ME ACROSS THE UNIVERSE IN AN INSTANT..."

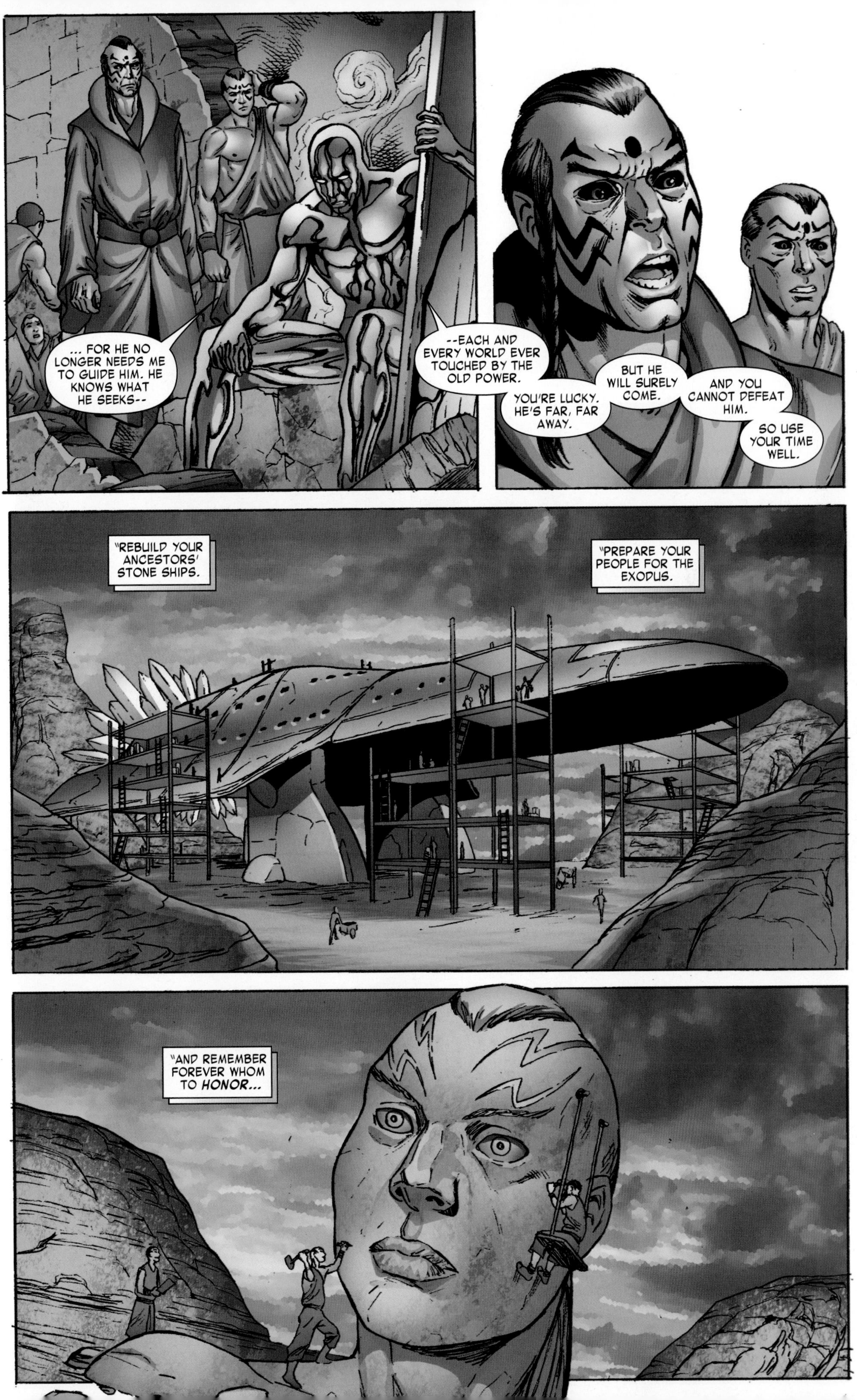
... FOR HE NO LONGER NEEDS ME TO GUIDE HIM. HE KNOWS WHAT HE SEEKS--
--EACH AND EVERY WORLD EVER TOUCHED BY THE OLD POWER.
YOU'RE LUCKY. HE'S FAR, FAR AWAY.
BUT HE WILL SURELY COME.
AND YOU CANNOT DEFEAT HIM.
SO USE YOUR TIME WELL.
"REBUILD YOUR ANCESTORS' STONE SHIPS.
"PREPARE YOUR PEOPLE FOR THE EXODUS.
"AND REMEMBER FOREVER WHOM TO *HONOR*...

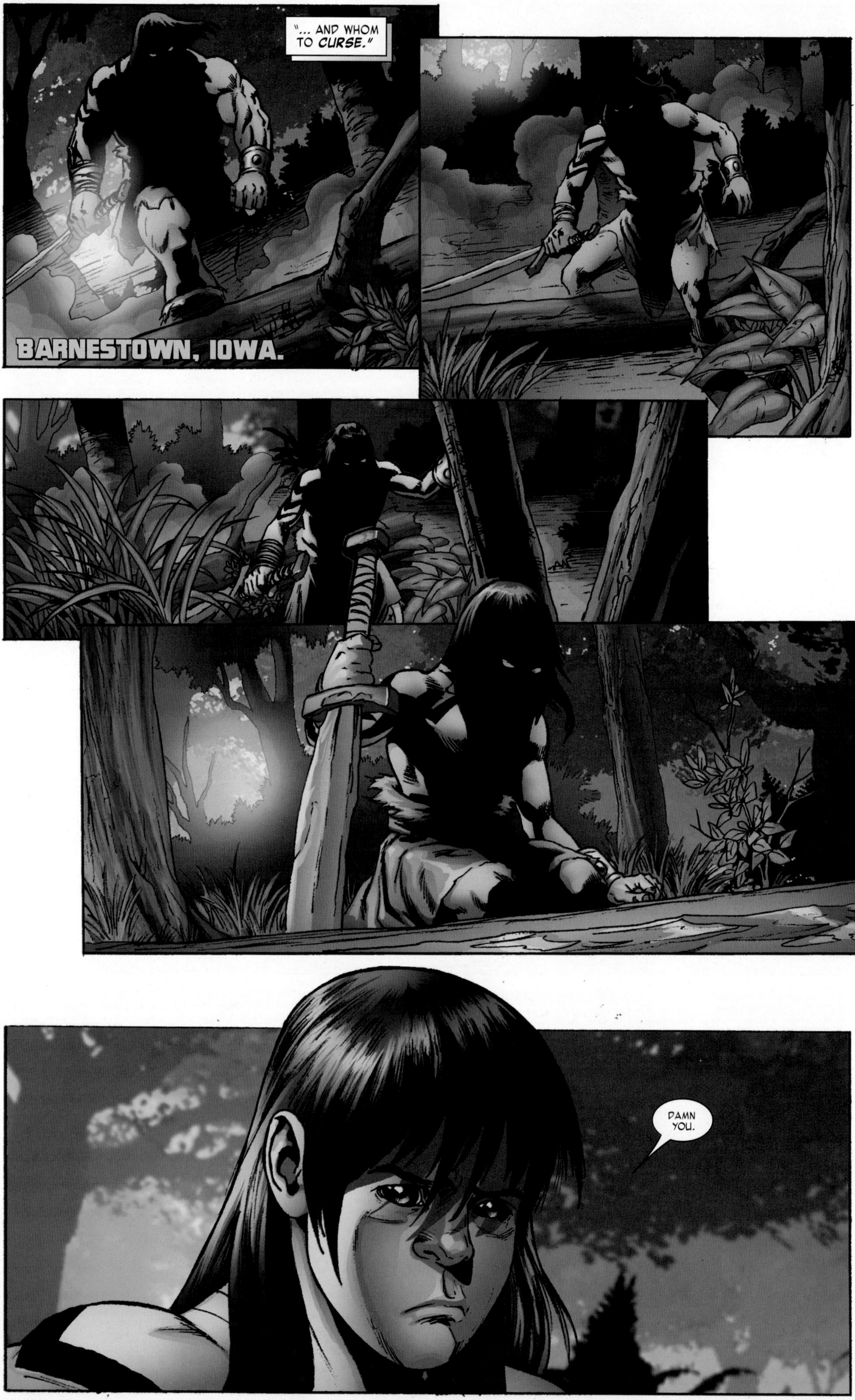
"... AND WHOM TO CURSE."
BARNESTOWN, IOWA.
DAMN YOU.

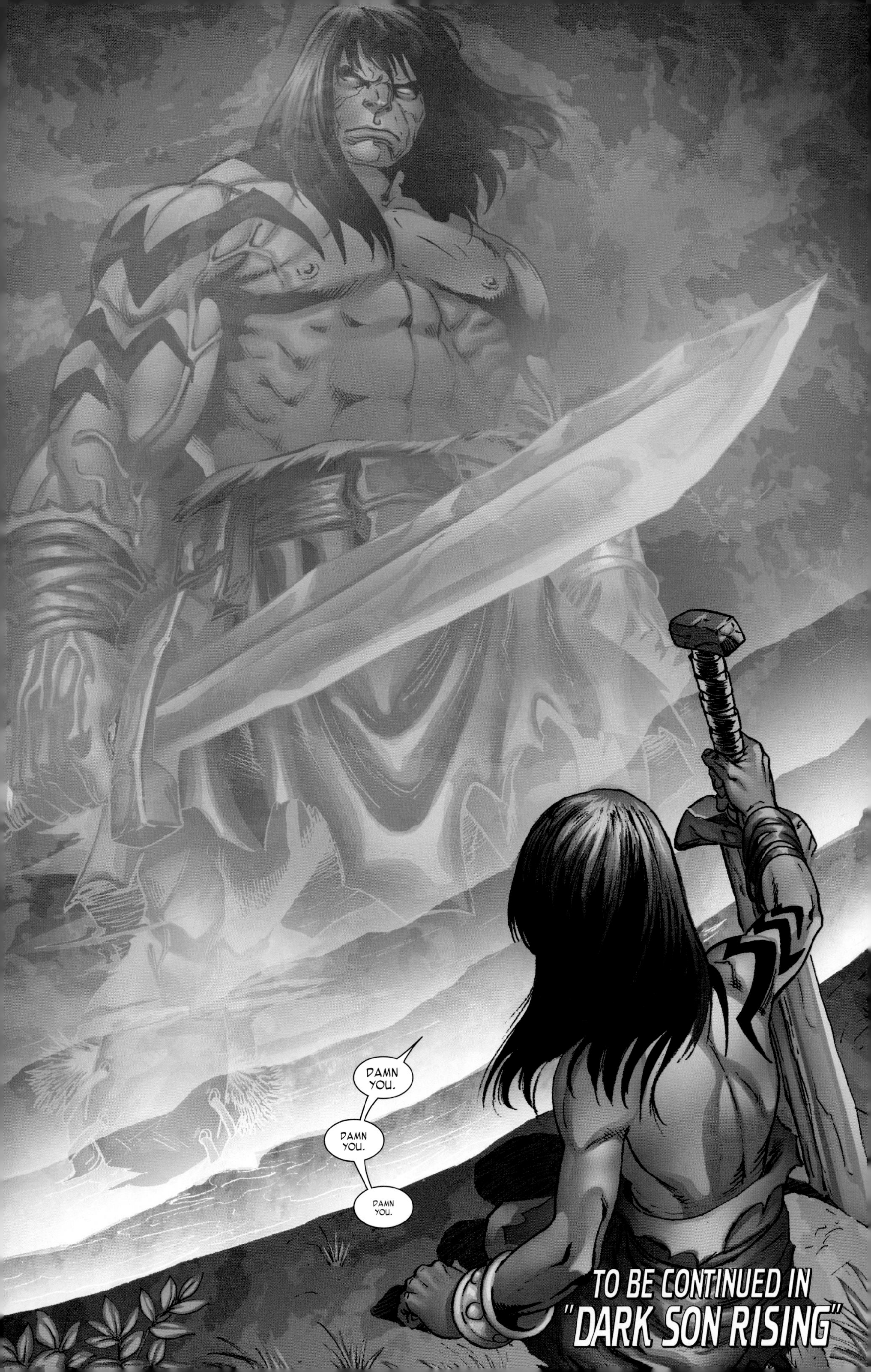
DAMN YOU.
DAMN YOU.
DAMN YOU.
TO BE CONTINUED IN "DARK SON RISING"

Son of Hulk #8
Pencils by
RON LIM

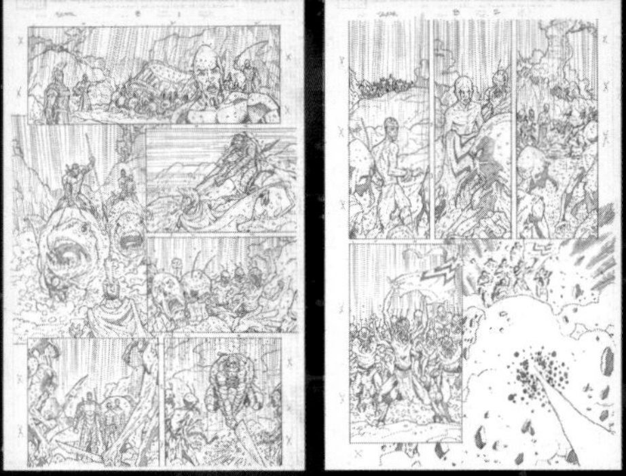

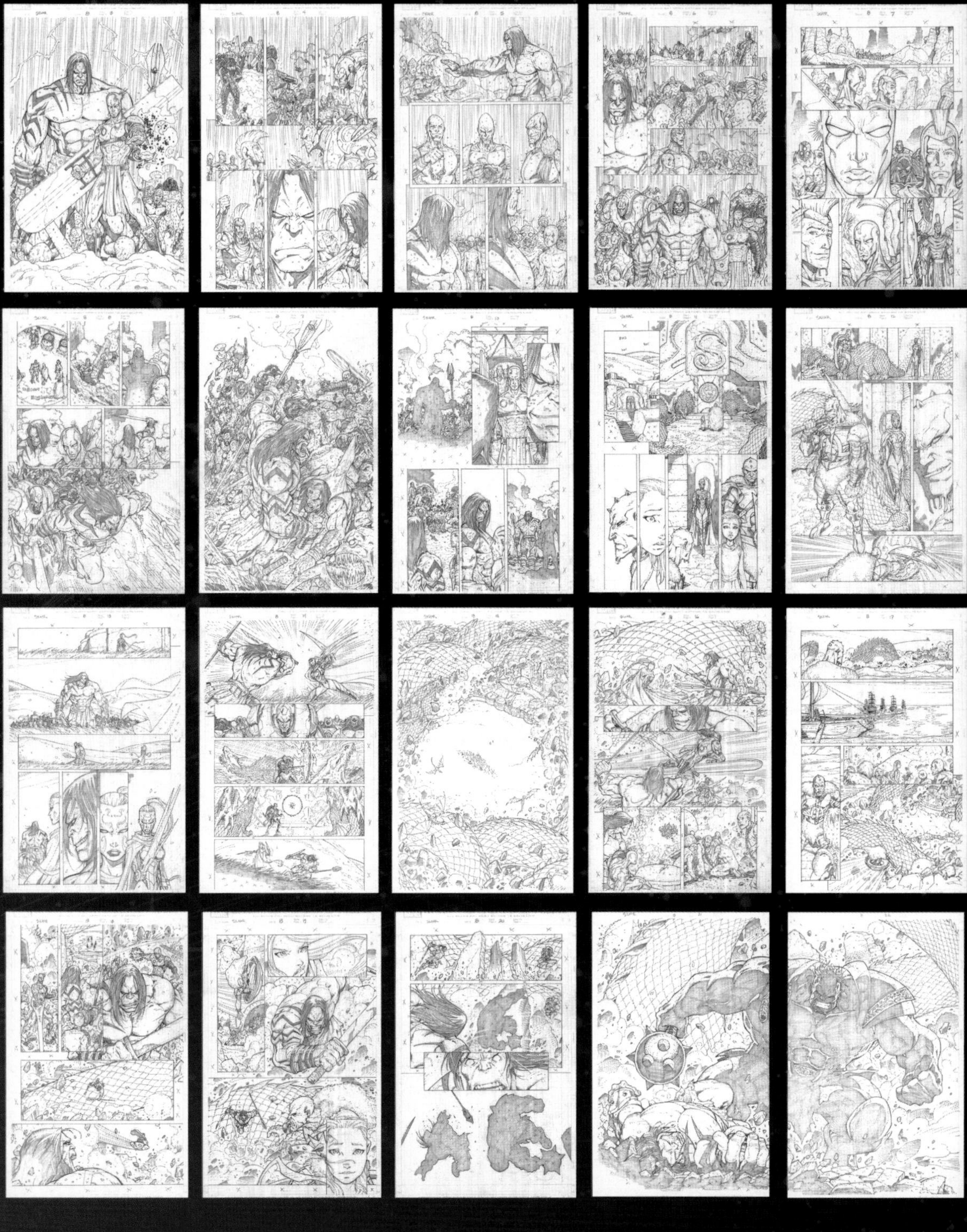

Son of Hulk #12 Pencils by

RON LIM

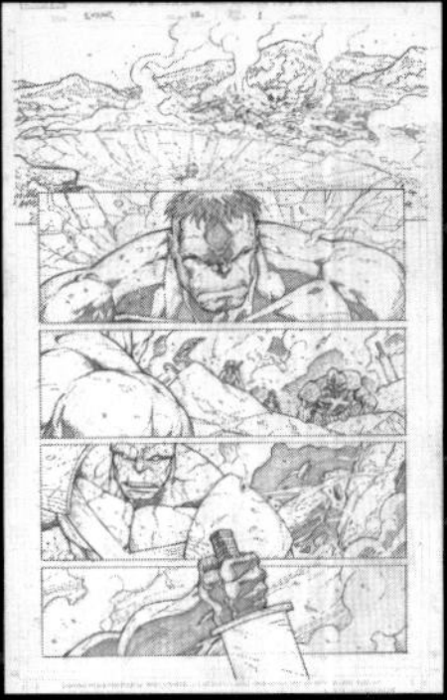
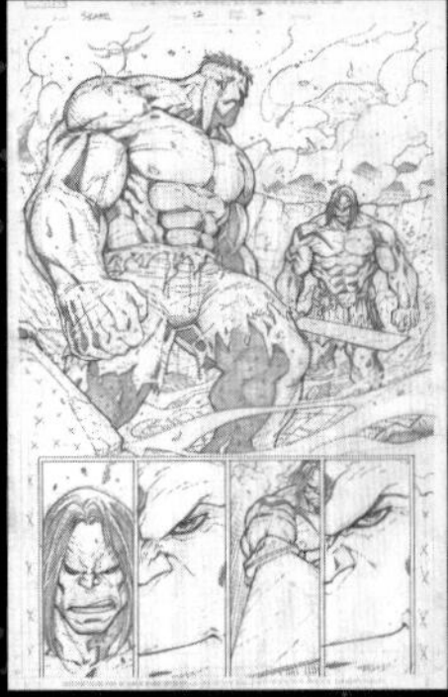
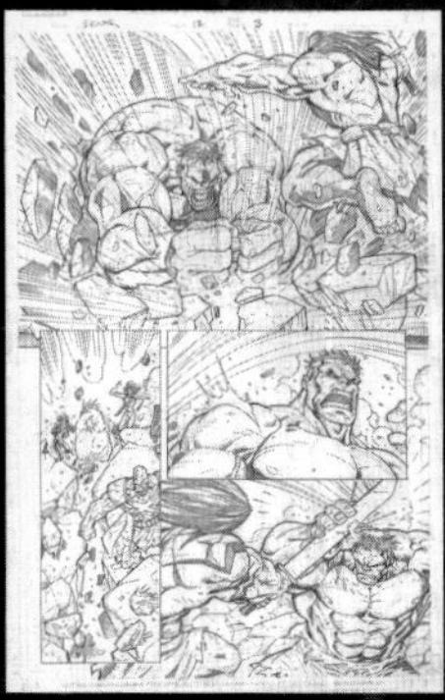
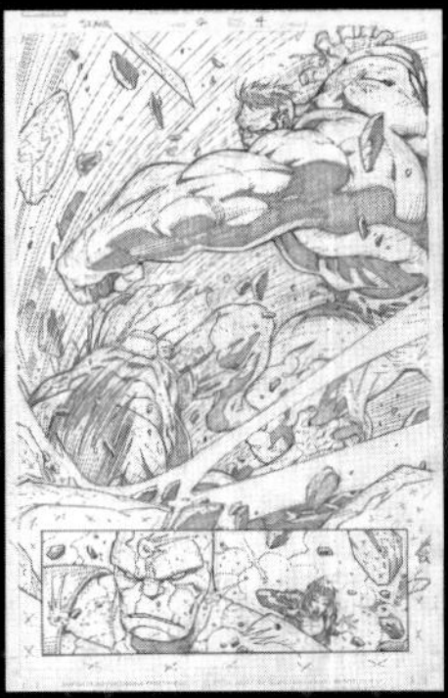
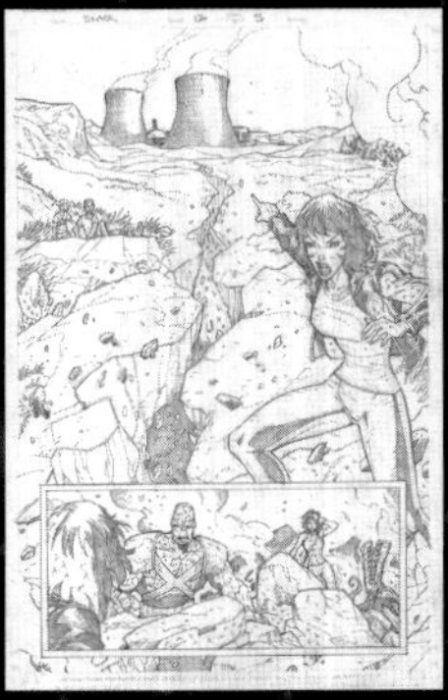
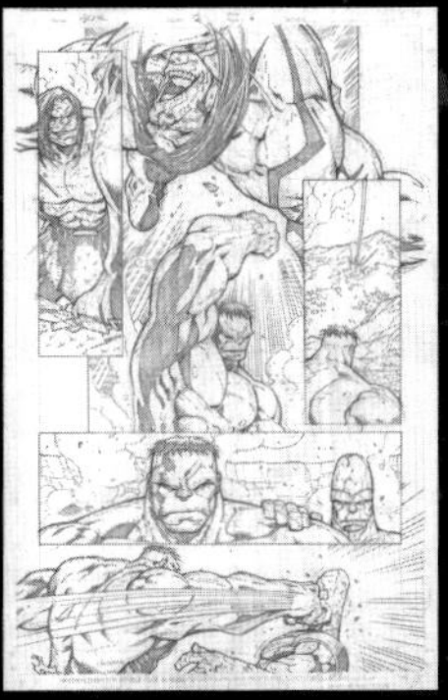
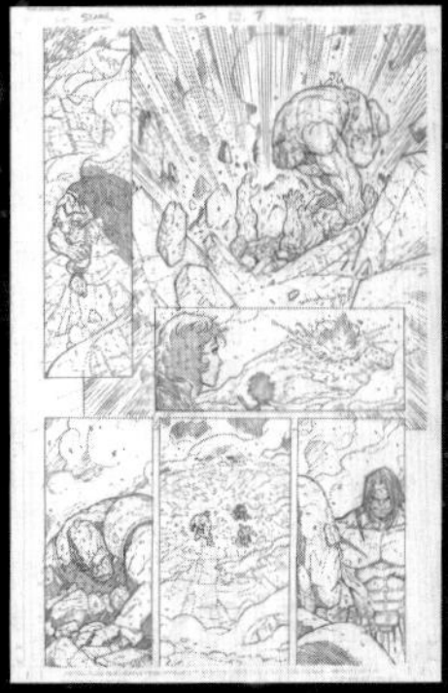
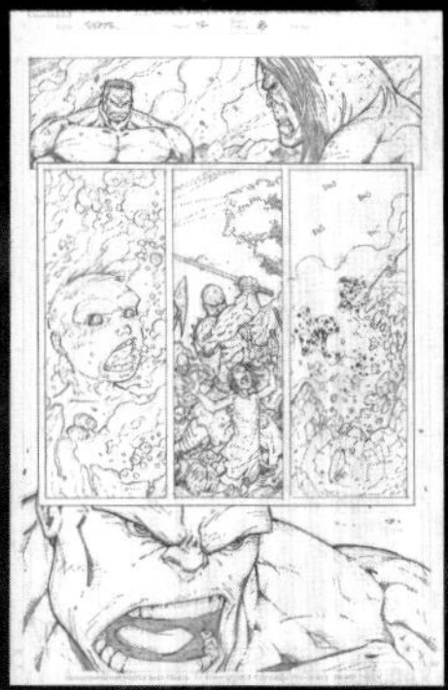
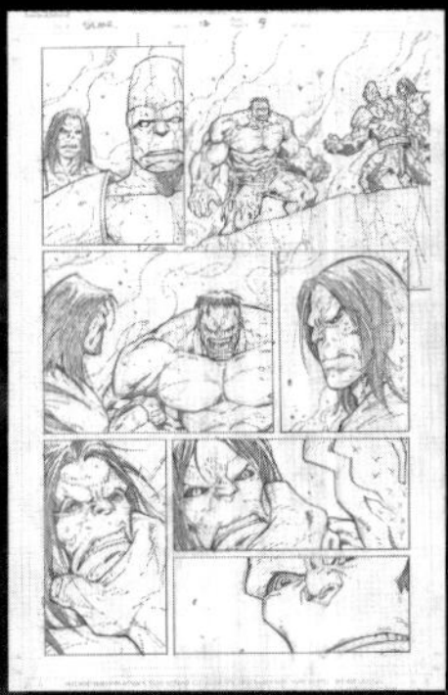
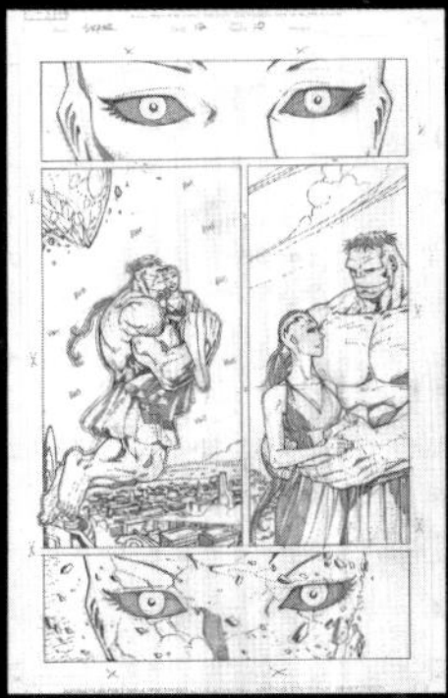
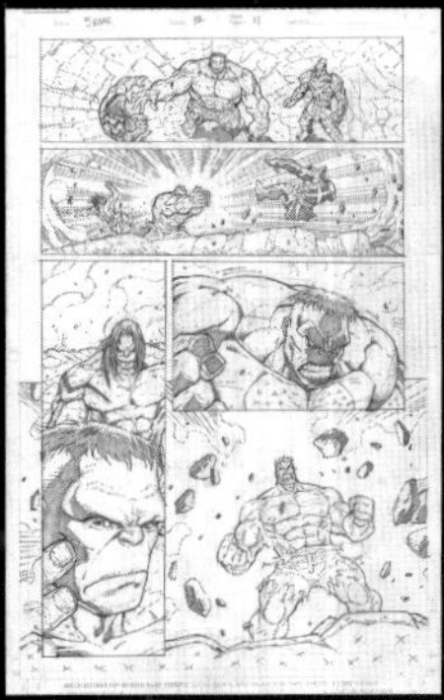
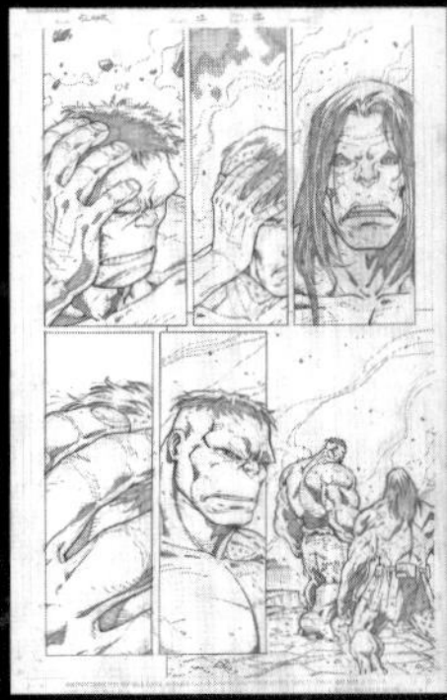
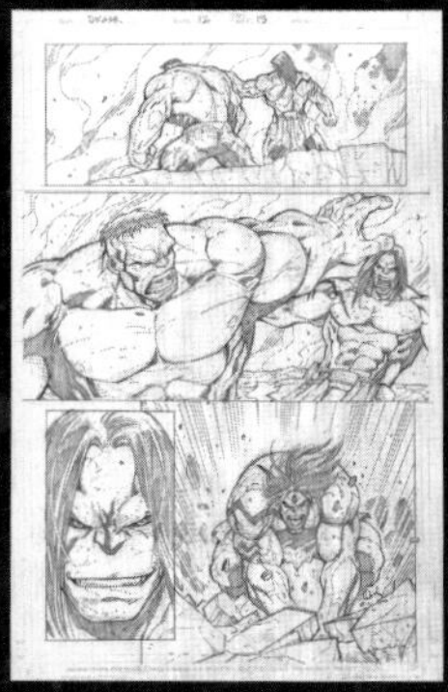
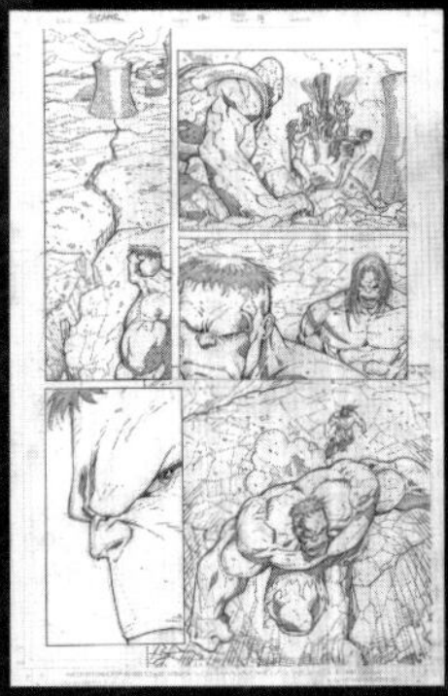
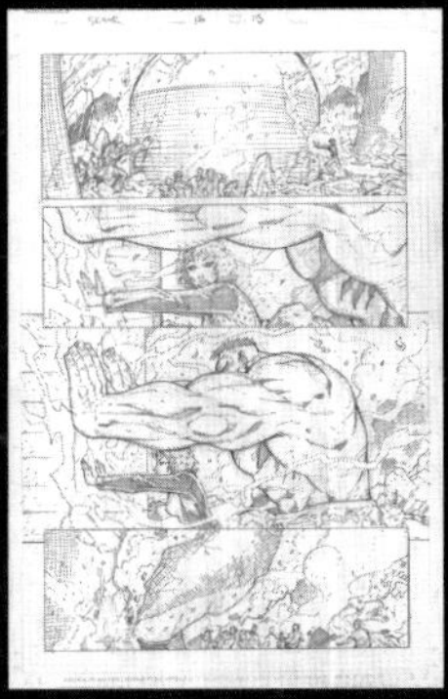
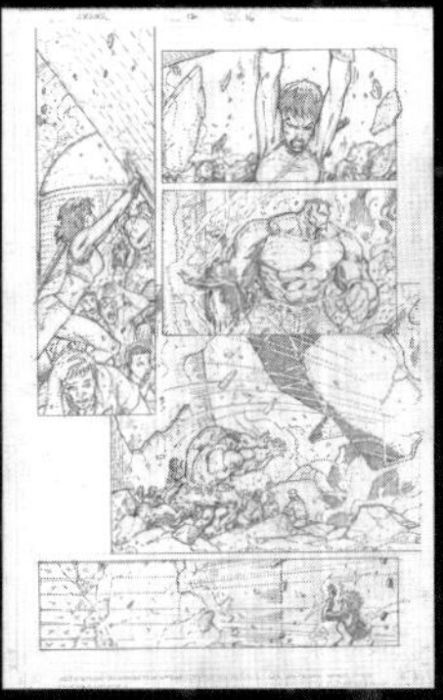
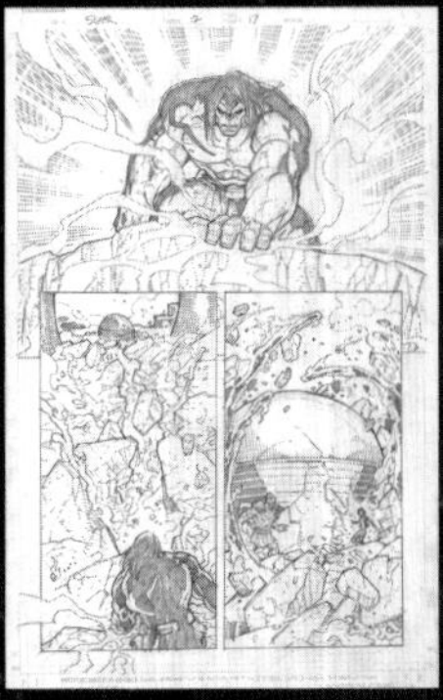
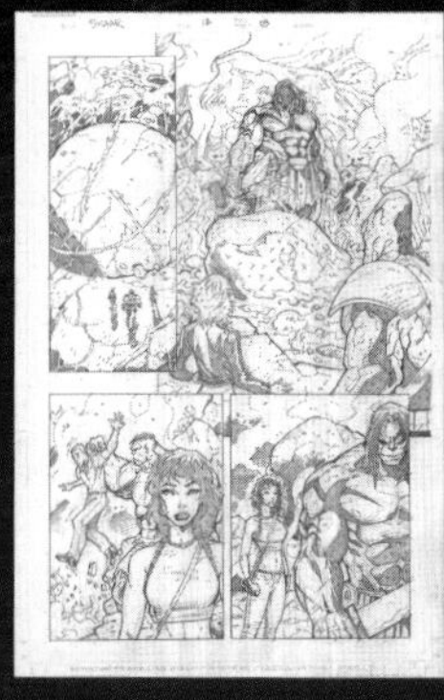
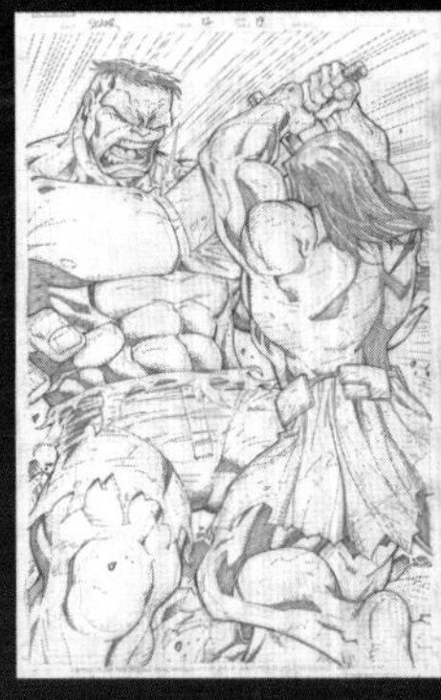
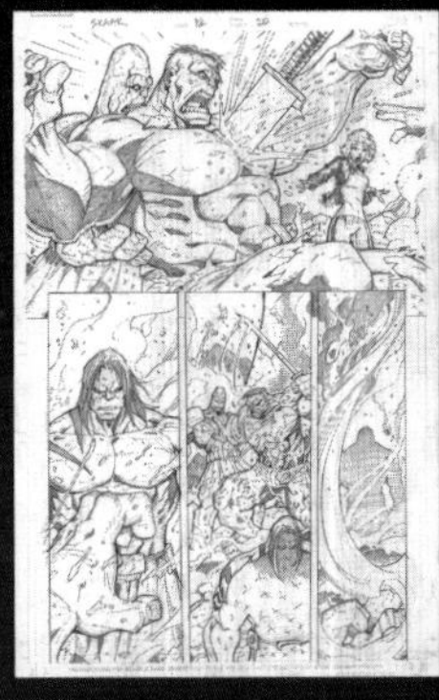
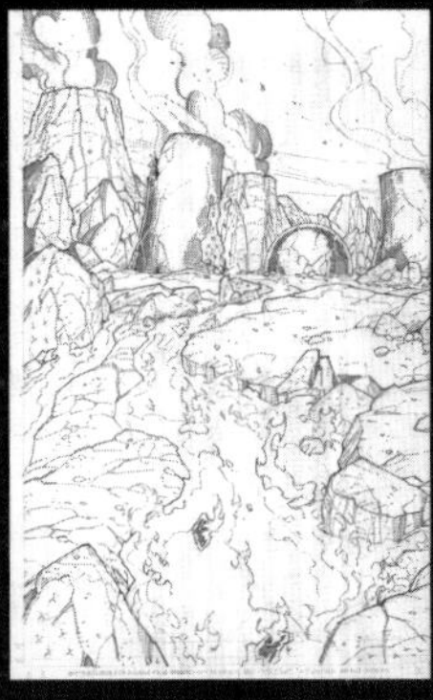
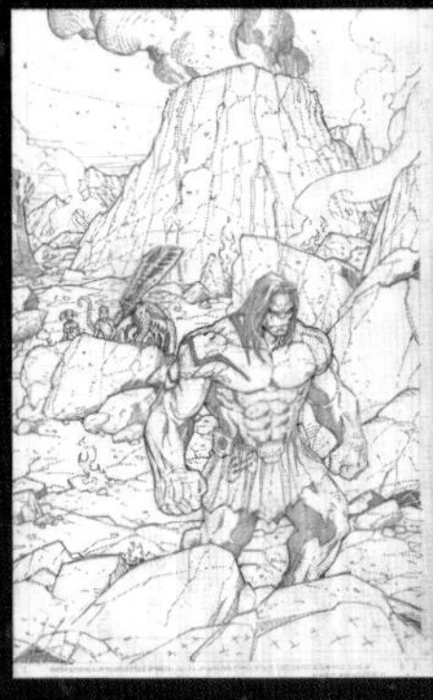

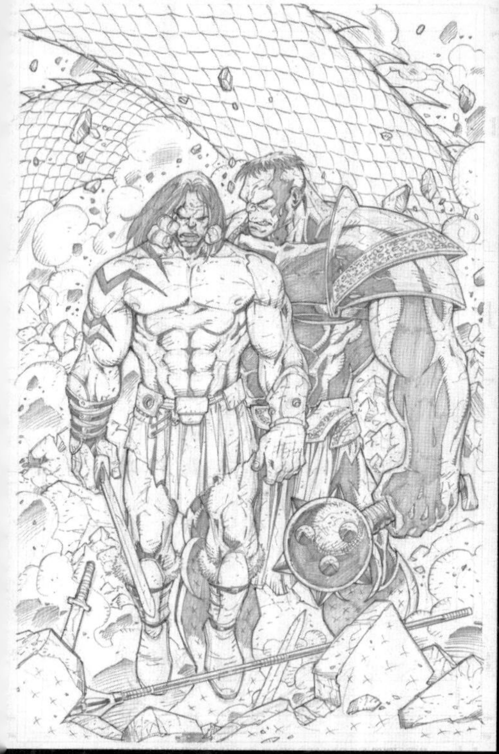
SKAAR
9
3

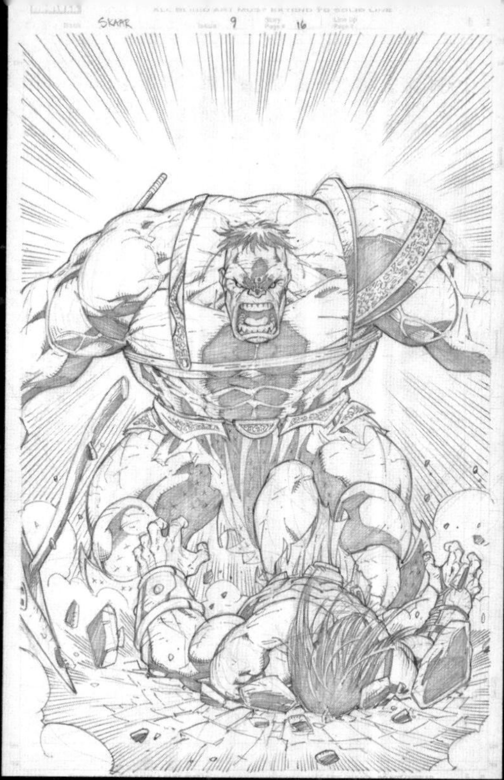
SKAAR
9
16

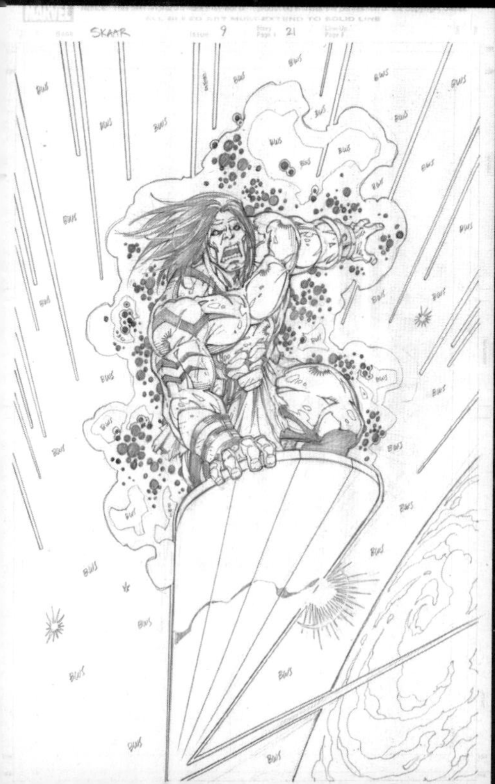
SKAAR
9
21

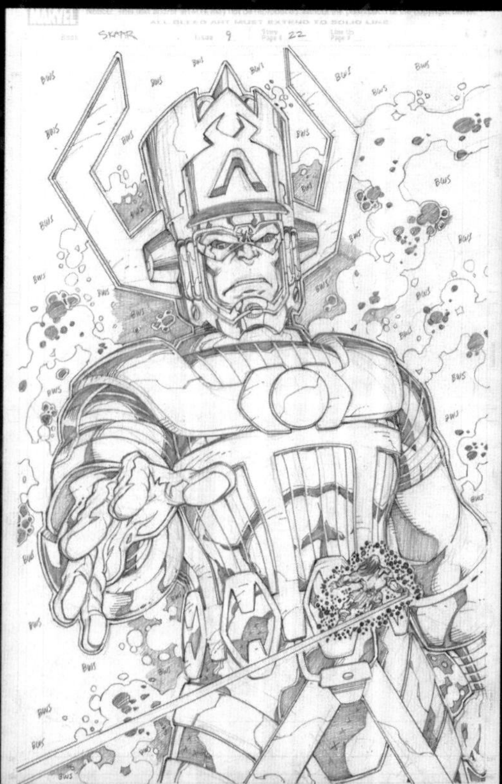
SKAAR
9
22